ROMAN SPLENDOUR ENGLISH ARCADIA

ROMAN SPLENDOUR
ENGLISH ARCADIA

The English taste for Pietre Dure and the
Sixtus Cabinet at Stourhead

Simon Swynfen Jervis and Dudley Dodd

PWP

To the National Trust
Historic Buildings Representatives
and the Members of the
National Trust Arts Panel

© National Trust, 2015

Published by Philip Wilson Publishers
an imprint of I.B.Tauris & Co Ltd
6 Salem Road
London W2 4BU
www.philip-wilson.co.uk

ISBN: 978-1-78130-024-4

Distributed in the United States and Canada
exclusively by Palgrave Macmillan
175 Fifth Avenue, New York NY 10010

Designed by E&P Design, Bath
Printed and bound in China by 1010 Printing

A full CIP record for this book is available from the British Library
A full CIP record is available from the Library of Congress
Library of Congress Catalog Card Number: available

The National Trust gratefully acknowledges a generous bequest from
the late Mr and Mrs Kenneth Levy that has supported the cost of
preparing this book.

Frontispiece and title page: View of the lake at Stourhead, showing
the Stone Bridge built in about 1762 after a design by Palladio and,
on the far side, the Pantheon, designed by Henry Flitcroft (1697–1769)
and built from 1753 to 1756.

Dedication pages: Colin Piper, conservator, working on the Sixtus
Cabinet in a specially constructed workshop, visible to visitors,
within the Column Room at Stourhead, in 2007.

CONTENTS

PREFACE

'A magnificent Cabinet' was Horace Walpole's encomium in 1762 after visiting Stourhead, whose garden he described as 'one of the most picturesque scenes in the World'. Since the eighteenth century, the garden at Stourhead has deservedly remained famous and has been repeatedly celebrated and analysed in print. But, admired as it was up to the early nineteenth century, Walpole's cabinet, then believed to have been made for Pope Sixtus v, has attracted little attention since that time. Its polychrome splendour of semi-precious stones, elaborate architecture and sculptural ormolu was ill calculated to appeal to twentieth-century English taste. And even well-informed English connoisseurs lacked knowledge of Italian furniture, to the extent that this quintessentially Roman masterpiece was considered Florentine. A reassessment was well overdue.

To establish the Cabinet's context has required an enquiry into the pronounced English appetite for pietre dure, a distinctive strain in the history of collecting, which resulted in riches unparalleled elsewhere. Florence, the best-known centre of production, has dominated the literature on pietre dure, and rightly so. But its precursor, Rome, deserves a larger share of the limelight with the Sixtus Cabinet – the *ne plus ultra* of all Roman pietre dure cabinets – as a focus. Pope Sixtus v's responsibility for several of Rome's famous landmarks, celebrated on the Cabinet's Pedestal, is well known. Less so is his Villa Montalto, the most extensive in Rome, now submerged under the Stazione Termini, where the Cabinet stood in the Palazzo Felice. Its patronage, purpose, design and setting need to be examined, as do the succeeding generations of the Peretti dynasty, whose decline, featuring a marital scandal of international no-toriety (an earlier episode provided the plot for Webster's *The White Devil* of 1612), led to that dispersal of the Montalto collections which brought a Discobolos to William Lock of Norbury, a Hadrian to Cobham Hall and Bernini's Neptune to Sir Joshua Reynolds and, later, to Brocklesby Park. Turning to England, the enquiry leads to the taste of Grand Tourists

and, above all, Henry Hoare, later called 'the Magnificent', who bought the cabinet in about 1740 – and to its history at Stourhead, as the principal ornament of the house, a 'grand observable', to reuse the phrase applied by John Loveday to its Florentine rival, the Badminton Cabinet.

The Sixtus connection was emphasized in Henry Hoare's scholarly new triumphal arch Pedestal, with English history providing a gloss in the form of an Armada medal, and again when his grandson, Sir Richard Colt Hoare, set the Cabinet in a new niche with a rich blue velvet curtains and a gilded cornice, supplied by Thomas Chippendale junior in 1802, carved with 'the Pope's tiara and other insignias'. William Beckford was envious and, a decade later, Wyatville created a special niche for the Badminton Cabinet in the sixth Duke of Beaufort's new Great Drawing Room there. The resonances of such pietre dure masterpieces, whether Roman or from elsewhere, be it at Stourhead and Badminton, Fonthill Abbey and Hamilton Palace or, in the case of Louis xiv's spectacular Cucci cabinets, in the Saloon at Northumberland House, are yet to be explored.

The vicissitudes of the Hoare family in the nineteenth century, when Stourhead almost lost its Cabinet in the Heirloom sales of 1883 before its rescue from the fire of 1902, usher this great Roman masterpiece into a period when a dominant taste for English oak, walnut, mahogany and satinwood furniture, still remarkably persistent in certain quarters, emerged – the 'patina' of old walnut being particularly admired. This cult of 'brown wood', as it is sometimes slightly termed nowadays, was often accompanied by a nationalistic admiration and preference for almost anything English and eighteenth century.

Such attitudes were echoed by complex counter-currents. The opening to the public of the Bowes Museum in 1896, of the Wallace Collection in 1900 and of Waddesdon Manor in 1959 established privileged 'continental' islands, but elsewhere, apart from Old Master paintings, which early received letters of denization, the fruits of Grand Tour and later collecting were often overlooked or underemphasized. It was not until the 1980s that the Beckford ingredient at Charlecote Park was fully celebrated, and the great assemblage of continental furniture at Longleat, much of it dispersed, has never received its due. While bringing sculpture into the fold, if recognition was lacking, posed few problems – crudely speaking, sculpture tends to have named subjects and/or named artists, as do Old Master paintings (the same holds for tapestry) – decorative art objects occupied a lower stratum in the hierarchy of things, partly because they were for practical use and taken for granted, and partly because, as ornaments, they were regarded as essentially secondary presences rather than as principals. An interest in such productions could be dismissed condescendingly as bricabracamania, in the spirit of Macaulay's categorization of Horace Walpole's collections as 'trinkets', 'baubles' or 'curiosities'.

Even to categorize the Sixtus Cabinet neutrally as 'furniture' is surely reductive: although secular and in a secular context, it has, arguably, more in common with a rich tabernacle or an elaborate reliquary than with any of the furniture in its vicinity. 'Decorative' it certainly is, but it seems, in its niche, more a cult object than a mere ornament. It is a challenge to anatomize this transcendence, whether it links umbilically to the cabinet's Roman origins, or reflects a sensual appeal derived from rich materials and elaborate craftsmanship, or the continuing pull of a living survivor of the Grand Tour cult of Italy. Its numinous afterlife may be an amalgam of these and other aspects, abstract or anecdotal, but, whatever the analysis, the Sixtus Cabinet is at once a paradigm and a proxy for that rare class of decorative art icons which can singly command attention and dominate a room.

To anatomize a work of art of such complexity and to trace its history from Papal Rome to Arcadian Wiltshire was evidently a challenge. The present writer may have been stung to take up this gauntlet by his experience in 1990, when, as Director and Marlay Curator of the Fitzwilliam Museum, Cambridge, he tried and failed to retain the Badminton Cabinet, a supreme example of Florentine

pietre dure, ordered by the third Duke of Beaufort in 1726, in this country. (It had been sold at Christie's for nearly £8.7 million, and was sold again in 2004 for over £19 million.) While subsequently serving as Historic Buildings Secretary (later Director of Historic Buildings) at the National Trust, the importance of its Roman rival, the Sixtus Cabinet at Stourhead, became ever more apparent. But, while he had some knowledge of Italian pietre dure, particularly in English collections, the patronage of the Hoare family at Stourhead was untrodden territory and he was thus fortunate to secure as a collaborator a former National Trust colleague, now also retired, Dudley Dodd, who was responsible, in 1981, for the first substantial guide book to the house, and has since pursued many facets of Stourhead, linking, for instance, the extraordinary *pulvinaria*, or sacred couches, based on Roman models and placed by Henry Hoare in his Temple of Flora in about 1746, neo-classical furniture long *avant le lettre*, to benches of about 1760 in his Pantheon, also of Roman inspiration, and painted with Roman subjects by William Hoare of Bath.

Rome and Wiltshire, Italy and England: Sir Richard Colt Hoare described Stourhead as an 'Italian villa'. The echoes and connections are protean; there are doubtless further avenues to be explored and evidence to emerge. But the Sixtus Cabinet surely merits the attention, as the greatest of all Roman pietre dure cabinets (and how remarkable the unexpected discovery that one of the greatest Roman tables, that in the gallery at Powis Castle, may also have been made for Pope Sixtus v) and as the centrepiece of Henry Hoare's original Cabinet Room at Stourhead, where it presided over paintings after Raphael and by Barocci, Poussin, Maratti and Dolci, an ensemble evoking an idealized Italian palace, just as the lakes and temples outside conjured up an idealized Italian landscape – in England.

Simon Swynfen Jervis

ACKNOWLEDGEMENTS

Our thanks go first to David Adshead at the National Trust, who early adopted this project and fostered it steadfastly to fruition. Other National Trust colleagues and friends, past and present, who have helped, include Alastair Laing, Christopher Rowell, James Grasby, Emily Blanchard and the staff at Stourhead, especially John Hayward and Mike Lucock, Margaret Gray and Ben Walker at Powis Castle, Rosie Thompson at Charlecote Park, and Carolyn Latham at Chirk Castle.

On the Roman dimension we are particularly grateful to Jennifer Montagu, Alvar González-Palacios, Xavier F. Salomon, Frank Dabell, Francesco Petrucci, Father Rupert McHardy, Thierry Crépin-Leblond, Matthias Quast, Anna Seidel, and the late Robert Oresko.

With regard to Stourhead and the Sixtus Cabinet itself we are indebted to Colin Piper, its conservator, to Nigel Israel and Monica Price, for identifying stones, to Dominic Gwynn for advice on the organ, to John Hammond for photography, and to the Leche Trust, whose generous grant enabled us to commission the revelatory series of drawings from Clifton Hepburn.

We are grateful to the partners at C. Hoare & Co. for permission to quote extensively from their archive and for the patience and help of Pamela Hunter, their Curator, and William Acton, their Genealogist. The enthusiasm and hospitality of Mr and Mrs Henry Hoare and Audrey Hoare have been an inspiration. The 1754 Stourhead Catalogue at Longleat House is included by permission of the Marquess of Bath. Janice Williams has generously allowed use of her unpublished research on Stourhead. The staff at the Wiltshire and Swindon Archives have been unfailingly helpful in providing access to the Stourhead and Ailesbury papers.

Elsewhere we have been assisted by Sir Hugh Roberts and Jonathan Marsden (The Royal Collection); Godfrey Evans (Hamilton Palace); Charissa Bremer-David (J. Paul Getty Museum); Mario Tavella (Sotheby's); George Drye (Lamport Hall); James Methuen-Campbell (Corsham Court); Sir Andrew Morritt (Rokeby Hall); Ian Wardropper (The Frick Collection); Deborah Gage (Firle Place); Father Michael Gill (St Dunstan's, Cranford); John Goldsmith (Cromwell Museum, Huntingdon), Jon Culverhouse (Burghley House), James Stourton; Craig Irving (Arundel Castle); Charles Cator (Christie's); Dr Christopher Ridgway (Castle Howard); Martha Andrews (Paxton House); Catherine McIntyre (London School of Economics, Archives and Special Collections); Adrian James (Library of the Society of Antiquaries of London); Craig Hartley (Fitzwilliam Museum, Cambridge); Meredyth Proby (Elton Hall); Dr David Pratt (Downing College, Cambridge); Hugh Brigstocke; Matthew Hirst (Chatsworth); Marjorie Trusted (Victoria & Albert Museum); Rupert Harris and Wil Roberts; Dugald Barr; Professor Elizabeth McGrath; Dr John Harrison; and Laura Ventimiglia.

The publishing process has been made painless thanks to the professionalism displayed by Anne Jackson and, in particular, David Hawkins, of Philip Wilson Publishers, by Claire Forbes, the National Trust Editor (Specialist Publishing), by Susannah Stone, picture researcher, and by Ian Parfitt, designer.

This book has been long in the making and we fear that these acknowledgements may have omitted many who have been generous with assistance in the past; if so we crave their forgiveness. Our final thanks, however, go to Fionnuala Jervis and Greg Walker, who have endured a prolonged period of gestation with patience and good humour.

ONE
THE ENGLISH TASTE FOR PIETRE DURE

… having whole tables […] set with Achates, Onyxes, Cornelians, Lazulis, Pearle, Turquizes & other precious stones.

JOHN EVELYN, 1644, ON THE DUCAL PALACE IN GENOA

In 1738 the new Bourbon king of Naples and Sicily, Carlo VII, founded a *Laboratorio delle Pietre dure* in Naples, emulating that in the *Galleria dei Lavori* in the Uffizi in Florence, founded by Ferdinando I de' Medici in 1588. In 1737 he had summoned from Florence Francesco Ginghi (1689–1762), a pupil of the great baroque sculptor, Giovanni Battista Foggini (1652–1725), to head his new enterprise. Ginghi had entered the Medici *Galleria* in 1704 and records in an autobiography, written in 1753, that, while in Florence, he worked for many foreign notables who came to admire the *Officina del travaglio di Pietre dure*, observing that: 'particolarmente si facevano distinguere come dilettanti e di buon gusto molti SSri Milordi Inglesi per i quali il Ginghi lavorava molto' [many English milords, for whom Ginghi executed much work, particularly disting-uished themselves as dilettanti and as possessing good taste].[1] This tribute from an accomplished master, who might well, before his departure to Naples, have worked on a pietre dure casket, or 'Florence box', which Henry Hoare probably purchased in Florence in 1739 or 1740,[2] is not to be taken lightly, and here prefaces a sketch of that English taste for pietre dure which supplies a larger context for Henry Hoare's acquisition of the Sixtus Cabinet.

A longer perspective takes in the pavement of the Trinity Chapel of Canterbury Cathedral, an elaborate geometric design in *opus alexandrinum*, rich in porphyry and usually said to date from about 1220, when the shrine of St Thomas Becket was moved there. An alternative theory proposes that this is the beautiful marble pavement which William of Malmesbury saw in 1125, preserved when the Trinity Chapel was rebuilt by William the Englishman in about 1180.[3] Even more celebrated are the Cosmatesque pave-ments in the Sanctuary (fig. 1) and Feretory of Westminster Abbey, and the shrine of St Edward the Confessor. This last was signed by 'Petrus … Romanus civis' and dated 1269, while the Sanctuary pavement is signed by 'Odoricus' and dated 1268; these are likely to be the same person, a Roman citizen, recorded, as 'Petrus Oderisius', as having made the tomb of Pope Clement IV in the church of San Francesco in Viterbo, in about 1270.[4]

THE SIXTEENTH CENTURY

Two and a half centuries later, Holbein's celebrated por-trait of two French ambassadors, Jean de Dinteville and Georges de Selve, executed in 1533, depicted a floor similar to and probably inspired by the Sanctuary pavement at Westminster.[5] Whether Holbein, his patrons or his audience were aware of its deeper cosmological meanings is dubious, but its prominence may reflect awareness of that revival of interest in porphyry which blossomed at the court of Cosimo I de' Medici in the 1550s, but which Vasari traced back to a porphyry tablet commemorating Bernardo Oricellario in Santa Maria Novella in Florence, which he erroneously attributed to Leon Battista Alberti (being dated 1511, it long postdates his death).[6] This possible link to English patronage of Roman craftsmen at Canterbury and Westminster in earlier centuries or to contemporary Italian stirrings finds no echo in the great inventory of Henry VIII's possessions compiled in 1547: only a single 'square table of stone' is noted in the 'Chambre within the Gallery' (the King's Gallery) at Greenwich.[7] Two tables made for Sharington's Tower at Lacock Abbey in the early 1550s were ideally adapted for pietre dure slabs, but their stone tops are plain.[8] However, a square English-made table base of chestnut with columnar legs at Aston Hall in Birmingham supports a fine pietre dure slab (fig. 4), which may have been imported to England before the creation of the Medici *Galleria dei Lavori* in 1588.[9] It comes from Melton Constable in Norfolk, and is likely to have descended to the Barons Hastings from John Astley (*c.*1507–1596), appointed a Gentleman of the Privy Chamber, Master of the Jewel-house and Treasurer of the Queen's Jewels and Plate, on the accession of Elizabeth in 1558.[10] Astley was an intimate of Roger Ascham, the Queen's tutor, who commended his Italian, and may have travelled in Italy in the early 1550s. Another contact was the Italian poet, historian and spy Pietro Bizzarri (1525–*c.*1586), who converted to Protestantism and lived in England for varying periods from 1549. Bizzarri's book of Latin verses, *Varia Opuscula* (Venice, 1565), included an ode

FIG. 1
The Great Pavement, onyx, porphyry, serpentine, limestone, glass, Purbeck marble, by Odoricus, 1268. 298 in, 758 cm square. Westminster Abbey.

FIG. 2
Two tables, the upper with a pietre dure border, pen and watercolour, folio 31 verso. 15½ x 11 in, 39.5 x 28 cm. In the Lumley Inventory, 1590.

FIG. 3
Three tables, that lower right with a pietre dure border, folio 32 verso. Size of sheet as fig. 2.

dedicated to Astley, praising him as the perfect courtier, in the mould of Baldassare Castiglione's *Il Cortegiano*, while the poet Gabriel Harvey dubbed him 'our Inglish Xenophon', in recognition of Astley's *The Art of Riding* (1584). Rich, cultivated, Italophile and connected to the trade in princely luxuries, Astley could have acquired such a slab as that at Aston, whose design – a complex geometric perspective with borders of peltate cartouches – suggests Rome in about 1570. There was also at Melton Constable a cushion-cover said to have been worked by Queen Elizabeth and given by her to Astley's first wife Katherine, *née* Champernowne, appointed Elizabeth's governess in 1547, increasing the likelihood that the pietre dure slab, whose base was probably made before Astley's death in 1596, was associated with this inheritance.[11]

If the suggestion that the Aston/Melton Constable table dates from about 1570 is accepted, the next milestone is the group of 13 tables in the Lumley inventory of 1590, three depicted with inlaid marble ornament, one rectangular with a polychrome geometric border (fig. 2), a second octagonal, with an inlaid chessboard surrounded by a geometric web of white lines with red reserves at their intersections, and a third (fig. 3) square with a border of scattered white flowers and red and blue rectangular panels in scrolled cartouches.[12] Although Rome and Florence were the leading producers of pietre dure slabs and it is tempting to attribute the Lumley slabs to the former on the grounds of their geometric design, none appears to be of fine quality, and it should be borne in mind that there were other centres of production. Jean Ménard, the leading craftsman in Rome from the early 1550s, was summoned to Paris in 1579 by Catherine de' Medici and was active there as a 'tailleur en marbre' until his death in 1582, when

his brother, son and son-in-law carried on this trade.[13] In 1620 Fra Francesco Buonarotti wrote of the inlaid marble tomb slabs for the knights of Malta being made in Messina, Palermo and Genoa, as well as Florence.[14] In late 1611, Sir Charles Somerset, a cultivated younger son of the Earl of Worcester, reported seeing in the Palazzo Doria in Genoa 'an other table of marble of sundrie sortes of coulours and of one intire peece which the prince that now is does much esteeme'.[15] Milan was another centre, as was Prague, but craftsmen migrated widely and undiscovered workshops may have existed elsewhere, producing slabs which, albeit possibly cruder, were recognizably Italianate and intended as such.

The Lumley tables may or may not have been Roman or Florentine, but most pietre dure tables mentioned at this period in England, and indeed France, were indubitably of Italian manufacture. In 1589, the possessions of Catherine de' Medici included 'Une grande table de marbre, marquetée de diverses sortes et couleurs de marbre, assize sur ung pied de bois doré et marqueté' [a large marble table, inlaid with various marble types and colours, set on a gilt and inlaid wooden base], almost certainly Florentine, given her origins (although it is conceivable that Ménard produced it before his death). While in 1599 Gabrielle d'Estrées, the mistress of Henri IV, owned 'Une table de marbre et jaspe de plusieurs couleurs, de quatre piedz de large ou environ, et de quatre doitz d'épaisseur, au milieu de laquelle il y a une ovale' [a table of marble and jasper of various colours, four feet wide or thereabouts and four fingers thick, with an oval in its centre], valued at 300 *écus* by Robert Mainart (or Ménard), brother of Jean Ménard, and Louis Leramber, keeper of the king's marbles.[16] With its oval centre this was of a Roman pattern. When Baron

FIG. 4
Table top, pietre dure, probably Roman, about 1570, formerly at Melton Constable, Norfolk. 47⅞ in, 121.5 cm square. Aston Hall, Birmingham.

FIG. 5
Table top (detail), pietre dure, probably Roman, about 1600,
59 x 30¾ in, 149.6 x 106.2 cm. Hatfield House, Hertfordshire.

FIG. 6
Table top (detail), pietre dure, possibly Florentine, about 1610,
48¾ in, 123.8 cm square. Hatfield House, Hertfordshire.

Waldstein visited Nonsuch in 1600, which Lord Lumley had ceded to the Queen in 1592, he saw 'an octagonal table, a gift to the Queen, made up of various sorts of different stones, all fitted together with the utmost skill'.[17] This might be a table sent to England by Francesco de' Medici before his death in 1587, recorded by the Dominican Agostino del Riccio, whose manuscript 'Istoria delle pietre dure' (1597) is the earliest account of the subject.[18] In 1592 Frederick, Duke of Württemberg, had seen 'tables of inlaid-work and marbles of various colours, all of the richest and most magnificent description' at Theobalds, Lord Burghley's great house in Hertfordshire, some of which may also have been Florentine.[19]

THE SEVENTEENTH CENTURY

The next survivors are two pietre dure slabs (figs 5 and 6) at Hatfield House in Hertfordshire, the house which Robert Cecil, Earl of Salisbury, built from 1607, having ceded the nearby Theobalds, his father's house, to James I.[20] The 1612 inventory of Salisbury House, Cecil's London residence, lists seven marble tables, possibly brought there from Theobalds, and later transported to Hatfield. Of the two slabs, one has its original base with a central pillar incorporating four addorsed satyr/lion terms, while the other has a nineteenth-century reproduction thereof. Because the evidence from inventories is unclear, it has been proposed that the latter was acquired by the third Marquess of Salisbury while in Italy in 1868.[21] That with the original base looks Roman, 1600 or earlier, while the latter, with more naturalistic ornament, might be Florentine and a little later. Although tables of this type were certainly on the market in the nineteenth century in London and Italy, it is possible that both slabs at Hatfield have been there since the beginning. In 1614 the Earl of Arundel visited the Medici court in Florence, where he was put up in the Palazzo Vecchio, and 'regolato d'un Tavolino di pietre commesse, che valeva circa scudi 600' [presented with a small table of pietre dure, which was worth about 600 *scudi*].[22] It is tempting to link this to the documented presentation in the same year of two tables, one to the Duke of Osuna, which survives in the Prado and is possibly an earlier Roman table with the Osuna arms added in 1614 in Florence, and the other 'al S. Conte Inghilese' [to the English earl].[23] It is tantalizing that the treatment of shields and trophies on an octagonal table (fig. 7) at Arundel Castle is similar to that on the Osuna table.[24] Could this be an Arundel relict from 1614 rather than, as previously supposed, one of the 15th Duke of Norfolk's purchases from Charles Davis?[25] In 1617 Arundel was considering ordering a version of his arms 'of rich stoanes inlayed', at a possible cost of '200 Crownes' in Florence, and landscapes, also in pietre dure, at a similar price.[26]

An enigmatic sketch in an album, bearing the date 1618, in the British Museum shows what may be an octagonal table with a geometric pietre dure top and, apparently, drawers round its base.[27] The album also contains a sketch of the arms of Thomas Cecil, Earl of Exeter, and a plan resembling Wothorpe, the house he built in about 1615,

FIG. 7
Table top, pietre dure, Roman, about 1570, 53½ in, 136 cm wide. Arundel Castle, Sussex.

FIG. 8
Cabinet, ebony, mounted in gilt bronze and pietre dure, Florence, about 1630, possibly acquired in Florence in about 1635 by William Cavendish, third Earl of Devonshire. 22½ x 42 x 17½ in, 57 x 106.8 x 44.5 cm. The Devonshire Collection, Chatsworth, Derbyshire.

according to Thomas Fuller, '*to retire to* (as he pleasantly said) *out of the dust, whilst his great house of* Burleigh *was a sweeping*'.[28] Less equivocal is 'One great Marble Table of Divers Colours' in the 'Inner Vault' at Chelsea, listed in the 1635 inventory of the first Duke of Buckingham's possessions.[29] If a superbly refined Florentine cabinet (fig. 8) at Chatsworth was indeed acquired by William Cavendish, third Earl of Devonshire, in about 1635 when he visited Florence with his tutor, Thomas Hobbes, it is one of the most important documents for an early English taste for pietre dure.[30] The inventories of Charles I's goods compiled under the Commonwealth in 1649–51 include, at Nonsuch, a 'Marble Inlaid Table' valued at £20: perhaps this is that which Baron Waldstein saw there in 1600.[31] Probably more modern was 'One Marble Table inlaied with many cullors upon a guilt frame square' at Denmark House, valued at £40, and noted as given to the Queen by 'ye Lady Banning'.[32] The likeliest candidate is Penelope, daughter of Sir Robert Naunton, who married the second Viscount Bayning in 1634 and was widowed in 1638, and married secondly in 1639 Philip Herbert, who succeeded as fifth Earl of Pembroke in 1650.[33] Nearby was:

A Marble Table inlaied with stone of divers cullors upon a frame suiteable, A Cabbonett of Marble suitable to the Table valued together at 60.00.00.[34]

The cabinet may have been a box or casket, or a cabinet of drawers in the modern sense. If the latter, it could have resembled the ebony cabinet (fig. 9) which the diarist John Evelyn, in self-imposed exile to avoid the Civil War, had made, probably in Florence, to display the 19 pietre dure panels he had purchased from Domenico Benotti in October 1644, and later had modified, probably in Paris in the late 1640s, to accommodate a set of brass reliefs by Francesco Fanelli.[35] If Henrietta Maria's 'Cabbonett' was, or resembled, a casket, a cabinet of casket form (fig. 10) in the Cromwell Museum, Huntingdon, presented to Oliver Cromwell by Ferdinando II de' Medici between 1653 and 1657, may provide a parallel.[36]

In 1671 Charles II visited Norfolk and was entertained by Sir Robert Paston, whom he created Viscount Yarmouth in 1673 and advanced to an earldom in 1679, at his great house of Oxnead. A pietre dure table (fig. 11) bearing the Paston arms (four times, within plain oval frames) without

FIG. 9
Cabinet, ebony, mounted with 19 pietre dure plaques purchased from Domenico Benotti in October 1644, and with Florentine gilt brass mounts, some with the Evelyn arms, originally made for John Evelyn (1620–1706) in Florence in 1644, with lacquered brass reliefs by Francesco Fanelli, probably added in Paris in about 1650. 36 x 48 x 15¾ in, 91 x 122 x 40 cm. Victoria & Albert Museum.

FIG. 10
Cabinet, of casket form, ebony and walnut with Florentine pietre dure panels, given to Oliver Cromwell by Ferdinando II de' Medici, Grand Duke of Tuscany, between 1653 and 1657, in return for a portrait of Cromwell by Peter Lely, in the Galleria Palatina (Palazzo Pitti). 11¾ x 16 x 14 in, 29.5 x 41 x 36 cm. Cromwell Museum, Huntingdon.

a coronet was sold in London in 1992, plausibly described as commissioned in Florence by Sir Robert before he was ennobled.[37] But his father, William Paston (raised to a baronetcy in 1642), may be a better candidate. On 31 July 1638 he arrived in Florence, where he met Nicholas Stone, the son of the sculptor of the same name, who had been employed by the Paston family since 1629. Nicholas junior was then on a foreign study tour with his elder brother Henry, a painter, and Nicholas's diary reveals a keen interest in the grand-ducal gallery, which he first visited on 24 June, and where he drew repeatedly up to his departure for Rome on 29 September.[38] On 10 July he and his bro-ther 'went amongst the inlayers', but while Henry received permission to copy paintings, 'for the inlaying itt was forbid by the great Duke'. After visiting the Cappella dei Principi 'which is began hauing rich stones all the worke being uery costly', Stone received written notification on 14 July that 'the Duke would give no leave for the learning of inlayd worke in the gallery', but there were no hard feelings: the Grand Duke repeatedly inspected Stone's drawings from sculpture, once calling him 'a gall-ant uomo'.

FIG. 11
Table top, pietre dure, Florentine, probably purchased by William Paston in Florence in 1638,
when his arms were added to a pre-existing top. 48¾ x 30¼ in, 124 x 77 cm.

Stone met Paston on 1 August, the day after his arrival and escorted him to various sites, including the Medici villa at Poggio Imperiale, and on 26 August Paston 'gaue me [Stone] a case with a knife with an agate haft to give to Sr Bastian Keper of the Gallery', suggesting that a relationship had been struck up. In the light of this incident and Stone's evident appreciation of pietre dure, it is likely that the table which surfaced in 1992 was commissioned by William Paston in 1638. Moreover, as the four small coats-of-arms are not well integrated into its design, they were probably inserted into black neutral spaces in a pre-existing slab. The table can be identified with 'a stone picture with the armes of the family' listed in the fragmentary Oxnead inventory of about 1670, which lists two other 'stone pictures'.[39] Before he left Florence Stone wrote a summary of the principal sights in Florence, including the Cappella dei Principi 'for cost and beautifull stone the richest worke on of all ye world'. On 3 October 1638 he arrived in Rome where he stayed, apart from a visit to Naples in March 1639, until May 1642. (An early visit, on 10 October 1638, was 'to the palace of Princeppe Parretta [Peretti] upon Mont Quirinalis, hard by the ruines of Therme Deoclesiana, where we saw diuers rare statuas and some paintings; a uery pleasant large garden with many fountains and statuas; in the pallace a uery fine library'.) On 6 November he received from England '3 scuchions of armes to be inlayed in marble for the monument of my Lady Barkley'. The first shield was commissioned on 25 January 1639 from 'one Sig: Domenica, stonecutter in Rome dwelling in the Coursa' for 22 crowns, the second on 28 April for 15 crowns and a third on 29 June for 30 crowns: all three (one altered shortly before dispatch) were sent off to England on 17 September. The tomb (figs 59 and 60) to Lady Berkeley (1574–1633), heiress of George Carey, Lord Hunsdon (1547–1603), appointed lord chamberlain of Queen Elizabeth's household in 1597, must have been supplied by Stone's father's workshop: it is in St Dunstan's, Cranford, with the three Roman pietre dure coats-of-arms in situ.[40]

Another early instance of an English commission of marble inlay in Rome in the mid-seventeenth century is a table in Canterbury with subjects from Ovid in white on black, made for Dr John Bargrave in 1660, accompanied by another made for Philip, Lord Stanhope, whom Bargrave had escorted to Italy in 1650.[41] In 1652 the young Dutch diplomat Lodewijk Huygens saw 'a table of pierres rapportées, a great piece of workmanship' at the house of Sir Walter Pye (1610–1659), whose father had been a great servant of the first Duke of Buckingham, and who himself travelled to Rome in 1642 to solicit support from the Pope for the royalist cause; perhaps he acquired his table there.[42] Englishmen noticed and admired pietre dure objects elsewhere than in Italy: in 1649 Robert Montagu, Lord Mandeville, saw in Cardinal Richelieu's lodgings in Richelieu 'a curious table all inlayed with pretious stones having in the middle an agate of an extraordinary bignest', now in the Louvre, and in 1652 in the Antiquarium in the Residence in Munich 'a most curious table made of inlayed stones as agates and the like', possibly the surviving Florentine table listed in the Kammergalerie of the Residence in 1641–2, inlaid with the Electoral arms of Bavaria, for Maximilian I and Elisabeth of Lorraine.[43] But Italy was the normal place of revelation, as when Richard Lassels described the Uffizi in Florence in 1654 as containing 'two Tables of inestimable valew, in which are xpressed to life birds and flowers in their severall colours, and all this by severall pretious stones sett together'.[44]

All these instances, whether observations, princely gifts or purchases, suggest that there existed in England, by the mid-seventeenth century, an awareness of and taste for commesso di pietre dure: witness lines in Mildmay Fane's 1651 thank-you poem to Lord Campden for the loan of his house in Kensington, which mentions, apparently in 'a room of state and audience':

> ... such tables as
> For curious marbles all surpass
> Wherein art doth the colours dress
> Into mosaic and pedri-commess,
> Appropriating to each stone
> His weight of admiration.[45]

THE RESTORATION

From 1665–70 Sir John Finch (1626–1682), whose portrait by Carlo Dolci is in the Fitzwilliam Museum, Cambridge, served as English resident at the court of the Grand Duke Ferdinando II de' Medici in Florence. In 1665 he supervised the Grand Tour of his nephew, Daniel Finch, later second Earl of Nottingham and seventh Earl of Winchilsea, who was recalled to London by his father in 1668. A cabinet (fig. 12) from Burley-on-the-Hill, incorporating pietre dure panels and marquetry, probably by Leonardo van de Vinne (now in the Gilbert Collection), was the product of this interlude.[46] Early pietre dure acquisitions may also include a relatively simple Florentine casket now at Burton Agnes Hall, Yorkshire, which Sir Griffith Boynton (1664–1731) kept in his London house at Great Ormond Street and described in his will as 'One other Cabinet or Box [...] consisting of Stone Inlayd with figures of Birds &c.' and a more elaborate casket at Drayton House, Northamptonshire, which may be identified with 'One stone cabinet upon a black frame' in the 1710 Drayton inventory, and could have been acquired by Henry Mordaunt, second Earl of Peterborough (1623–1697), who travelled to Italy in 1673 to negotiate the marriage of Mary of Modena to the Duke of York.[47] Another diplomatic episode took place in the winter of 1683–84 when John Cecil, fifth Earl of Exeter, and Lady Frances, his wife, née Manners, were in Florence at the court of the Grand Duke Cosimo III de' Medici, who presented the Earl with a magnificent cabinet (fig. 14) incorporating pietre dure panels framed by floral marquetry also attributed to Leonardo van der Vinne.[48] By 1688 it had been supplied with an English carved and gilt stand. Also at Burghley, on a similar stand, is a smaller Florentine cabinet, with a grid of 12 drawers fronted with pietre dure panels, presumably acquired by the Earl at about the same time. A cabinet (fig. 13) at Chirk Castle with a central pietre dure panel depicting Orpheus, surrounded by 12 further panels depicting animals, may

FIG. 12
Cabinet, ebony, mounted with Florentine pietre dure plaques, and with marquetry, probably by Leonardo van de Vinne, Florence, about 1668, from Burley-on-the-Hill, Rutland. 30 x 45½ x 16 in, 76.5 x 115.9 x 40.3 cm. The Gilbert Collection.

FIG. 13
Cabinet, ebony, mounted with Florentine pietre dure plaques, Florence, about 1650, at Chirk Castle, Clwyd. 24 x 41¾ x 14⅜ in, 61 x 106 x 36.5 cm. National Trust.

FIG. 14
Cabinet, ebony with marquetry, probably by Leonardo van de Vinne, mounted with Florentine pietre dure plaques, given to John, fifth Earl of Exeter, by Cosimo III de' Medici, Grand Duke of Tuscany, in winter 1683–4. 39 x 68⅞ x 20⅞ in, 99 x 175 x 53 cm. The Burghley House Collection, Stamford.

have been acquired by Sir Thomas Myddelton in Florence before his return from his Grand Tour in 1672, although its stand is early eighteenth century. Comparable motifs decor-ate a- richer Florentine cabinet with the arms of Cardinal Maffeo Barberini, who became Pope Urban VIII in 1623.[49] When John Loveday went to Chirk in 1733 he described in the gallery there 'two curious Cabinets; one has some Lapis Lazuli in the front of it, the other represents several Beasts and that by means of several kinds of stones, advantageously inlaid according to their native colours'.[50] The first of Loveday's two cabinets is evidently that with the Orpheus panel; perhaps the second resembled one (fig. 16) at Belton House in Lincolnshire, also on an early eighteenth-century gilt stand, lavishly revetted in lapis lazuli, with pewter stringing. Possibly Roman, it may have been acquired by Sir John Brownlow, later Lord Tyrconnell (1690–1754), during the Grand Tour which took him to Rome in 1711.[51] Cabinets and caskets incorporating pietre dure seem to have been increasingly popular purchases, but table slabs continued to be collected. In 1677, while on his Grand Tour, Sir Thomas Isham of Lamport received news from Giovanni Remigio (c.1638–1695) that 'Your Tabels are perfectly done and putt up in theyre Caseses and indeed are two Jewels' (fig. 58).[52] Remigio, a copyist and art agent in Rome, who also worked for the fifth Earl of Exeter, was a son of Remi van Leemput (1607–1675), a key figure in the London art world as painter, dealer and collector.

SCAGLIOLA

A reflection of the late seventeenth-century English taste for pietre dure is the scagliola chimney piece (fig. 15) and window sill, decorated with scrolls and flowers, in the Queen's Closet at Ham House. These were executed by a Roman craftsman, Baldassare Artima, for the Duke of Lauderdale in about 1673.[53] Artima was probably responsible for a table from Warwick Castle now in the Victoria & Albert Museum, for a set of table, mirror and candle-stands at Drayton House, made for the second Earl of Peterborough, and for an unprovenanced cabinet sold by Sotheby's in 2010, clearly based on Florentine pietre dure prototypes.[54] Artima was a 'scene-keeper' in the King's Company of Players from 1670, together with another Italian, Diacinto Corcy, but when, in 1672, their playhouse was burned, they turned to scagliola, Artima working for grand patrons in London and Corcy, an inferior craftsman, for less grand ones in Suffolk.[55] This seems to have been an isolated episode. Later, from the 1720s, in an unrelated development, the Benedictine friar, Don Ferdinando Hugford (1695–1771), son of Ignazio Hugford, watchmaker to Cosimo III de' Medici, developed a refined form of scagliola, often applied to table tops incorporating pictorial or heraldic elements, along with the birds and flowers on a black ground, typical of seventeenth-century Florentine pietre dure; he worked at the convent of Santa Reparata at Marradi, the abbey of Vallombrosa and the

FIG. 15
Chimney piece, scagliola, of the Queen's Closet at Ham House, Surrey, made by Baldessare Artima, 1673.
47¼ x 52½ x 1⅛ in, 120.1 x 133.4 x 2.8 cm. National Trust.

FIG. 16
Cabinet, ebony, mounted in lapis lazuli, on slate, probably Rome, about 1640, at Belton House, Lincolnshire.
35⅝ x 47⅞ x 19⅞ in, 90.5 x 121.5 x 50.5 cm. National Trust.

monastery of San Pancrazio near Florence. His assistant, Don Pietro Belloni, also produced table tops of this ilk (fig. 17). They were much in demand from Grand Tourists, and Hugford's only pupil, Lamberto Gori (1730–1802) stated that the 'più culte nazioni, e in specie gli Inglesi' [the most cultivated nations, and especially the English] competed for Hugford's works.[56] In 1742 Sir Horace Mann paid Hugford 25 zecchins for a table top which he gave to Horace Walpole.

THE EIGHTEENTH CENTURY

In 1725 there certainly were in the 'best dressing room' and the 'best chamber' at Cannons, the seat of James Brydges, Duke of Chandos, tables described almost identically as 'A Mozaick table wth a rich Guilt frame', each valued at the extraordinary figure of £250.[57] The descriptions in the 1747 Cannons sale catalogue (one reads: *A most magnificent large marble sideboard table 5 ft. 1 by 3 ft. 3, embellished with* lapis lazuli *and variety of curious* Italian *stones, inlaid in so beautiful manner as to represent birds, fruit, flowers and insects; and supported by a frame richly carved and gilt, and elegantly ornamented with figures, festoons, masks, shells, &c.*)[58] reveal that these must be Florentine pietre dure slabs, probably those acquired for Cannons by Henry Davenant, who acted as an agent to James Brydges, then Earl of Carnarvon (1674–1744), in Italy in 1715–17, and shipped by John Fuller of the firm of Gould Harriman & Fuller at Leghorn.[59] Presumably similar to the 'stone pictures' at Oxnead were 'Two pictures composed of different sorts of Marble, out of the Duke of *Florence*'s Collection. This Work is called, in Italian, *Pietra Commessa*', described by James Kennedy in 1769 in the Lobby at Wilton; they had probably been acquired by Thomas Herbert, eighth Earl of Pembroke (1653–1733), the great collector who purchased part of the Mazarin collection of antique sculpture, probably in 1714.[60]

One of a set of landscape panels for a cabinet, celebrated for their later incorporation in that (fig. 18) designed by Robert Adam and made by Mayhew and Ince, with mounts by Matthew Boulton, in about 1771–5, for the Duchess of Manchester, is signed by Baccio Cappelli, a Florentine craftsman, and dated 1709.[61] The 11 panels may have been acquired by William Montagu, Viscount Mandeville, later second Duke of Manchester (1700–1739), in 1720, while on his Grand Tour.[62] A similar set ornaments a cabinet on an early eighteenth-century gilt stand at Welbeck Abbey, purchased by Mr Lee for £3.12.6 on behalf of the third Duke of Portland at the famous sale of his mother's collection in 1786.[63] The 1740s inventory of Barbavilla, Co. Westmeath, lists '1 marble cabinet with mahogany frame and glass doors', recorded in a photograph which shows an evidently Florentine cabinet fitted with 11 comparable landscape pietre dure panels, on a characteristically Irish mahogany stand.[64] Another object designed by Robert Adam, a casket made for the writer and painter George Keate (1729–1797) in 1777, incorporates Florentine panels, one signed 'Matteo Crebolans' and dated 1711;[65] perhaps Keate acquired them during his Grand Tour of

FIG. 19
The Badminton Cabinet, ebony with gilt bronze mounts, among them figures of the Seasons by Girolamo Ticciati, and incorporating Florentine pietre dure, including one panel inscribed and dated by Baccio Cappelli 1720, ordered by Henry, third Duke of Beaufort in Florence in 1726 and finally delivered in 1733. From Badminton House, Gloucestershire. 152 x 91½ x 37 in, 386 x 232.5 x 94 cm. Gartenpalais Liechtenstein, Vienna.

FIG. 20
Casket, ebony with gilt bronze mounts incorporating hardstone fruit, with panels of Florentine pietre dure, probably acquired by John Chute in Florence in about 1741. At The Vyne, Hampshire. 11¾ x 17½ x 15 in, 30 x 44.5 x 36.6 cm. National Trust.

FIG. 21
Cabinet, japanned black and gold, mounted with ivory medallions and with Florentine pietre dure plaques, probably acquired by Sir Matthew Fetherstonhaugh Bt in Florence in 1751–2, the cabinet possibly by William Hallett, London, about 1754. At Uppark, Sussex. 63 x 40⅛ x 23⅝ in, 160 x 102 x 60 cm. National Trust.

1754–5, but they may have arrived in England closer to their date of manufacture. A less equivocal parallel is a mahogany cabinet of bookcase form, made for the Hon. Charles Hope-Weir, whom Robert Adam accompanied on his Grand Tour in 1755, which displays 18 Florentine panels and a medallion of Hope inscribed 'Roma 1755'. It was probably made in Edinburgh after Hope's return in 1756, to show these Grand Tour trophies.[66]

Doubtless other cabinets incorporating pietre dure panels were acquired by or assembled for English, or Scottish, patrons in the early eighteenth century: in 1727 the Marquess of Carmarthen had '1 Large Cabt. Inlaid. wth Ston & Marble. Pillars' in the Wrought Bedchamber at Kiveton, Yorkshire;[67] and in 1735 John Loveday noticed at Ditchley, Oxfordshire, 'a Cabinett curiously inlaid with different stones in such a manner that their native Colours represent Birds, Beasts, Fruits &c.', and at Burley-on-the-Hill, Rutland, 'The front of a Cabinet of inlaid Stones in their native Colours representing flowers and birds'.[68] But undoubtedly the Badminton Cabinet (fig. 19) was, and remains, the *ne plus ultra* of Florentine cabinets made for an English patron; indeed, it is the swan-song of the genre. It was made for Henry Somerset, third Duke of Beaufort, who seems to have ordered it in Florence in 1726: it was finally delivered in 1733. After its sale in 1990 two inscriptions were discovered on the reverse of pietre dure panels, both with the name 'Baccio [or 'Bacchio'] Cappelli', also found on the Duchess of Manchester's cabinet, and one with the date '1720'.[69] The date is on the central panel of the cabinet and, long antedating the Duke's order, suggests that this was probably made speculatively, not necessarily for a cabinet; a group of five comparable panels in the Green Vaults in Dresden are framed as pictures.[70] Smaller than the Badminton Cabinet, but of a similar quality, is a group of pietre dure caskets with gilt mounts influenced by Foggini in the Royal Collection (acquisition date unknown, but on a stand of about 1720), at The Vyne, Hampshire (acquired by John Chute in Florence in the 1740s) (fig. 20), and at Strawberry Hill (lost, a present to Horace Walpole from Sir Horace Mann (1706–1786), the British representative in Florence).[71] Two caskets of the same ilk later in the collection of William Beckford may have had earlier English provenances: one is now at Charlecote Park, Warwickshire, having been purchased by George Hammond Lucy at the 1823 Fonthill Abbey sale.[72] At Stourhead itself there were at least three Florentine caskets, for one of which Henry Hoare commissioned a marble stand from Benjamin Carter in about 1759: Hoare had almost certainly acquired it during his stay in Italy from 1739–40;[73] any or all of the Stourhead caskets may also have been Fogginian. However, after the extinction of the Medici line of Grand Dukes in 1737, the stock of such objects gradually dried up and there was no further production. Thus, if, as seems likely, it was while in Florence in 1750–1 that Sir Matthew Fetherstonhaugh acquired the seven fine pietre dure panels of seventeenth-century type which he incorporated into a sprightly and elaborate chinoiserie cabinet (fig. 21) still at Uppark, Sussex, he may well have counted himself fortunate on their availability.[74] That comparable products may not have been easy to obtain, even earlier, is suggested by a letter written from Florence in 1720 to his friend, Sir John Percival, Baron Egmont, later first Earl of Egmont (1683–1748), by the philosopher, George Berkeley (1685–1753): 'You wrote to me for a series of marbles. I have been told this was the proper place to get them in; accordingly I have made it my business to enquire for them, but could only find one set in the whole town. It contains about one hundred sorts, being small oval pieces';[75] in 1768, however, Sir Watkin Williams Wynne bought 'a chequer table of all sorts of Marble' from the sculptor Francis Harwood, who specialized in coloured marbles, in Florence.[76] Thirteen apparently seventeenth-century Florentine pietre dure panels were reused on a commode attributed to Pierre Langlois, probably made in about 1765; whether these were recently acquired from Florence or cannibalized from an existing, but unfashionable, cabinet is impossible to tell.[77] A bold and earlier Langlois commode incorporated five landscape pietre dure panels, of good quality and probably early eighteenth century, and another of about 1770, probably by Pierre Langlois junior, with eight possibly slightly later landscape panels using *pietra paesina*, exemplify similar reuse.[78] In the late 1760s Richard Dalton (1720–1791), the Royal Librarian, acquired a small cabinet (fig. 23) incorporating 11 Florentine pietre dure panels, mainly in relief, in Rome for George III; it looks as if it was assembled there, perhaps quite recently, rather than in Florence.[79] Also worth mentioning is a cabinet in the Ashmolean Museum converted or created for Charles Watson-Wentworth, second Marquis of Rockingham (1730–1782), in about 1770, which incorporates both landscape pietre dure panels and others with flowers and birds, likely to have been acquired when, as Lord Malton and keenly in pursuit of marble tables, he was in Florence in 1749.[80] An acquisition worthy to conclude this account of Florentine purchases was that of two pictorial slabs from the Grand-Ducal Galleria designed by Antonio Cioci (1732–1792), its in-house designer, by George, third Earl Cowper (1738–1789), who lived in Florence from 1760 until his death; depicting the interior of the Colosseum in Rome and the port of Leghorn (fig. 22) they were based on oil paintings delivered by Cioci on 25 February 1775.[81] Straying from furniture, when in Florence in 1725, the Roman Catholic Sir Edward Gascoigne (1697–1750) commissioned a monument to his parents from the architect Alessandro Galilei (1691–1737): displayed in Florence to much acclaim in 1728, it incorporated pietre dure, notably lapis lazuli, but the church in which it was erected in 1729, in Barwick-in-Elmet, was pulled down in 1858, and the monument lost.[82]

ROME

Florence was the focus of English patrons of pietre dure. But Rome has been unjustly overlooked. The shields ordered from 'Sig. Domenica' in 1639 (fig. 60) and Thomas Isham's table of 1677 (fig. 58) are early instances. Attention should also be drawn to a reference in Vertue's notebook covering his 1738 tour to Kent, Sussex and Hampshire to 'A beautiful Cabinet of Ebony finely wrought and adorned

FIG. 22
Table top (detail), Florentine pietre dure with a view of the port of Leghorn, designed by Antonio Cioci in 1775, acquired in Florence by George, third Earl Cowper, in about 1780. From Panshanger, Hertfordshire. 57¼ x 29½ in, 145.5 x 75 cm. Private collection, UK.

FIG. 23
Cabinet, ebony mounted with Florentine pietre dure panels of about 1650, probably assembled in Rome in about 1670, purchased there for George III and Queen Charlotte, by Richard Dalton, the King's Librarian, in the late 1760s. 26 x 31¾ x 17⅛ in, 66 x 80.5 x 43.5 cm. The Royal Collection Trust.

FIG. 24
Cabinet, ebony, mounted in gilt bronze and pietre dure, Rome, probably about 1610, possibly acquired in Rome by Sir Francis Dashwood Bt in 1740. At West Wycombe Park, Buckinghamshire. 36 x 46½ x 16⅜ in, 91.25 x 118 x 41.5 cm. National Trust.

FIG. 25
Table top, pietre dure, Rome, about 1570. Probably purchased by Sir Thomas Robinson of Rokeby in Rome in 1730. 45 x 36 in, 114.4 x 91.5 cm. Rokeby Park, Yorkshire.

with limmings all the panells. slipps &c views of Rome most curiously drawn' at Cowdray House, Sussex.[83] Vertue rarely noticed furniture so it is plausible to identify the Cowdray object with a remarkable late seventeenth-century Roman cabinet, on a carved and gilt frame, sold in London in 2007.[84] This was one of four matching cabinets (fig. 72) exhibited in about 1669 by the celebrated Roman cabinet-maker of German descent, Giacomo Herman, although completed later with the insertion of an octave virginal by Giovanni Battista Maberiani, dated 1676; the journeyman responsible for the cabinet work was Johannes Meisser from Freiburg, who dated another of the cabinets 1678. In 1739 Cowdray belonged to the Roman Catholic Anthony Browne, sixth Viscount Montagu (1686–1767), who had inherited in 1717 and soon afterwards employed Giovanni Antonio Pellegrini (1675–1741) and Louis Goupy (c.1674–1747) to execute murals there.[85] Montagu, who later commissioned Jacopo Amigoni (c.1685–1752) to paint an altarpiece of the *Resurrection* for his chapel, would surely in about 1720 have thought this splendid and relatively modern cabinet, clad in lapis lazuli and jasper, an ideal complement to Italianate murals in a Roman Catholic house.[86]

The next Roman episode concerns, again, the young third Duke of Beaufort: after having ordered the Badminton Cabinet in Florence he travelled to Rome, where he spent most of the seven months from May to mid-December 1726, and where he continued to evince a fascination for coloured marbles and hard stones. At Badminton is a catalogue of marbles issued by the dealer Antonio Vinelli in about 1727, and the correspondence of the Duke's agent, the Scottish painter Patrick Coburn, mentions no fewer than '13 Tables of different kinds of Marble'.[87] However, the Duke's most remarkable commission was a small room clad in coloured marbles, said to come from a temple of Nero in the gardens of the Villa Farnese and from a property of the Marchese Sacchetti at Ostia. While in Rome the Duke lodged in the palazzo of Giovanni Francesco Guernieri (1665–1745), an architect and stuccoist, who acted as his agent in dealing with the execution, by Francesco Tedesco (or François Allemand), of the marble room or 'cabinet', as he called it in French, and its delivery to England. In 1701 Guernieri had been summoned to Germany by Landgrave Karl of Hesse, who had just, in 1699–1700, undertaken a Grand Tour to Italy. Guernieri's works in Kassel included a massive engraving, published in 1706, of his scheme for the great garden ensemble at Wilhelmshöhe. It seems likely that Guernieri, who had also worked for the Elector Palatine at Düsseldorf, designed the marble room. He related that it was admired in Rome as 'un ouvrage exquis et parfait', but after its arrival at Badminton, sadly, it lingered unerected, although elements were in 1783 incorporated into the new chapel (Appendix II, p. 202). In a linked episode the Duke was sent notice of a forthcoming sale at Mr Cock's auction room in Poland Street, Golden Square, to be held on 25 January 1728, at which numerous objects, including 'Fine Granet, Marble and Curios inlaid Tables […] lately collected in Rome, Venice and other parts of Italy', were to be sold on behalf of William Philips, a Jacobite who had been the Duke's governor in Italy: the suspicion was that Philips, with whom the Duke had a

FIG. 26
Cabinet, ebony, mounted in gilt bronze and pietre dure, Rome, probably about 1600, possibly acquired in Rome by Sir Hugh Smithson Bt in 1733–4, its stand by Morel & Hughes, London, 1825, incorporating three Florentine pietre dure panels of about 1650. From Northumberland House, London. 33⅝ x 43⅝ x 15 in, 85.5 x 111 x 38 cm (cabinet only).

FIG. 27
Cabinet, ebony, mounted in gilt bronze, including crowned eagles (Borghese), and pietre dure, Rome, probably about 1610, possibly acquired in Rome by Henry, fourth Earl of Carlisle, in 1738–9. 49¼ x 36⅝ x 17⅛ in, 125 x 93 x 43.5 cm. The stand, mahogany parcel gilt, probably of about 1800, incorporates figures similar to those supporting a Boulle coffer at Blenheim, formerly in the collection of Lord Gwydir (1754–1820). The Castle Howard Collection, Yorkshire.

FIG. 28
The matching cabinet. The Castle Howard Collection.

difficult relationship, was selling works belonging to his master, a charge he met with obfuscation and evasion.[88] Two years later Sir Thomas Robinson (*c.*1702–77), owner and architect of the Palladian Rokeby Park, Yorkshire, was in Rome on his Grand Tour, accompanied by his wife, *née* Lady Elizabeth Howard, sister of the fourth Earl of Carlisle (see below), and is likely then to have purchased a fine early Roman pietre dure slab (fig. 25) still at Rokeby, a 'Curios inlaid Table' indeed.[89] That another Roman table, probably slightly later, was probably acquired in Rome in 1755 by Admiral John Forbes (1714–1796), suggests an enduring taste for this particular type.[90]

In purchasing the Sixtus Cabinet in Rome in about 1740 Henry Hoare might have been emulating the Badminton Cabinet, which had arrived in England as recently as 1733 and which John Loveday called a 'grand observable' when he visited Badminton, some 30 miles north of Stourhead, in 1752.[91] But Hoare may have been more directly influenced by a taste for cabinets of the Roman type among contemporary or near-contemporary Grand Tourists. At Syon Park was a fine Roman cabinet (fig. 24), which could have been acquired by Sir Hugh Smithson, later Duke of Northumberland (1715–1786), who was in Rome as a Grand Tourist in 1733–4; it was formerly at Northumberland House and has a stand, incorporating three seventeenth-century Florentine pietre dure panels, made by Morel & Hughes in 1825.[92] In 1738–9 Henry Howard, fourth Earl of Carlisle (1694–1758), who had just inherited the title on his father's death, visited Rome (not for the first time, having been there in 1715), and during that stay that he is likely to have acquired two impressive Roman cabinets (figs 27 and 28) now at Castle Howard; their mounts include crowned eagles, suggesting a Borghese provenance. While in Rome Carlisle was in touch with antiquaries and dealers including Baron Philip von Stosch (1691–1757), Francesco Ficoroni (1664–1747) and his rival Belisario Amidei.[93] In 1743 Ficoroni sent Carlisle a letter enclosing an account for 1739 mentioning 'due tavole di Musaico ottangole giallo e nero, casse, et altro' [two octagonal mosaic tables, yellow and black, cases &c.], which may also have been pietre dure objects. In 1772 Horace Walpole described Castle Howard as containing: 'the finest collection in the World of antique tables of the most valuable marble, & some of old Mosaic, & one of Florentine inlaying', adding: 'There are two fine Cabinets of the same work & materials', presumably the Roman pair, which Walpole evidently could not distinguish from Florentine products.[94] Sir Roger Newdigate (1719–1806), in Rome in 1739–40, is likely then to have purchased a 'near-pair' of Roman cabinets, smaller than Carlisle's and now at Arbury Hall, Warwickshire.[95] Sir Francis Dashwood, later Lord Despencer (1708–1781), was also in Rome in 1740, when he probably secured the elaborate Roman cabinet (fig. 22) now at West Wycombe Park, Buckinghamshire. Dashwood, Newdigate and Sir John Rawdon (1720–1793) collaborated in the purchase of a granite column on the Palatine Hill, which they planned to slice into table tops; a deal was negotiated by the antiquary Mark Parker (*c.*1698–1775), guide and agent to many young Englishmen (see pp. 133–4).[96] Another possible collector is Thomas Duncombe

of Duncombe Park, who was on Grand Tour in 1747, and two years later married Lady Diana Howard, daughter of the fourth Earl of Carlisle: he may have bought a small but fine Roman cabinet (fig. 71) with a plausible Duncombe Park provenance.[97] To this group of Roman cabinets should be added the two lesser examples at Stourhead (figs 68 and 73), inevitably overlooked because outshone by the Sixtus Cabinet; one is a Stourhead heirloom, quite probably also acquired by Henry Hoare in about 1740, while the provenance and descent of the other is uncertain (see Appendix VI). The 1747 sale of the first Duke of Chandos's London house in Cavendish Square included a 'large Cabinet, most beautifully embellished with Lapis Lazuli, agate and Italian stone and brass ornaments gilt', which sounds very Roman; it is not evident in the 1725 inventory of his St James's Square house and may be a later acquisition.[98]

NAPLES

Grand Tourists explored other sources than Florence and Rome. At Burghley House are two slabs on six-legged neoclassical tables, of parcel-gilt mahogany enriched with paterae, lion's mask capitals and lion's paw feet. The slabs themselves, displaying a distinctive pattern of interlocking circles enclosing different coloured stones, were described in 1797 as 'two beautiful large slabs, composed of the lava, highly polished, which flowed from an eruption of Mount Vesuvius'.[99] These must have been brought from Naples by Brownlow Cecil, ninth Earl of Exeter (1725–1793), after his Grand Tour of 1763–4: in the latter year he presented a similar but larger slab (fig. 29) incorporating various sorts of lava from Vesuvius to the British Museum.[100] It rests on an early neoclassical base of mahogany, liberally fluted and perhaps designed by Robert Adam, and it is notable that this slab, and probably the two at Burghley, were acquired by Exeter in Naples before that obsessive volcanologist, Sir William Hamilton (1730–1803), arrived there in November 1764. They may all have been supplied by Giuseppe Canart (active 1738–91), a Roman sculptor of French origin, who had been summoned to Naples by Carlo VII in 1739, and was heavily involved with the conservation and repair of the ancient marbles being excavated in quantity; in 1783 he was responsible for two comparable tables, earlier at Portici, and now in the Palazzo Reale in Naples, and in 1759 he had delivered four, probably similar, to the Palazzo Reale.[101] Another candidate is Giovanni Atticiati.[102] William Constable (1721–1791) of Burton Constable acquired a table of this type in Naples in 1771; its base was supplied by Thomas Chippendale in about 1778.[103] Further similar tables are at Badminton House, at Castle Howard and at Florence Court, County Fermanagh, this last probably brought back by John Viscount Cole, later second Earl of Enniskillen (1768–1840) after his Grand Tour of 1792. Particularly notable are a pair (fig. 32) at Paxton House, Berwickshire, on bases by the Edinburgh cabinet-maker, William Trotter (1772–1830). These were acquired by Patrick Home (1728–1808) in Naples during his second stay there in 1774–5; they were originally made for

FIG. 29
Table top, Neapolitan
pietre dure, composed of
lava specimens from Vesuvius,
possibly made by Giuseppe
Canart, purchased in Naples
by Brownlow Cecil, ninth Earl
of Exeter, in 1763–4, and given
by him to the British Museum,
London, in 1764. 45 x 30⅛ in,
114.5 x 76.5 cm. Trustees of
the British Museum.

FIG. 30
Table top, Neapolitan pietre dure, late seventeenth century, in the manner of Cosimo Fanzago, possibly acquired in Naples by Marmaduke, fifth Baron Langdale, in 1763–4, or by his daughter, Apollonia Langdale, in 1787–8 or 1790–2. 54½ x 27½ in, 138 x 70 cm.

FIG. 31
The matching table top.

FIG. 32
Table top (detail), Neapolitan pietre dure, composed of lava specimens from Vesuvius, made for Louis-Charles-Auguste, Marquis de Matignon, in about 1773, and purchased by Patrick Hume in Naples in 1774–5. 57 x 30¾ in, 145 x 78 cm. Paxton House, Berwickshire.

Louis-Charles-Auguste Goyon, Marquis de Matignon (1755–1773), who had died young in Naples, while staying with his father-in-law, the Marquis de Breteuil, French Ambassador there.[104] The transaction was probably expedited by Hamilton, who had a low opinion of Breteuil.[105] It is worth adding that in 1805 Christie's sold 'A pair of ditto [slabs] inlaid with various beautiful specimens of lava, and giallo border, 3 feet by 1 foot 7 each', which had been 'Collected by a Man of Fashion During a recent Visit to Rome and Naples'.[106] In the same year Peter Beckford described the principle articles of trade in Naples as 'silk stockings, soap, tortoise-shell boxes, lava, fiddle-strings, and diavolonies'.[107] A complete contrast to Neapolitan neoclassical slabs with lava specimens is supplied by a near-pair of pietre dure slabs (figs 30 and 31) with a Langdale provenance recently sold in London:[108] boldly polychrome and baroque, they are likely to be late seventeenth-century Neapolitan products, their style reflecting that of Cosimo Fanzago (1591–1678) as displayed in an altar frontal and an overdoor of 1631 in the Cappella di San Bruno in San Martino.[109] They may have been acquired by Marmaduke, fifth Lord Langdale, while on Grand Tour in 1763–4. With regard to such products it is interesting that, whereas in 1670 Richard Lassels described the marble decoration in the Certosa di San Martino as 'the most sumptuous thing in all *Europe*', in 1730 Edward Wright published his observation of the 1720s that while the Neapolitan 'Profusion of Marbles is scarcely

to be imagin'd […] the Disposition of it in Incrustations is not so well judg'd as it is in the Churches of Rome'.[110]

FLORENCE AND ROME

A remarkable octagonal pietre dure table (fig. 33) sold recently from Wrotham Park and recorded in the 1847 inventory of the London house of George Byng MP (1764–1847) at 5 St James's Square is a trophy of the first water.[111] Its scale and complexity, and its very shape, place it in contention with the greatest of all pietre dure tables, that designed by Ligozzi for the centre of the Tribuna in the Uffizi.[112] The recent publication of documents revealing that in 1797 its then owner, a Florentine nobleman named Adriano Benotti, offered it to the Grand Duke Ferdinando III, and was subsequently given permission to sell it abroad, has established its provenance.[113] The purchaser was almost certainly George Byng MP who had it supplied with its present base, attributed to George Bullock (1778(?)–1818), with four gilt griffins, the ensemble evidently intended as a cynosure in his St James's Square drawing room. Most other great pietre dure slabs in English houses at this period were Roman. A typical Roman slab of moderate size from Woodhall Park, a house acquired by the nabob Sir Thomas Rumbold (1736–1791) in 1774, and rebuilt for him to the design of Thomas Leverton (1743–1824), is likely to

FIG. 33
Table top, Florentine pietre dure, early eighteenth century, sold by Adriano Benotti, Florentine noble, in 1797, and purchased, directly or indirectly, by George Byng for his house in St James's Square, London. Later at Wrotham Park, Hertfordshire. 52¾ in, 134 cm wide.

FIG. 34
Table top, pietre dure, Roman, about 1580, possibly acquired in Rome by Roger Palmer, Earl of Castlemaine, in 1685, but more probably by George Herbert, second Earl of Powis, in 1775–6 or 1782. At Powis Castle, Powys, since at least 1793. 100⅜ x 53½ in, 255 x 136 cm. National Trust.

FIG. 35
Table top, pietre dure,
Roman, about 1580, purchased
by George Lucy at the 1823
Fonthill Abbey sale for £1,890,
when said to have come from
the 'Borghese Palace'. At
Charlecote Park, Warwickshire.
108 x 54 in, 274 x 137 cm.
National Trust.

have been purchased by Rumbold while on Grand Tour to Italy in 1786.[114] Its base may have been supplied by Mayhew and Ince, who worked for Rumbold in 1775 and 1776.[115] Less renowned than it deserves is the much larger Roman table (fig. 34) in the Gallery at Powis Castle, although Lord Torrington did not approve, when he saw it in 1793:

> In the gallery are busts of the 12 Caesars, of great size, and weight, with a vast, inlaid, table.—These, and other *wonderful* marbles have been brought from Italy at a great expence; and must add much to the comforts of the castle, in which there is not one carpet, not one bed fit to sleep in, nor, probably one hogshead of wine!! What abominable folly is all this?? I should exchange the Caesars for some comforts; and the inlaid Roman table should go *towards* the purchase of a good English dining table.[116]

Its date of acquisition is not recorded, although family tradition suggests a papal gift and the Palazzo Borghese.[117] A possible purchaser is George Herbert, second and last Earl of Powis of the second creation (1755–1801), whose Grand Tour took him to Rome in 1775–6, when he was painted by Batoni, and which he visited again in 1782.[118] However, it is also possible that the table arrived at Powis alongside a set of 12 marble busts of Caesars, delivered in 1704 from Powis House in Lincoln's Inn Fields, sold to the Duke of Newcastle in 1705.[119] These busts were seen at Powis in 1772 by the architect Thomas Farnolls Pritchard (1723–1777). If the table did arrive from London in about 1704 its acquisition in Rome may have connected with the 1685 embassy to Pope Innocent XI conducted by Roger Palmer, Earl of Castlemaine (1634–1705), who was first cousin to William Herbert, third Lord Powis, and first Earl, Marquis and titular Duke of Powis (c.1626–1696), and was buried in the Herbert vault at Welshpool. The lions on its base might have been seen to echo the lions rampant conspicuous in Herbert heraldry (but see p. 103, for further observations).

THE EARLY NINETEENTH CENTURY

Better known than that at Powis is the similar but slightly larger Roman slab now at Charlecote Park, Warwickshire, purchased, in competition with, among others, George IV and the Marquess of Westminster, by George Hammond Lucy (1798–1845) at the 1823 Fonthill Abbey sale for a prodigious £1,890; it had stood prominently in King Edward's Gallery there (fig. 35). The sale catalogue gave it a 'Borghese palace' provenance (could the family tradition at Powis be an echo of this?) and Mary Elizabeth Lucy added that it had been taken thence 'in the time of Napoleon', probably a reflection of Prince Camillo Borghese's enforced sale of many works of art to his brother-in-law, Napoleon, in 1807.[120] About the same time as the Fonthill sale the Abbé Luigi Celotti (1759–1842), best known for dealing in manuscripts, sold an equally if not more remarkable pietre dure table to the dealer Edward Holmes Baldock (1777–1845), probably the Florentine example described in Giustiniano Martinioni's supplement

in the 1663 edition of Francesco Sansovino's *Venetia Città Noblissima*: 'à lavoro di Firenze [...] una tavola di diligente fattura, per il disegno industrioso d'Orfeo, che col soave della sua Lira, favoleggiano traesse à se le piante, e gli Animali, dispostivi eglino al vivo, con patiente maestria' [of Florentine work [...] a table of careful workmanship, thanks to its painstaking design of Orpheus, who is said to have used the sweetness of his lyre to attract the plants and the animals, these being arranged as to the life, with patient mastery]' standing in the loggia of the Palazzo Cavazza.[121] In 1824 George Lucy bought another Roman slab, smaller than that from Fonthill, which had been offered to him by the picture dealer, Thomas Emmerson, who claimed that it had been for many years in Germany 'in the family of an Italian banker'.[122] At Attingham, Shropshire, is a further apparently Roman slab of about 1600, with two small landscapes, possibly added later, in border cartouches; it was probably acquired by William Noel-Hill, third Baron Berwick (1773–1842), during his long diplomatic career in Italy from (Sardinia) 1807–33 (Naples).[123]

From the very late eighteenth century there was a flood of acquisitions of pietre dure in England. In 1793 the Council Chamber at Carlton House contained 'A Superb Commode of Inlaid Marble imitating Fruits enrich'd with Or Molu Ornaments', and its companion, purchased by George Prince of Wales at the 1791 sale of goods imported by the *marchand mercier*, Dominique Daguerre, who spent part of the year in England from 1788 and settled there in 1792.[124] This commode may have been that in the Small Blue Velvet Room at Carlton House in 1818, moved thence to Windsor in 1828.[125] Signed by Adam Weisweiler, its front displays six pietre dure panels, all Florentine seventeenth century, apart from a relief of fruit made at the Gobelins, which must have come from a cabinet made for Louis XIV. A more spectacular display of Gobelins fruit in relief is on a commode (fig. 36) made for Daguerre by Martin Carlin, which George IV acquired in Paris in 1828;[126] one of its panels is signed on the back by Gian Ambrogio Giacchetti, a Florentine craftsman who worked for the Gobelins manufactory in Paris from 1670.[127] But even this must yield to the unique surviving pair of Louis XIV cabinets (fig. 37) produced by Domenico Cucci at the Gobelins, which are now at Alnwick Castle, Northumberland, having in 1822 been purchased by Hugh Percy, third Duke of Northumberland (1785–1847), from Robert Fogg, 'Chinaman to his Majesty', for £2100: they had been sold at the Louvre on the orders of Louis XV in February 1751 as old fashioned.[128] Their survival, virtually intact, is remarkable, in a period of re-employment, new combinations and, frequently, a search for more lavish effects. At Powis Castle, for example, was a commode (now at the J. Paul Getty Museum, Los Angeles), one of pair originally veneered in lacquer, stamped by Guillaume Beneman, with bronzes chased by Pierre-Jean [Philippe] Thomire, delivered by Jean Hauré to Louis XVI's bed chamber at Saint Cloud in 1788, where they remained until shortly before inclusion in a revolutionary lottery in 1795. The Powis commode (its companion is in the Palacio Real, Madrid) was probably acquired by Edward Clive, future second Earl of Powis of the third creation (1785–1848), perhaps while in Paris in 1815. It is, however,

FIG. 36
Commode, oak and ebony, with gilt bronze mounts and Gobelins pietre dure plaques, two signed 'Gachetti' for Gian Ambrogio Giachetti, Paris about 1670–5, the commode by Martin Carlin and Dominique Daquerre, Paris, about 1778, bought for George IV in Paris in 1828. 41½ x 60 x 23 in, 105.2 x 152.5 x 58.4 cm. The Royal Collection.

no longer veneered in lacquer, but was adjusted to exhibit 13 variegated pietre dure panels, mostly seventeenth century.[129] Clive's father had been in Italy in the late 1770s and may have acquired some of these panels then. Reuse, rather than embellishment, may be exemplified by the bath cabinet (fig. 38) supplied by Morel & Seddon for George IV's bathroom at Windsor in 1828: attributed to François-Honoré-Georges Jacob-Desmalter (1770–1841), it incorporates 22 Florentine pietre dure panels, probably derived from a rosewood cabinet made for Carlton House by Tatham & Bailey in 1810, a case of double reuse.[130]

In 1824–5 William Beckford's artistic adviser, factotum and friend, Gregorio Franchi (1770–1828), corresponded with his patron concerning a pair of low cabinets (fig. 39) under construction in Paris: lavishly mounted in ormolu incorporating the Hamilton cinquefoil, they required the import of porphyry panels, jasper slabs and agate bacchic masks from Rome, albeit centred on Gobelins relief pietre dure panels, depicting vases filled with fruit.[131] Cosmopolitan in origins, the cabinets reflect a particularly English taste for such luxurious confections. Robert Hume and his son of the same name seem to have specialized in their manufacture; they worked for William Beckford from about 1811, and Robert, the son, became his principal agent.[132] The Humes were also involved with Beckford's son-in-law and cousin, Alexander, tenth Duke of Hamilton (1767–1852), to whom in 1824 they supplied a clock cabinet, mounted with pietre dure, now in the Gilbert Collection.[133] Another Hume client was the extravagant George Watson Taylor (1771–1841), whose furniture, sold in two sales, in

FIG. 37
Cabinet, one of a pair, ebony, with gilt bronze mounts and Gobelins pietre dure plaques, produced by Domenico Cucci, head of the Gobelins workshops, in 1679–83, at a cost of 10,000 *livres* the pair, the sole survivors of Louis XIV's Versailles cabinets, sold by Louis XV in 1751, purchased from Robert Fogg in 1828 by Hugh Percy, third Duke of Northumberland. Formerly at Northumberland House, London. 118 x 77⅛ x 25½ in, 299 x 196 x 65 cm. Alnwick Castle, Northumberland.

FIG. 38
Bath cabinet (detail), purplewood and satinwood with gilt bronze mounts and Florentine pietre dure plaques, of about 1650 (from a rosewood cabinet made by Tatham & Bailey for Carlton House, London, in 1810), made by Morel & Seddon for the King's bathroom at Windsor Castle, Berkshire, in 1828. 40⅛ x 91 x 45¼ in, 102 x 231 x 115 cm. The Royal Collection.

FIG. 39
One of a pair of cabinets, ebony with gilt bronze mounts, incorporating the Hamilton cinquefoil, Gobelins pietre dure plaques of about 1680, porphyry, jasper and agate, acquired in Rome in 1824, commissioned by William Beckford about then, their design supervised by Gregorio Franchi and Robert Hume junior, the cabinet work executed in Paris, possibly by Alexandre-Louis Bellangé, sold by Beckford in about 1831, and subsequently acquired by the Duke of Sutherland for Stafford House, London. 41 x 26½ x 15¼ in, 104 x 67 x 38.5 cm.

1825 from his London House in Cavendish Square, and in 1832 from Erlestoke Park, Wiltshire, his country house, was to be distributed among collectors with similar taste, including George IV.[134] The entry for a cabinet, one of a pair or near-pair, sold from the Grand North Drawing Room at Erlestoke provides, in its very puffery, a flavour of what was on offer:

> **25** A very MAGNIFICENT EBONY CABINET, of splendid classic design, the CENTRE DOOR REPRESENTING ONE OF THE FINEST SPECIMENS OF BOLD FLORENTINE MOSAIC, displaying a vase filled with fruit, flowers and birds, the centre compartments of the wings composed of Mosaics equally fine, on a smaller scale, with lapis lazuli borders, the upper and lower panels and entablatures formed of choice specimens of Oriental agates and lapis lazuli, beautiful Italian rosso antico marble slab, supported by 4 very fine sienna marble fluted Corinthian columns, the whole most splendidly mounted with or-molu, chased shell, gadroon and scroll mouldings, capitals and bases, 5 feet 6 wide and 3 feet 7 high.[135]

The 1882 sale of the contents of Hamilton Palace by the tenth Duke's grandson, the 12th Duke, provided a coda to this opulent Regency taste, including no fewer than 16 significant pietre dure tables, caskets or cabinets.[136] This tally omits a superb Roman slab, given at some date to St Mary's Episcopal Church, Hamilton, and sold in 1993, and the key document of early Roman pietre dure, the Farnese Table (fig. 53), acquired by the tenth Duke at an unknown date after 1796 from a convent in Verona and already in 1844 at Hamilton Palace, whence it was sold in 1919.[137]

Grand early Roman table slabs, such as that from the church at Hamilton, or those still at Powis Castle and Charlecote, evidently appealed to this Regency or post-Regency taste. (One extra worth singling out is a rare early Roman table from the Westminster collection, comparable to another delivered to Spain in 1587: it is likely to have been purchased by Robert, second Earl Grosvenor, later Marquis of Westminster (1767–1845), who collected on the grand scale, buying the collection of paintings formed by Welbore Ellis Agar (1735–1805) in 1806 and others at the Watson Taylor sale in 1822.[138])

ROMAN MOSAIC

The contemporary Roman products which most attracted this generation of Grand Tourists and collectors were the mosaics formed of glass tesserae made at the Vatican Studio di Mosaico founded by Pope Benedict XIII in 1727, with Pietro Paolo Cristofari (1685–1743) as its first director, exploiting the vast range of colours developed by the chemist Alessio Mattioli. (At this period, confusingly, the term 'mosaic' might, as in the Erlestoke lot description quoted above, be applied to pietre dure, as well as to the tesserae-based compositions which the word nowadays describes.) From the mid-eighteenth century the development of *smalti filati* [spun enamels] allowed the production of ever smaller

FIG. 40
Panel of Roman mosaic, signed and dated by Cesare Aguatti, 1774, purchased in Rome, through his agent, Thomas Jenkins, in 1775 by Brownlow Cecil, ninth Earl of Exeter. 15⅝ x 21½ in, 42 x 54.6 cm. The Burghley House Collection, Stamford.

tesserae, which were used in micro-mosaics incorporated in objects from chimney pieces to jewellery. In 1795 the architect and designer Charles Heathcote Tatham (1772–1842) wrote from Rome to Henry Holland (1745–1806) of a chimney piece, recently purchased by Prince Augustus Frederick, later Duke of Sussex (1773–1843), for no less than £350, that: 'The mosaic is inimitable. And comes so near to painting it is literally a deception'.[139] The leading masters were Giacomo Raffaelli (1743–1836) and Cesare Aguatti; Aguatti signed a chimney piece supplied to Thomas Mansel Talbot in 1771, now at Penrice Castle, Glamorgan, and two panels, depicting the Colosseum (fig. 40) and the Temple of Vesta at Tivoli, procured for Brownlow Cecil, ninth Earl of Exeter (1725–1793), who, on Grand Tour in Rome in 1775, described Aguatti as 'certainly the best workman that ever was in Mosaick'.[140] Notable later masters included Michelangelo Barberi (1787–1867) (fig. 41) and his brother Gioacchino (1783–1857). The latter is among those from whom the painter and dealer James Irvine (1757–1831) procured objects (in Barberi's case ten mosaics, including six destined for another dealer, William Buchanan (1777–1864)) for his client and fellow dealer, Arthur Champernowne (1767–1819).[141] In 1805 Peter Beckford, stating that the Florentine pietre dure tables at the Pitti might have cost three years' labour and 20,000 crowns, pronounced: 'The Mosaic at Rome answers a better purpose; it will faithfully render the paintings of the best masters to the latest posterity.'[142] A further critical step was taken by Sydney, Lady Morgan (1783–1859): after her visit to Italy in 1819–20 she castigated Florentine pietre dure and described the Cappella dei Principi at San Lorenzo as 'by far the most tasteless and the most splendid edifice in Italy'.[143]

ROME, AGAIN

Rome continued a principal source for marbles of every variety, as well as mosaics. James Irvine's notes of 1800–6 mention several dealers as supplying marbles, sometimes in the form of table slabs, and Gregorio Franchi has been noted buying porphyry, jasper and agate there.[144] Irvine specifies Blasi as providing a round table of specimens in 1803. This particular type was much collected: the cargo of the frigate *Westmorland*, captured by the French in January 1779 and sold in Malaga to the Compañía de Longistas, a Spanish firm, contained, among other Grand Tour trophies destined for English patrons, 'muestras de piedras, petrificaciones y lavas del Vesubio' [specimens of stones, fossils and lavas from Vesuvius], and in 1783 these, including a Roman table top with marbles arranged in a rectangular grid (fig. 42), were allocated to the Gabinete de Ciencias Naturales, while two Roman tables, with marbles in a hexagonal grid, were sent to the Real Academia de Bellas Artes; all remain in Madrid.[145] Almost certainly while on honeymoon in 1827, Sir Clifford Constable (1806–1889) of Burton Constable acquired a large and elaborate pair of slabs (fig. 43) by Giacomo Raffaelli, with a key to the specimens, following 'Avocato Corsi's work on ancient marbles'.[146] It is surely no coincidence that, also in 1827, the

FIG. 41
Table top, Roman micro-mosaic, with the arms of the 13th Duke of Norfolk, supplied by Chevalier Michelangelo Barberi of Rome in 1847 (its walnut and giltwood base by Morant & Co. of London). 39 in, 99 cm. diameter. Arundel Castle, Sussex.

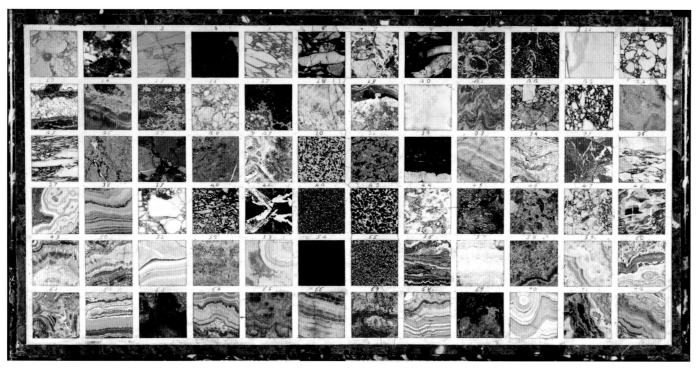

FIG. 42
Table top, Roman, with numbered specimen stones, originally destined for an unknown English collector but captured as part of the cargo of the frigate *Westmorland* by the French in January 1779, sold to the Compañía de Longistas of Malaga. 31¾ x 62¼ in, 80.5 x 158 cm. Museo Nacional de Ciencias Naturales, Madrid.

FIG. 43
Table top, one of a pair, each with about 150 stone specimens, accompanied by manuscript keys based on Faustino Corsi, *Catalogo ragionato d'una collezione di pietre di decorazione* (Rome, 1825), almost certainly purchased in Rome by Sir Clifford Constable, while on his honeymoon in 1827. 61 x 27 in, 155 x 69 cm. The Burton Constable Foundation, Yorkshire.

collection of marble specimens assembled by Faustino Corsi (1771–1845) was purchased in Rome by Stephen Jarrett, a wealthy undergraduate at Magdalen College, Oxford, and presented by him to his university.[147] In 1844 the Sixth (Bachelor) Duke of Devonshire wrote of 'Two round tables of marble [...] got up for me at Rome by poor Gabrielli' as 'too like tailors' pattern books, but they are satisfactory to refer to' and notes that 'A vellum-bound catalogue gives the names of all in the Roman tables.'[148] Table slabs, whether early or modern, with specimens, were not the only Roman pietre dure objects noted in English collections of the early nineteenth century. In 1812 William Beckford had at Fonthill 'a rich cabinet of ebony, inlaid with lapis-lazuli, and other precious stones, designed by Bernini' (fig. 44), which, having passed through the 1823 Fonthill sale, reappeared in Beckford's 1841 Lansdowne Tower sale, still attributed to Bernini, and made 150 guineas.[149] A comparable but more elaborate Roman cabinet (fig. 70) 'with columns of lapis lazuli in relief, inlaid all over with slabs of rare agates, jaspers and onyx' was in the 1882 Hamilton Palace sale, its design attributed, even more implausibly, to 'M. Angelo'; it is likely to have been acquired by Beckford's son-in-law, the tenth Duke.[150] Even more remarkable is a cabinet (fig. 65) formerly in The Royal Collection purchased by George IV from Edward Holmes Baldock (1777–1845) in 1827, and then said, quite plausibly, to have been the property of Prince Borghese; of all the surviving Roman cabinets it bears the closest comparison to the Sixtus Cabinet at Stourhead.[151] A less imposing but nonetheless exquisite example of Roman pietre dure acquired at this period is a house altar, containing a Nativity painted on lapis lazuli, at Corsham Court (fig. 62), which was probably purchased by the Revd John Sanford (1777–1855), who was in Italy, mainly Florence, from 1815–37.[152] In 1856 the South Kensington Museum bought a very similar altar, with the Flight into Egypt on lapis lazuli (fig. 63), for only £16.[153]

MALTA

All travellers to Malta remember the extraordinary floor of the Co-Cathedral of St John in Valletta and that, only slightly less remarkable, in the Cathedral of St Paul in Mdina, covered in pietre dure monumental slabs of, respectively, knights of Malta and Maltese nobles. After the expulsion of the Order of St John by Napoleon in 1798 and the island's transformation into a British colony, formalized in 1814, Giuseppe Darmanin (1779–1863), descended through his mother from the Durante dynasty of marble workers, established a business which, from about 1830, produced numerous inlaid table tops, mainly with coats of arms of British clients, although shells, vases of flowers and the Doves of Pliny, a favourite subject for Roman micro-mosaic, also crop up.[154] A table (fig. 45) with the Royal Arms of Queen Victoria and Prince Albert, now in Buckingham Palace, was one of a group awarded a medal at the Great Exhibition of 1851; the jury report observed that such products were executed 'on a plan imitative of that pursued in Tuscany', but hinted that they did not always match their Florentine models in refinement.[155]

FIG. 44
Cabinet, ebony, mounted in gilt bronze and pietre dure (the horses on its base are recent additions), Rome, probably about 1630, acquired by William Beckford, who attributed its design to Bernini, by 1812 and eventually sold by him from Lansdowne Tower, Bath, in 1841. 59¾ x 48 x 20½ in, 152 x 122 x 52 cm.

FIG. 45
Table top, marble inlay with the Royal Arms of Queen Victoria and Prince Albert, by Darmanin & Sons of Valletta, Malta, shown at the Great Exhibition of 1851 and, through the good offices of Sir John Le Marchant, Governor of Malta, delivered to Buckingham Palace in 1858. 49 x 37 in, 124.5 x 94 cm. The Royal Collection.

DERBYSHIRE

Another nineteenth-century pietre dure industry was
based at Ashford in Derbyshire, where in 1748 Henry
Watson (1714–1786), son of Samuel Watson (1663–1715),
the carver celebrated for work at Chatsworth, established
a marble works and, according to his memorial in Holy
Trinity, Ashford 'was the first who formed into ornaments
The *FLUORS* and other *FOSSILS* Of this County'.[156] In
1751 Watson submitted a patent application for a water-
driven machine for cutting and polishing marble, and he
advertised *inter alia* 'Tables curiously inlaid and decorated
with a Variety of Colours in Stone, the produce of this
Island'. From about 1785 his nephew, White Watson
(1760–1835), a provincial polymath with a bent for
geology, produced increasingly sophisticated 'tablets' in
which geological strata are represented by specimens of
the actual rocks, inlaid into Ashford black marble. These
idiosyncratic educational tools preceded the introduction,
in 1834, of marble inlay on the Florentine model, whose
pioneer was William Allan, manager of the Old Royal
Museum in Matlock, about ten miles from Ashford. This
development was encouraged by the sixth 'Bachelor' Duke
of Devonshire' (1790–1858), who had, as a boy, received
lessons in mineralogy from White Watson and was a
passionate collector of marbles. He not only patronized
this new local industry, but also gave access to his collection
of pietre dure at Chatsworth, and helped the makers
obtain the foreign marbles necessary for the production
of their newly polychrome wares. By 1840 the best maker,
Thomas Woodruff of Bakewell and, later, Buxton, had sold
a table top to the Duke of Cambridge (1792–1850), Queen
Victoria's uncle, and in about 1850 the Dresden-born
designer, Ludwig Gruner (1801–1882), given Woodruff's
address by the Duke of Devonshire, commissioned from
him two highly refined table tops (fig. 47), now at Osborne,
which were shown by Prince Albert at the 1851 Great
Exhibition and awarded a Prize Medal, along with John
Vallance of Matlock Bath and George Redfern of Ashford,

FIG. 48
Table top, its walnut frame enclosing an inlaid marble slab incorporating a large Florentine pietre dure plaque with a parrot, probably about 1650, and four smaller plaques with birds, probably mid-nineteenth century, designed by William Burges in 1867 for his chambers in Buckingham Street, London, and later at Tower House, Melbury Road, Kensington. 54 x 32 in, 137 x 81 cm. Lotherton Hall, Yorkshire.

who also exhibited inlaid tables.[157] Although Samuel Birley of Ashford won a medal for a remarkably elaborate and sophisticated table (fig. 46) shown at the 1862 London Exhibition, purchased by the South Kensington (now Victoria & Albert) Museum for £240, no small sum, the Derbyshire industry was by the mid-1880s largely reduced to the production of small souvenir wares, such as paper weights, thermometers and pen-trays, and was around 1900 in terminal decline.[158]

ENAMELLED SLATE

Another shorter venture deserves mention. In 1840 George Eugene Magnus (1801–1873), the proprietor of slate quarries in Wales and Ireland, patented a method of enamelling slate and founded the Pimlico Slate Company; it barely outlived him.[159] However, in 1842 the Duke of Wellington bought a billiard table, still at Stratfield Saye, from Magnus for 200 guineas and in 1847 Prince Albert designed a Magnus table for Osborne House. Magnus won medals at the London 1851 and 1862 Exhibitions, his enamelled slate being said on the latter occasion to have been patronized 'by the Empress of the French' and 'by the Princes of India' and used 'in the seraglio at Constantinople'. Wall panels shown in 1862 incorporate birds and flowers on a black ground, clearly inspired by Florentine pietre dure, and the same motif is on the enamelled slate tops of three bookcases designed by the Gothic architect Charles Forster Hayward (1831–1905) for the collector John Jones (1799–1882), and made by Howard & Sons of Berners Street in around 1860, one signed underneath 'MAGNUS' in red.[160]

THE LATE NINETEENTH AND TWENTIETH CENTURIES

A greater Gothic architect than Hayward, William Burges (1827–1881), incorporated several panels of Florentine pietre dure in tables (fig. 48) designed for his Buckingham Street rooms in about 1867.[161] Fourteen years later, in January 1881, the renowned connoisseur John Charles Robinson (1824–1913, knighted 1887) bought two Roman pietre dure tables, then regarded as Florentine, at Christie's, the one, rectangular, for £38, the other, octagonal (fig. 49), for £40, and these he passed on to the South Kensington (now Victoria & Albert) Museum; he prided himself on their cheapness, a snowstorm having deterred other bidders.[162] The sale was of the stock of a New Bond Street firm, Messrs Toms & Luscombe, makers of luxury furniture in the French style, who had shown 'Buhl cabinets and tables' at the 1862 London Exhibition.[163] Joseph Toms had worked for and succeeded Messrs Town & Emanuel, manufacturers and dealers established in about 1830, who sold up in 1849, having been active buyers at the 1842 Strawberry Hill and 1848 Stowe sales.[164] That the tables Robinson bought for South Kensington were indeed bargains is suggested by the prices charged to the 15th Duke of Norfolk in 1883 by the dealer Charles Davis, £580 for 'A fine Mosaic table' and £400 for 'a very fine Florentine table'.[165] A more modest price, £42, paid by Davis for 'Another [handsome Italian cabinet] with niche in the centre, two columns with ormolu capitals and five drawers on each side, the front of lapis lazuli, agates & c.', is worth noting, especially as this was in the Stourhead Heirlooms sale, also of 1883, and must have resembled the two lesser Roman cabinets at Stourhead (figs 68 and 73, see also Appendix VI).

FIG. 49
Table top, pietre dure, Rome, about 1570, purchased by John Charles Robinson for £42 in 1881 at the stock sale of Messrs Toms & Luscombe of Bond Street, London, and passed to the South Kensington Museum. 55 in, 139.5 cm diameter. Victoria & Albert Museum.

It should also be remembered that English patrons continued to purchase modern Florentine pietre dure: an example is a fine carved ebony and boxwood cabinet made by Nicodemo Ferri and Carlo Bartolozzi to display six panels of floral pietre dure acquired from the Opificio by Henry Martin Gibbs (1851–1928), then of Tyntesfield and later of Barrow Court, Somerset, in 1876.[166]

Roman pietre dure slabs such as those the 15th Duke of Norfolk acquired for Arundel Castle, which he was rebuilding, might seem a curious complement for Victorian Gothic, but they were evidently expressions of grandee status. Another, earlier, purchaser of grand Roman pietre dure, James Morrison (1789–1857) was no duke but a radical dissenter. He seems to have been captivated by William Beckford's taste from the 1823 Fonthill Abbey sale onwards, and bought a major Roman pietre dure slab at Beckford's 1845 Bath sale for £388.10s.; this was much admired by Gustav Waagen.[167] James Morrison's son, Alfred (1821–1897), relished the exotic, rich and mannered, echoing and intensifying the taste of his father, whose collections he retained. Unmistakeable evidence of a reaction by the following generation is afforded by an *Illustrated Description of Some of the Furniture at Goodrich Court* (Oxford, 1928) compiled by Alfred Morrison's nephew, Harold Moffatt (1859–1945), a devotee of old English oak and walnut. A nadir in the appreciation of pietre dure was reached in 1936 when, another generation onwards, John Granville Morrison (later Lord Margadale, 1906–1996) sold some objects from Fonthill (by now the 1902 Detmar Blow house, Little Ridge, built for his father, Hugh Morrison (1868–1931), in a provincial late seventeenth-century style and enormously enlarged, also by Blow, in 1921). They included 'A Giltwood Centre Table, the frieze carved with foliage, supported on eight legs boldly carved with lions' heads and skins united by an interlaced stretcher, surmounted by an inlaid marble slab', which was knocked down to Lipitch for a mere £6.16.6.[168] The slab received no detailed description. Nonetheless, the dimensions and the date identify it as a table (fig. 50) purchased by his fellow Guards' officers in 1936 as a wedding present for John Alfred Codrington (1898–1991), who in 1984 presented it to All Souls College, Oxford, where it now stands in the Codrington Library, endowed by his ancestor, Christopher Codrington (1668–1710).[169] Its giltwood support is indeed handsome, being close to that of the celebrated table now in the Galerie d'Apollon at the Louvre, which was confiscated from the Château de Richelieu in 1800.[170] But the slab itself is a magnificent Roman example, and is, moreover, signed, 'M·PIETRO·CARLI·FĪO·FECIT'. Codrington, widely travelled, had become interested in art in the 1920s, while at Christ Church, Oxford, where the short-lived Uffizi Society attracted a group with aesthetic inclinations.[171] One of its members, Ralph Dutton (1898–1985, later eighth and last

Lord Sherborne), was to collect pietre dure for his country house, Hinton Ampner, Hampshire, where he employed as his architect a friend, Lord Gerald Wellesley (1885–1972, later seventh Duke of Wellington), who had been a member of the Magnasco Society, founded by the Sitwells in 1924 to reawaken interest in baroque art, and was himself a keen collector of marble and pietre dure.[172] The first stirrings of a revived English taste for pietre dure may thus be traced, along with that for the baroque, to the 1920s.

CONCLUDING REMARKS

This account began by citing Ginghi's 1753 observation that the English were particularly active and discriminating patrons of pietre dure. He had in mind purchases of contemporary products by Grand Tourists. But Henry Hoare, when he acquired the Sixtus Cabinet in about 1740, secured an object he believed to be some 150 years old, with historic associations. The 'Borghese palace' provenance of the great Fonthill table now at Charlecote, and the Abbé Celotti's reference to the Palazzo Cavazza in Venice as the origin of a Florentine slab he sold to Edward Holmes Baldock, suggest that the attraction of pietre dure included its weight of history and associations. Behind this, in a world steeped in classical learning, was the sense of marble as a noble Roman material. Its permanence lent it further appeal. In this respect the iconography of the Badminton Cabinet is particularly explicit: on its drawers and door everlasting materials drawn from Nature, marbles and hard stones, dazzlingly mimic the evanescent figure of a butterfly's wing, the feathers of a bird or the petals of a flower, and so, thanks to Art, Nature itself has triumphed over Time. The clock and the statues of the four seasons placed above reinforce this temporal theme, but Nature, Art and Time are yoked together in homage to the Beaufort arms (essentially the royal arms of England) set topmost, with their proud motto, 'Mutare vel timere sperno' [I scorn change or fear].

When the dowager Duchess of Beaufort visited Stourhead in 1762 she remarked 'in ye Cabinet room Cabinet very fine of precious stones, & a coffer of the same'.[173] The high value of the materials of pietre dure constituted an essential element of its prestige, as did the virtuoso craftsmanship involved in its manufacture. In 1726 the philomath Richard Neve claimed of architecture, with which he linked 'the *Mechanicks* of *Handicrafts*', that 'This Noble *Art* makes *Marble*, and other *Stones* become the Delights of Men, of which are made our Glorious Palaces, and the Ornaments of our most splendid Churches, and the most durable Monuments which the Ambition of Man could ever invent, to render themselves and their Grandure known to future Ages.'[174]

1. González-Palacios 1993, I, p. 141.
2. Jervis 2007, pp. 247–8.
3. Dudley 1990, chapter 3.
4. Foster 1991, pp. 22–3, 80.
5. Foister, Roy and Wyld 1997, p. 43.
6. Butters 1996, p. 141.
7. Starkey 1998, p. 205, no. 9541.
8. Jourdain 1924, figs 20 and 21.
9. Wolsey and Luff 1968, figs 79 and 80.
10. On Astley see Collins 1955, pp. 199–223, and *ODNB*, 'John Astley (*c*.1507–1596)', 'Katherine Astley (d. 1565)' and 'Jacob Astley, first Baron Astley of Reading (1579–1652)'.
11. Collins 1955, p. 218.
12. Jervis 2010, pp. 47–50. The 1588 inventory of Robert Dudley, Earl of Leicester's London house includes 'a square table layd in with marble stone, standing upon a frame', which may be an earlier mention of a pietre dure slab (Bracken 2003, p. 218, note 101).
13. Ronfort 1991–2, pp. 139–47.
14. Hay 2010, p. 185, note 2.
15. Brennan 1993, p. 180, where it is noted that later, in 1644, Evelyn observed, in the same palace, 'whole tables […] many of them set with Achates, Onyxes, Cornelians, Lazulis, Pearle, Turquizes, & other precious stones'.
16. Bonnaffé 1874, pp. 137–8, no. 685; Havard 1887–90, III , col. 607.
17. Gross 1981, pp. 157–9.
18. González-Palacios (catalogue entry 7) 1988, p. 90.
19. Rye 1865, p. 45.
20. González-Palacios 2001, illus. pp. 87 and 91.
21. Cornforth 1988, p. 164. However, Coleridge 1967, p. 64, cites in the 1621 Hatfield inventory '1 square table of stone inlaid with colours', '1 square table with a frame of walnut tree' and '1 faire square table inlaid with a frame to it', which might include two marble slabs. But in 1761 Horace Walpole remarked only a single 'fine table of inlaid marbles, Italian' at Hatfield (Toynbee 1928, p. 35).
22. Chaney 1985, pp. 313–14.
23. González-Palacios 2001, p. 86.
24. Jervis 1978, p. 209, where a second Roman table at Arundel, in this case rectangular, is also illustrated.
25. Jervis 2005, p. 244, cites among the Duke's purchases from Davis '5 February 1883 "A fine Mosaic table" £540' and '11 May 1883 "a very fine Florentine table" £400'. But Arundel Inventory 1816 includes in the First Floor Gallery 'A Marble Slab' and, in the Best Staircase or entrance hall, another. These might just be those still at Arundel.
26. Hervey 1921, p. 130.
27. British Museum, BM 1917-6-12v. A somewhat comparable table with a central chess-board and drawers in its frieze in the collection of the Principe d'Avalos in Naples is illustrated by González-Palacios 1981, p. 10, fig. 1.
28. British Museum, BM 1917-6-10r.; quotation after Summerson 1966, pp. 60–1.
29. Jervis 1997, p. 69.
30. Barker, Devonshire and Scarisbirck 2003, pp. 84–5. This cabinet has much in common with a Florentine example now in the National Gallery of Canada (González- Palacios 1986, I, pp. 64–5, pls II–III).
31. Millar 1972, p. 418 (33).

32. Millar 1972, p. 120, no. 333.
33. Jervis 1989, p. 288.
34. Millar 1972, p. 121, no. 335.
35. Radcliffe and Thornton 1976, pp. 254–63.
36. Jervis 2007, pp. 247 and 257, fig. 1.
37. Christie's, London, 19 March 1992, lot 119; also Sotheby's, London, 5 July 2006, lot 6; see also Ketton-Cremer 1944, pp. 35–6.
38. 'Diary of Nicholas Stone, Junior', in Spiers 1919, pp. 160–200.
39. Repton 1844, p. 152; Wenley 1990–3, p. 136.
40. White 1999, pp. 123, 134–5.
41. The Bargrave table is inscribed 'Per il Sigr Giovanni Bargrave A Roma 1660' (Harris 1986, p. 278).
42. Bachrach and Collmer 1982, p. 58.
43. Brennan 2004, pp. 111 and 138; Alcouffe, Dion-Tenenbaum and Lefébure 1993, pp. 332–3; Langer and von Württemberg 1996, pp. 68–72.
44. Chaney 1985, p.168.
45. Fowler 1994, p. 239.
46. González-Palacios and Röttgen 1982, pp. 86–7.
47. Jervis 2007, p. 247. The 1710 quotation is, however, more likely to refer to a cabinet from Drayton House whose drawer fronts are decorated with *pietra paesina*, which was with Jonathan Harris in 1991; a related casket was sold at Christie's, South Kensington, on 8 September 2009.
48. Impey 1998, pp. 192–3.
49. Koeppe 2008, pp. 176–7. Even closer are the pietre dure panels on a cabinet in the Detroit Institute of Arts (1994.77) with a Frescobaldi provenance. In the Cabinet Room at Corsham Court, Wiltshire, is another cabinet with animal panels, acquired by the Revd John Sandford in Florence, probably in the 1830s (illus., Methuen-Campbell 2004, p. 9).
50. Markham 1984, p. 155.
51. Rowell 2011, pp. 4–5.
52. Burton 1960, pp. 14–16. The two tables referred to are probably the handsome slabs, now in the Entrance Hall and the Hall at Lamport, with double rectilinear borders, but no complex pietre dure decoration; the Roman table illustrated may be among 'yr past tabels' mentioned in the same letter.
53. Nino Strachey, in Rowell 2005, p. 67.
54. Sotheby's, London, 7 December 2010, lot 7.
55. Rowell 2013, pp. 204–21.
56. *Gori Relazione* 1771–9, cited by Massinelli 1997, p. 256.
57. Jenkins 2005, pp. 121, 123. The adjective 'rich' is missing from the first description.
58. Cock 1747, p. 42, The State Bed Chamber, lot 8. The other table, with an identical description, apart from the omission of any mention of *lapis lazuli*, is lot 7 on p. 21, The Drawing Room, next the state bed-chamber.
59. Collins Baker and Collins 1949, pp. 75, 79, 165.
60. Jervis 2006, p. 140; Michel 1999, p. 328.
61. Tomlin 1972, pp. 106–7.
62. Ingamells 1997, p. 634.
63. Lot 1725.
64. Peill 2007, p. 119. Yet another cabinet of this type with 11 pietre dure landscape panels is in the Gilbert Collection (González Palacios and Röttgen 1982, pp. 96–7). Lacking an early provenance it was, up to its sale at Christie's

in 1967, on a Kentian stand (illus., Beard and Goodison 1987, p.79), later replaced with its present gilt gesso stand, of an early eighteenth-century character.
65. Jervis 2007, p. 249.
66. Pryke 1996, pp. 44–5.
67. Murdoch 2006, p. 258.
68. Markham 1984, pp. 201, 365.
69. Christie's 2004, p. 46.
70. Syndram 1994, pp. 28, 121.
71. Jervis 2007, pp. 249–50.
72. Ibid., p. 250.
73. Ibid., pp. 247–9.
74. Coleridge 1968, plate A.
75. Luce and Jessop 1955, p. 114.
76. Ingamells 1997, pp. 472 and 1030.
77. Rieder 1974, pp. 11–13.
78. Thornton and Rieder 1974, pp. 107–10, fig. 5; Christie's, London, 8th July 1999, lot 110.
79. Roberts 2004, p. 255, no. 261, illus.
80. Illus., Penny 1991, p. 8.
81. González-Palacios, 'La Galleria nel tardo Settecento. Antonio Cioci', in González-Palacios 1986, pp. 85–8. The tables, once at Panshanger, are now in a private collection in the United Kingdom.
82. Friedman 1975, p. 847.
83. Vertue 1955, p. 90.
84. *A Magnificent Roman Baroque Cabinet by Giacomo Herman*, Sotheby's, London, 4 December 2007.
85. Croft-Murray 1970, pp. 2113, 254–5.
86. For Amigoni, Croft-Murray 1970 pp. 164–5. White 1984, p. 248, floats James Gibbs as a possible architect for the remodelled chapel at Cowdray, where very fine plaster fragments survived the 1793 fire. Vertue 1955, p. 90, can be taken to imply that the cabinet stood in the 'Bed chamber, where Queen Elisabeth lay'.
87. Abel Smith 1996, pp. 25–30; Cockburn, quoted by Alvar González-Palacios, 'The Badminton Cabinet', in Christie's 2004, p. 63.
88. Sitwell 1942, p. 116.
89. Rokeby 1986, endpapers.
90. Christie's, London, 10 July 2014, lot 40.
91. Markham 1984, p. 390.
92. Illus., Syon Park 2003, p. 51.
93. Scarisbrick 1987, pp. 90–104
94. Toynbee 1928, p. 72.
95. Although it should be noted that in 1775, during a later stay in Rome, Newdigate purchased a pietre dure cabinet from an Antonio Lucchese (Wood 1962, p. 43).
96. Ingamells 1997, p. 278.
97. Ibid., p. 320.
98. Jenkins 2007, p. 147.
99. Illus., Jackson-Stops 1985, p. 303 (as 'probably Roman'); Jervis 2006, p. 96.
100. British Museum, BM 1764, 0928.1.
101. Porzio 2001, pp. 6–19, 32–41.
102. González-Palacios 2001, pp. 273–4, where the name of Mattia Valenziani, who in 1786 sold Goethe a number of objects formed of lava, is also mentioned.
103. Gilbert 1978, 1, p. 278, 2, fig. 287.
104. Rowan 1993, fig. 39; Ingamells 1997, p. 516.
105. Fothergill 1969, pp. 131–2.
106. Christie's, London, 29 March 1805, lot 18.
107. Beckford 1805, 2, p. 384.
108. Sotheby's, London, 6 July 2011, lot 11.
109. Fittipaldi 1995, pp. 32–3.
110. Quoted by Chaney 1998, pp. 113 and 135.
111. Christie's, London, 9 June 2005, lot 50;

Annamaria Giusti, in Koeppe 2008, pp. 208–9.
112. Colle 1997, pp. 145–6, pl. 11.
113. González-Palacios 2011, pp. 51–6.
114. 136.5 cm x 79 cm; Sotheby's, 13 March 1931, lot 105; with Carlton Hobbs, New York.
115. *Treasures from the Royal Collection* 1988, pp. 102–3.
116. Andrews 1936, p. 296.
117. I am grateful to Christopher Rowell for this information.
118. Ingamells 1997, p. 785.
119. Gray Long Gallery Report 2010.
120. Wainwright 1989, p. 217; Jervis 2004, pp. 400–4.
121. Jervis 2004, pp. 400–4.
122. Wainwright 1989, pp. 222–4.
123. In the Picture Gallery in 2011: 106 cm x 123 cm (3 ft 5¾ ins x 4 ft ½ in). Another finer Roman table (48 in, 122 cm square) of the about the same date in the Walker Art Gallery, Liverpool, was formerly at Nostell Priory, Yorkshire, for which it was probably acquired by Charles Winn (1795–1874), a passionate collector, who inherited in 1817.
124. de Bellaigue 1995, pp. 157–79
125. *Carlton House* 1991, pp. 76–7, pl. XI. In 1818 George IV also bought the small cabinet mounted with Florentine pietre dure panels, which Richard Dalton had acquired for his parents in Rome in the late 1760s, at the sale of his mother, Queen Charlotte's possessions (see note 79 above).
126. Roberts 2002, pp. 178–9.
127. González-Palacios, 'I Fiorentini del Re Sole', in González-Palacios 1993, I, pp. 19–60.
128. Baxter 1992, pp. 350–2.
129. Wilson 1985, pp. 38–45.
130. Roberts, 2002, pp. 163–4.
131. McLeod and Hewat Jaboor 2002, pp. 135–43.
132. Alexander 1957, p. 191; Gemmett, 2000.
133. Tait 1983, pp. 395–6; Massinelli 1997, pp. 49–50.
134. Roberts 2000, pp. 115–37. See Cordier 2012, p. 368, for an attribution of this group to Alexandre Bellangé.
135. Robins 1832, lot 25.
136. Christie's, London, 17 June–20 July 1882, lots 181, 182, 520, 540, 666, 876, 877, 896, 992, 995, 996, 1276, 1278, 1287, 1439 and 1440.
137. Sotheby's, London, 10 December 1993, lot 70 (I am grateful to Godfrey Evans for this reference); the Hamilton Church table is described by Alvar González-Palacios in Sarti 2006, pp. 65–9; Koeppe 2008, pp. 120–2.
138. Chancellor 1908, pp. 260–74. Another similar table formerly at Belvedere, County Meath, was probably acquired by Charles Brinsley Marlay (1829–1912), the benefactor of the Fitzwilliam Museum, Cambridge (Guinness 1971, p. 297), while a further specimen (Sotheby's, London, 15 December 1999, lot 46) was on an English stand of about 1830, suggesting that it was in England then.
139. Stillman 1977, p. 85.
140. Newman 1995, p. 509; Impey 1998, p. 130.
141. I am grateful to High Brigstocke for this reference.
142. Beckford 1805, I, p. 171; Simond 1828, p. 101, went even further: 'I have heard of fifteen, twenty, and twenty-five years spent by a set of artists working together to finish a single table!'
143. Morgan 1821, 2, p. 94.
144. As well as Barberi, Irvine mentions Blasi, Cartoni, Coredore, Giustiniani, Bernadino Ledus, Count Leoncelli, Magaoli, Magrola, Mazzei, Palmaroli and Ravaglioni. I am grateful, again, to Hugh Brigstocke for these names.
145. Nogué 2000, p. 20: González-Palacios 2001, pp. 276–9.
146. Gilbert 1998, pp. 681–4.
147. Price 2007, pp. 11–12.
148. In his *Handbook of Chatsworth*, quoted in Devonshire 1982, p. 143.
149. Sotheby's, London, 10 June 1998, lot 20.
150. Christie's, London, 4 July 1882, lot 996.
151. Roberts 2001, pp. 248 and 269. I am grateful to Jonathan Marsden for the information that the cabinet bears Paul V's arms, surmounted by a tiara and crossed keys.
152. Illus., Methuen-Campbell 2004, p.16.
153. Museum number 1556-1856.
154. Hay 2010, pp. 157–88; Horace Walpole had 'A snuff-box with mosaic pigeons, from the antique; a present from her royal highness the duchess of Gloucester' in the Great North Bedchamber at Strawberry Hill (Walpole 1798, 2, p. 503).
155. Hay 2010, pp. 167–70, fig. 11.
156. Brighton 1995, pp. 58–67; Tomlinson 1996, *passim* and p. 10.
157. Marsden 2010, pp. 254–5.
158. Illus, Jervis 1983, pl. viii.
159. Cockcroft 1979, pp. 493–4.
160. Waring 1863; a bird motif is already visible on a Magnus bath shown at the 1851 Great Exhibition (illus. London, 1851, p. 229; Jervis 1972, pp. 52–7; the bookcase (ibid., fig. 3) is in the possession of the author.
161. Crook 1981, pl. 199 (now Lotherton Hall, Leeds, 32/71), and Birmingham Museum and Art Gallery M134.71.
162. V&A museum file 403/1881; Christie, Manson & Woods, 18 January 1881, The Valuable Stock of Mr Joseph Toms (Formerly of Messrs Toms and Luscombe of New Bond Street), lots 313 and 314.
163. Litchfield 1907, p. 309.
164. Collard 1996, pp. 81–9; Westgarth 2009, pp. 174–5.
165. Jervis 1978, p. 206, pls G and H, and Jervis 2005, p. 244.
166. González-Palacios 1986, I, p. 154, pl. xxxi.
167. Dakers 2010, p. 197, and Dakers 2011, p. 184.
168. Christie's, London, 7 May 1936, J.G. Morrison, Esq., of Fonthill House, Tisbury, Wilts., lot 130: the next lot, another smaller giltwood table, from its description neoclassical, was also 'surmounted by an inlaid marble slab' and bought by Lipitch, for only £3.13.6 (the prices and buyers noted in the National Art Library copy of the catalogue).
169. I am grateful to Norma Aubertin-Potter for information and access. She showed me a smaller Roman slab given by Codrington to All Souls, which *might* be the second slab in the 1936 sale (see previous note), although the base is different and the dimension does not tally exactly.
170. Marot *c.*1660: 'Dans le Milieu dudit Salon, il y a une table de pierres pretieuses de raport, entre-autre, une Agathe d'une prodigieuse grandeur la fait estimer une des plus belles tables du monde.' It had earlier been admired by Lord Mandeville, see note 43 above.
171. Codrington 'Gathering Moss' 1947: his military career never matching his father, Lt Gen. Sir Alfred Edward Codrington (1854–1945), he was later successful as a landscape gardener. In 1952, his ex-wife, Primrose Harley, divorced in 1945, married his friend, Lanning Roper (1912–1983).
172. Ford 1988, p. 44; Dutton 1969, p. 81.
173. Harris 2000, p. 41.
174. Neve 1726, p. vi.

TWO
ROMAN PIETRE DURE

Marmoream se relinquere quam latericiam accepisset.
SUETONIUS, *DIVUS AUGUSTUS*, 28

The Emperor Augustus's well-known claim, recorded by Suetonius, that he found Rome a city of brick and left it one of marble, reflects the imperial taste for that noble material.[1] Marble was sometimes used in Rome earlier, but tended to be associated with the luxurious appetites frowned on by those who cherished the *mos maiorum*, the set of ancestral attitudes, including frugality, which constituted the bedrock of republican virtue. In his *Exempla*, or anecdotes, Cornelis Nepos (*c.*100–*c.*24 BC) stated that the first person to introduce marble wall revetments and columns of solid marble to a private house in Rome was Mamurra, who had served as a supervisor of engineers in Gaul under Julius Caesar, and was notorious for extravagance and other vices zestfully attacked by Nepos's close friend, the poet Catullus. In the third quarter of the first century AD the encyclopaedist Pliny the Elder preserved this anecdote in his *Historia Naturalis*. He also noted, as an earlier symptom of Rome's decline towards decadent luxury, that Lucius Licinius Crassus, who served as consul in 95 BC, had incorporated six columns of marble from Mount Hymettus, near Athens, in his house on the Palatine Hill, leading to his being nicknamed the 'Venus Palatina' by Marcus Junius Brutus, the father of the tyrannicide.[2] White – or whiteish – marbles were the most commonly used in Roman architecture, ornament and sculpture. Their ancient sources included Mount Hymettus, Mount Pentelicos, also near Athens, and the islands of Paros in the central Aegean Sea, Thasos in the northern Aegean and Proconnesus in the sea of Marmara, but from the mid-first century BC Rome began to intensify the exploitation of the quarries, now known as Carrara, near the Etruscan town of Luni. About a century later Seneca the Younger was bemoaning modern luxury, citing the employment of coloured marbles from the sands of Egypt, from the deserts of Africa, from Alexandria and Numidia. Some hint of the variety of marbles available in Rome is provided by the *Edictum de maximis pretiis* [edict on maximum prices] promulgated by the emperor Diocletian

in AD 301, in an early and vain attempt to control inflation, which lists 19 varieties, with prices for a cubic foot ranging from 250 *denarii* for Egyptian red and Greek green porphyry to 40 *denarii* for Proconnesian white marble and 'Potamogalleno', identified as an ash-coloured Bithynian marble.

From the reign of Tiberius, who succeeded Augustus in AD 14, the Luni quarries were imperial property, and eventually most of the important quarries of the Roman empire came under imperial control, the most celebrated including Mons Claudianus in the eastern Egyptian desert, the source of the grey granite of the great columns of the Pantheon's portico, and, also in Egypt but even more remote, Mons Porphyrites, the exclusive source of the red or purplish porphyry reserved for imperial use in Rome and later in Constantinople. Marble extraction, distribution and allocation fell to a central administration, the *statio marmorum* [marble department]. The Egyptian quarries, which were connected to the Nile and the Red Sea by a web of roads and way stations, ceased production around the middle of the fifth century. Thus, in the sixth century, it was later claimed, a pious widow named Marcia sent Justinian six great porphyry columns from the temple of the Sun on the Quirinal, founded by Aurelian in the late third century, for use in Hagia Sophia in Constantinople. The detail may be unreliable, but recycling was certainly the only way of acquiring porphyry at this period. In imperial Rome there was a central marble depot by the Tiber at what is still called Via Marmorata and a wharf further up by Tor di Nona near a concentration of marble-workers' workshops.

The attraction of marbles lay not only in their colours and figure. Some were also supposed to possess magical, religious or curative properties. But particular weight was often given to their provenance in regions, often remote, with rich historic and mythological associations. Thus when the poet Statius (*c.*45–*c.*96) thanked the emperor Domitian for inviting him to a spectacular dinner, he describes how in the banqueting hall:

FIG. 50
Table top, pietre dure, Rome about 1600, signed by Pietro Carli, from Florence, formerly at Fonthill House, Wiltshire, whence purchased in 1936 for £6.16.6 as a wedding present from his fellow Guards' officers to John Alfred Codrington, who gave it to All Souls College, Oxford, in 1984. 76⅜ x 52¾ in, 194.5 x 134 cm.

Aemulus illic
Mons Libys, Iliacusque nitent, et multa Syene,
Et Chios, et glauca certantia Doride saxa
Lunaque portandis tantum suffecta columnis[3]

[there marble from a Libyan mountain strives to excel, and marble from Troy, and many panels from Syene shine out, and marble from Chios, and stones that vie with the blue Sicilian sea, and Luna, only supplied for the supporting columns]. This makes a distinction between white Luni marble used for construction and coloured marbles used, it must be presumed, on the floors and walls. On floors marbles were often used in the form of *opus sectile* [cut work], in which sawn elements of contrasting colours were used to create predominantly geometric patterns, ranging from the simple to enormously complex and variegated polychrome designs. The bow saw allowed the introduction of discs and other curved elements, and yet greater variation and elaboration, and on occasion the inclusion of flowers, leaves and other naturalistic motifs. Roman marble wall decorations have a dramatically lower survival rate than floors, floors in *opus sectile* surviving in most parts of the Roman empire (there are even some fragments in England, where the cheaper mosaic is prevalent).[4] On walls marble was used as plain slabs and in mainly rectilinear panelled schemes. A famous example of this type survives, restored, on the upper walls of the Pantheon, erected under Hadrian from 118 to 125 AD. But in the reign of Claudius, who succeeded as emperor in 41 AD, according to

FIG. 51
Wall elevation of the Basilica of Junius Bassus (Sant'Andrea Catabarbara) by Giuliano da Sangallo, Rome, from Codice Barberini Lat. 4434. 17⅞ x 15¼ in, 45.4 x 38.8 cm. Biblioteca Apostolica Vaticana, Rome.

Pliny the Elder, who did not approve of this development: 'coepimus et lapide pingere' [we also began to paint with marble].[5] Sadly there are no early survivals of pictorial *opus sectile* schemes. Indeed until 1969, when a complex partly Christian scheme excavated near the Porta Marina at Ostia was published, the only extensive example was in the former secular basilica of Junius Bassus, dedicated in 331 AD, when he was consul, which became a church thanks to a generous bequest from a high-ranking Goth, Valila, in the 470s during the pontificate of Simplicius (468–483). Remarkably, the conversion did not obliterate Bassus's rich but pagan decorations, which survived to be drawn (fig. 51) by Giuliano da Sangallo (c.1445–1516) late in the fifteenth century.[6]

While the Basilica of Junius Bassus was being converted into a church *opus sectile* was still being used to decorate the walls of other Christian buildings, notably the narthex of the Lateran Baptistry and the nave of Santa Sabina in Rome, and the inner walls of the Arian Baptistry in Ravenna, which incorporate peltate forms similar to those shown in Sangallo's Junius Bassus drawings.[7] But power and riches had migrated to Constantinople, the new Rome, where Roman marble *spolia* were used extensively as wall decoration in Hagia Sophia, and prized, porphyry above all, for their divine and imperial significance, as well as for the rarity and beauty celebrated in Paul the Silentiary's poetic description of the great church, delivered in 563. In Rome there was a long period of massive destruction and loss. In the ninth century, however, there was some revival of *opus sectile*, at least for floors, notably in San Prassede, where a great porphyry disc is surrounded by a chequer pattern formed by small squares of contrasting marbles.[8] Porphyry discs or *rotae*, essentially slices sawn from porphyry columns, are a regular feature of floors, liturgical fittings and wall decorations produced by Roman *marmorarii* [marble workers] from about 1100–1300 AD. They carried echoes of the great *rota porphyretica* set in the nave floor of Constantine's Old St Peter's, and associated with imperial coronations.[9] The layout of such *opus sectile* ornament was exclusively geometric, and often, as with the Great Pavement (fig. 1) of Westminster Abbey executed by Petrus Oderisius in 1268, very complex.

The technique is indelibly associated with the Cosmati family, first documented in 1264 and thus relative latecomers to a tradition which dwindled away for lack of patronage after the transfer of the papacy to Avignon in 1309. Antiquity and early Christian associations were doubtless behind the incorporation of a porphyry *rota* on the marble table in the Old Sacristy of San Lorenzo in Florence above Buggiani's 1433 tomb to Giovanni di Averardo de' Medici and his wife Piccarda, and the larger and more prominent porphyry *rota* with a superimposed white marble knot placed before the high altar of San Lorenzo in 1465 as a tomb marker for Cosimo de' Medici. The Vatican Sistine Chapel and the Carafa Chapel in Santa Maria sopra Minerva were given Cosmatesque *opus sectile* floors in the 1480s, an example followed in about 1510 in the Stanza della Segnatura where the floor, which complements Raphael's ceiling, is inscribed with Julius II's name.[10]

ROMAN TABLES: JEAN MÉNARD

In Rome the *Universitas Marmorariorum et Sculptorum* [guild of marble workers and sculptors] had statutes dated 1206, and must have provided some continuity. Nonetheless, after its adoption in the Stanza della Segnatura, the Cosmatesque style of *opus sectile* was eclipsed and around 1550 a new manner emerged, influenced by ancient examples and marked by a wider and more colourful range of marbles, in arrangements still predominantly geometric but now usually incorporating scrolls, cartouches, peltate forms, multiple borders and oval rather than circular centres, regularly of richly figured alabasters. Tops of this type are depicted, sketchily but unmistakeably, on three drawings of about 1554 by the little-known Giovanni Colonna da Tivoli, whose notes seem to credit one to a specialist in fine brick floors identifiable as Giovanni di Nono (or Giovanni Pietro Annone), who was working for Cardinal Giovanni Ricci di Montepulciano (1498–1574) at his palazzo in the Via Giulia (now the Palazzo Sacchetti) and is later documented as a 'scarpellino' [stonemason].[11] Ricci was evidently a connoisseur of pietre dure tables. The sculptor Flaminio Vacca (1538–1605) later recorded that the Cardinal had purchased recently excavated transparent alabaster columns, part of which he incorporated in pietre dure tables dispatched to the King of Portugal (in fact the Crown Prince) but lost at sea. This episode must have happened in early 1564 just before a 'M.ro Giovanni Franzese m.ro di tavole' received payments from the Cardinal. This 'table master' has been identified as Jean Ménard (*c*.1525–1582). Ménard was first mentioned as 'Franciosino scultore' in 1552, when he was working on the fountain of Pope Julius III's Villa Giulia, designed by Bartolomeo Ammanati (1511–1592), where Vasari and Vignola were also involved and whose nymphaeum incorporated a semi-circular floor with a fan-like arrangement of coloured marbles.[12] In 1555 Ammanati wrote a description of the Villa to a Paduan patron, the scholar and collector Marco Mantova Benavides (1489–1582), mentioning two very large pietre dure tables, over 11 feet long and over four feet wide, each with three inlaid marble bases, on which Ménard may have worked. When, in the 1560s, Ménard was engaged on the Ricci Chapel in San Pietro in Montorio, one of his colleagues was named as 'Mastro Ludovico delle Tavole', which suggests that working on tables was an established speciality. In 1568 Francesco de' Medici, through his secretary, Bartolomeo Concini, asked Cardinal Ricci to recommend him a stoneworker capable of carving or mounting stones. Ricci replied that he had found someone, meaning Ménard, 'perfettissimo per inserirle' [absolutely perfect at fitting stone together] and offered to suggest another who could carve, while drawing attention to the availability of a mass of carved stones assembled by his banker, Gerolamo Ceuli, whose son, Tiberio (see p. 97), was eventually to acquire Ricci's palazzo. Ménard's skill seems to have been sought to supervise the completion of a richly inlaid table designed by Vasari, being executed by a Florentine expert, Bernardino di Porfirio da Leccio, who had made another for Francesco's father, Duke Cosimo de' Medici, which suggests that Rome was in 1568 perceived as commanding greater skill in this art than Florence. In the event, Ménard was too busy to go to Florence. Ricci, referring to him as this 'franciosetto', another diminutive of 'Frenchman' (he must have been small) and reiterating that he was the best at his craft in Rome, attributed to him 'un poco del fantastico' [a touch of the fantastic], implying that he was a creative artist as well as a supreme craftsman.

Ménard may also have been something of a thug, having been involved in a 1568 knife brawl in the house of Michelangelo with whom Ménard seems to have had prolonged contacts, including in about 1560 an involvement attested by Vasari in the wooden model for the dome of St Peter's. In 1570 he travelled to Naples to work on tables for the Viceroy, Pedro Afán de Ribera, assisted by a restorer, Giuliano Menichini from Carrara. In 1580 another Roman maker of tables, a Fleming named Niccolò Musterdi, sent three pietre dure chess boards to Naples, so this was probably a regular trade. In the 1570s Ménard was active as a restorer and/or dealer in antique sculpture. In 1579, however, he moved to Paris to serve the Queen Mother, Catherine de Médicis: he had dispatched a load of marble and antique sculpture by sea (this was captured by an Algerian galley but eventually, in 1581, returned). In 1582 he died in Paris, leaving behind a dynasty of marble workers. It is possible that the 'grande table de marbre' (see p. 4) in Catherine's 1589 inventory may have been made by Ménard, whether in Paris or sent earlier from Rome.[13] His career suggests that by his death grand pietre dure tables had been produced in Rome for around 30 years and had gained international renown.

ROMAN TABLES: FERDINANDO DE' MEDICI

Annone and Ménard were not the only makers of pietre dure tables patronized by Cardinal Ricci. The 'Ludovico delle Tavole' mentioned above had a brother, Francesco di Bastiano de' Rossi, born in Florence, who worked on tables for Ricci in the mid-1560s, while a Francesco di Baronio was paid in connection with tables destined for Cardinal d'Avalos d'Aragona, for Prince Orsini and for a queen, probably Catherine de Médicis. Ricci indeed had a reputation for wheeling and dealing fitter for a merchant than a prince of the church.[14] A native of Montepulciano in Tuscany, he became close to the young Cardinal Ferdinando de' Medici (1549–1609), whose 1563 appointment as a cardinal he had supported and to whom he had given lodging several times before he settled in Rome in 1569 at the age of 18. In 1576 Ferdinando purchased Ricci's splendid villa on the Pincio, and embellished it to become the Villa Medici. In 1587 he resigned the purple and moved to Florence to succeed his brother, Francesco, as Grand Duke of Tuscany. Inventories of the Villa Medici taken in 1588 and 1598 record the presence there of six pietre dure tables, indubitably Roman, and probably a combination of his own commissions and others taken over from Ricci. Two have been identified, one in the Sala di Venere of the Palazzo Pitti, and another at the Villa del Poggio Imperiale, possibly that made by Ménard using the transparent alabaster acquired by Ricci in about 1564, while a third, in this case oval, table with the signs of the zodiac, now in the Museo degli Argenti in Palazzo Pitti, made in Rome before 1587, may be from the Palazzo Firenze, Ferdinando's town house in Rome, or from the Villa Medici, but for some reason not recorded in its inventories.[15] In 1588 Ferdinando founded the Galleria dei Lavori (Opificio delle Pietre Dure since 1860) in Florence, combining the various court workshops in the Uffizi. The Galleria's particular focus on pietre dure echoed the tastes of his father, Cosimo, and his brother, Francesco, and harks back to the much earlier taste for hard stones displayed by Piero de' Medici 'Il Gottoso' (1416–1469) and his son, Lorenzo 'Il Magnifico' (1449–1492),[16] but there is no doubt that under the auspices of Ferdinando and later generations Florentine pietre dure became increasingly sophisticated. In 1588, however, Ferdinando had spent almost all his adult life in Rome, and Roman pietre dure was what he knew and, judging by his acquisitions, admired. And the first director of his Galleria dei Lavori was a Roman noble, Emilio dei Cavalieri (c.1550–1602), who was active in securing Roman marbles for Florence.[17] It is worth noting that Ferdinando was a friend and supporter of Cardinal Felice Peretti during his years of disfavour and campaigned for his election as pope, when the Medici cause was lost, and that the Villa Medici was a beneficiary of the Acqua Felice, when its waters began to flow.

ROMAN TABLES: GIOVANNI ANTONIO DOSIO

Communication between Rome and Florence was so easy and contacts so close, apart from the fact that in 1537 most of the members of the Roman Università dei Marmorari were of Tuscan origin, that too much should not be made of contrasts between the two.[18] In 1569 Cardinal Ricci wrote to the Medici secretary, Concini, about a recently excavated large white slab which he had fitted with a green marble border and was sending to Florence to receive extra decoration there.[19] Once complete was this Roman or Florentine? Another case is the architect, sculptor and antiquary, Giovanni Antonio Dosio (1533–1611), who was born in San Gimignano, but moved to Rome at 15 and, although he often worked elsewhere for brief periods, was only in Florence regularly from about 1575–90, renting a house there in 1576, but still spending time in Rome.[20] In 1596 he was living in Naples and he died at Caserta in 1611, but during these years he was still involved with Roman projects (including, in 1609–10, maintenance work on the Palazzo Firenze for Grand Duke Ferdinando). Dosio's archaeological activity (in 1562 he discovered parts of the *Forma Urbis Romae*, the ancient marble map of Rome, from the Templum Pacis) led him to deal in antique sculpture and *spolia* and to provide drawings of antiquities, some used for engravings published by Bernardo Gamucci in 1565 and by Giovanni Battista de' Cavalieri in 1569. It was thus predictable that he had contacts with the prodigiously rich Florentine banker and collector, Niccolò Gaddi (1537–1591), who advised both Francesco and Ferdinando de' Medici. Gaddi used Dosio as an agent in purchasing

FIG. 52

Design for two table tops, by Giovanni Antonio Dosio, Rome, about 1565. From the collection of Niccolò Gaddi. Pen and watercolour over pencil, 16⅛ x 10⅞ in, 41 x 27.6 cm. Galleria degli Uffizi, Florence.

antiques and employed him to decorate the Cappella Gaddi in Santa Maria Novella, executed from 1575–7.[21] Although preceded by the more modest marble dado of the Cappella Cavalcanti in Santo Spirito, executed in about 1560, which has been attributed to Dosio,[22] and by Vasari's 1563 proposal that the Cappella dei Principi at San Lorenzo be 'tutta di vari marmi mischi a musaico' [all in various polychrome marbles in the manner of mosaic (that is pietre dure)],[23] the Cappella Gaddi was the first spectacular instance of pietre dure chapel decoration in Florence.

Predictably Agostino del Riccio (1541–1598), the author of a manuscript *Istoria delle Pietre* [History of Stones], the first comprehensive work on the subject, singled out the Cappella Gaddi for praise, noting no fewer than 18 different marbles.[24] He was a Dominican monk of Santa Maria Novella and, while he recognized the Roman origin of many stones, his work was first dedicated 'All'onorati ed industriosi Fiorentini' [to the honoured and industrious citizens of Florence], and he always stressed the Florentine dimension. The floor of the Cappella Gaddi incorporated fan-like motifs reminiscent of the nymphaeum of the Villa Giulia and was revealingly compared by Riccio to a series of 'tavolini' [little tables]. It was indeed Roman in materials and design, as was its successor and rival, the Cappella Niccolini in Santa Croce, on which Dosio began to work in 1579.[25] His client, the rich diplomat and collector, Giovanni Niccolini (1544–1610), was appointed as ambassador to Sixtus v in 1587 and remained in Rome almost to his death. In that final year Dosio recommended to him Benetto Balsimelli, then also in Naples, to finish off the marble work: earlier elements included the altar table produced by Giulio Balsimelli in 1584, whose border is of a clearly Roman character and resembles a table design by Dosio in the Uffizi, part of a group of drawings from the collection of Niccolò Gaddi acquired in 1778.[26]

The dating of Dosio's designs is difficult: one sheet (fig. 52) incorporating an octagonal table with a predominance of curved peltate motifs has on its verso a rectangular table with a mainly rectilinear schema and has been convincingly assigned to the 1560s.[27] Both approaches were evidently contemporary. Another Uffizi design, clearly related, with regard to its oval centre and flanking scrolls, to the Palazzo Pitti Sala di Venere table, has a rectilinear border in strong contrast to the executed design, while a further sheet has a variation on the executed border but a different arrangement of the central oval.[28] To introduce a different and later witness, a design for the floor monument of Giovanni Vincenzo Cardinal Gonzaga (1540–1591) in S. Alessio by the sculptor Nicolas Piper d'Arras (d.1599), who had worked on the Cappella Sistina in Santa Maria Maggiore, displays a fine central cast bronze armorial set on a marble slab with a relatively simple geometric pietre dure border with some peltate elements which could easily be assigned to the 1560s.[29] Such evidence tends to suggest that this repertoire of ornament was interchangeable and long lived. The most celebrated example, the very large Farnese Table (fig. 53), now in the Metropolitan Museum of Art, New York, has been dated between 1566, when Cardinal Alessandro Farnese (1520–1589) began to display the arms incorporating the fleurs-de-lys inlaid on its top and carved on its triple marble bases, attributed to Guglielmo della Porta, and the year of death of its supposed designer, the architect Jacopo Barozzi da Vignola (1507–1573).[30] In the Palazzo Farnese are a number of smaller and simpler tables which display similar ornament and must be roughly contemporary.[31]

ROMAN TABLES: GIOVANNI VINCENZO CASALE

New light was thrown on Roman tables of the late sixteenth century with the publication of an album of drawings in the Biblioteca Nacional in Madrid assembled by Giovanni Vincenzo Casale (c.1539–1593), a Florentine Servite brother and sculptor.[32] The album, arranged after 1593 by his nephew, the engineer Alessandro Massai (d.1630), includes drawings collected by Casale's master, the sculptor Giovanni Angelo Montorsoli (1499–1563), by Casale himself and by Massai. From about 1565–77 Casale was in Rome, where he worked for both Cardinal Alessandro Farnese and Cardinal Fernando de' Medici. In 1577 he moved to Naples, but was still in touch with Rome, and later, in 1586, to Spain and

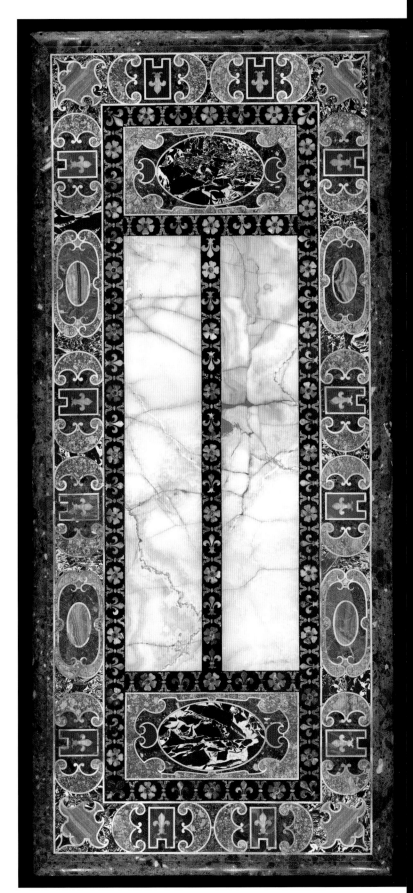

FIG. 53

The Farnese Table, pietre dure, Rome, about 1568–73, designed by Jacopo Barozzi da Vignola, possibly made by Jean Ménard, at Hamilton Palace, Lanarkshire, until 1919, when bought by Viscount Leverhulme. 149¼ x 66¼ in, 379.1 x 168.3 cm. Metropolitan Museum of Art, New York.

FIG. 54
Design for a table top, by Giovanni Vincenzo Casale, Rome, about 1570. Pen and sepia ink, 13 x 7⅜ in, 33.2 x 18.7 cm. Biblioteca Nacional, Madrid.

thence, in 1589, to Portugal. The album includes drawings of pietre dure floors, including a variation on that of the Sala Regia in the Vatican, completed in 1573 under Matteo Bartolini da Castello (c.1530–after 1597), and no fewer than nine designs for tables. One, densely geometric (fig. 54), is related to two exceptional tables, one formerly in the collection of the Duke of Westminster and the other formerly with the Corsini Gallery in New York, and slightly less to a superb table given to Philip II of Spain by Michele

Bonelli, Cardinal Alessandrino (1541–1598), great nephew of Pius V, in 1587, this last the subject of a complex Latin description by the antiquary and dealer, Vincenzo Stampa, celebrating the virtues of its stones.[33] These three tables have been likened to the Sixtus Cabinet, and their intensity of ornament, colour and rich materials is similar, although the detail of pattern and technique is different. However, five of the Casale table designs (figs 55, 56 and 57), one for an octagonal table with two variants, and four for table

FIG. 55
Design for a table corner, by Giovanni Vincenzo Casale, Rome, about 1570. Pen and sepia ink, 12¼ x 8¼ in, 31.2 x 20.9 cm (size of full pieced-together sheet of which this table corner forms a part). Biblioteca Nacional, Madrid.

FIG. 56
Design for a table corner, by Giovanni Vincenzo Casale, Rome, about 1570. Pen and sepia ink, 5⅜ x 7 in, 12.9 x 17.7 cm (a cut-down sheet). Biblioteca Nacional, Madrid.

FIG. 57
Design for octagonal table tops (two variants) and two designs for table corners, by Giovanni Vincenzo Casale, Rome, about 1570. Pen and sepia ink, 14⅜ x 11 in, 36.7 x 28 cm. Biblioteca Nacional, Madrid.

FIG. 58
Table top, pietre dure, Rome, about 1570, probably acquired by
Sir Thomas Isham at Rome in 1677. 57½ x 40 in, 146 x 101.6 cm.
The Lamport Hall Trust, Northamptonshire.

corners, are richer than Dosio's, the familiar peltate forms, often alternating with cartouches, being filled or embellished with leaves, flowers, scrolls and trophies of arms.[34]

When Casale's nephew, Massai, wrote a list, in Portuguese, of the album's contents, he described the designs just mentioned as being of jasper tables 'que se uzão fazer em Roma' [which used to be made in Rome], suggesting that, by 1630 at the very latest and probably much earlier, the fashion for such tables had passed, and that any temptation to push the dates of more elaborate examples well into the seventeenth century should be resisted.[35] Alvar González-Palacios has convincingly proposed that the table in the Prado which once belonged to the Duke

of Lerma's doomed favourite, Don Rodrigo Calderón (d.1621), should be dated to about 1600.[36] The comparable (fig. 50) table in the Codrington library of All Souls, Oxford, which is, uniquely, signed on the underside of its border 'M.PIETRO.CARLI.FĪO.FECIT', must be contemporary and Pietro Carli, evidently a Florentine working in Rome, may have been related to Bartolomeo Carli, 'Camerlengo' [treasurer] of the Roman Università dei Marmorari in 1598.[37] The presence on tables of natural elements, flowers and birds in particular, has often been interpreted as evidence of Florentine manufacture. But, albeit not in the highly naturalistic Florentine manner of which Ferdinando I boasted in a letter of 1601 to his ambassador in Rome concerning a pietre dure portrait of Clement VIII Aldobrandini, such motifs were sometimes present on Roman products – for example, a charming table of about 1600 in New York, inlaid with birds, flowers, a comb and a mirror.[38] The Roman production of pietre dure tables thus seems to have petered out not long after 1600, when Florence became dominant, and some early tables previously credited to Florence may merit reallocation to Rome. The Roman tables brought to England, described in the last chapter, were probably almost all old at the time of their acquisition, including that (fig. 58) bought by Sir Thomas Isham in 1677.

ROMAN MARBLE DECORATION

A revealing exception is not a table but the colourful marble coats of arms (figs 59 and 60) by 'Sig: Domenica, stonecutter in Rome, dwelling in the Coursa', supplied for Lady Berkeley's tomb in 1639. These fit into the continuing

FIG. 59
Tomb of Elizabeth, Lady Berkeley, by Nicholas Stone the Elder.
St Dunstan's, Cranford, Middlesex.

FIG. 60
Berkeley tomb (detail), the arms inlaid in marble by 'Sig.Domenica',
Rome, 1639. 17½ x 15 in, 44 x 38 cm (a single shield).

Roman tradition of marble decoration in churches and chapels, which, as noted in the case of Dosio's designs for the Gaddi and Niccolini chapels in Florence, overlaps with the history of secular Roman pietre dure production.[39] An early precursor was the Cappella Chigi in Santa Maria del Popolo designed by Raphael for the Sienese banker, Agostino Chigi, called 'Il Magnifico' (1466–1520), with relatively restrained wall revetments of coloured marbles set in panels reminiscent of the upper parts of the Pantheon. But this taste only made its first spectacular appearance in the Cappella Gregoriana in St Peter's, decorated from 1572–83 for Sixtus v's predecessor and adversary, Gregory XIII Boncompagni, who gathered in much of the finest ancient marble available in Rome, under the supervision of Giacomo della Porta.

COMPARANDA FOR THE SIXTUS CABINET

Further references to such ecclesiastical ornaments will be in the next chapter, which concentrates on the Sixtus Cabinet, but it is now time to search for its parallels. As will emerge, this is a complex creation, which owes its impact to a combination of ebony, pietre dure and gilt bronzes, as well as sheer scale and elaboration. The first object to have been proposed as a parallel is an extraordinary reliquary (fig. 61) surmounted by a crucifix, in the museum of the Basilica di San Petronio in Bologna, but originally given to the church of San Francesco there by the Bolognese Pope Gregory XV Ludovisi (1554–1623) in 1622 to form the centrepiece of an extraordinary assemblage of reliquaries assembled in Rome by an energetic Franciscan, Michele di Michelangelo Miserotti (1576–1630).[40] Apart from this papal gift, 13 of the reliquaries in San Petronio are of ebony or ebonized wood, with pietre dure and gilt bronze mounts and/or figures, all produced in Rome around 1622, in response to Miserotti's campaign. Competent but formulaic and all about 30 inches (75 cm) high, they give the impression of a flourishing industry. The big reliquary 'della Passione di Cristo' is on a quite different scale, being about 90 inches (227 cm) high. It has clearly been assembled from three disparate parts, a bottom Corinthian section of rectangular cabinet form with the Ludovisi arms of Gregory XV in a gilt bronze frame affixed to the centre of its frieze; a central Doric stage formed as a pedimented tabernacle with flanking wings and scrolls set on gilt bronze lions; and, perilously set on a narrow neck above that pediment, a lofty crucifix.[41] There are stones or jewels set in bezels and ebony veneers and mouldings on all three stages, but alabaster pilasters are confined to the bottom, ivory scrolls and terms to the centre, and wave mouldings to the crucifix at the top, where Christ, the Virgin and St John are in silver. Wave mouldings were invented in Rothenburg ob der Tauber or Nuremberg in about 1600 by Johann Schwanhardt (d.1613) and popularized by his son-in-law Jacob Hepner, both cabinet-makers: 1622 is an early date for their appearance in Rome. The panels of pietre dure on the reliquary are of simple design and coarse execution compared to the Sixtus Cabinet. The ensemble makes a

FIG. 61
Reliquary called 'della Passione di Cristo' [of the Passion of Christ], ebony, mounted in silver, gilt bronze and pietre dure, Rome, completed in 1622, given by Pope Gregory XV Ludovisi to San Francesco, Bologna. 89⅜ in, 227 cm high. Museo di San Petronio, Bologna.

FIG. 62
House altar, ebony mounted in silver-gilt and pietre dure with silver stringing, framing an Adoration of the Magi
painted on lapis lazuli, Rome, about 1620, probably purchased in Italy by Revd John Sanford, between 1815 and 1837.
20 x 13½ in, 51 x 34.3 cm. Corsham Court Collection, Wiltshire.

FIG. 63
House altar, ebony mounted in gilt bronze and pietre dure with silver stringing, framing a Flight into Egypt painted on lapis lazuli, Rome, about 1620, purchased by the South Kensington Museum in 1856 for £18. 19⅞ x 12 in, 50.4 x 30.5 cm. Victoria & Albert Museum.

FIG. 64
House altar, ebony, mounted in gilt bronze (including the finial formed as a cross set on three mounts, possibly Peretti, comparable to that crowning the pediment of S. Girolamo degli Schiavoni (fig. 192), rebuilt by Martino Longhi the Elder in 1588–9 under the aegis of Sixtus v) and pietre dure, containing an Annunciation by Peter Aertsen, purchased by Count Antoine Seilern in Brussels in 1929 and placed in this frame, bought from Alessandro Orsi, Milan, in 1969. 22⅞ x 13⅜ in, 58 x 34.8 cm. Courtauld Gallery, London.

spectacular first impression but close examination reveals its improvised nature, the gilt bronzes, including no fewer than 22 angels at different scales, eight with instruments of the Passion, lending a hectic veneer of unity.

The smaller reliquaries at San Petronio are related to an extended family of small ebony house altars incorporating pietre dure with gilt bronze mounts, represented in England by those at Corsham Court (fig. 62), the Courtauld Institute (fig. 64) and the Victoria & Albert Museum (fig. 63), the last plausibly associated with a 1623 payment to an 'ebanista' [cabinet-maker], Ermanno Fiammingo, based near Santa Maria sopra Minerva.[42] The accounts of Cardinal Francesco Barberini (1597–1679) for 1630–40 include mentions of several craftsmen who supplied comparable objects, including Remigio Chilozzi, a German 'ebanista', Francesco Bottaciolo, 'coronaro' [rosary-maker], Francesco Baldini, 'coronaro', Francesco Spagna, 'argentiere' [silversmith], Francesco Benelli 'gioielliere' [jeweller] and Giovanni Battista Venturini, 'coronaro'.[43] In 1625 Pietro Gotti 'ebanista' supplied something similar to Cardinal

Scipione Borghese (1517–1633), as did Baldini in 1629, Chilozzi in 1630 and Giovanni Cheller, 'orafo' [goldsmith], in about 1633. Cheller, evidently a German, did similar work for Urban VIII Barberini in 1624, as did Raniero Bruch, 'orefice' [goldsmith], a Fleming, in 1626: Urban also employed Bottaciolo, Chilozzi and Spagna. The picture emerging from this recitation, which could be enlarged, is of an elite group of craftsmen, cabinet-makers, gold- and silversmiths, jewellers and rosary-makers, often of Flemish or German origin, who assembled and sold these complex confections, which were usually on a small scale. A more prominent producer was Gaspare Mola (c.1567–1640), a goldsmith from Como, who held important posts in Milan and Florence before being appointed engraver to the Papal Mint by Urban VIII in 1625. In this capacity he produced many medals, but also made small pietre dure objects, which were thus no monopoly of marble workers.[44]

An exceptionally large specimen of this type of production is the cabinet (fig. 65) formerly in the Royal Collection at Windsor Castle with the arms of Paul v Borghese

FIG. 65
Cabinet, ebony, mounted in silver and gilt bronze, one mount with
the arms of Pope Paul V Borghese, and pietre dure, Rome, about 1620,
its stand attributed to Alexandre-Louis Bellangé, Paris, about 1625.
Purchased by George IV from Edward Holmes Baldock in 1827
and formerly in the Grand Corridor, Windsor Castle, Berkshire.
Sold in 1959. 51 in, 129 cm wide.

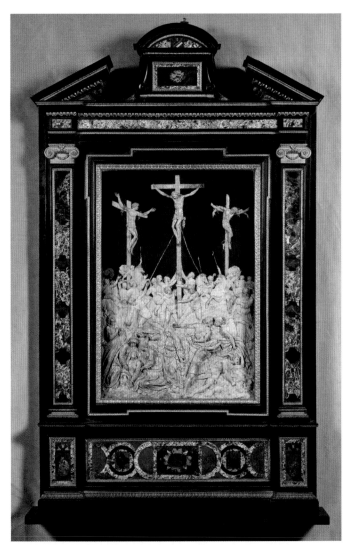

FIG. 66
Frame, ebony monted in gilt bronze and pietre dure, Rome, possibly
about 1610 for Cardinal Scipione Borghese, to house a Crucifixion,
wax relief on slate, by Guglielmo della Porta (d.1577). 27 x 18½ in,
68.5 x 47 cm (the relief). Galleria Borghese, Rome.

(1552–1621), who reigned from 1605, and is the closest
Roman comparison to the Sixtus Cabinet.[45] Its base has
panels of stone within moulded ebony frames similar to
those on the Victoria & Albert Museum's house altar. The
1830 repair account from George IV's cabinet-makers,
Morel & Seddon, mentions 'lapis lazuli, agate, coral and
other gems', 'ormolu enrichments', 'silver figures', 'ebony
mouldings' and 'inlaid silver lines', thus underlining its
resemblance to the Cabinet at Stourhead. However, while
the silver figures are a richer feature, and apparently of
higher quality than the gilt bronze figures on this latter,
other detailed comparisons do not favour the Windsor
example. Its panels of pietre dure are simpler, its gilt
bronze mounts less varied and lavish, its columns, splendid
as lapis lazuli may be, less of a virtuoso achievement than
alabaster, it is lower and there is a hint of the formulaic
about its composition. Nonetheless, it is a splendid object
and its more ample proportions, its open central niche and
broad segmental pediment could be seen as contributing

to a more baroque presence. In 1588 its patron, Paul V,
while still Camillo Borghese, was appointed vice-legate
of Bologna by Sixtus V, while its legate was Sixtus's great-
nephew, Cardinal Alessandro Peretti Montalto.[46] Five
papacies later, in 1605, Montalto proposed the candidature
of Borghese, a Cardinal since 1596, for the pontificate.
Such close links make it probable that the new Pope would
have known the Sixtus Cabinet, presuming that, as will be
suggested, it was made earlier, and even possible that the
cabinet formerly at Windsor was produced in emulation.
In 1613 Paul employed Pompeo Targone, the son of a
goldsmith and active as both founder and engineer, to
supply a stand decorated with pietre dure to fit an earlier
cabinet, and he would be a plausible candidate to have
orchestrated its manufacture.[47] (An interesting successor
is a small cabinet, of the same character albeit much less
splendid, made for Gregory XV Ludovisi (1554–1623),
who followed Paul V and was the donor of the large San
Petronio reliquary discussed above: it incorporates a pietre

FIG. 67
Cabinet, ebony, mounted in gilt bronze and pietre dure, Rome, about 1620. Listed at Schloss Ambras, Tyrol, in 1821.
19⅛ x 30⅞ x 11¼ in, 48.7 x 78.4 x 28.7 cm. Kunsthistorisches Museum, Vienna.

FIG. 68
The Wavendon Cabinet, Roman, early seventeenth century. Stourhead, Wiltshire. 21⅝ x 38½ x 15½ in, 55.5 x 97.7 x 39.5 cm. National Trust.

FIG. 69
Cabinet, ebony, with gilt bronze and silver-gilt mounts and pietre dure plaques, Rome, about 1630, its parcel gilt ebony stand designed by Filippo Schor and carved by Franz and Dominik Stainhart, Rome 1678–80. 102⅜ x 82⅝ x 31½ in, 260 x 210 x 80 cm. Palazzo Colonna, Rome.

dure relief portrait of the Pope, within a wave-moulded ebony frame.[48])

Paul v's artistic advisor was his nephew, Cardinal Scipione Borghese (1576–1633). In the chapel of his Villa Borghese, built from 1608, is a relief of the Crucifixion, wax on slate, attributed to Guglielmo della Porta (d.1577) and possibly acquired in 1609 as part of the collection of Giovanni Battista della Porta (d.1597).[49] Its elegant, even severe, ebony frame (fig. 66) is decorated with spare gilt bronze mounts and very geometric panels of pietre dure, and may be an exemplar of this taste at its most refined. The geometric elements are outlined by narrow silver borders, a regular feature on Roman cabinets and a simplified version of the technique used on the Sixtus Cabinet (see p. 101). Unfortunately, there is a dearth of documented examples. The six cabinets of this ilk in the Capitoline Museums (two at present shown in the Museo di Roma, Palazzo Braschi) were bequeathed by Conte Francesco Cini in 1881, and a small example (fig. 67) in the Kunsthistorisches Museum in Vienna has not been traced beyond the 1821 inventory of Schloss Ambras. Sequences are thus speculative, but it seems likely that the small 'Duncombe' cabinet (fig. 71), whose pietre dure panels are articulated by bezel-like gilt mouldings rather than silver stringing, may be a late-sixteenth-century successor of the Sixtus Cabinet. Its central door is surmounted by a fan- or shell-like arrangement of pietre dure common to most Roman cabinets including the finer of the two secondary Stourhead cabinets (fig. 68), which incorporates wave mouldings and should probably be of at least 1622, when this feature appears on the big San Petronio reliquary (fig. 61).[50] The famous pietre dure cabinet (fig. 69) in the Palazzo Colonna was acquired from the papal *dispensiere* [steward], Lorenzo Paribeni, in 1678 during Innocent xi Odescalchi's austere reign, and then supplied with an ebony stand incorporating three Moors, designed by Filippo Schor (b.1646), and partly executed by the Stainhart brothers, Franz (1651–1695) and Dominik (1655–1712), woodcarvers from Weilheim in Bavaria, who executed the reliefs on the grander baroque ivory and ebony cabinet in the same palazzo, designed by Carlo Fontana (1638–1714).[51] The Colonna pietre dure cabinet is unique in that its panels are predominantly floral, with only a minority geometric: it may be supposed that, albeit distinctively Roman, these floral panels were a riposte to the Florentine mastery of this genre. Although of superb quality (Count Nicodemus Tessin the Younger (1654–1728) wrote of its 'grandissime beautè') as to execution and materials (the figures which surmount it are silver-gilt), its design seems timid beside its present baroque companion and it seems likely to be much earlier.[52] Similar floral panels are central to a cabinet (fig. 44) which belonged to William Beckford and to another (fig. 70), similar but more elaborate, sold at the 1882 sale of his son-in-law, the Duke of Hamilton (when implausibly described as 'From the design of M. Angelo'), but the remaining pietre dure of these two cabinets is exclusively geometric.[53] Indeed, the picture which emerges is not one of marked stylistic progression, but of a set of components – pietre dure columns, pilasters and panels, in geometric variations or, much less frequently, floral or foliate, and

FIG. 70
Cabinet, ebony, mounted in gilt bronze and pietre dure, Rome, probably about 1630. From the collection of the Duke of Hamilton, sold from Hamilton Palace, Lanarkshire, in 1882, when this photograph was taken for the Christie's catalogue. 50 x 53½ x 20 in, 127 x 136 x 50.8 cm. The Elton Hall Collection, Peterborough.

FIG. 71
Cabinet, ebony, mounted in gilt bronze and pietre dure, Rome, probably about 1590, possibly acquired in Rome in 1747 by Thomas Duncombe and said to come from Duncombe Park, Yorkshire. 20⅞ x 33½ x 14⅛ in, 53 x 85 x 36 cm.

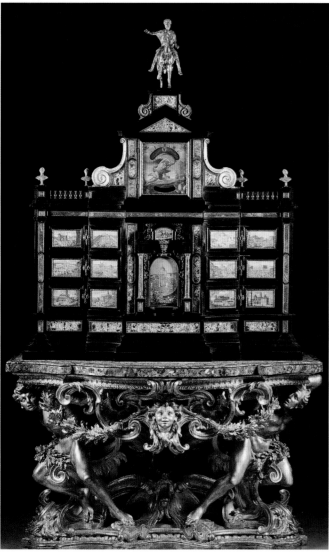

FIG. 72

Cabinet, ebony, mounted in gilt bronze, lapis lazuli and jasper, with miniature views of Roman monuments, surmounted by a clock signed Giovanni Wendelino Hessler, and containing a virginal by Giovanni Battista Maberiani, dated 1676, the cabinet by Giacomo Herman, Rome, about 1669–75. 72½ x 60¼ x 19¾ in, 184 x 153 x 50 cm. Set on a carved and gilt console table, with a veneered verde antico and lumachella marble slab, Rome, about 1725. 42⅛ x 67¾ x 28½ in, 107 x 172 x 72.5 cm.

gilt bronze mounts and figures, set within ebony frames, sometimes with ivory inlay, and with more or less elaborate internal complications – all of which could be combined for greater or lesser expense and impact. The lesser of the two secondary Stourhead cabinets (fig. 73) may represent the lower end of this scale, although not as low as a cabinet in the Museo Canonica, from the collection of the sculptor Pietro Canonica (1869–1959), which replicates the stock geometrical pattern of drawers, with central ovals, in painted glass.

AN EXTINCT TECHNIQUE?

In 1669 the German cabinet-maker, Giacomo Herman, who was also involved in the two Colonna cabinets mentioned above, exhibited an extraordinary but incomplete group of four matching ebony cabinets to Cardinal Giacomo Rospigliosi (1628–1684), nephew of Clement IX.[54] Two were inscribed, before completion, by a craftsman named Johannes Meisser, from Meissen. One, from Wilanów Palace, is in Warsaw, two are now in Denmark, in Rosenborg Castle and Fredensborg Palace, and the fourth in private hands (fig. 72). Their drawers are decorated with miniatures but, while other elements are veneered in lapis lazuli and jasper, these are used in unarticulated panels with no geometrical patterning. Earlier, in 1668, Herman had made a great ebony cabinet, similarly decorated, but with scenes from the life of the Emperor Constantine on copper rather than miniatures, presented by Cardinal Friedrich von Hessen-Darmstadt (1616–1682) to the Emperor Leopold I of Austria, of which Friedrich was cardinal protector. This, like the set of four, has a night clock in its attic, a feature not present in earlier Roman pietre dure examples, but its overall design, recalling a great triumphal arch, is much grander and bolder, suggesting the hand of an architect. The group of four, all later, revert to a design formula comparable to the Beckford cabinet mentioned above, or those at Castle Howard (figs 44, 27 and 28). Perhaps Herman, who died in 1685 aged 70, and is first noted as active in Rome in 1651 but could well have arrived a decade or more earlier, was adopting the forms of his youth in designing his four cabinets, which seem to have been a speculation rather than a commission.[55] Artisan conservatism is a constant. It may be that furniture decorated with Roman pietre dure in the tradition of the Sixtus Cabinet was by the mid-century a thing of the past. That particular technique, setting small panels of variegated hard stones, frequently backed by foil and separated by silver stringing, within ebony frames, was largely distinct from the methods used on tables or on wall-cladding, floors and funerary monuments within churches and chapels with rich marbles. This latter trade continued to be practised by those who belonged to the 'Confraternità delli Statuari et Lapicidari di Roma' [confraternity of the statuaries and lapidaries of Rome], active as a religious offshoot of the ancient guild of marble-workers, masons and sculptors from at least 1570 and awarded its own statutes in 1597.[56] Doubtless certain more specialized lapidaries could produce the miniature shaped slices of stone required for furniture, but it may be suspected that the skills needed were at least equally available to luxury metalworkers and jewellers. The Sixtus Cabinet certainly belongs within a great and ancient Roman tradition, but it is also a very specialized achievement.

FIG. 73
The Stourhead Cabinet, Roman, mid-seventeenth century. Stourhead, Wiltshire. 23⅝ x 42½ x 16¼ in, 60 x 108 x 41 cm. National Trust.

1. See Gnoli 1988, and Borghini 2004, for much of this account.
2. *Naturalis Historia*, 36:48, 17:6, 36:7.
3. *Silvae*, IV, 2, lines 26–9.
4. Peacock and Williams 1995, pp. 353–7.
5. *Naturalis Historia*, XXXV.1.3.
6. Kalas 2013, pp. 279–302.
7. These also recur in the *opus sectile* from Ostia: see Guidobaldi 2003, figs 56 and 78.
8. McClendon 1980, p. 157, and pl. XXXa.
9. A parallel is provided by the Omphalos or Omphalion in Hagia Sophia, a square section of the floor associated with imperial ceremony, centred on a great disk of grey granite, with 28 smaller discs surrounding it, 14 of red or green porphyry, probably ninth century in origin (see Pedone 2011, pp. 759–68).
10. A porphyry panel dated 1482, surrounded by Cosmati work, in the Roman palazzo of Cardinal Giuliano della Rovere, the future Pope Julius II, is illus. di Castro 1994, fig. 2.
11. See Tuena 1988, pp. 54–69, and Ronfort 1991–2, pp. 139–47.
12. Illus., di Castro 1994, fig. 16.
13. Bonnaffé 1874, pp. 137–8.
14. Tuena 1988, p. 67, from a Venetian ambassador's report of 1565 'più tosto bon mercante che gran prelato'.
15. See Colle 1997, pp. 104–5, 100–1 and 102–4.
16. See Dacos *et al.* 1980.
17. His fame is as a composer: see Kirkendale 1979.
18. Leonardo 1997, pp. 269–300.
19. Tuena 1988, p. 67
20. Barletti 2011, pp. 746–8.
21. See Morrogh 2011, pp. 299–323.

22. Bosman 2005, pp. 361–6.
23. Baldini 1979, p. 317.
24. Gnoli and Sironi 1996.
25. Spinelli 201, pp. 345–73.
26. Morrogh 1985, fig. 65.
27. Ibid., figs 32 and 38.
28. Ibid., figs 66 and 67. Morrogh attributes fig. 66 to Dosio's patron, Niccolò Gaddi, but it might be a Dosio workshop product.
29. Di Castro 1994, figs 7 and 8.
30. See Koeppe 2008, pp. 120–2, for references and an attribution of the top to Jean Ménard, who may have worked on the two almost equally large tables at the Villa Giulia described by Ammanati in 1555.
31. One is illus. Raggio 1960, p. 230, and another in Giusti 2003, fig. 2.
32. Bustamente and Marías 1991, pp. 212–90. See also Lanzarini 1998–9, pp. 183–202, and Aguiló Alonso 2009, pp. 262–4.
33. Bustamente and Marías 1991, no. 114; González-Palacios 1981, p.14; Giusti 1988, pp. 92–3; González-Palacios 2001, p. 59; *Alexandrinae mensae descriptio*, see Furlotti 2010, p. 393, which notes that Stampa wrote a pamphlet in praise of the Aqua Felice, *De aquaeductu Felici* (Rome, 1589).
34. Bustamente and Marías 1991, nos 99, 115 and 119.
35. Ibid., p. 221.
36. González-Palacios 2001, pp. 69–73.
37. Di Castro 1994, p. 119.
38. Zobi 1853, pp. 187–8; Koeppe 2008, pp. 130–1 (entry by Annamaria Giusti).
39. For this see, for example, Ostrow 1990, pp. 253–76, and Di Castro 1994.

40. See Fanti 2003 and Buitoni 2010.
41. It is, of course, a solecism to place Doric above Corinthian.
42. González-Palacios 1991, p. 150.
43. For these names and those which follow see González-Palacios 2010, pp. 28–135.
44. González-Palacios 1988, pp. 49–50.
45. Roberts 2001, pp. 244, 248 and 269.
46. Granata 2012, p. 27.
47. González-Palacios 2010, p. 65.
48. Colle and Bartolozzi 2005, pp. 16–20, entry by Annamaria Giusti.
49. Middeldorf 1935, pp. 90–6.
50. This cabinet has features in common with one of the Cini cabinets (630) now in the Sala d'Ercole of the Pinacoteca Capitolina, although this displays no wave moulding.
51. Strunck 2008, p. 17; Valeriani 1999, pp. 256–7.
52. Waddy 2002, p. 261.
53. Sotheby's, London, 10 June 1998, lot 20; Christie's, London, 4 July 1882, lot 996. A cabinet from the Demidoff Collection (Sotheby's, Monaco, 20 June 1992, lot 810) displays a similar combination, with predominantly geometrical panels, but for a cartouche with foliate scrolls in its centre and floral panels in its twin gables.
54. Sotheby's, London, 4 December 2007, A Magnificent Roman Baroque Cabinet by Giacomo Herman (entry by Alvar González-Palacios and Mario Tavella).
55. Colle 2000, p. 455, summarizes the known facts about Herman.
56. Di Castro 1994, pp. 11–12, 133–51.

THREE
THE SUPREME EXAMPLE:
THE SIXTUS CABINET

Sixtus the Fifth's cabinet is divine, I know.
WILLIAM BECKFORD, 1814

The two earliest descriptions of the Cabinet at Stourhead date from the 1750s, the first in a manuscript catalogue of the Stourhead paintings in the archive at Longleat and the second by Jonas Hanway, published in 1756.[1] Their accounts of the Cabinet's provenance coincide in the essentials: the Cabinet formerly belonged to Pope Sixtus v and was bought in Rome by Henry Hoare from a convent to which it had been left by a nun, the last of the Peretti family, descended from that Pope's nephew.

FIG. 74
Relief of Francesco I de' Medici, Grand Duke of Tuscany, receiving a model for the façade of Florence Cathedral, gold on amethyst (in a later seventeenth-century gilt bronze frame), designed by Giambologna and executed by Antonio Susini and Cesare Targoni, Florence, 1585–7, originally intended to decorate an ebony cabinet, the 'Studiolo Nuovo', in the form of a circular temple, designed by Bernardo Buontalenti for the centre of the Tribuna of the Uffizi, made by Bartolomeo d'Erman, a German cabinet-maker, in 1584–6. 3¼ x 4⅜ in, 8.3 x 11 cm. Museo degli Argenti, Florence.

This story, repeated again and again with minor variations, has commanded scant attention in the years since Stourhead was given to the National Trust in 1946. It is easy to understand a measure of scepticism and neglect: highfalutin traditional provenances are often fanciful, and for many years all Italian cabinets incorporating marble inlay were regarded as Florentine (indeed the Cabinet was published as such in the 1968 and 2005 National Trust guide books to Stourhead), and manufacture in Florence would have seemed to distance the Cabinet from Sixtus v, a pontiff closely identified with Rome, although born in the Marches. The recent recognition that the Cabinet is a quintessentially Roman product prompted research into its provenance. Henry Hoare would not have been the first or last Grand Tourist to have been sold a pup by some silver-tongued art agent in Rome. But could the truth be simpler and the story he told of the Cabinet – and there is no doubt that this was Henry Hoare's own account, as he lived until 1785 – be based in fact? But before attempting to trace the Cabinet's provenance, its description and analysis must be the priority.

In 1585 Giambologna (1529–1608), the great Flemish sculptor who had been in regular Medici service since 1561, designed a set of eight exquisite reliefs representing the acts of Francesco I, Grand Duke of Tuscany since 1574. Modelled in wax the reliefs were then cast in gold from bronze moulds made by Giambologna's assistants, Antonio Susini and Cesare Targone, and set on backgrounds of semi-precious stones. One (fig. 74), on an amethyst ground, depicts Francesco seated, surrounded by members of his court, surveying what might be taken for a cabinet, set on a cloth-covered table slightly too small for it.[2] This miniature work and its seven companions were made to decorate the drawers of an ebony cabinet designed by Bernardo

FIG. 75
The Sixtus Cabinet, ebony, mounted in gilt bronze and pietre dure, Rome, probably about 1585. At Stourhead, Wiltshire. 84¼ x 49⅝ x 33½ in, 214 x 126.2 x 84.9 cm. National Trust.

FIG. 76
Cabinet (*escritorio*), with its fall-front closed, walnut inlaid with bone, depicting the Eleven Ages of Man (derived from a print; a later version London, Thomas Jenner, 1630s), Spanish, about 1600. Castle Drogo, Devon. 21¾ x 36⅛ x 18⅜ in, 55.3 x 91.8 x 47.5 cm. National Trust.

Buontalenti (*c.*1531–1608), the Grand Duke's architect and designer-in-chief. The object shown on the table, however, is not a cabinet, but a model of Buontalenti's own design for the façade of Florence Cathedral. A church could look like a cabinet, and a cabinet like a church. The Sixtus Cabinet is a case in point.

In its essence the cabinet started as a box filled with drawers, and many early – and later – cabinets have a simple rectilinear form. The type seems to have first developed in Spain, where a Moorish tradition of fine woodwork pieced together in small geometric units was in contrast to the more massive carpentry techniques typical of Northern Europe. The Spanish cabinet usually had a fall-front (fig. 76) which did not lend itself to architectural articulation. But once the form had spread, above all to the mercantile cities of Germany, particularly Nuremberg and Augsburg, twin doors tended to replace the fall-front, the drawers and compartments within were arranged as a centralized composition, and before long the confines of the box were transcended and the way was open for formal innovation, invariably of an architectural character. The earliest German cabinets, of the mid-sixteenth century, were decorated with marquetry (fig. 77) but soon, above all in Augsburg, a taste for ebony dominated. Memorably described during an Augsburg demarcation dispute in 1588 as 'selbst teur und solche Arbeit nit für den gemeinen Mann, sondern durch Potentaten und Herren angefrimbt und verschickt' [expensive in itself, and such work not for the common man, but made to the order of and dispatched to potentates and gentlemen], ebony's black sheen might

FIG. 77
Cabinet, oak, marquetry of various woods, boxwood reliefs, probably Augsburg, about 1570, its stand, incorporating Tudor royal heraldry, probably confected in about 1810, to support the myth that the cabinet was designed by Hans Holbein for Whitehall Palace, possibly on the orders of William Beckford. From Fonthill Abbey, Wiltshire. 54⅞ x 37⅜ x 24 in, 139.5 x 95 x 61 cm. Victoria & Albert Museum.

FIG. 78
Cabinet, ebony with silver and silver-gilt mounts, by Boas Ulrich (1550–1624), Augsburg, about 1610. 15 x 14½ x 11½ in, 38 x 36.8 x 29.3 cm.
Victoria & Albert Museum.

be enjoyed unembellished for its own sake, but also lent itself to ornamentation in contrasting materials, be it mounts of silver, silver-gilt (fig. 78) or gilt bronze and/or inlay incorporating ivory (bone was a cheaper substitute) or marbles and semi-precious stones, as in the case of the Sixtus Cabinet.[3]

It should be added that, just as the word 'cabinet' may, in both French and English, mean a small room dedicated to study and/or housing a collection, or a cabinet in the furniture sense, the Italian 'studiolo' covers a similar spectrum.

DESCRIPTION OF THE SIXTUS CABINET

Because the Sixtus Cabinet is the richest and most elaborate of all surviving Roman cabinets (or *studioli*) its description and anatomy pose a challenge. As hinted above, the obvious metaphor for the Cabinet's elevation is a church and in particular a Roman church of the late sixteenth century, the two most conspicuous and important exemplars being the Gesù (properly 'Santissimo Nome di Gesù all'Argentina') and the Chiesa Nuova ('Santa Maria in Vallicella').[4] The Gesù (fig. 79) was originally projected by St Ignatius Loyola from at least 1550, and finally commenced in 1568, thanks to the patronage of Cardinal Alessandro Farnese, to a design by Jacopo Barozzi da Vignola (1507–1573), whose façade design was modified by Giacomo Della Porta (1532–1602) and completed in 1577. The Chiesa Nuova was commenced in 1575 by St Philip Neri (1515–1595) under the aegis of Pope Gregorio XIII Boncompagni; its façade,

to the design of the little-known architect and cartographer Fausto Rughesi, was built from 1594–1606. The progeny of the Gesù formula, a façade in which the wider ground floor is articulated by a grand order and the narrower upper floor by another, the two visually linked, at the upper level, by lateral scrolled volutes, were legion, an early successor being Santa Maria dei Monti in Rome, designed by Giacomo Della Porta in 1580, while Martino Longhi's version at San Girolamo degli Schiavoni of 1587–90, constructed under the patronage of Sixtus V, is included among the works recorded on the Cabinet's pedestal (figs 188 and 192).[5] Earlier versions tended to low relief and restraint, but the façade of Santa Susanna (fig. 80), designed in 1597 by Carlo Maderno (1556–1629), who had by 1576 journeyed to Rome from his native Lugano to work for his uncle, Pope Sixtus V's friend and favoured architect, Domenico Fontana (1543–1607), enlivened the model by introducing a richer vocabulary of ornament and, in the lower storey, three-quarter Corinthian columns. Maderno later designed a similar façade for San Andrea della Valle, commissioned in 1608 by Cardinal Alessandro Peretti Montalto (1571–1623), Sixtus's great-nephew: this was executed with variations by Carlo Rainaldi (1611–1691) in 1656–65 at the expense of Cardinal Alessandro's late nephew, Cardinal Francesco Peretti Montalto (1597–1655).[6] These churches provide a point of reference for the Sixtus Cabinet, although its composition, taller and narrower, with four storeys on a podium, has a more mannerist and less baroque flavour.

The Cabinet's visible wooden surfaces (not including its back) are clad in veneers and mouldings of ebony.[7]

FIG. 79
The façade of the Gesù, Rome, designed by Jacopo Barozzi da Vignola and Giacomo della Porta, completed in 1577. Etched by Ambrogio Brambilla, published by Nicolas van Aelst, Rome, 1589. 18¾ x 15⅛ in, 47.5 x 38.4 cm. The British Museum.

This dense and very hard timber has been ident-ified as African blackwood (*Dalbergia melanoxylon*), which does not belong to the family of ebenaceae, but at the time of the Cabinet's manufacture this taxonomic distinction would not have been recognized.[8] The invisible carcase wood is a broad-grained pine, as was normal in Roman furniture at this period. The mouldings are without exception of exquisite neatness and refinement, while the invisible pine parts range from the highly precise for drawer linings to the solid and straightforward for unseen structural members. It hardly needs adding that the front elevation of the Cabinet is completely symmetrical, and its side elevations match one another.

THE PODIUM

The Sixtus Cabinet rests on an integral podium, the bottom-most of its five separable sections (fig. 241) and the only one to have undergone serious modification: the mid-eighteenth-century descriptions state that the Cabinet originally comprised an organ and mention a series of wax portraits behind glass depicting Sixtus V and his family, features lost but not without trace.[9] There is external evidence, confirmed by internal examination, that the podium, which breaks forward nearly 8 inches (20 cm) for nearly two-thirds of its width, originally incorporated a central keyboard concealed by a removable lid and front cover, the latter fitted with a slightly off-centre lock. When these elements were removed, the exposed edges and surfaces proved to be veneered in ebony or, where less likely to be visible, ebonized, while the carcase on either side of the putative keyboard was in oak, with its grain set vertically, presumably to provide a more secure and solid housing for this delicate instrument than the nearby pine could afford. The top of the podium is decorated with ivory stringing forming simple rectangles at each end and three more complex rectilinear panels with well-spaced double

FIG. 80
The façade of Santa Susanna, Rome, designed by Carlo Maderno, 1597–1603. Engraved by Giovanni Maggi, published by Giovanni Orlandi, Rome, 1609. 12½ x 8⅜ in, 31.7 x 21.3 cm. The British Museum.

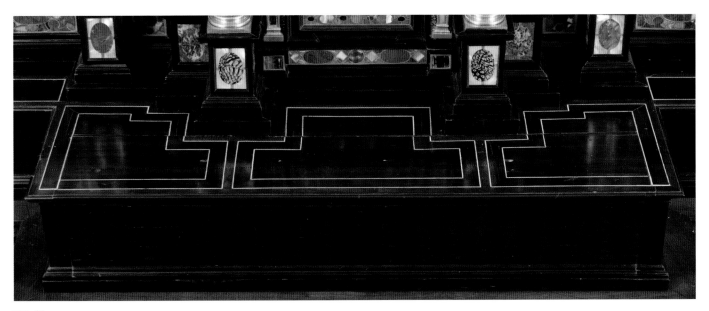

FIG. 81
Central projection of podium from above, showing the original edges (now sealed) of the removable lid and front cover which concealed the organ's keyboard.

FIG. 82
Ionic first storey, detail showing alabaster *a tartaruga* columns flanking the fourth bay.

FIG. 83
Ionic first storey, detail of a gilt-bronze capital. Actual size 1⅜ x 2¼ in, 3.4 x 5.8 cm.

stringing adapted to the architecture of the façade on the central projection (fig. 81). At some stage, probably when the organ was removed, perhaps because it was no longer working or had become unfashionable, or both, the lid and front were firmly glued into place. Then or thereafter the portrait waxes were fitted into 11 circular apertures cut into the vertical faces of the podium, four on the central projection, one each on its returns and two, more tightly spaced, on each front end. When the waxes were removed and sold, between 1838 and 1894, and probably in 1883, the apertures were mostly filled with pine and all covered, somewhat crudely, with ebonized panels (in 2006 these were removed and the apertures veneered in ebony).

THE IONIC FIRST STOREY

Above the podium rises the slightly narrower Ionic first storey (fig. 84), whose most striking architectural feature is an order of ten alabaster *a tartaruga* columns with gilt bronze bases and capitals (fig. 83), demarcating the five bays of the elevation. Two pairs, whose inner columns are stepped forward (fig. 82), flank a central 'doorway', while a further two pairs, whose outer columns are stepped back, provide lateral terminations. Between these inner and outer pairs, whose pedestals are linked, single columns on single pedestals, set towards the centre, separate the outer bays containing 'side windows' from two narrower bays with tiers of four panels, which prove to be drawers. The fronts of the pedestals of all the columns, the dados between them and the front of the central door's 'threshold' are set with panels of pietre dure, while the visible flanks of all the pedestals are set with panels comprising a single stone. Behind the columns are pilasters with unarticulated ebony bases and capitals, formed of single slabs of Spanish *broccatello* on both their front and return faces, apart from those behind the two central columns, which are of alabaster inlaid with a vertical tier of ten discs, lozenges and ovals of jasper, lapis lazuli and mother-of-pearl.

The arched central door is set within a frame whose entablature, supported by gilt bronze caryatid terms facing diagonally outwards, supports a narrow tablet flanked by scrolls and surmounted by gilt bronze scrollwork. The tablet, door and spandrels are decorated with pietre dure and there are jewels on the frieze of the door frame, and on the bases of the caryatid terms and their tapering shafts. The tablet and terms are set against a background of green Roman millefiore glass, also incorporated in the pietre dure panels on the plinths of the columns flanking the door, and on those of the forward columns of the

FIG. 84 ▶ OVERLEAF
Podium and Ionic first storey, frontal view. Heights: 5⅜ in, 13.8 cm (podium), 23 in, 58.5 cm (Ionic storey).

FIG. 85
Panel (part) of polychrome glass inlay, possibly from the Villa of the Emperor Lucius Verus, Rome, second century AD. *c*.18½ x 22½ in, 47 x 57 cm. Museo Nazionale Romano, Palazzo Massimo.

lateral pairs. Its use in these prominent positions suggests a particularly prized specimen of Roman *spolia*: the material closely resembles the background of a panel of glass inlay (fig. 85), dated to the second century AD, in the Museo Nazionale Romano, Palazzo Massimo.[10] The two outer bays contain 'windows' flanked by smaller gilt bronze caryatid terms, with entablatures supporting segmental pediments, above which are rectangular tablets in scrollwork gilt bronze frames (fig. 86); there are also small scrollwork gilt bronze ornaments below the 'windows'. These latter, and the tablets above, are mounted with pietre dure panels, and are on a background of lapis lazuli. The frieze in the entablature which surmounts the Ionic first storey is also mounted with pietre dure, with jewels at regular intervals.

The *interior* of the Ionic first storey is complex (fig. 87). The interconnected pedestals and dados of the colonnade pull out to form three shallow drawers, that in the centre, corresponding to the 'threshold', narrower and shallower. The four drawers in each of the second and fourth bays have already been noted (fig. 89). In the outer bays the 'windows' and tablets pull out as drawers, the former each with a secret drawer at the back, originally released by pressing a bone spring (fig. 88).[11] On either side of

FIG. 86
Ionic first storey, detail showing a panel of pietre dure within a gilt-bronze frame, above the right 'window'.
Actual size of frame 4¼ x 5⅜ in, 10.9 x 13.8 cm.

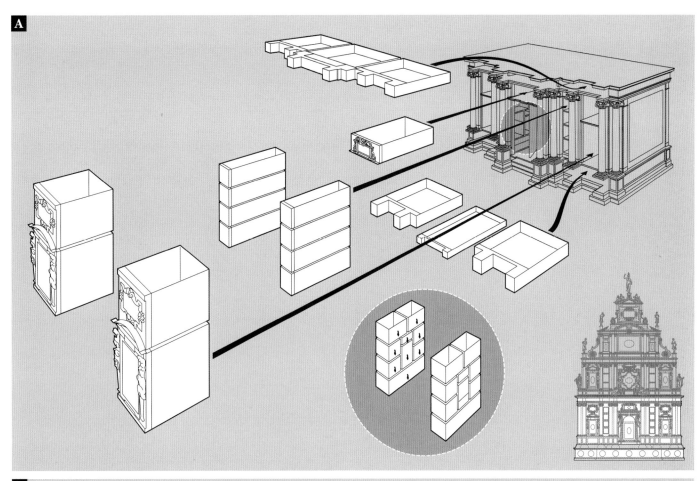

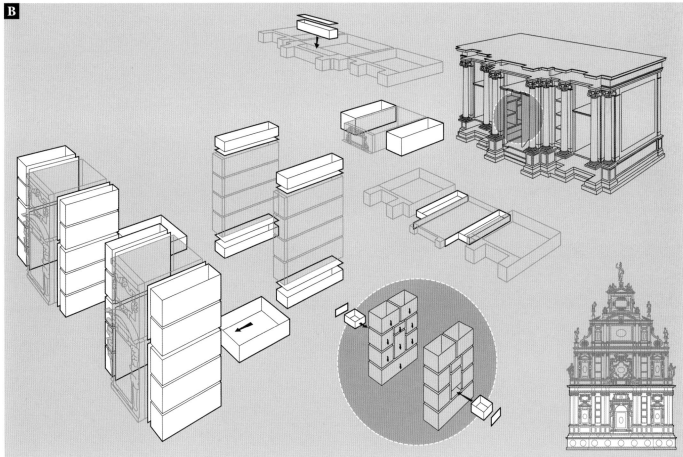

FIG. 87
Exploded drawings of the Ionic first storey, showing arrangement of drawers (A) and arrangement of drawers and compartments within drawers (B).

FIG. 88
Ionic first storey,
detail showing right 'window' drawer,
with secret drawer at back.

the 'windows' and tablets are tiers of five secret drawers, three flanking the 'windows' (fig. 91) and two the tablets. The central door, in appearance arched, is in operation rectangular including spandrels, entablature and caryatids. It is veneered on the inside in partridge wood with four L-shaped ebony panels outlined in ivory to its corners, partly overlaid in the centre by an oval panel of *fiorito* alabaster in a raised ebony bezel. When the central door is opened, sliding out on the extended and concealed leaves of a blued steel double hinge which prevents clashes with the alabaster column on the right and whose visible inner plates have a delightfully curved profile *en arbalète*, an open central compartment is revealed. Its back is veneered with ebony and partridge wood, as a Doric aedicule containing an arched niche, whose triangular pediment, capitals and bases are formed of ivory engraved to depict shadowed mouldings (fig. 90). The central compartment's floor and ceiling are veneered in the same pattern as the inside of the door, but with a central rectangle of ebony outlined in ivory (henceforward only as stringing or turned knob pulls) instead of the alabaster oval. Its sides are similarly treated, but in their case the central rectangle is broken into a central ebony lozenge surrounded by four ebony triangles. The sides prove to be removable and to have a similar pattern on their hidden faces. They conceal two

FIG. 89
Ionic first storey, detail showing four concealed drawers in the fourth bay partly pulled out (compare with fig. 82).

FIG. 90
Ionic first storey, detail of the back of the central compartment, showing aedicule of ebony, partridge wood and engraved ebony.

FIG. 91
Ionic first storey, detail showing three secret drawers flanking the right 'window' drawer.

FIG. 92
Crucifix with Saints, ebony with gilt and silvered bronze mounts and panels of lapis lazuli, its sculptural elements (with the exception of the corpus of Christ, a later replacement, following a model created by Bernini) attributed to Jacob Cornelisz Cobaert, including four reclining cherubs of the same model as the putti on the Sixtus Cabinet, Rome, about 1590. 65¾ x 38⅜ x 9⅛ in, 167 x 7.6 x 23.2 cm. Museo Nazionale del Palazzo di Venezia, Rome.

matching nests of nine small drawers, with fronts veneered in ebony with neatly moulded borders, with single ivory stringing within and central multicolour silk pulls. The drawers are in four tiers, one in the bottom, two in the top, while the central tiers comprise two short lateral drawers and, between these, a shallower upper and deeper central drawer, the latter with a secret drawer at its back, concealed by a removable panel of pine. The central panel above the door also pulls out as a single drawer. The frieze of the Ionic first storey comprises three shallow drawers, the central drawer wider and concealing in its front a removable lidded tray. This storey thus contains no fewer than 61 drawers, of varying degrees of secrecy, and one secret lidded tray.

Although it is structurally part of the Corinthian second storey, the central broken triangular pediment is visually and architecturally an integral part of the Ionic first storey (fig. 84). The chubby gilt bronze putti who recline on each of its ends, that to the left with crossed legs, that to the right with legs drawn up, both propped on their outer elbows with their inner arms resting by a knee, closely resemble four cherubs, two of each kind, which are set on the ends of two broken scrolled pediments forming part of an elaborate ebony and lapis lazuli crucifix base (fig. 92), decorated with gilt and silvered bronze mounts, acquired by the Museo Nazionale, Palazzo Venezia in 2004.[12] The only significant difference between the models is that those in Rome had wings attached, as befitted their sacred identity. The putti on the Sixtus cabinet fit more snugly on their straight sections of pediment than the Palazzo Venezia cherubs on their scrolled bases. Pietro Cannata has attributed the sculptural elements of the crucifix base to Jacob Cornelisz Cobaert (1530/5–1615), a Flemish sculptor who came to Rome in the early 1550s and entered the studio of the sculptor and architect Guglielmo della Porta (c.1515–1577) and was known as 'Coppe Fiammingo' or variations thereof.[13] This attribution rests on close resemblances to the sculpture, including cherubs, on a gilt bronze tabernacle (fig. 93) commissioned by Cardinal Matthieu Cointerel (1519–1585), italianized as 'Matteo Contarelli', for San Luigi dei Francesi, a church whose façade was designed by Guglielmo's cousin, Giacomo della Porta (1532–1602), in the early 1580s but completed by Domenico Fontana in 1589. In 1585 the tabernacle commission was adopted by Cointerel's heir, Virgilio Crescenzi, but disputes over the cost of gilding delayed this until 1597 and final delivery was in 1602. Cobaert was unhappy on a large scale, but had a substantial output of small works, which might be used for ornamental purposes by goldsmiths and others, and indeed reused over a number of years.[14] Nonetheless, if the attribution of the putti on the Sixtus Cabinet is accepted, this would fit comfortably with a date in the mid-1580s.

It is worth adding that the late Donald Garstang attributed the wooden element of the Palazzo Venezia crucifix to a Flemish craftsman, possibly Jan van Santen (c.1550–1621), better known as Giovanni Vasanzio, of whom Giovanni Baglione wrote 'fece studioli di ebano, e d'avorio, & alcuni di gioie ne commesse, e con grandissima diligenza componevali' [he made cabinets of ebony and ivory, & some mounted with jewels, and assembled them with the greatest diligence].[15] Vasanzio probably arrived

FIG. 93
Tabernacle, gilt bronze, attributed to Jacob Cornelisz Cobaert, commissioned for the high altar of San Luigi dei Francesi by Cardinal Matthieu Cointerel before his death in 1585, its completion delayed by long disputes over the cost of gilding, finally effected in 1597, before delivery in 1602. It incorporates six cherubs close to the putti on the Sixtus Cabinet. 37½ x 17⅜ in, 95 x 45 cm. San Luigi dei Francesi, Rome.

in Rome in the early 1580s, and ran a cabinet-making workshop in the Via Giulia, hence his nickname 'Giovanni degli Studiuoli'. He later developed a career as an architect, with a speciality in fountains. In 1613 he worked on a fountain in the Via Giulia with the hydraulic engineer Giovanni Fontana (1540–1614), elder brother of Domenico, Sixtus V's favourite architect.[16] With such skills and such connections Vasanzio would be a plausible candidate for involvement in the Sixtus Cabinet.

THE CORINTHIAN SECOND STOREY

After this excursus the Corinthian second storey needs description (fig. 94). Again the dominant feature is a parade of eight alabaster, here *fiorito*, columns with gilt bronze capitals and bases, but at this level they are shorter,

FIG. 94 ▶ OVERLEAF
Corinthian second storey, frontal view. Height 16⅝ in, 42.2 cm.

FIG. 95
Corinthian second storey, detail showing gilt bronze mask on the central panel. Actual size of mask 1⅞ x 3⅝ in, 4.8 x 9.3 cm.

fewer and slightly different in plan (fig. 98). The outermost columns have been suppressed, reducing the width of the façade, but their pedestals are echoed. These now support giltwood statues of St Peter, right, and St Paul, left, evidently supplied in 1743 at the same time as the Cabinet's Pedestal (Appendix v, pp. 215–6).[17] The outer columns of the pair flanking the central bay are set slightly forward of those below and those flanking them laterally, thus stressing the importance of the centre. As below all the columns are backed by pilasters, here alabaster slabs with plain ebony bases and capitals. The dadoes of each bay are set with pietre dure panels, but the pedestals of the columns, and of the two lateral statues, are variously set with pietre dure panels, single stones and cut jewels. On this Corinthian level the narrow second and fourth bays contain tiers of three pietre dure panels, the central ones taller, which again prove to be drawers. They are surmounted, at capital level, by beribboned gilt bronze swags. The two outer bays contain 'windows', filled with pietre dure panels, their frames with flanking gilt bronze caryatid terms set on exquisite tiny ebony brackets, their heads, facing frontally, supporting bunches of fruit in which pears are prominent, plausibly a reference to Sixtus v's family name, 'Peretti' [little pears], while their tapering shafts are mounted in lapis lazuli (fig. 97).[18] Above, jewel-mounted entablatures with triangular pediments filled with lapis lazuli support symmetrical pairs of gesturing gilt bronze putti. The central bay is flanked by slender gilt bronze female figures standing on ebony brackets incorporating gilt bronze volutes at dado level: their inner arms, crooked at the elbow, rest elegantly on a complex ebony frame, whose basic outline is a square with narrow rectilinear projections, indented, to each side and semi-circular projections at top and bottom (see also p. 126). This frame, set against an alabaster background,

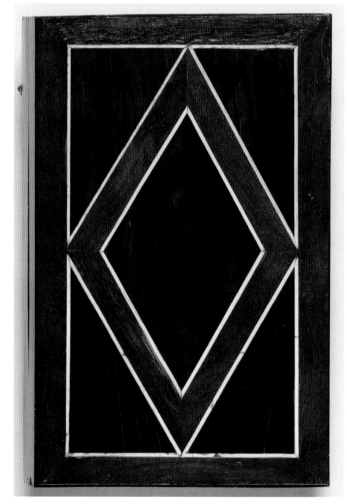

FIG. 96
Corinthian second storey, detail showing back of the left 'window' panel, removed (see fig. 97, facing page).

FIG. 97
Corinthian second storey, detail showing left 'window' panel, removed. 8¾ x 6¼ in, 22.2 x 15.8 cm.

FIG. 98
Corinthian second storey, detail showing *fiorito* alabaster columns flanking the fourth bay.

FIG. 99
Three concealed drawers in the fourth bay pulled out.

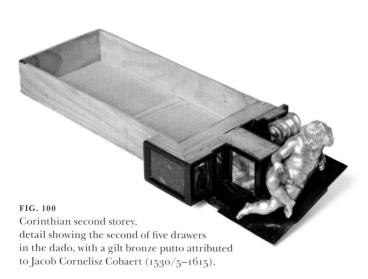

FIG. 100
Corinthian second storey,
detail showing the second of five drawers
in the dado, with a gilt bronze putto attributed
to Jacob Cornelisz Cobaert (1530/5–1615).

is surmounted by a scrolled and winged grotesque mask of gilt bronze (fig. 95), below a jewelled segmental pediment, filled with pietre dure and set on a lapis lazuli background. The frieze of the Corinthian storey's entablature contains pietre dure, like that below.

Now to turn to the *interior* of the Corinthian second storey, which rivals the Ionic in complexity (fig. 101). Its dados and pedestals are differently combined to pull out as five, rather than three, drawers (fig. 100), while the frieze above contains three drawers which only extend across the central bay and its flanking columns. The second and fourth bays, as noted above, contain three drawers each (fig. 99). In the outer bays the pediments supporting putti open as single drawers, but the panels below, including the caryatid terms, can be removed – a most unusual feature – revealing their reverses to be veneered with partridge wood, a central ebony lozenge being set within a rectangle whose corners are formed as ebony triangles, all these figures being outlined in ivory stringing (fig. 96). The panels conceal compartments whose ceilings, flanks and floors are veneered in this same pattern, while their backs contain nests of eight drawers in three tiers, the lowest with two drawers and the rest with three, those in the centre comprising a deep lower drawer below a shallower (fig. 102): the deep drawer has a secret drawer at its back, concealed by a pine panel (fig. 103). The frame of the nest and the drawer fronts are veneered in partridge wood and

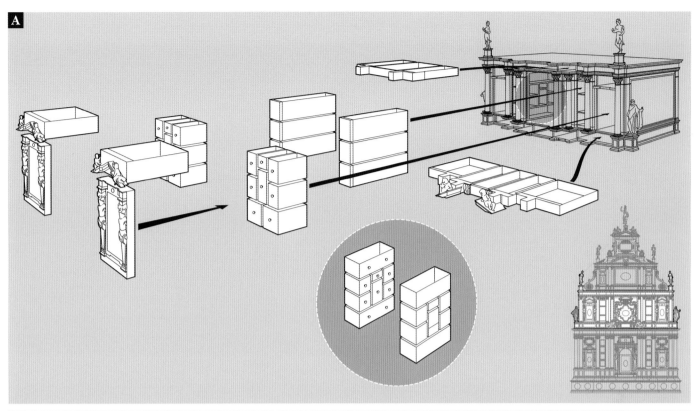

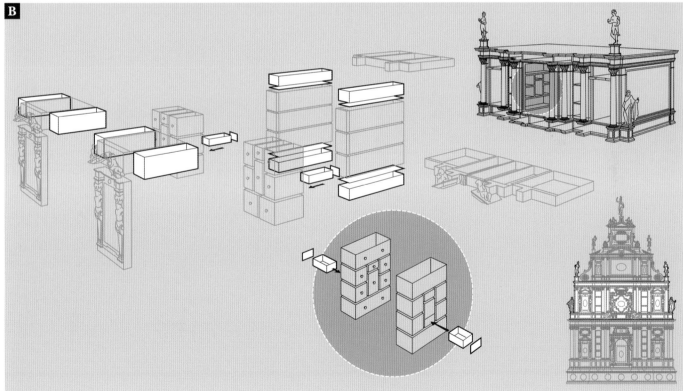

FIG. 101
Exploded drawings of the Corinthian second storey, showing arrangement of drawers (A)
and arrangement of drawers and compartments within drawers (B).

FIG. 102
Corinthian second storey, detail showing nest of drawers at the back of the compartment behind the left 'window' panel.

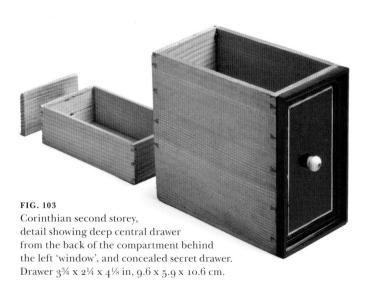

FIG. 103
Corinthian second storey, detail showing deep central drawer from the back of the compartment behind the left 'window', and concealed secret drawer. Drawer 3¾ x 2¼ x 4⅛ in, 9.6 x 5.9 x 10.6 cm.

all drawers are framed by neat ebony mouldings, with ivory stringing within, and a turned ivory knob in their centres. The whole front of the central Corinthian bay opens as a door, with double hinges (the only hinges outwardly visible) to avoid clashes between the right-hand female figure and the nearest alabaster column. The back of the door is now veneered in plain ebony with signs of mends. It seems virtually certain that this door was once held in place by friction and gravity, like its lateral companions, that the projecting elbows of the female figures on its front served as handles to ease its removal (the whole façade was thus once enigmatically devoid of visible hinges), and that it was once veneered in an elaborate pattern.[19] The back of the compartment it conceals is veneered in a complex geometric pattern formed by partridge wood borders and bands outlined in ivory separating ebony fields, in essence a central lozenge set in a rectangle with projecting corners and quadrants to each outer corner. Its ceiling and floor are veneered in a variation on this theme, a rectangle with incurved corners forming its centre. On either side are nests of – apparently – ten drawers in four tiers, their fronts, within an ebony frame, with ebony edge mouldings, two lines of ivory stringing enclosing a band of partridge wood around a partridge wood panel with a central turned ivory knob. However, the top and bottom tiers are single drawers, with fictive double fronts. Similarly to the lateral bays, the two central tiers are of three drawers each, with, in the centre, a deeper drawer, with a secret drawer and panel at the back, and a shallower above. The Corinthian second storey thus has 50 drawers, some more secret than others.

THE COMPOSITE THIRD STOREY

The Composite third storey is narrower than those below, the outside bays being eliminated, a change normal a storey lower on a church façade (fig. 105).[20] At either end are gilt bronze female figures on hexagonal ebony bases, these bases not original but probably supplied in England in the eighteenth century. The Composite storey itself is fronted by five columns of alabaster *a tartaruga*, with gilt bronze bases and capitals; shorter and slenderer than those below, they stand against pilasters with plain ebony bases and capitals formed, with their returns, of slabs of pale Egyptian alabaster. Their pedestals are set with stone panels or jewelled and the three dados are filled with panels of pietre dure. The entablature contains a frieze which is jewelled against an onyx marble background and projects beyond the lateral columns below which there are downward extensions resting on the single top scrolls of S- or reverse S-shaped gilt bronze open brackets, which incorporate bearded masks and vegetal and grotesque engraved ornament (fig. 110). These brackets, whose fronts are painted blue to resemble lapis lazuli, within gilt bronze borders, terminate, after an angular break, in flattened triple scrolls, at which level they have a slightly improvised and ungainly appearance. However, their flattened and broken form can be directly compared to scrolls surmounting a 'Mausoleo' or *castrum doloris* designed

FIG. 104
Composite third storey, detail showing central gilt bronze bracket with pendant bunch of – presumably Peretti – pears.
Actual height 3⅜ in, 8.5 cm.

FIG. 105 ▶ OVERLEAF
Composite third storey, frontal view. Height 12⅜ in, 31.5 cm.

FIG. 106
Composite third storey, detail showing the compartment behind the
central drawer with two drawers to one side.

FIG. 107
A drawer from the side of the central compartment of the Composite
third storey, 4¼ x 8⅛ x 7⅜ in, 10.8 x 20.7 x 18.8 cm, contrasted
with another from the back of the left 'window' compartment of
the Corinthian second storey (see fig. 102), 1⅝ x 2¼ x 4⅛ in,
4.4 x 5.8 x 10.5 cm.

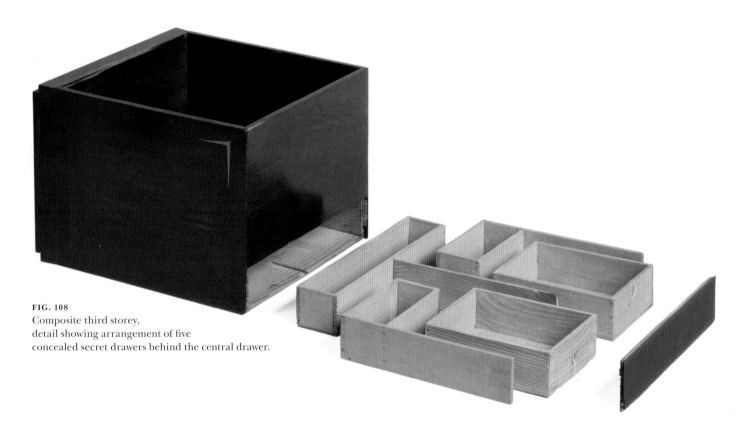

FIG. 108
Composite third storey,
detail showing arrangement of five
concealed secret drawers behind the central drawer.

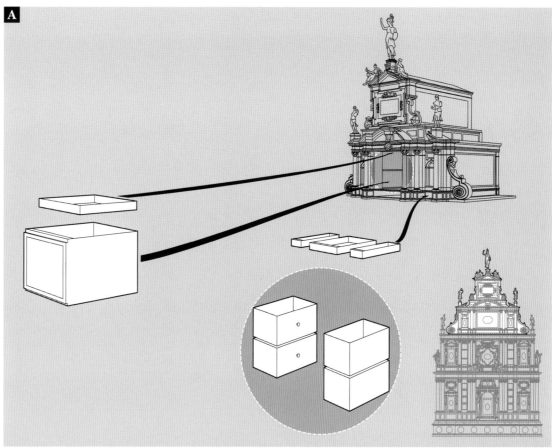

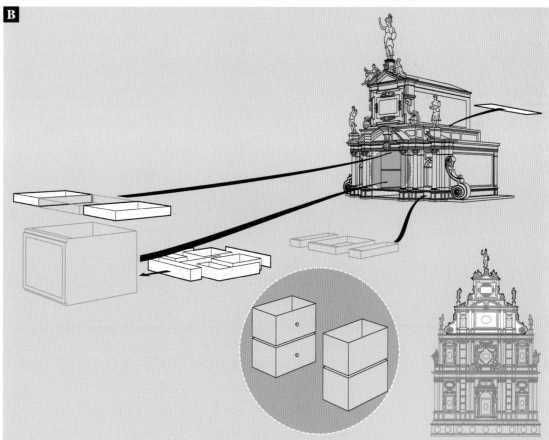

FIG. 109
Exploded drawings of the Composite third storey, showing arrangement of drawers (A)
and arrangement of drawers and compartments within drawers (B).

FIG. 110
Composite third storey, detail showing left gilt bronze bracket with engraved ornament. Height 8¾ in, 22 cm.

FIG. 111 ▶ FACING PAGE
Attic, frontal view. Height 26¾ in, 68 cm.

by Domenico Fontana for the funeral of his patron, the Conde de Lemos, Spanish Viceroy in Naples in 1601.[21] That they are original elements is further suggested by the careful finish of their low plinths, firmly attached to the Corinthian storey, economically veneered in ebony where visible and in cheaper walnut where not. The presence of crude narrower housings for some earlier fitment cut in the flanking dados of the Composite third storey behind these scrolls is a puzzling feature.[22] The narrow outer bays contain ebony-framed arched 'windows' and, above these, tablets, both filled with pietre dure, set against a background of onyx marble. And the central bay is a spectacular panel of pietre dure, with a central oval of foiled amethyst. Above the entablature the outer bays are surmounted by the triangular ends of a very broken pediment and the centre by a bold segmental pediment, filled to each side by panels of pietre dure, mainly mother-of-pearl and coral, with a projecting centre mounted with a jewel and a gilt bronze scroll, from which hangs a beribboned, conspicuous and unmistakeable – and presumably Peretti – bunch of pears (fig. 104).

Turning to the Composite *interior* (fig. 109), the dados pull out as three drawers but neither the frieze nor the side bays contain drawers. However, the central panel pulls out as a single large drawer all of whose surfaces, except its outer base, are finely veneered in ebony, inside and out, with ebony parquetry on its outer sides. At its lower back is an ebony-covered slip which can be slid off to give access to five secret drawers, the first two rectangular and at right angles to the back, the second pair, behind, rectangular and parallel to the back, with extended L-shaped linings, and the fifth, further behind, again parallel to the back with an extended T-shaped lining, these extensions serving as handles for extracting the drawers (fig. 108). Once removed the main drawer reveals a compartment veneered in partridge wood on its back and ceiling (the floor, invisible at this height, is economically unveneered) with ivory stringing forming four L-shaped panels round a central rectangle. The ceiling can be pushed backwards and then slides down and out to reveal a shallow secret drawer, while the compartment's sides each contain two drawers, their fronts with deep ebony mouldings, double ivory stringing enclosing a partridge wood band, and central ebony panels with turned ivory knobs (figs 106 and 107). The Composite third storey thus contains 14 drawers of varying degrees of secrecy.

THE ATTIC FOURTH STOREY

The fourth storey, or rather Attic, rests on a plinth with incurved ends, set behind and projecting beyond the central segmental pediment of the third Composite storey (fig. 111). At its sides the tops of this plinth may be slid out to reveal open compartments. The front of the plinth is faced with rectangular pietre dure panels at each end, which die into the pediment, and is flanked by square ebony pedestals, which support slender gilt bronze female figures.[23] The Attic, of a similar width to the central panel of the Composite storey, is flanked by open scrolled gilt

bronze brackets, lighter than, but of a similar profile to those on the Composite storey, but their base scrolls ornamented with sunflowers. The Attic is surmounted by a triangular pediment, which breaks forward at each end, where repose female gilt bronze figures. On its centre is an ebony pedestal mounted with a Corinthian pilaster capital (the Attic order is essentially one of pilasters, not necessarily tied to any one of the standard orders). The pedestal is octagonal and probably a later introduction, comparable to the two at the ends of the Composite third storey below, while the pilaster capital has been borrowed from the Wavendon cabinet (see fig. 68), where it has been replaced by a copy.[24] The façade of the Attic contains an ebony-moulded rectangular frame with projecting corners. In the frieze above its centre is a long panel of pietre dure. Between the ebony frame and a second inner frame of the same shape the border is filled with alabaster mounted with oval lapis lazuli 'jewels' set in silver bezels, and to the four sides of the inner frame gilt bronze scrollwork mounts, that below the frame incorporating a drapery swag, and that above a mask. The inner frame contains a single panel of onyx marble, with pietre dure corners. There is no access to the interior of the Attic, beyond the two compartments in its plinth.

THE SIDE ELEVATIONS

The side elevations of the Sixtus Cabinet, largely identical, are less richly and architecturally articulated than its façade, although with dados and pedestals at almost every level (fig. 112). This lack of articulation allows the display of larger stone or pietre dure elements. Starting with the ebony plinth, there are five varied alabaster stone panels to each side set in alternately long and short oval silver bezels (fig. 113). The dados of the Ionic first storey are filled by long panels of pietre dure, incorporating vertical ovals of lapis lazuli in silver bezels. At the back are pedestals, with *fiorito* alabaster panels, for alabaster pilasters with plain ebony bases and capitals. Similar pilasters towards the front lack pedestals, arguably an architectural solecism and the first to be noted. Between these pilasters, in ebony frames, are large panels of pietre dure centred on spectacular ovals of *fiorito* alabaster. The Ionic friezes are also veneered in alabaster, in this case *di Palombara*, with 11 gems to each side, alternately small circles and ovals, set in silver bezels. On the Corinthian storey the dados are veneered in Spanish *broccatello* set with nine stones in silver bezels on each side, alternately large and small ovals (fig. 114). The pedestals at the back are both set with green Roman millefiore glass. The alabaster pilasters they support are similar to those on the Ionic storey. However, in between these, in ebony frames, are pietre dure panels of exceptional elaboration and of an unparalleled coloration, predominantly light alabaster motifs on light alabaster grounds. The friezes above, with alabaster grounds, alternate ten small vertical ovals of lapis lazuli or mother-of-pearl, unframed, with nine larger oval stones in silver bezels, set horizontally. The dado of the Composite storey is simply panelled in alabaster *a pecorella*, while the back pedestals for alabaster pilasters

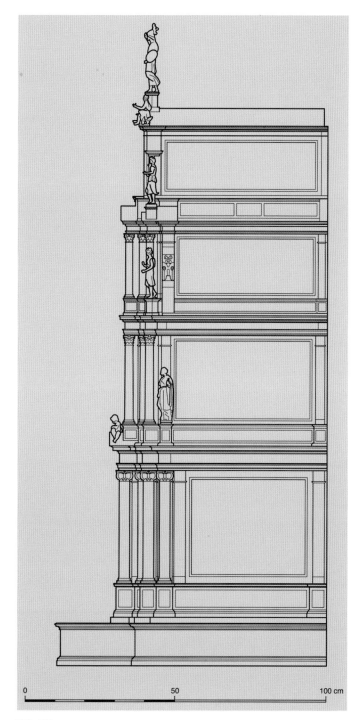

FIG. 112
Drawing of the right side elevation.

FIG. 113
Podium and Ionic first storey, right side.

FIG. 114
Corinthian second storey, left side.

FIG. 115
Attic, left side.

FIG. 116
Composite third storey, left side.

are again panelled in green Roman millefiore glass (fig. 116). The main fields are filled with large and spectacular panels of *fiorito* alabaster. The narrow Composite frieze is panelled with alabaster *a tartaruga*. As for the Attic, the sides of its plinth are divided into two long and one central short panels of partridge wood by ebony framing, and the sides of the Attic itself at the back, without pedestals, are filled with large and striking panels of *pecorella* alabaster with deeply chamfered edges, in ebony frames (fig. 115).

THE GILT BRONZES

All the gilt bronzes on the Sixtus Cabinet have been mentioned in the foregoing account, and it has been noted that there is a strong case for the attribution of the two putti who recline on the broken pediment of the Ionic first storey to Jacob Cornelisz Cobaert and for the dating of this model to the mid-1580s. The four small gesturing putti in the Corinthian second storey, whose gestures would be more meaningful if attributes survived, are not easily pinned down, although Cobaert is possible.[25] The Cabinet's gilt bronze capitals and bases may seem generic, but had to be tailored to the diminishing diameters of the columns, and were almost certainly custom-made (for example fig. 83). The same applies to the beribboned swags between the Corinthian capitals, and it may be observed that Domenico Fontana placed beribboned swags (admittedly not a rare formula) between the Corinthian capitals on his tombs to Pius v (1586–1588) and Sixtus v (1588–1590) in Santa Maria Maggiore. The ribbon motif is repeated on the central mount on the Composite pediment hung with particularly conspicuous pears, presumably, with this Peretti reference, made for the Cabinet.[26] The pears above the heads of the ten caryatids, of three models, at Ionic and Corinthian levels, suggest that these too were made as part of a suite. Domenico Fontana seems to have been fond of the caryatid term motif: it is used on both the papal tombs just mentioned and, monotonously, on the third floor of the Lateran Palace courtyard (1586–1589). Unlike their smaller chunkier companions, the caryatids flanking the central door of the Ionic first storey are slender, even willowy, and have much in common with the five standing and two reclining female figures on the Composite and Attic storeys, not to speak of the two poised by the central panel of the Corinthian storey, surely custom-made for this position. A general reference point for such elongation is provided by the four lively but lanky adolescents cast in bronze in 1585–8 by the Florence-born sculptor and architect, Taddeo Landini (*c*.1561–1596) for the Fontana delle Tartarughe, itself designed by Giacomo Della Porta, 'architetto delle fontane di Roma' since 1567. Closer parallels, at least for the standing figures, are the angels, supplied in 1589 by Flaminio Vacca (1538–1605) and Pietro Paolo Olivieri (1551–1599), flanking Sixtus v's arms in the attic of the Fontana del Mosè, far above its 'mastodontico' Moses.[27] Their garments tend to hang rather than flutter or billow; stockier angels with slightly billowing garments, supplied in 1610 by Ippolito Buzio (1562–1634) to support the arms of Pope Paul v Borghese

FIG. 117
Pax, the Risen Christ, gilt bronze, attributed to Guglielmo della Porta, Rome, about 1570. 5⅜ x 3⅝ x 2 in, 13.8 x 9.4 x 5.1 cm. Metropolitan Museum of Art, New York.

on the Fontana dell'Acqua Paola, supply a contrast.[28] The figures on the Sixtus Cabinet are small (the largest, at its top, is about 10 inches (24.5 cm) high, the smaller ones about six and a half inches (16 cm) high) and, although they are not finished to the highest degree, their garments (which tend to the droopy) are textured or punched with scrolling patterns. Unfortunately, many have lost attributes, and the Cabinet's iconographic programme is thus obscure. The top figure, armoured, with shield and helmet but lacking her lance, may be Minerva or Athena, possibly flanked by the reclining Medicine, with a snake, and Navigation, with an anchor. An extra unattached figure, probably a survivor of the pair which preceded St Peter and St Paul, has a book and a bag (?). With nine locations, the Cabinet could have presented many variations on the arts and sciences.[29] Perhaps the most impressive gilt bronzes on the Cabinet are the scrollwork frames and mounts, especially those incorporating masks. Albeit small, they are boldly designed and vigorously executed. The caryatid terms, and particularly their scrolled terminations, may be compared in design to the smaller equivalents forming part of a pax (fig. 117) by Guglielmo Della Porta in New York, elements which may well have been worked on by Cobaert.[30] The Cabinet sports 96 gilt bronze elements, and there were once two more in this expensive material. The production of such a large and varied set of custom-made figures and mounts was a substantial task. A chain of detailed resemblances, as well as practical considerations, suggests that a single Roman workshop was responsible.

A general point is that bronzes were often a conspicuous feature of ambitious early cabinets. That made in Rome in the early 1560s for Cesare Gonzaga incorporated at least 18 antique bronze statuettes assembled by Giovanni Antonio Stampa, a prominent dealer from about 1554, and the ebony cabinet made for Giovanni Grimani's Venetian palace after 1568 was similarly embellished.[31]

THE PIETRE DURE

What renders the Sixtus Cabinet spectacular is the presence of an overwhelming quantity of pietre dure. This may well reflect Sixtus v's own taste for rare and/or ancient marbles and precious stones. He was a patron of Michele Mercati (1541–1593), physician, scholar and collector, whom he employed as a herbalist in 1587. In 1588 Mercati's ill-health led to his retirement from this activity, but he concentrated instead on the development of the Metallotheca, intended as a complement to the Vatican Bibliotheca [library], and consisting of a systematic assembly of the products of the earth in 19 labelled cabinets, including 'XI Marmora' [marbles].[32] In 1589 Mercati dedicated his *Degli obelischi di Roma* to Sixtus, the great re-erector of obelisks. But Sixtus's interest in marbles was more than intellectual: he is notorious for having in 1588 ordered the demolition of the Septizonium, a famous ornamental façade with three orders of columns erected by the Emperor Severus in AD 204 at the foot of the Palatine Hill, and appropriated its materials, including rare marbles, for his own building projects, among them the Cappella Sistina in Santa Maria Maggiore. This may be seen as emulating the Cappella Gregoriana in St Peter's, which Sixtus's predecessor and adversary, Gregory XIII Boncompagni, had initiated after his election in 1572 and which was completed under the supervision of Giacomo della Porta in 1583; it was described by Agostino del Riccio in 1597 as 'la più ricca di marmi vari et la più ornate che sin qui sia veduta' [the richest in variety of marbles and the most ornate so far seen].[33] In the Cappella Sistina (fig. 118), commenced in 1585, rich and varied marble inlays arranged in geometrical patterns clad the walls and the facing tombs of Pius v and of Sixtus v himself, both designed by Domenico Fontana. Their kneeling statues are set in round-headed niches inlaid in polychrome marbles in a scallop pattern, comparable to that on the central door of the Ionic first storey of the Sixtus Cabinet. The *scalpellino* [stone-mason] Lorenzo Bassani, who was head of the Sistine workshop, was responsible for this marble inlay.[34] The central focus of the Cappella is a tabernacle (see fig. 193), almost certainly designed by Domenico Fontana, formed as a *tempietto* carried by four gilt bronze angels by Bastiano Torrigiani (d.1596), a Bologna-born sculptor who had entered Guglielmo della Porta's workshop in 1573 and took it over after his death in 1577. The *tempietto* itself was supplied by the Sicilian bronze-founder Ludovico del Duca, who described its elements as 'gentili e minuti' [delicate and minute], adjectives applicable to the many pietre dure panels it incorporates, smaller than, but of a similar geometric character to, the cladding of the Cappella's walls.[35]

The geometric patterns of the pietre dure on the Sixtus Cabinet, though even more 'gentili e minuti', have a general resemblance to those on the tabernacle in the Cappella Sistina, but the effect is much richer, with a lavish use of lapis lazuli and other precious materials, including, as has been noted, green Roman millefiore glass. Its decorations also incorporate a large number of jewels, and a few engraved gems. A parallel may be provided by 'un' studiolo […] fatto di diverse pietre gemme, et altre cose' [a cabinet […] made of various stones gems, and other things], which was given to Cardinal Scipione Borghese in 1609, when valued at 3,500 crowns, by his uncle, Pope Paul v Borghese.[36] This long-lost cabinet had belonged to the enormously wealthy Pisan-born Roman banker, Tiberio Ceuli, who bought what is now the Palazzo Sacchetti in 1576 and assembled a magnificent collection of 'gioie, statue, pitture, e infinite altre cose' [jewels, statues, paintings and infinite other things], including the Ares Borghese, now in the Louvre, which had to be sold by his impoverished sons after his death in 1605.[37] The splendour of the *studiolo* was such that in 1610 Paul v commissioned for his nephew a stand to support it 'di diverse pietre dure come diaspri, lapislazzari, et altre simili nel studiolo' [of various hard stones such as jaspers, lapis lazuli and others similar to the cabinet], employing Pompeo Targone at a cost of 2,000 crowns.[38] Targone (1575–c.1630) trained as a goldsmith under his father, but also had an important career as architect, engineer and bronze-caster. Along with the goldsmith, Curzio Vanni, Targone was responsible for the gilt bronze tabernacle designed by the sculptor and architect, Pietro Paolo Olivieri (1551–1559), for the Sacrament altar in San Giovanni in Laterano, executed from 1598–1600.[39] This was another *tempietto* but with wings, and not in the round, being set against the altar's reredos, and incorporated a considerable display of pietre dure. In the context of tabernacles, close to cabinets, it is worth drawing attention to an exceptional unfinished cabinet in the will of Niccolò Gaddi (1537–1591), 'lo studiolo di gioie' [the cabinet of jewels].[40] Gaddi, a wealthy Florentine banker, landowner, collector and art adviser to the Medici, whose chapel in Santa Maria Novella, executed in 1575–7 to the design of Giovanni Antonio Dosio (1533–1611), who also supplied rare and beautiful stones from Rome, was the earliest in Florence to be clad in coloured marbles, maintained 'segatori e pulitori di pietre bellissime e di gioie' [sawyers and polishers of beautiful stones and jewels] in his *palazzo*.[41] In his will he specified that his *studiolo* could only be alienated if Santa Maria Novella wanted it 'per ciborio per il Santissimo Sacramento' [as a ciborium – that is, tabernacle – for the most holy Sacrament].[42] In his 1597 *Istoria delle Pietre* [History of Stones] Agostino del Riccio described it as incorporating 'rare pietre preziose' [rare precious stones] and 'tutto adornato con profile d'oro che vanno coprendo le commettiture delle pietre' [all decorated with mouldings of gold which serve to cover the joins between the stones].[43] In the *Istoria* del Riccio justifies his inclusion of gems as well as stones by stating that these

FIG. 118

The Sistine Chapel in Santa Maria Maggiore, Rome, designed by Domenico Fontana from 1584–7: on the left the tabernacle cast by Ludovico del Duca, supported on the shoulders of four angels, cast by Bastiano Torrigiani, the whole completed in 1590; on the right the tomb of Sixtus V. The walls of the chapel are clad with marbles, executed under the direction of the *scalpellino* [mason], Lorenzo Bassani.

too are used to ornament structures 'massimamente nelle fabbricche picciole, che sono imitazioni delle grandi, come astucci, tavolini e studiuoli'[above all on small structures which are imitations of large ones, such as cases, small tables and cabinets].[44]

The Gaddi cabinet and its probable contemporary, if not precursor, the Ceuli cabinet, and the Sixtus Cabinet, could each be categorized as a 'studiolo di gioie', and it may be noteworthy that the great early seventeenth-century pietre dure cabinet in the Palazzo Colonna, purchased from the papal *dispensiere*, Lorenzo Paribeni, in 1678, for which Filippo Schor, son of Bernini's ornamental adjudant, 'Giovanni Paolo Tedesco', designed a stand incorporating three figures of Indians, was admired in 1679 as 'lo Studiolo gioiellato' [the jewelled cabinet], an echo perhaps of its kinship with this earlier type.[45]

The pietre dure on the Sixtus Cabinet may be divided into four main categories. The simplest, which comprises its columns and pilasters and the panels within many pedestals, consists of unarticulated slabs or, in the case of the columns, cylinders whose interest and appeal lies in the colour and figure of the material, predominantly alabasters (the lateral pediments of the Corinthian second storey and the culminating pediment of the Attic, all three filled with slabs of lapis lazuli, are further instances). This ostensibly simple approach is most dominant on the sides of the Cabinet, where the dado and frieze of the Composite third storey, as well as its large central panels, and the large panels filling the sides of the Attic or fourth storey, are all slabs of strongly figured stone (fig. 119). These are the areas furthest from the spectator and least subject to scrutiny: fine work would be wasted at this distance, whereas bold figuring tells. But why 'ostensibly' simple? A correspondence between Cesare Gonzaga (1536–1575) of Mantua and later of Guastalla and his antiquarian adviser, Geralomo Garimberto (1506–1575) concerning a coin cabinet made for the former in Rome from at least 1562–5, to the design of the architect, Francesco Capriani da Volterra (1535–1594), demonstrates that the production of alabaster columns was not straightforward: there were technical challenges and it was difficult to secure alabaster of the right quality.[46] Some alabaster supplied by Paolo del Bufalo, who had just sold part of his family's collection of antique sculpture to Cardinal Alessandro Farnese, proved rotten, and some columns had to be made of green marble, the task involving two craftsmen, a recalcitrant Silvestro and a more productive Alberto (Garimberto used some imperfect columns in a cabinet of his own, designed by a pupil of Volterra). The cabinet was seen by Giorgio Vasari (1511–1564) in Mantua in 1566, who described it in glowing terms as of ebony and ivory. An early example of this taste, it was also, in 1571, described by Ulisse Aldrovandi (1522–1605), the famous Bolognese botanist and collector, while in about 1567 the antiquary Jacopo Strada (1507–1588) sent a drawing of the cabinet to his then master, Albrecht v of Bavaria (1528–1579). It may well have directly or indirectly influenced the Sixtus Cabinet.

The next category comprises panels conforming to the normal pattern of Roman work, as found on tables or in churches, in which the stone inlays or veneers butt

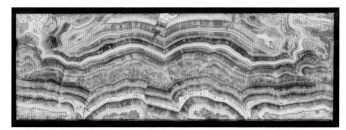
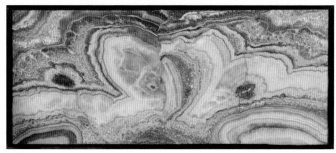

FIG. 119
(Top) Attic, detail showing right side panel of alabaster *a pecorella*, and (bottom) Composite third storey, detail showing right side panel of *fiorito* alabaster.

FIG. 120
Ionic first storey, detail showing main left side panel, with a central oval of *fiorito* alabaster.

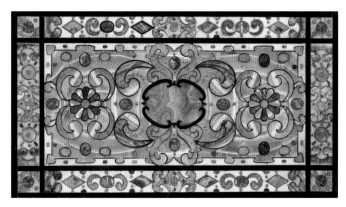

FIG. 121
Corinthian second storey, detail showing main left side panel, predominantly of variegated alabasters.

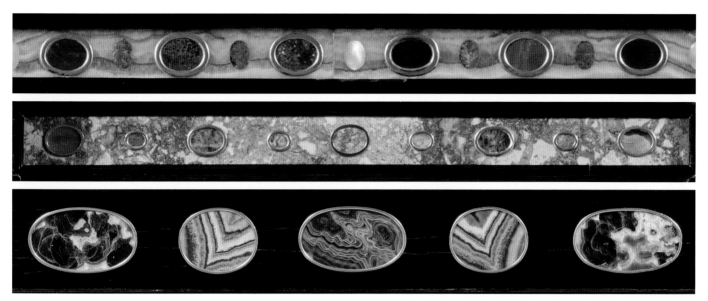

FIG. 122
(Top and centre) Corinthian second storey, details showing the right side frieze and dado with various stones in silver bezels, and (bottom) podium, detail of right side showing alabasters in silver bezels.

against one another or the ground. This technique is scarce on the façade of the Cabinet, being confined to the lateral pediments of the Ionic first storey, the panels in its pedestals, and the pilasters behind its two central columns, and to the pediment of the Composite third storey and the central panel of the Attic. On the Cabinet's sides, however, it is dominant, the dados of the Ionic first storey being simple friezes of ovals in this manner surmounted by main panels with quadrant corners and central ovals of alabaster with dotted borders (fig. 120), a motif to be compared to the centre of a table in the Palazzo Farnese plausibly dated to the 1560s, and repeated many times on a table in Madrid presented to Philip II of Spain in 1587 by Cardinal Alessandrino, Michele Bonelli (1541–1598), great-nephew of Sixtus v's great supporter, Pius v.[47] These handsome panels are transcended by those above which flank the Corinthian second storey (fig. 121). These have borders whose black *paragone* edgings intersect to form corner squares, each with a central lapis lazuli disc surrounded by four coral dots on a Spanish *broccatello* ground. The remainder of the borders and the central grounds display a variety of predominantly abstract motifs, scrolls, lozenges, dots, ovals and peltate forms. However, there is more than a hint of naturalism, not so much in the highly formalized rosettes which flank the central cartouches filled with alabaster, as in the scrolls above and below, which seem explicitly to represent sprouting foliage. These are accompanied by scrolls formed of coral dots of diminishing size, a motif reminiscent of the *cosses de pois* ornament fashionable among Parisian goldsmiths and jewellers from about 1615 to the 1630s, but already present on the 1587 Madrid table just mentioned and, in greater profusion, on a late-sixteenth-century Roman table top from the Corsini collection in the J. Paul Getty Museum.[48] The general design of the two panels is reminiscent of a number of Roman tables of the late sixteenth century, although they are, comparatively, on a tiny scale.[49] Thus, although the larger borders are in black *paragone*, as on

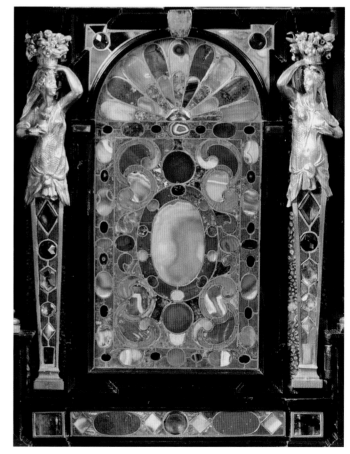

FIG. 123
Ionic first storey, detail showing the central 'door' panel of pietre dure.

many a full-scale table, the smaller borders are executed in bone, ebonized with added paint, much faded or lost. It is tempting, because they are livelier than the other side panels, to speculate that these panels may have been conceived and manufactured for another purpose and then enlisted for the Cabinet, but their fit is so precise, if not perfect, that they must surely have been custom-made. In the Cabinet context – and in a wider perspective – they are distinctive not only in design but also in their colour palette and tonality: light backgrounds are rare in pietre dure tables, and the strange alabaster polychromy displayed, partly light on light, is unparalleled.

The third category of pietre dure on the Cabinet comprises stones or gems set in silver bezels of roughly astragal profile (fig. 122), predominantly on its side elevations, in rhythmic alternations of larger and smaller ovals or discs, five (large) of alabaster on each side of the podium, four of lapis lazuli on the dadoes of the Ionic first storey, in this case alternating with ovals set as standard unbezelled pietre dure, 11 on the Ionic friezes, nine on the dados of the Corinthian second storey and nine on its friezes, again alternating with unbezelled ovals. On the front elevation of the Cabinet the only long sequence of bezels – in this case gilt – is on the frieze of the Composite third storey (and briefly on its returns), where lapis lazuli ovals alternate with carnelian rectangles. Further lapis ovals in gilt bezels are set in the corners of the border of the Attic storey's central panel. All these bezels, especially when they contain jewels, whether cut or cabochons, afford the Cabinet extra sparkle. The use of bezels is paralleled, on a larger scale, by the silver-gilt specimens (fig. 124) supplied in 1601 by the goldsmith Bartolomeo de' Bardi to frame panels of lapis lazuli, agate, jasper and other stones incorporated in the pietre dure of the chapel of San Filippo Neri in Santa Maria in Vallicella (the Chiesa Nuova).[50] Some of these decorations were designed by Giovanni Guerra (1544–1618), one of Sixtus v's principal painters, and executed by two *scalpellini* [stone-masons], Marchione Cremoni and Bartolomeo de' Laurenzi, the former probably connected to Melchiorre Cremona who had worked on the monument, completed in 1587, which Sixtus erected to his patron, Pius v, in Santa Maria Maggiore.[51]

The fourth and final category of pietre dure on the Sixtus Cabinet is confined to its front elevation, apart from short frieze returns on the Ionic first and Corinthian second storeys. Its defining feature is the use of narrow silver borders round every stone element, producing an effect comparable to earlier *cloisonné* enamels (fig. 125).[52] This technique required that spaces be cut for all the stones in a panel, be it a small drawer front or a large door, into a single sheet of silver which was held by a concealed metal frame of copper or iron (both were used). To cut such lace-like patterns into silver sheet must have demanded considerable skill. The polished stones were then fitted into their prepared spaces in what was effectively a tray, and secured by a sticky mixture of rosin: the tray was then filled and levelled with plaster, forming a rigid panel. The more transparent stones were regularly backed with gold foils which, albeit now partly oxidized, reflect light

FIG. 124
Detail of the pietre dure decoration of the Chapel of San Filippo Neri in Santa Maria in Vallicella (the Chiesa Nuova), Rome, showing the silver-gilt bezels supplied by the goldsmith Bartolomeo de' Bardi in 1601 to contain lapis lazuli, agate, jasper and other stones.

FIG. 125
Ionic first storey, detail showing the topmost of the tier of four small drawers in the second bay. This photograph, taken in 2008 during conservation, reveals the metal frame of this representative pietre dure panel, which is normally concealed by ebony mouldings. Metal frame and pietre dure panel 2⅜ x 2¼ x ¼ in, 6.1 x 5.7 x 0.7 cm.

and are particularly effective in flickering candlelight. The decorative vocabulary of these panels includes many circles and ovals and the occasional quatrefoil, octagon and lozenge, but the most distinctive and frequent motifs are comma-shaped scrolls, often linked or intertwined (fig. 123), and contributing to complex patterns reminiscent of certain designs for table tops by Giovanni Vincenzo Casale (c.1539–1593), probably executed while he was working for Cardinal Ferdinando de' Medici in Rome during the 1570s (fig. 57).[53] It has been suggested that the combination of the Cabinet's gilt bronzes with the dominant colours of the pietre dure on its façade, the blue of lapis lazuli and the reds of carnelian and coral, may have been intended to evoke the tinctures of Sixtus v's heraldic arms.[54] It may be added that the elements of mother-of-pearl – and the silver borders – may have been conceived as echoing the silver of his three heraldic mounts. But beyond doubt there is an explicit reference to Sixtus's family name, Peretti [little pears], already detected in certain gilt bronze mounts, in the small pear-shaped pietre dure elements which surround the irregularly shaped foiled agate set behind glass at the centre of the central panel of the Corinthian second storey, arguably the cynosure of the whole Cabinet (fig. 126).

THE PEDESTAL OF THE CABINET

The original pedestal of the Cabinet is an absence, not a presence, unlike its fine and elaborate successor, created in England (see Chapter 8). The documents of 1655 and 1665 (Appendix I) refer to 'suo piede con figure indorate' [its foot with gilt figures] and that of 1713 to 'un gran Piedestallo di legno negro e dorato' [a large pedestal of black and gilt wood]. At an early stage cabinets were rarely provided with integral or matching stands, and often set on tables or simple improvised supports. It can be surmised that the Sixtus Cabinet must have been set at least at table height to allow the organ to be played, whether seated or, more probably, standing. It is possible that the pedestal described in 1655, 1665 and 1713 was a baroque addition. However, it should be noted that the magnificent Roman pietre dure table now at Powis Castle has a massive gilt and painted stand (fig. 127), distinctly sixteenth-century in style and conformation, incorporating fluted Ionic columns whose capitals contain upright pears, a most unusual feature which may allude to the Peretti arms, and lion and lioness monopods, possibly relating to the Peretti lion. Certainly a number of pietre dure tables are listed in various Peretti inventories, which would render a Peretti provenance possible. Perhaps the Powis stand may provide an indication of the character of the original pedestal of the Sixtus Cabinet.

CONCLUDING REMARKS

The Sixtus Cabinet was and is first and foremost an object of display, designed to amaze, impress and entertain, through its synthesis of rich and elegant architecture and sculpture, of exquisite craftsmanship, and of luxurious, colourful

FIG. 126
Corinthian second storey, detail showing the central panel, its pietre dure pattern incorporating little pears, presumably for 'Peretti'.

FIG. 127
Base of table (detail), including a lion and, in the Ionic capital, a pear ('upside down') flanked by two leaves, all echoing Peretti heraldry, gilt and painted (possibly to resemble green porphyry) wood, probably Roman, about 1580. At Powis Castle, Powys. 36¾ in, 93.5 cm high (including table top shown in fig. 34). National Trust.

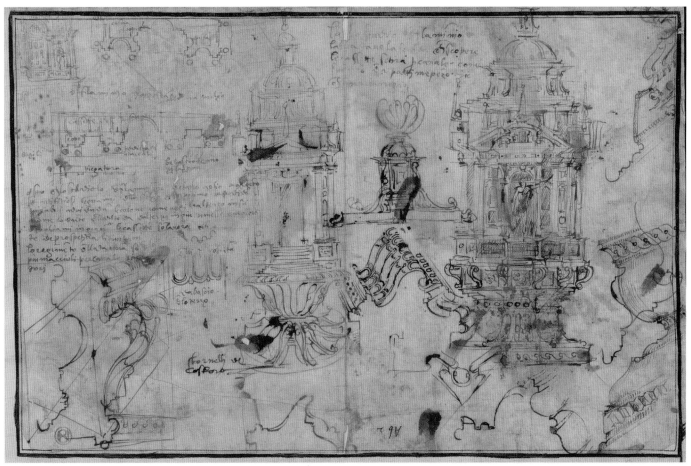

FIG. 128
Sketches including (top left) details of a 'studiolo' [cabinet] by 'Flaminio francese' (Boulanger), attributed to Giovanni Colonna da Tivoli, Rome, about 1570. Pen and sepia ink, 10½ x 16⅛ in, 26.6 x 41 cm. Biblioteca Nacional, Madrid.

and rare materials drawn from nature (but for Roman glass), the antique associations of many of the stones – *spolia* – lending them extra resonance. A contemporary audience would have relished the Cabinet's variation and modulation of ornamental patterns, on different scales, its careful matching or calculated contrasts of stones, both as to colour and figure, its orchestration of a whole range of skills, including cabinet-making, pietre dure, bronze casting, chasing and gilding, jewellery and silversmithery, engraving (on ivory) – and organ-building. The layered ingenuity of its interior lends it further interest and fascination, and many of its internal spaces and fitments, though normally hidden from view, are objects of display themselves, with their stylish livery of ebony, partridge wood and ivory. The Cabinet's organ, while it survived, was another feat of ingenuity, more admirable on that account, it may be suspected, than for musical excellence.[55] The Cabinet's practical functionality should not be overstated: that its drawers show little sign of use speaks for itself.[56] Its function was in sum more symbolic and performative than practical: it would be possible to reconstruct a plausible choreographic scheme for putting the Cabinet through its paces before a privileged audience, culminating, perhaps, in the extraction of the Composite third storey's beautifully veneered drawer and a demonstration of its five secret drawers – if not in a tune on the organ.

It was normal for cabinets produced in many European cities to use ornament derived from classical architecture, but surprisingly few follow an architectural model as faithfully as does the church-like façade of the Sixtus Cabinet. The cabinet designed in about 1562 by Francesco da Volterra, who was a skilled woodworker, for Cesare Gonzaga, has already been noted:[57] as it incorporated columns, pedestals and niches it is likely to have had an architectural character. In about 1578 Guglielmo Bos, agent to Alvise Mocenigo, writing to Niccolò Gaddi, stated that he had offered for sale to Francesco I de' Medici a coin cabinet designed by Andrea Palladio (1508–1580) for Lunardo Mocenigo (1522–1575) described as a 'bellissimo arco d'ebano fatto a simiglianza di quello di Constantino' [most beautiful ebony arch made in resemblance to that of Constantine], evidently a piece of miniature architecture.[58] An ebony cabinet of similar ambition designed by an unknown architect, quite possibly Palladio again, was made soon after 1568 by a Flemish cabinet-maker for Giovanni Grimani (1506–1593) as a central focus for the study in his new apartment in his Venetian palace near Santa Maria Formosa.[59] An architectural Roman cabinet (fig. 129), devised by the Farnese antiquary, Fulvio Orsini (1529–1600), and probably detailed by Giacomo della Porta, who had succeeded Vignola as the Farnese architect in 1573, was made by the French carver and cabinet-maker, Flaminio Boulanger, active in Rome since 1552, in 1578 to contain the manuscript encyclopaedia of Rome and collection

FIG. 129
Cabinet, walnut, devised by Fulvio Orsini, made by Flaminio Boulanger for Cardinal Alessandro Farnese, Rome, 1578.
90½ x 83⅞ x 32¼ in, 230 x 213 x 82 cm. Musée national de la Renaissance, Château d'Écouen.

of medals which the Neapolitan painter, architect and antiquary Pirro Ligorio (*c*.1512–1593) had in 1567 sold to Cardinal Alessandro Farnese.[60] This walnut cabinet, part *palazzo*, part triumphal arch, may be compared to a cabinet (fig. 128) with a complex architectural façade, incorporating a central niche and pairs of columns flanking lateral bays, attributed to 'Flaminio francese' and said to have been executed in 'debano aolio e argeto e artifitiosi legnami e mischio' [ebony ivory and silver and skilfully worked woods and coloured marble] in inscriptions on a drawing in Giovanni Vincenzo Casale's album in Madrid: it must date from before Boulanger's death in 1584, and probably from Casale's principal Roman period in the 1570s.[61] Other examples include the lost 'Studiolo Nuovo' designed by Bernardo Buontalenti for Francesco I de' Medici to stand in the centre of the Tribuna of the Uffizi and executed by the German cabinet-maker, Bartolomeo d'Ermann, from 1584–6: in the form of a *tempietto* (or tabernacle) this was of ebony with alabaster columns and pilasters, and silver-gilt mounts, richly jewelled and containing a multiplicity of drawers for antique coins and medals.[62] Cabinets of predominantly architectural form, as well as ornament, were thus, albeit uncommon, no novelty when Sixtus was elected Pope in 1585. It may be added that the façade of the Sixtus Cabinet reads consistently and convincingly in both detail and overall design, suggesting that an architect was responsible, in which case the obvious candidates would be Sixtus's friend and favourite, Domenico Fontana, and/or his nephew, Carlo Maderno, who succeeded to the family business in Rome when his uncle left for Naples in 1594. Of the two Maderno, a livelier designer, seems the more likely, and the task could well have been delegated to him: he had been in his uncle's employ since 1576, and, as noted earlier, the Cabinet bears resemblances to both his Santa Susanna (from 1597) and his San Andrea della Valle (about 1620). The side elevations of the Cabinet are not as architecturally

impeccable as its façade.[63] It seems likely that these visually less prominent aspects had not been fully detailed and the cabinet-maker had to improvise. At a more technical level the carcase displays a number of alterations or hesitations in the positioning of the housings for the drawer divisions, where they engage the base and sides, suggesting that their maker was finding the incorporation of so many drawers and divisions a challenge. Another criticism which might be levelled is that the Cabinet's gilt bronze mounts are of uneven quality. It is tempting to put this down to impatience on the client's side: Sixtus was the quintessential old man in a hurry.

Throughout this chapter, which has attempted to combine a full, although by no means exhaustive, description of the Sixtus Cabinet with some sidelights and parallels focused on his reign, the implication has been that the Cabinet was made for Sixtus. That it was worthy of such a client, who was a considerable grandee in Rome while a cardinal and, once Pope, both a temporal and a spiritual sovereign, is evident from its ambition, elaboration and opulence, while iconographic hints point to Peretti patronage. There is no obvious internal evidence to reject a commission in the 1580s, while the story which Henry Hoare bought with the Cabinet in 1740 merits, prima facie, some credence. The next chapter will explore Sixtus and the Peretti dynasty, and pursue questions of patronage, date and provenance, but this one will conclude by citing the presence, in a list of objects sold in 1591 as part of a tidying-up exercise after Sixtus's death, of 'Un' studiolo piccolo d'Ebano Intersiato di dentro e di fuora d'osse lavorate' [a little cabinet of ebony inlaid inside and out with wrought bone] and 'Una tavola di pietra di diverse colori con il piede di pietra intersato' [a table of stone of various colours with a base of inlaid stone].[64] These may be minor objects, but they demonstrate that Sixtus had a taste for ebony cabinets and pietre dure.[65]

1. See Appendix II, p. 197–9.
2. Heikamp 1963, p. 221 illus.
3. Hellwag 1924, p. 69.
4. The comparison of a cabinet and a church is not new: the 1597 inventory of the Palazzo Pitti includes a 'Studiolo grande a forma d'una facciata di chiesa' [large cabinet in the form of a church façade] decorated with Venetian style black and gold japanning and painted with the story of Perseus (Bohr 1993, p. 266).
5. See p. 164.
6. Maderno's original designs were engraved in Sandrart 1690, pls. 41–4.
7. Much of what follows draws on the observations of Colin Piper, who was responsible for the conservation of the Sixtus Cabinet carried out in 2006–7.
8. For the rest of this account the wood will be referred to as ebony.
9. See Appendix V, p. 213.
10. From the Stroganoff Collection, no. 60327. Two comparable examples of Roman glass ('Pasta antica') were illustrated by Pier Leone Ghezzi in 1726 (Coen and Fidanza 2011, nos 243 and 255).
11. Many of the lining panels, some missing, which concealed nests of secret drawers, and the drawers themselves, were released by bone springs, now mainly fragmentary; in this instance the aperture in the pine base of the drawer, through which the spring could be pressed to release it, is fitted with a neat sliver of ebony veneer, whose hardness would protect the soft pine from being damaged by repeated use, a signal refinement.
12. Cannata 2011, pp. 142–54, especially pp. 150–2 illus. I am grateful to Jennifer Montagu for drawing this to my attention.
13. Ibid.
14. One example may be the cruder variations on the putti model, with added wings and wreaths, transforming them into cherubs, which surmount the tabernacle frame of an Agony in the Garden signed and dated by Jacopo Ligozzi (1547–1627) in the Allen Memorial Art Museum, Oberlin (illus. Koeppe 2008, p. 141).
15. Garstang 2003; Baglione 1733, p. 165.
16. d'Onofrio 1957, p. 153.
17. See Chapter 8 below for the Pedestal and Boson, and Appendix V for St Peter and St Paul.
18. The suggestion of a visual pun on Peretti was made by Xavier F. Salomon. The second caryatid term from the left is apparently a replacement, cruder than the rest.
19. The likeliest explanation for this brutal alteration is that the door was dropped and damaged, and a more secure fixing and simpler veneered surface replaced its original insecure elaboration.
20. An exception is Buontalenti's 1587 model for Santa Maria del Fiore, Florence Cathedral, in the Museo dell'Opera del Duomo, which has curved brackets in this position. The gold relief mentioned at the beginning of this chapter seems to show a different and odd solution, sloping balustrades, also shown in a drawing (66.510) by Cigoli (Ludovico Cardi) (1559–1613) of a variant 1589 scheme in the Metropolitan Museum, New York (1559–1613).
21. Verde 2008, p. 92, fig. 10. Related scrolls are to be seen on the Fontana del Prigione designed by Fontana for the Villa Montalto in

the late 1580s, but re-erected in 1923 as an eye-stopper at the top of the Via Luciano Manara in Trastevere (illus. Quast 1991, pl. 33).
22. A possible explanation is that the present scrolls were mislaid during some move, necessitating the provision of alternative mounts, but that they were subsequently rediscovered and reinstalled in their rightful places.
23. That on the left appears to be an aftercast, of lower quality than the other figures.
24. See Appendix VI.
25. See Cannata 2011, pp. 138–9, an entry on two not dissimilar gilt bronze putti, unattributed, which mentions the Stourhead four.
26. It is worth mentioning that the Arco di Sisto V, part of the Acqua Felice aqueduct on the Via Marsala, north of Stazione Termini, has Sixtus's heraldic pears in the spandrels of its lower side arches and is popularly called the Arco delle Pere.
27. d'Onofrio 1957, pl. 66 and p. 93 (for 'mastodontico').
28. d'Onofrio 1957, pl. 123.
29. An alternative reading might see the top-most figure as Fortitude, flanked by Prudence and Hope, but a theological theme is belied by the absence of wings on the secular putti below.
30. Walker 1991, p. 168, fig. 1 (see also fig. 6, detail of a scheme by della Porta for San Silvestro al Quirinale, Rome, c.1556–7, drawn by Giovanni Antonio Dosio (1533–1609), Oxford Ashmolean Museum, Largest Talman Album, fol. 37, incorporating caryatid terms also comparable to those on the Cabinet).
31. Brown and Lorenzoni, 1993, pp. 13, 235; Thornton 1997, p. 71.
32. It was finally published as *Michaelis Mercati Samminiatensis Metallotheca Opus Postumum* (Rome, 1717), edited by the papal physician, Giovanni Maria Lancisi (1654–1720).
33. Quoted di Castro 1994, p. 18.
34. di Castro 1994, p. 19.
35. Montagu 1996, p. 24.
36. González-Palacios 2010, p. 65.
37. Camiz 1991, p. 214, citing Florence as Fondo Mediceo del Principato, F 3761.
38. González-Palacios 2010, p. 65.
39. di Castro 1994, pp. 24–5, and Peccolo 1994, pp. 169–76.
40. Barletti 2011, p. 497.
41. Ibid., pp. 299, 345, 320.
42. Ibid., p. 475.
43. Gnoli and Sironi 1996, p. 164.
44. Ibid., p. 87.
45. Strunck 2008, pp. 17–18.
46. Brown and Lorenzoni 1993.
47. Illus., Koeppe 2008, p. 14, fig.17; González-Palacios 2001, pp. 59–64.
48. For *cosses de pois*, see Fuhring and Bimbinet-Privat 2002, pp. 1–224; the Getty table is illus. Giusti 2006, p. 14: I am grateful to Charissa Bremer David for the information on provenance. Similar, but more naturalistic, dots are present on the Roman slab at Lamport Hall (see fig. 58).
49. A comparable table is illus. González-Palacios 1982, p. 15.
50. Incisa della Rochetta 1972, p. 47. The chapel was paid for by a Florentine, Nero del Nero, with an estate at Porcigliano, and the stones were partly sent from Florence and partly from Venice, the latter sawn and polished by a craftsman named Donato from

the Abruzzi. The chapel was said in 1601 to involve 'spese incredibili' [incredible expenses].
51. Ibid., p. 48; Barbieri, Barchiesi and Ferrata 1995, pp. 106–16; Fagiolo and Madonna 1992, p. 554, entry on Melchiorre Cremona.
52. In 2006 Rupert Harris Conservation commissioned extensive XRF analysis of the metal, revealing a silver content ranging from 88.9 per cent to 52.2 per cent.
53. Lanzarini 1998–9, pp. 190, fig. 10, and 192.
54. This possibility was floated by Xavier F. Salomon in 2007. Sixtus's arms were 'Azure, a lion rampant or holding a branch of pears slipped and leaved, overall a bend gules charged with a star, or, in chief and three mounts, argent, in base.'
55. See Appendix V.
56. Although the discovery of miniatures in the drawers after the Cabinet came to England suggests a modest modicum of practical use (see Appendix V).
57. See p. 99 above.
58. Brown and Lorenzoni 1999, pp. 59–60, 74.
59. Thornton 1997, p. 71.
60. Coffin 2004, pp. 76–7.
61. Lanzarini 1998–9, pp. 197, fig. 22, 198 and 202, no. 97, where she attributes this sheet to Giovanni Colonna da Tivoli; Petraccia 2011, pp. 85–100. The present reading of the inscription differs slightly from that given by Bustamente and Marias 1991, p. 297.
62. Heikamp 1963, pp. 209–17; Bohr 1993, pp. 137–8.
63. As noted, the forward side pilasters of the Ionic first storey lack plinths, unlike those at the back.
64. Mobili nel Palazzo Montalto 1591, f. 12 verso and f. 14.
65. It is also suggestive of Sixtus's taste that when, on 12 October 1589, he attended a great feast at Terracina at the southern end of the Pontine marshes, which he planned to drain, a notable feature was a 'studiolo' [cabinet] of ebony, inlaid with gold (Orbaan 1910, p. 67).

FOUR
SIXTUS V, THE VILLA MONTALTO AND THE PERETTI DESCENT

Fra ttutti quelli c'hanno avuto er posto
de vicarj de Ddio, nun, z'è mmai visto
un papa rugantino, un papa tosto
un papa matto, ugualea Ppapa Sisto.
GIUSEPPE GIOACHINO BELLI, 1834

In the epigraph above, the poet Belli, writing in Roman dialect, sums up Pope Sixtus v's popular reputation, two centuries after his death: 'Of all those who have held the office of vicar of God, there has never been seen a rough pope, a tough pope, a savage pope, the like of Pope Sixtus.' Eighty years earlier the 1754 Stourhead paintings catalogue in the archive at Longleat said of Sixtus: 'This Pope was contemporary with Elizabeth Queen of England, and was originally a pig driver' (see Appendix II). Both statements are accurate, although the latter a slight exaggeration. Sixtus (fig. 130) was born Felice Peretti in December 1521 at Grottamare, north of Pescara on the Adriatic coast of Italy, north-east from Rome. His father rented a smallholding and his mother worked as a servant for their landlord. The family's impoverished origins were in Montalto, a village 20 miles back from the coast, between Ascoli and Fermo. As a small boy Felice Peretti carried out chores on the family farm, including looking after his father's pigs. However, his education was taken firmly in hand by a Franciscan uncle and in 1530 he entered that order's house at Montalto, taking Franciscan vows in 1534. Ordained a priest in 1547 he was in 1548 awarded a doctorate in theology at the University of Fermo, after studies in Rimini and Siena. Thenceforward Peretti established a reputation as a preacher and moved upwards in the Franciscan hierarchy, with spells in Naples and Venice. From 1560 he was mainly based in Rome in the convent of the Santi Apostoli, becoming Procurator General of the Franciscan order in 1561, its Vicar General in 1566 and Apostolic President in 1567. The convent and basilica of the Santi Apostoli were under the protection of the powerful Princes Colonna, whose palace they adjoined, and Peretti taught philosophy to Marcantonio Colonna, elected archbishop of Taranto in 1560 and created a cardinal in 1565. He formed an even more fruitful friendship with Cardinal Michele Ghislieri,

who was elected to the papacy as Pius v in 1566 and died in 1572, having raised Peretti to the purple in May 1570. In 1565, however, he had made a powerful enemy in Cardinal Ugo Boncompagni, who was leading a legation, to which Peretti was attached, to investigate a heresy case in Spain. In 1572 Boncompagni succeeded Pius v as Pope Gregory XIII, and Peretti's hopes of advancement were stifled for the next 13 years. Gregory XIII died on 10 April 1585 and on 24 April Peretti was elected to succeed him as Sixtus v.

Sixtus v, over 64 at the time of his election, was a compromise candidate: the college of cardinals had been split between supporters of the Farnese faction, who looked back to the papacy of Paul III, Alessandro Farnese, from 1534–49, and the Medici supporters, who recalled the papacies of Leo x, Giovanni de' Medici, from 1513–21, Clement VII, Giulio de' Medici, from 1523–34, and Pius IV, Gian Angelo de' Medici, from 1559–65 (his family, from Milan, was probably unconnected to the Medici of Florence, but he was nonetheless recognized as belonging to the clan). The new Pope, an ageing Franciscan from an obscure family, was not expected to survive long, still less to establish himself as a force to be reckoned with. In the first respect expectations were vindicated, as Sixtus died in August 1590, barely five years after his election, but in the second they could scarcely have been more delusive: Sixtus v proved himself energetic, forceful and dominant. He is best remembered now for his creation of many of the major landmarks and thoroughfares of Rome, some commemorated on the English eighteenth-century pedestal of the Cabinet at Stourhead (see Chapter 8 below). He also extirpated the bandits who plagued his realm, and built up the papal treasury. But Sixtus, a serious collector of books, was also theologically formidable and lent his full weight to the completion of a new version of the Vulgate, the Latin Bible. This project, initiated by Pope Pius IV in

FIG. 130
Sixtus v, surrounded by the medals issued during his pontificate, engraved by Matteo Greuter, for Alphonso Ciacconio, *Vitae et Res Gestae Pontificum Romanorum*, Rome, 1630. 13 x 8⅞ in, 33 x 22.5 cm. Society of Antiquaries of London.

SIXTI. V.
PONT. MAX.
NVMISMATA

VADE FRAN·REPARA

1588 B. DIDACVM HISP·IN
REVILIT · WAN·SS·

Diffi- / cillimis / tempori- / bus Pon- / tificatu / adeptus.

Religi- / onis am- / plificādæ / studi- / um.

FECIT IN MONTE CONVIVIVM PINGVIVM

VIGILAT SACRI THESAVRI CVSTOS 1586

Iustitia, / Pax, et / Vbertas.

Aerariū / supplen- / di cura.

VRBE LAVRETO 15 86

CVRA PONTIFICA

Lauretū / ciuilibus / honori- / bus cu- / mulat.

Apertis / directis / vijs Vrbem / exornat.

EXALTAVIT HVMILES 1587

PERFECTA SECVRITAS

Religio / et decor / Vrbi quæ- / situs.

Grassato- / ribus Pō- / tificia / ditione / depulsis.

SACRA PROPHANIS PRÆFERENDA

SVPER HANC PETRAM ROMA

Propha- / nas mo- / les pieta- / tis in / usum / uertit.

Tholum / Vaticani / Templi / absoluit.

PONTINAS PALVD·SICCARI CONCESS· 1588

PVB. BENEFICIVM

Agrorum / fertilita- / ti con- / sultum

Aquarū / copia Vr- / be locu- / pletata.

MONTALTO 15 88

ECCE·REGNVM·DEI

Patriæ / dignita- / tem et / Religio- / ne addit.

Pontifi- / catū uni / Deo ac- / ceptum / fert.

FOELIX PRESIDIVM

NOXIIS   TANTVM

PONS FELIX

Pontifi- / cia Clas- / se instr- / ucta.

AD·LATERA·P·CONCIS·CELEBRAV   QVARTVM ANNO QVARTO ERE[X]IT 1586

Publicæ / commo- / ditati / prospec- / tum.

Latera- / nensi Ba- / silicae / decus / addit.

AN·DOM·M·D· LXXXIX·

Vrbem / religiose / illustrat.

SIXTO · V · PONT · MAX
OB QVIETEM PVBLICAM
COMPRESSA SICARIORVM EXTINQVĒ
LICENTIA RESTITVTAM
ANNONAE INOPIAM SVBLEVATAM
VRBEM AEDIFICIIS VIIS AQVAEDVCTV
ILLVSTRATAM
S · P · Q · R

Illustrissimo Principi D. Francisco Pereito Abbati Syxti V Pronepoti
Franciscus Gualdus Arim eg S. Steph. deuoti animi gratia D.D.

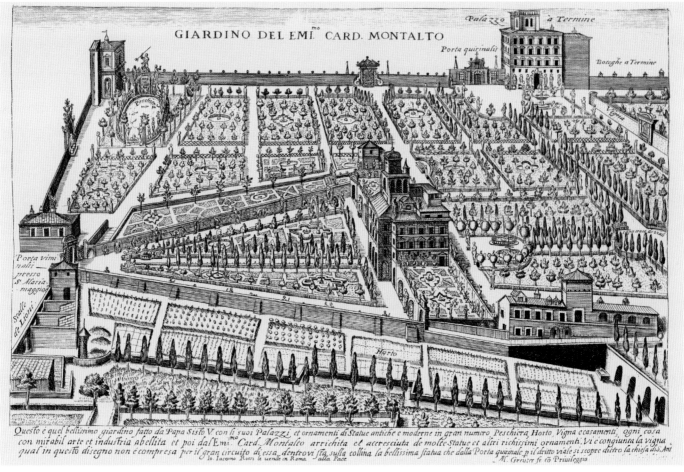

FIG. 132
The Villa Montalto, bird's-eye view of the north-west portion with the Palazzo Felice in its centre, engraved by Matteo Greuter, originally published by Greuter and Gotfried de Scaichi, Rome, 1623. 9¼ x 14 in, 23.6 x 35.5 cm.

1561 during the Council of Trent, had made little progress. It was revived by Pope Pius V in 1569 in the aftermath of the Council, but again faltered. Sixtus's commission for the revision was set to work in 1586, but he rejected their recommendations and took the editorial work in hand himself. The new three-volume edition, produced in a hurry and promulgated in 1590, was deemed so full of errors that it was ordered to be destroyed; its successor the Sixto-Clementine, more usually called Clementine, Vulgate, first published in 1592, by Pope Clement VIII Aldobrandini, was by contrast accepted as definitive and endured until 1979. Ironically, Sixtus's name survived on the title-page as having commissioned the work. Ruthless though he could be, Sixtus was no philistine. He would discuss Roman coins late into the night with the humanist bibliophile and collector, Fulvio Orsini (1529–1600), who dedicated to the Pope his edition of *De Triclinio Romano* (Rome, 1588), by the Toledo-born antiquary Pedro Chacón (1525–1581).[1] Sixtus collected books and one of his great projects was the Sala Sistina of the Vatican Library, built to Domenico Fontana's design in 1587–9 and frescoed with the Pope's achievements.

THE VILLA MONTALTO

The site of Stazione Termini, Rome's railway station, and the adjoining swathes of late-nineteenth-century developments were until the late sixteenth century a remote and uninhabited tract within Rome's ancient Aurelian walls, largely vineyards.[2] In 1576 Sixtus V, then Cardinal Felice Peretti-Montalto, purchased the Vigna Guglielmini, a short distance north-west from Santa Maria Maggiore, for 1,500 *scudi*, his sister Camilla being the ostensible buyer. This was an awkward U-shaped plot, but under two years later, in 1578, Sixtus purchased the Vigna Cappelletti, which filled in the central gap, for 450 *scudi* and in 1580 added the Vigna Zerla, a larger plot to the north-east, with an entrance opposite the Baths of Diocletian, at a cost of 1,700 *scudi*. The principal works on the site were initiated after the acquisition of the Vigna Cappelletti and comprised the first steps towards extensive landscaping and the erection of a casino, a relatively modest five-bay house, which became known as the Palazzo Felice, on a central axis between the west end of the Vigna Guglielmini and the highest point in Rome, a hill to the north-east.

◄ FIG. 131
The Palazzo Felice of the Villa Montalto, engraved by Natale Bonifacio da Sebenico for Domenico Fontana, *Della trasportatione dell'Obelisco Vaticano et delle fabriche di Nostro Signore Papa Sisto V*, Rome, 1590. 15⅛ x 9½ in, 38.4 x 24.2 cm. Society of Antiquaries of London.

His architect, Domenico Fontana (1543–1607), one of a dynasty of masons and *stuccatori* from Ticino, had arrived in Rome in 1563, and gradually worked upwards, being appointed a papal architect by Gregory XIII in 1577 along with his brother Giovanni (1540–1614), although only in a technical, surveying capacity. A commission of 1574 from Sixtus to execute a monument in Santa Maria Maggiore to Nicolas IV (1288–1292), the first Franciscan pope, established their relationship, and in about 1577 Fontana worked on the then Cardinal's town house on the corner of the Via dei Leutari and the Piazza del Pasquino. In 1578, when commencing works at the Villa Montalto, Sixtus was still in receipt of a monthly subsidy of 100 *scudi* ordained by his late patron, Pius V, as a 'cardinale povero' [poor cardinal], but in early 1581 this was withdrawn by his foe, Gregory XIII. By then the principal works on the Palazzo seem to have been complete but Sixtus continued to improve 'la sua bella fabrica' [his beautiful building], partly with money lent, remarkably, by his architect.[3] For the next four years, still in disfavour, Sixtus lived at the Palazzo. And once elected Pope he pursued an inexorable policy of expansion, whether by purchase or gift, involving no fewer than 16 acquisitions of land, the last secured a bare month before his death, and the Villa Montalto (fig. 132) became, at almost 160 acres, the largest such estate within Rome's ancient walls.[4]

To acquire a villa, a suburban retreat with rural connotations, was by 1576 a common ambition among Roman grandees of every stamp. But it was an ambitious move for a Franciscan cardinal with no family background, and limited means. Sixtus's choice of site, on the Esquiline hill above Santa Maria Maggiore, had several advantages: the neglected area was relatively cheap, it was close to that basilica, which had been reconstructed by the Franciscan Nicholas IV, whose tomb Sixtus, his papal name chosen to recall the intervening Franciscan pope, Sixtus IV (1471–1484), had erected there in 1574, and, being near the highest point in Rome, it was a real 'montalto', reflecting the name of his birthplace, on which, when he died in 1590, Sixtus was planning to build a 'Palazzo bellissimo' with views over all Rome and its countryside.[5] A further attraction was that Sixtus, who celebrated his own agricultural past, could indulge in some real husbandry, although he also went in for seriously grand gardening. An early great project of his papacy was the Acqua Felice, so called, as was his Palazzo, after his baptismal name, an ambitious hydraulic scheme masterminded by Giovanni Fontana, incorporating an aqueduct which went underground on the Villa Montalto, and whose ceremonial culmination, nearby, was the Fountain of Moses or 'Mostra dell'acqua Felice', designed by Fontana's brother Domenico, and inaugurated in 1587.[6] The waters had begun to flow on the Villa Montalto in October 1586, allowing a constant sequence of aqueous embellishments in the form of fish-ponds and fountains, shrubberies and walks lined with cypresses. As Domenico Fontana observed in 1590, the casino, the Palazzo Felice (fig. 131), was 'alquanto picciolo, rispetto la corte grande, che ricerca un tal Principe' [somewhat small, with regard to the great court required by such a prince], but, this notwithstanding, Sixtus loved to spend time there, particularly in the summer, enjoying the beauty of its architecture, ornaments and paintings, the wealth of views afforded by the garden he had created and the wholesome sweetness of the air.

While the Palazzo Felice was a retreat secluded from the new roads Sixtus had created, in 1588–9 he also had built on the side of the new Piazza Termini, opposite the Baths of Diocletian, the substantial Palazzo alle Terme, which his family could occupy. Its street façade was of seven bays, with a lower three-bay wing to the north, succeeded by a row of 18 shops and a granary, all with a very urban flavour, the Palazzo itself verging on the bleak, although Domenico Fontana, its architect, called it 'bellissimo'. The whole Villa Montalto estate was eventually sold by auction in 1696 to the recently created Cardinal Francesco Negroni (1629–1713), treasurer to Innocent XI. His family later lived in Genoa, neglecting their Roman property, which was in 1784 purchased by a merchant, Giuseppe Staderini, who cut down the timber and in 1786 sold the sculpture to the English antiquary and dealer, Thomas Jenkins (1722–1798), the greatest coup of his long and successful career. In 1789 the dilapidated villa was bought by Prince Camillo VII Francesco Massimo (1730–1801), and held by his family until the 1860s when expropriated to provide a site for Rome's new station, an act which hastened the death of its owner, Prince Camillo IX Vittorio Emanuele Massimo (1803–1873), a distinguished scholar who loved the place and had in 1836, before inheriting, published an extraordinarily full history of what was then the Villa Massimo.[7]

THE LOGGIA

In his description of the Palazzo Felice he knew so well (Appendix 1, p. 196) Massimo pronounced the loggia on the *piano nobile*, some 41 feet (12.5m) long and approaching 16 feet (4.9 m) wide and facing north-east over the villa's gardens 'la più magnifica stanza del Palazzo' [the most magnificent room in the palace].[8] This was partly for its painted decorations, but also reflected its central position as the culmination of the ceremonial route which led up the stairs and along the central corridor separating the two principal apartments; an upstairs loggia was frequently the greatest ornament and delight of such a casino. In his poem *Perettina sive Sixti v Pont. Max. Horti Esquilini* [On the Peretti Villa or Esquiline Gardens Belonging to Pope Sixtus V], published in Rome in 1588, but already composed, albeit not in its final form, in 1583,[9] Aurelio Orsi described the dawn light shining through the loggia's three arches, and the cool breezes and views of flowers and water enjoyed by its noble proprietor, taking, as it were, a springtime stroll within his palace; it is perhaps more than coincidence that the Latin word Orsi used for loggia, 'xyxtus', is close to 'Syxtus', as he spelled his patron's papal name.[10] The loggia's vault was decorated with three scenes, the Nurture of Jupiter, the Choice of Hercules and Hercules crowned by Virtue, subjects readily referred by Orsi to Sixtus's career, the first, depicting Jupiter's rustic upbringing on Mount Ida being particularly *à propos*. The ceiling was exceedingly colourful and incorporated elaborate grotesque and emblematic

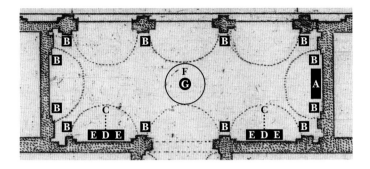

FIG. 133
Plan of the loggia of the Palazzo Felice,
with a possible arrangement of its principal contents.

A. Sixtus Cabinet and its canopy
B. 12 painted pedestals supporting antique marble statues
C. Two ebony side cupboards
D. Two Giambologna bronze groups (lion and horse, lion and bull)
E. Four Giambologna bronze animals (two horses, two bulls)
F. Circular pietre dure table
G. Giambologna bronze group, The Rape of a Sabine

vornament surrounding four ovals with mythical subjects, while in its corners four pairs of genii supported allegories in rectangular cartouches.

Massimo published extracts from the description of the loggia's contents in the 1655 inventory of the Palazzo Felice (see Appendix I) commencing with:

> a Cabinet made in the form of a Tabernacle with an organ inside with ten columns of alabaster on the first floor eight on the second and six on the third with seven small figures, and two seated with panels of various precious stones with its base with gilt figures and its Canopy of red Cotton with gold lace and fringes.

The recent recognition that this was indubitably the Sixtus Cabinet immediately removed the mid-eighteenth-century account of its provenance from the realm of possible myth to a firm basis in reality. The English traveller, Francis Mortoft, who visited the Palazzo Felice on 20 January 1659, was not as good at counting columns but 'A very high and Rich Cabinett of inlaid worke, with many Aggat pillars to the number of 15', which he noted, confirms the Sixtus Cabinet's presence.[11] Although the inventory is dated 1655 there are strong reasons to believe that it copied one of 1631, only a generation or so after Sixtus's death.[12] Evidently the inventory was still valid in 1655, and the existence of a close but not identical version dated 1665 (see Appendix I) extends that validity, which is further prolonged by an inventory of the sculpture (but including the Sixtus Cabinet) of about 1680 (see Appendix I), which shows its contents unchanged. Such continuity suggests that the loggia was piously preserved as an historic ensemble. Perhaps because they would be somewhat exposed to the elements there were no easel paintings – with one exception: 'Un ritratto in Tavola isolata di D. Alvaro' [A portrait of D. Alvaro on an isolated panel]. It was tempting to suppose that this represented Don Alvaro I, King of Congo from 1568–87, whose ambassador, the Portuguese merchant Duarte Lopez, was received by Sixtus V in late 1588.[13] But in fact this was Don Alvaro Nano, a dwarf, who crops up in another painting listed in the Palazzo alle Terme in 1655.[14] The other ornaments of the loggia included 12 wooden pedestals painted and gilt with arabesques and the arms of Cardinal Montalto, arguably Sixtus before his elevation, which must have resembled the surviving pedestal of the Torrigiani bust of Sixtus in the Victoria & Albert Museum, plausibly associated with his great-nephew, Prince Michele Peretti (fig. 134), and predominantly red, blue and gold,

FIG. 134
Sixtus V, gilt bronze, by Bastiano Torrigiani, Rome, about 1585–90, its pedestal, of painted and gilded wood, incorporating Peretti heraldry, possibly made for Prince Michele Peretti. 34½ x 23⅜ x 14⅛ in, 87.5 x 59.5 x 36 cm (bust), 18¾ x 15⅛ in, 47.5 x 38.4 cm (pedestal). Victoria & Albert Museum.

FIG. 135
Bull, bronze, by Giambologna, this cast by Girolamo di Zanobi Portigiani, Florence, 1573, 8½ x 10¼ in, 21.7 x 26 cm. Collection of Mr and Mrs J. Tomilson Hill.

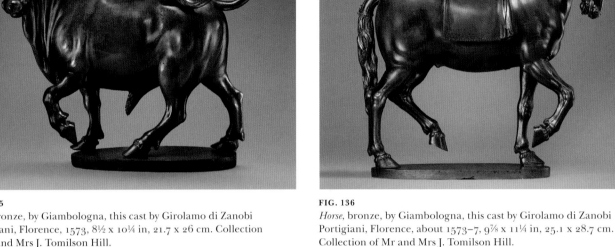

FIG. 136
Horse, bronze, by Giambologna, this cast by Girolamo di Zanobi Portigiani, Florence, about 1573–7, 9⅞ x 11¼ in, 25.1 x 28.7 cm. Collection of Mr and Mrs J. Tomilson Hill.

echoing his heraldic tinctures. These pedestals supported 12 antique marble statues, all about three feet high, two Apollos, three Venuses and so on, identified in the *c.*1680 inventory. Sixtus was a collector of antique sculpture.[15] More significant may be the bronzes which stood on two side-cupboards inlaid with ivory, ebony and tawny wood, perhaps partridge wood, and thus displaying the same palette as the Sixtus Cabinet.[16] They comprised two small bulls, two small horses (figs 135 and 136), a lion attacking a horse and a lion attacking a bull (figs 137 and 138), all on ebony or ebonized bases and immediately recognizable as Giambologna models. His contribution to the loggia is confirmed by the presence of a bronze group listed in the 1655, 1665 and *c.*1680 inventories merely as composed

of three figures: the suspicion that this must be a bronze reduction (fig. 139) of his *Rape of a Sabine* of 1583 is confirmed by the statement in the manuscript, *Roma ornate dell'architettura, pittura e scoltura* [Rome adorned with Architecture, Painting and Sculpture], by the historian and topographer Fioravante Martinelli (1599–1667) of 1660–3 that in the loggia: 'Il Ratto di una Sabina di metallo è di Giovan Bologna' [the bronze Rape of a Sabine is by Giambologna].[17] A significant detail in the 1655 and 1665 inventories is that elements of this group and/or its base (described as of carved wood in *c.*1680) were gilt. Given that Francesco de' Medici, Grand Duke of Tuscany, had given money to the then Cardinal Montalto in 1583,[18] the year when the *Rape of a Sabine* was unveiled, by his

FIG. 137
Lion Attacking a Horse, bronze, after a model derived from the antique by Giambologna, Florence, 1580s, this version possibly French, early seventeenth century. 9⅝ in, 24.5 cm high. Patricia Wengraf Ltd.

FIG. 138
Lion Attacking a Bull, bronze, after a model by Giambologna, Florence, 1580s, this version possibly French, early seventeenth century. 8¾ in, 22.5 cm high. Patricia Wengraf Ltd.

FIG. 139
The Rape of a Sabine, bronze, attributed to Gianfrancesco Susini, after a model by Giambologna, Florence, about 1620–50. A bronze of this type, reduced from Giambologna's marble of 1583, now in the Loggia dei Lanzi, Florence, stood in the loggia of the Palazzo Felice in the Villa Montalto. 23½ in, 59 cm high.

court sculptor, Giambologna, it seems probable that the group of seven bronzes was a grand-ducal gift, touches of gilding on the *Rape* and/or its base underlining its quality and significance. (In the same year Francesco's brother, Cardinal Ferdinando de' Medici, gave his friend Sixtus the *Virgin and Child with Saints Francis and Lucy* by Alessandro Allori (fig. 140) which was installed as the altarpiece of the Palazzo's chapel, then on the same floor as the loggia.) The *Rape* stood on a round pietre dure table with a carved base, which was in 1683 described as standing in the middle of the loggia, the logical position. The only other furnishings were a table cover of red leather with gilt fringe, probably for this table, four stools for seating, covered in red Cordova leather, quilted with yellow silk and with yellow and red silk fringes, and the blue canvas hangings for the three arched openings of the loggia, with their cords and iron fitments, all in a decayed state. The heraldic red, blue and gold thus recur.

The loggia, as designed by Fontana, was articulated by 12 Ionic pilasters painted with Peretti mounts and stars on a red ground, with a richly marbled dado below. Given the Peretti palette it seems likely that the main walls were blue. The four lunettes below the vaulted ceiling on the entrance and end walls (but not that over the door, which probably contained an heraldic achievement) were filled with landscapes incorporating lions: *Samson and the Lion*, *Daniel in the Lions' Den*, *The Disobedient Prophet* and a scene Massimo could not interpret (the building had been struck by lightning in 1835), showing a contemplative man in a rocky landscape, surely *St Jerome and the Lion*. As Cardinal Peretti Montalto, Sixtus had a particular devotion to St Jerome, and the first door encountered ascending the stairs to the *piano nobile* of the Palazzo Felice was surmounted by a painting of him in the guise of St Jerome, who was usually depicted as a cardinal and whose lion Sixtus had chosen as the central charge on the coat of arms he devised when raised to the purple in 1570.[19] That Jerome was responsible for the Vulgate which Sixtus was to re-edit was no coincidence; he was, moreover, an irascible character who never ceased to beat his chest with a stone during four years in the wilderness, according to the *Golden Legend*, a practice the irascible Sixtus commended as having secured his sainthood. While the other lions in the loggia's landscape lunettes were at once biblical and heraldic, St Jerome's, albeit not biblical, thus carried a profounder personal significance for Sixtus. Although some doubt must remain as to the date and attribution of these lost landscapes, they are such an integral part of the loggia's decoration, echoing the arches of its windows with their views of greenery, that they seem unlikely to be later additions.[20] Massimo describes them as being flanked in the adjoining spandrels by gilt female nudes 'a guisa di accademie' [in the manner of academy figures], evidently unable to decipher their significance, and as being separated by an upper tier of Ionic pilasters, painted with arabesques and emblems of the Cardinal in chiaroscuro on a yellow ground, except the pairs in the corners which had white arabesques on blue.

The purpose of this account of the loggia where the Sixtus Cabinet stood is to draw attention to its extraordinary

FIG. 140
Madonna and Child with Saints Francis and Lucy, by Alessandro Allori, Florence, 1583, given to the future Sixtus V
to serve as the altarpiece of the chapel in the Palazzo Felice of the Villa Montalto by Cardinal Ferdinando de' Medici,
also in 1583. Oil on canvas, 101¾ x 66 in, 265.5 x 167.6 cm. National Museum of Wales, Cardiff.

quality, in terms of complexity, of colour – almost all with a Peretti dimension, of design – equally suffused with Peretti iconography, and of artistry, if Massimo is to be believed. It is surely remarkable that in the grandest room in his casino Sixtus should have himself represented as Jupiter and as Hercules, that it was surrounded by 12 antique statues, predominantly of Roman deities, and that Giambologna's *Rape of a Sabine Woman* should be its central focus. Christianity only intrudes directly in the landscape lunettes, where the lions double as heraldic and that of St Jerome was additionally a very personal emblem. For a cardinal in disfavour, a cardinal risen from poverty, the whole ambitious ensemble reads as an act of self-assertion, if not defiance. His loggia is a sculpture gallery, ancient and modern, the creation of a princely connoisseur and humanist, presided over by his Cabinet, set at one end under a red canopy with gold fringing (fig. 133). The cabinet was 'a tabernacolo' [in the form of a tabernacle], suggesting that it represented the altar of this miniature temple of art, in which the ebony sideboards surmounted by Giambologna bronzes were the equivalent of side altars, and that the figure on its top is indeed Minerva, who was depicted in the vault of the ground floor entrance below, presiding over the sciences and the arts.[21] That it contained an organ complicates and enriches the image (see Appendix v). If the Sixtus Cabinet was, as seems quite plausible, commissioned for the loggia of his Palazzo by the future pope in the early 1580s, while he was still a cardinal, it should perhaps be rechristened as the 'Studiolo Felice'.

THE PERETTI DYNASTY

By 1700 a myth had arisen that the Peretti family were of Dalmatian origin, descended from a Zanetto Peretti, a native of Cruscizza or Krujkica, 'little pear', the equivalent of 'Peretti' in Croat, who had fled from the Turks in the fourteenth century. In fact Sixtus v, albeit his parents were certainly of very modest means, had respectable Peretti ancestors in Montalto from at least 1290. But, though respectable, his family was by no means noble or distinguished. As Sixtus was, by definition, celibate, the survival of his family and the creation of a dynasty worthy of a Pope (see diagram, p. 220) depended on his younger sister, Camilla, born in 1524. By 1549 she had married Giambattista Mignucci, a citizen of Montalto, whom Sixtus, not yet a cardinal, adopted in 1562 and who was dead by 1566. By him Camilla had two children, Francesco and Maria Felice Mignucci Peretti, born in 1549 and 1552, nephew and niece to the future Pope. In 1574, by which time Sixtus was a cardinal, Francesco married Vittoria Accoramboni, who belonged on her father's side to a family of minor nobility from Gubbio and on her mother's to the noble Roman family of Albertoni, with a palazzo on the Piazza di Campitelli. Beautiful and extravagant, Vittoria attracted many admirers, among them Paolo Giordano Orsini, Duke of Bracciano, whose first wife, Isabella de' Medici, daughter of Cosimo i de' Medici, Grand Duke of Tuscany, had been strangled on Braccciano's orders in 1576, in revenge for her adultery with his cousin, Troilo

FIG. 141
Cardinal Alessandro Damasceni Peretti Montalto, marble, by Gianlorenzo Bernini, Rome, about 1620–3, formerly in the Palazzo alle Terme of the Villa Montalto but perhaps originally intended for the Cardinal's tomb, never executed, in the Sistine Chapel of Santa Maria Maggiore. 31 x 25⅝ in, 79 x 65 cm. Kunsthalle, Hamburg.

Orsini. Vittoria's brother, Marcello, and her mother, Tarquinia, favoured her grand alliance with Bracciano and accordingly, in 1581, had Francesco Mignucci Peretti murdered. After delays and protests, Vittoria's marriage to the Duke of Bracciano finally took place on 24 April 1585, the day of Sixtus's election to the papacy. The pair then fled to Venetian territory, where Bracciano died that November and, after a bitter dispute over his Orsini inheritance, Vittoria was assassinated by a gang of thugs on Christmas Eve. This episode formed the basis for John Webster's tragedy, *The White Devil*, published in 1612.

In 1570, fortunately, Sixtus's niece, Maria Felice Mignucci Peretti, had contracted a more fruitful marriage to a Roman merchant named Fabio Damasceni, bearing him four children from 1571–7. After their mother's death Sixtus adopted them and had them brought up by Lucrezia Salviati, a natural daughter of Cardinal Bernardo Salviati, himself an uncle to Cosimo i de' Medici, Grand Duke of Tuscany; her husband, Latino Orsini, who was killed in Cyprus in 1586 fighting the Turks, was a legitimized natural son of Camillo Orsini, Governor of Rome in 1559. In 1585 the first-born of the four, Alessandro Peretti Damasceni, was created a cardinal at the age of 14, barely a fortnight after his great-uncle's coronation as Sixtus v. Cardinal Montalto, as he became known, was a close confidant of the Pope, and proved himself a discreet, efficient and faithful servant.[22] Not everyone saw him in this light: in 1598 the Venetian ambassador described him as a 'giovane morbido e dato a' piaceri in tal modo che trascura quasi tutti le cose' [an effeminate youth, devoted to pleasures to such a degree

FIG. 142
Cardinal Andrea Baroni Peretti Montalto, by Ottavio Leoni, Rome, 1626.
Red and black chalk heightened with white on blue paper, 8½ x 6 in,
21.5 x 15.2 cm. Downing College, Cambridge.

that he neglects almost everything].[23] His rewards included
an income of some 100,000 *scudi* and, in 1587, the Villa
Lante at Bagnaia. He was a major patron of painters, at
the Palazzo della Cancelleria and the Palazzo alle Terme,
as well as elsewhere. His bust (fig. 141), by Bernini, is now
in the Kunsthalle in Hamburg; it was probably intended
to form part of a monument to the Cardinal in the Sistine
Cappella del Presepio in Santa Maria Maggiore, where he
was buried in 1623, but this project was never executed.
Montalto also commissioned Bernini's *Neptune and Triton*,
now in the Victoria & Albert Museum, to preside over a
basin at the Villa Montalto. He evidently had a pronounced
taste for pietre dure, witness many entries in his accounts
for objects incorporating lapis lazuli, jasper and alabaster,
including, in 1614, 190 *scudi* to Persio, a silversmith, for a
'Madonna con il figliolo in braccio d'argento con diverse
pietre commesse et finimento d'ebano' [Madonna and
Child in a silver frame decorated with various inlaid stones
and ebony veneer].[24] In November 1602 he visited the
Opificio in Florence where he would probably have seen
Matteo Nigetti's recent design for the tabernacle in the
Cappella dei Principi.[25] Cardinal Montalto is the most likely
patron for the Sixtus Cabinet, if it was not, as proposed
here, made for Sixtus himself.

Another member of the Peretti family should be
noticed. Andrea Baroni was born in 1573, the son of a
first cousin of Sixtus, and in 1589 formally taken into
the Pope's household as a Peretti (fig. 142). After Sixtus's
death Andrea was in 1596 created a cardinal by Clement
VIII Aldobrandini, who owed much to Sixtus and, indeed,
to Andrea's cousin, Cardinal Montalto. Andrea himself,
liked and respected, sometimes lived as part of the
Montalto household, but died in 1629 in a rented palazzo
in the Borgo. Although poor by the standards of many
cardinals Cardinal Peretti, as he was known, assembled
antique sculpture and over 100 paintings, which he left
to Francesco Damasceni Peretti, son of his executor,
Prince Michele Peretti. His taste echoed that of his cousin,
Cardinal Montalto.[26]

After Cardinal Montalto, to return to the main line,
the next two Damasceni Peretti children were girls,
Felice Orsina, born in 1573, and Flavia, a year younger.
In an heroic feat of papal diplomacy Sixtus arranged
the marriage of both great-nieces on the same day, 20
March 1589, to representatives of the two greatest –
and perennially feuding – families in Rome, Orsina to
Marcantonio Colonna, Grand Constable of the kingdom of
Naples, and Flavia to Virginio Orsini, Duke of Bracciano,
son by his first, murdered, Medici wife to the preceding
Duke of Bracciano, who had been implicated, eight years
earlier, in the killing of the Pope's nephew, Francesco
Mignucci Peretti. Each bride received a dowry of 80,000
scudi as well as pin-money of 20,000 *scudi* and other gifts.
Marcantonio Colonna died in 1595 and that same year the
childless Orsina was remarried to her late husband's first
cousin, Muzio Sforza, Marquis of Caravaggio, who had in
1594 founded the Accademia degli Inquieti in Milan, of
which Ludovico Settala was a leading light.

The male line depended on the fourth Damasceni
Peretti child, Michele, born in 1577. He was much favoured
by Sixtus, being appointed Captain General of the Papal
Bodyguard and Governor of the Borgo, the district
between the Vatican and the Tiber in 1585, when he was
eight. He is prominent, in armour, in a mural of about 1588
by Pietro Facchetti in the Biblioteca Apostolica Vaticana
depicting its architect, Domenico Fontana, presenting
his plan for the library to the Pope. And in that year,
aged 11, Michele was married to Margherita Cavazzi della
Somaglia, only daughter and therefore heiress of a wealthy
Milanese noble and his Spanish wife, Maria Leonora de
la Cerda y Bobadilla, daughter of a Count of Chinchon
prominent at the court of Philip II. In 1605 Michele's pious
grandmother, Sixtus's sister Camilla Peretti, died. Sixtus's
acquisition and expansion of the Villa Montalto had been
effected in her name and in October 1586 he formally
confirmed his transfer of the villa to her, securing it for his
Peretti descendants.[27] The actual donation he had made
a little earlier in a surprise after-dinner speech following
a day they had spent together at the Vatican, in which
Sixtus proclaimed his responsibility and fondness for the
villa, but associated it with his period as cardinal. He also
stated that in the previous month he had ordered it to be
more nobly furnished than hitherto, so as to befit Camilla's
princely status, although he stressed that her court should

FIG. 143
Prince Michele Peretti, attributed to Pietro Facchetti, Rome, about 1608. Oil on canvas, 70⅞ x 48¾ in, 180 x 124 cm.
Galleria Nazionale d'Arte Antica, Palazzo Corsini, Rome.

FIG. 144
Cardinal Francesco Damasceni Peretti, by Ottavio Leoni, Rome, 1622.
Red and black chalk heightened with white on blue paper, 9⅜ x 6½ in,
23.8 x 16.4 cm. Accademia Toscana di Scienze e Lettere, 'La Colombaria'.

FIG. 145
Cleria Cesarini, by Jacob Ferdinand Voet, Rome,
possibly painted at the time of her marriage to
Filippo Colonna, Prince of Sonnino, in 1671.
Oil on canvas, 27½ x 23⅝ in, 70 x 60 cm.
Private collection.

be of a modest character.[28] It is theoretically possible that the Sixtus Cabinet was part of this 1586 campaign. The focus of Camilla's personal patronage had been the convent and church of Santa Susanna, close to the villa, where she was responsible for the chapel of San Lorenzo, completed in 1591 and richly embellished with marbles.[29] She had always been devoted to her brother (in 1586 one of his physicians, Castore Durante, dedicated his *Il Tesoro della sanità*, a medical primer, to her as an aid to her care of the Pope) and Sixtus had given her further possessions, to which she added significantly after his death, notably Celano and Piscina in the Kingdom of Naples, purchased from Costanza Piccolomini in 1591, with the assistance of Michele's brother, Cardinal Alessandro Montalto. One of her titles was Marchesa di Venafro, from another Neapolitan property she had purchased for 86,000 *scudi* in 1586, and after her death Philip III of Spain granted Michele the title of Prince of Venafro. In 1594 Michele purchased Mentana, a castle and estate near Rome, from Fabio and Virginio Orsini for 250,000 *scudi*. He is shown in princely guise in a dashing portrait in armour (fig. 143) of about 1608, now in the Galleria Corsini, by Pietro Facchetti, who had painted him in the Biblioteca Vaticana some 20 years earlier. When he inherited the Villa Montalto from his great-aunt Camilla, he ceded its use to his elder brother, the Cardinal.

Prince Michele Peretti's wife, Margherita Cavazzi della Somaglia, bore him three children, Francesco in 1595, Camilla in 1596 and Maria Felice in 1603. Margherita was involved in negotiations for Francesco to marry Anna Maria Cesi, daughter of Cornelia Orsini and Andrea Cesi, first Duke of Ceri, with a dowry of 160,000 *scudi*, when, in 1613, Margherita died and Prince Michele, still in his early 30s, married his son's intended. The marriage was celebrated later, in 1614, under his brother Cardinal Montalto's aegis, at a great feast in the Palazzo della Cancelleria. Prince Michele doubtless hoped for more sons by his rich new wife and Francesco entered the priesthood, eventually, in 1641, being made a cardinal. But his father's second marriage was childless and when he died in 1631 Francesco became his heir. A drawing by Ottavio Leoni (fig. 144) dated 1622 depicts him as a young abbé, while in an engraving by Cornelis Bloemaert, dated 1645, he is a cardinal; both suggest a milder character than his cardinal uncle. The 1655 inventory, even if copied from an earlier document, was produced in response to his death in that year. The survival of the Peretti line depended on his two sisters. The first, Camilla, had taken the veil in 1617 at the Dominican convent of Santa Caterina a Magnanapoli, where she died in 1668, her benefactions having included 1,000 *scudi* for the spectacular relief of *Santa Caterina in Ecstacy* designed by Melchiorrè Caffa (1636–1667) above the high altar of its church.[30] But in 1620 the second sister, Maria Felice, had married a rich Roman nobleman, Bernardino Savelli, second Prince of Albano and first Duke of Ariccia, and was to produce four sons and a daughter. On her death in 1656 she was buried in the Capuchin cemetery in Rome, where her monument states that she had passed the titles and honours of the Peretti, 'gentis quidem suae jam extinctae' [of her own family, now extinct], to the Savelli.[31]

Maria Felice's first and third Savelli sons, Francesco and Alessandro, died young, and the second, Paolo, born in 1622, renounced his rights of primogeniture in 1646, when he became a priest; he was made a cardinal in 1664 and died in 1685. The male line thus devolved on the fourth son, Giulio, Prince of Albano and of Venafro, born in 1626. He had an only son, Bernardino, by his first wife, who was also his first cousin, Anna Aldobrandini; a second marriage to Caterina Giustiniani was childless. But Bernardino died in 1672 before his 20th year, and his father, Prince Giulio, was left as the last male representative of the Savelli, Peretti and Somaglia families. By his death in 1712 he was also a Spanish grandee, having succeeded a cousin as ninth Count of Chinchon, thanks to his Somaglia great-grandfather's marriage to Maria Leonora de la Cerda y Bobadilla. Prince Giulio's inheritance was tainted by accumulated debt. There had been sales before his father's death in 1658, and more may have taken place before the 'vile subasta' [despicable auction] of 1696, which Giulio had done his best to fend off, thanks to which Cardinal Negroni acquired the Villa Montalto.[32] The sale was ordered by the Congregazione dei Baroni, the body charged by the Apostolic Camera with discharging the nobility's debts. A recently published inventory establishes that, when the contents of the Palazzo Felice were sold, along with the other assets of the Villa Montalto, the Sixtus Cabinet was not among them. The loggia, reduced to the 'Corridore que segue' [adjacent corridor], contained eight gilt and painted stands, survivors presumably of the 12 listed in 1655, but now all but one supporting busts rather than statues, the same four quilted leather stools as 1655, the same two ebony sideboards (now described as 'tavolini' [small tables]), and, presumably, the central round pietre dure table, although its shape is not specified, and, finally, the portrait of a dwarf (see Appendix 1).[33] The removal of the five Giambologna bronzes and the Sixtus Cabinet suggests that these had been spirited away to avoid the sale, and without them the loggia, with its reduced number of stands, and with a less homogeneous display of sculpture, must have lost both integrity and grandeur.

In 1713, over a year after Prince Giulio Savelli's death in 1712, some furniture, paintings and sculpture, and other items, rescued from the continuing enforced debt recovery, were transferred to his widow's family home, the Palazzo Giustiniani, and thence to her home as a widow, opposite the convent of San Egidio in Trastevere (some items were left behind and these, including 'studioli' [cabinets] she gave to her nephew and future heir, Monsignor Andrea Giustiniani, in 1723, a year before her death).[34] The very first item in the 1713 transfer (see Appendix 1 for this and subsequent entries) catches the eye:

> A ciborium about ten palms high, richly decorated with small agate columns, with gilt bronze capitals and bases, and its entire material composed of various fine stones of value, and mounted in the manner of rings in large quantity in bronze or copper, or gilt brass decorated with various statues of bronze, gilded as above, and the said ciborium is set on a large pedestal of ebonised and gilded wood.

In Italian 'ciborio' usually refers to a canopy above an altar, but it may also refer to a tabernacle, and as the Sixtus Cabinet had already been described as in the form of a 'tabernacolo', the meaning may be identical. Related to the Sixtus Cabinet this 1713 description is certainly inaccurate and incomplete, specifying agate instead of alabaster (a repetition of Mortoft's mistake in 1659), and failing to mention ebony or drawers. But to a hasty eye the drawers were invisible, and the panels of pietre dure and the plethora of stones set in bezels, like rings, may have seemed the salient features. However, it is the height, about ten palms equating to about 85 inches (216 cm), which most strongly suggests that this must have been the Sixtus Cabinet, spared from the 1696 sale. Its preservation within the family, however contrived, suggests particular significance. The other ten cabinets listed in 1713, six of them annotated as missing, seem to have been smaller more standard products, mainly of ebony or ebonized, with ivory inlay. However, the first, more elaborate than the others, and not marked as lost, is described as 'completely full of various little old portraits in copper about 50 in number'. The question must arise whether these could have been the miniatures, actually 73, later found in the Sixtus Cabinet (see Appendix v). The absence of the Sixtus Cabinet from the inventory taken on the death of Caterina Giustiniani Savelli in 1724 suggests that she had passed it on, plausibly to the Sforza Cesarini Savelli line, then, as will emerge, representing the main Peretti descent, or to a convent.[35]

Meanwhile, the female line continued: in 1635 Prince Giulio Savelli's sister, Margarita, had married Giuliano Cesarini, third Duke of Civitanova, also effectively the last of his line. Although his only brother, Filippo Cesarini, a priest, outlived him to be laicized and succeed as the fourth Duke of Civitanova, he died childless in 1685. However, before his death in 1665 Margarita Savelli and Giuliano Cesarini had had two sons and eight daughters (after his death she joined her aunt, Camilla Peretti, in the convent of Santa Caterina a Magnanapoli, dying there in 1690). The two Cesarini sons and a daughter died young and all but one of the remaining daughters became nuns in various convents. The exception was Cleria (fig. 145), who married Filippo Colonna, Prince of Sonnino, in 1671 (his great-uncle Marcantonio Colonna had married Orsina Damasceni Peretti in 1589), and all seemed set fair for her to inherit the accumulated family possessions. In 1673, however, her elder sister, Livia Cesarini, up to then an oblate at the convent of Santa Maria dei Sette Dolori, married Federico Sforza, Duke of Onano.[36] This alliance was the focus of an international furore, which divided Rome, its incidents including an arquebus attack on the Patriarch Giacomo Altoviti (d.1693), superintendent of the convent, but eventually the Colonna family and faction lost. In 1681 rights of primogeniture were granted to Livia Sforza Cesarini by the Sacra Rota, the supreme court of the Church. When her uncle, Filippo Cesarini, died in 1685 the way was clear for Livia to reclaim from her sister Cleria and her Colonna husband the Cesarini properties which Filippo had allocated to them. This prompted a further lawsuit, adjudicated in Livia's favour in 1697. Even then legal proceedings dragged on as Livia pursued the Cesarini silver, furniture, money and manuscripts appropriated by Cleria. Her final victory came in 1709.

Although neither Livia Sforza Cesarini, who died in 1711, nor her husband, Federico, who died in the following year, lived long to enjoy their spoils, the new house of Sforza Cesarini continued in tail male. The second Duke, Gaetano, a godson of Louis xiv, born in 1674, had in 1703 married Vittoria Conti, niece of the future Pope Innocent xiii. In 1704 they had a daughter, Margherita, who proved so lively that in 1721 Pope Clement xi (Albani) had her sent to the convent of Santa Maria dei Sette Dolori, a sentence reversed by her great-uncle, Cardinal Conti, after he had succeeded as Pope that same year. In 1726 she married Valerio Santa Croce, Duke of San Gemini. If the Sixtus Cabinet was returned to the Savelli line before the death of Caterina Giustiniani Savelli in 1724, Gaetano Sforza Cesarini, her great-nephew by marriage, would have been the one to receive it. His son, Giuseppe, was born in 1705 and succeeded his father as the third Sforza Cesarini Duke in 1727. He died in 1744.

By 1744 the Sixtus Cabinet was in England and there is no need to pursue the Peretti descendants further. But there are conclusions to be drawn from this long and complicated recital. The first is that Sixtus v's project to build his family's wealth and position was extraordinarily successful. When Livia Cesarini, of the fifth generation to follow Sixtus's own, married Federico Sforza in 1673 she was already linked by blood or marriage to most of the leading families in Rome, and moved in a world of princes and dukes, cardinals (five in five successive generations among Peretti descendants alone) and popes, with close connections to both Spain and France, the powers which vied for influence in Rome at this period. This was a world in which the possession and display of fine works of art and rich furnishings, whether acquired by inheritance, purchase or commission, was, if not obligatory, certainly expected and celebrated. The family, a term with a much wider application than at present, was the central focus, and ideally it acted as a collective. It would be expected that family members who entered the Church and thus became celibate would ultimately contribute their wealth to the family estate and, reciprocally, that they would be allowed to enjoy their appropriate share of the family fortune, while they lived. The fact that Sixtus v was a Franciscan, committed to simplicity – and indeed practised a degree of austerity in his personal life – was evidently far from inhibiting his promotion of his family. For the first two generations which succeeded him he was able to ensure, by adoption, the survival of the Peretti name, and his grandson Prince Michele Damasceni Peretti's children preserved it for another. In that sense Maria Felice Peretti Savelli's claim on her monument to be the last of that name was justified, overlooking her cloistered sister, Camilla, who survived her by 12 years. But Sixtus's achievements had left such a stamp on Rome that the Peretti legacy and its descent was unlikely to be forgotten quickly. Certainly Sixtus himself did his best to make sure that his great projects were commemorated by inscriptions, and by paintings in the Lateran Palace and elsewhere.

A CODA

Such is the general genealogical and dynastic context for the Cabinet's association with Pope Sixtus v and his family. It is an important detail that nuns and convents have cropped up repeatedly, lending some plausibility to the eighteenth-century account of the Cabinet's acquisition by Henry Hoare, which stated that he bought it from a convent in Rome to which it had been left by a nun who was the last of Sixtus's family. The principal possibilities are two: Santa Caterina a Magnanapoli and Santa Maria dei Sette Dolori. Santa Caterina took in many girls or widows from the noblest families in Rome. Camilla Peretti Damasceni (1596–1668), whose younger sister, Maria Felice (1603–1656), described herself as the last of the Peretti on her tombstone, has been mentioned as taking the veil there in 1617: she was followed in 1623 by her first cousin, Camilla Sforza Caravaggio (d.1659). All this took place while the Sixtus Cabinet was still in the Palazzo Felice. However, the family links to Santa Caterina continued in the next generation, when in 1668, after the death of her husband, Giuliano Cesarini (1618–1665), Margarita Savelli Cesarini (d.1690) entered the convent. There was also a close link to the Giustiniani family, who in 1656 donated 100 *scudi* to secure two rooms for their female descendants.[37] If Caterina Giustiniani Savelli gave the Cabinet to a convent between 1713, when it was in her possession, and 1724, the year of her death, when it was hers no longer, Santa Caterina might have been the obvious choice, with its combined Peretti and Giustiniani associations.

However, the convent of Santa Maria dei Sette Dolori has a strong claim. This was founded in 1641 by Camilla Virginia Savelli Farnese (1602–1665), the elder sister of the Bernardino Savelli (1604–1658) who married Maria Felice Peretti, and thus the aunt of the Margarita Savelli Cesarini just mentioned. Camilla employed Francesco Borromini (1599–1667) as the convent's architect in 1642 but work stopped in 1655 for want of money, being resumed in 1659–65 under Francesco Contini (1599–1669). After her husband, Pierfrancesco Farnese, last Duke of Latera, died in 1662, Camilla Savelli Farnese retreated to her foundation for her final years, which overlapped in 1664 with the profession there as an oblate of her great-niece, Livia Cesarini, daughter of Margarita, under the religious name of Suor Maria Pulcheria. Livia spent nearly ten years there before leaving in 1673 to contract the controversial marriage with Frederico Sforza recounted above. Once she was married Pope Clement x, whose adopted nephew, Cardinal Paluzzo Altieri (1623–1698), had been an early supporter during her marital travails, but in the end a broken reed, gave permission to Livia to make 12 visits of a few days each to various convents every year. These close links, briefly renewed when her naughty grand-daughter, Margherita Sforza-Cesarini, was briefly detained there in 1721, as noted earlier, might have made Santa Maria the family's choice as a destination for the Cabinet, if Caterina Giustiniani Savelli handed it back to the main line of Peretti descent, before her death in 1724. It would be desirable to pin down one of these candidates, although it is possible that the Cabinet went to another of the convents in Rome.

1. Orbaan 1910, p. 105. Ancient coins and papal generosity combined when, in 1587, imperial coins were discovered, 'divinitus' [by divine inspiration], during the demolition of the Lateran Palace and distributed by Sixtus to contemporary rulers, as depicted in the Salone degli Imperatori of the rebuilt palace (Mandel 1994, p. 221, fig. 147, pl. VIII).
2. This account of the Villa Montalto is based on Quast 1991.
3. Ibid., p. 52. See also Bedon 2008, pp. 39–40, for a more nuanced but in essence confirmatory account of their financial relationship. A subvention of 1,000 *scudi* from Francesco de' Medici, Grand Duke of Tuscany, received at Christmas 1583 (Quast 1991) also helped.
4. Coffin 1991, p. 143.
5. Fontana 1590, p. 37.
6. The fountain is at right angles to the church of Santa Susanna, whose chapel of San Lorenzo, rich in marbles, was executed under the patronage of Camilla Peretti, Sixtus's sister, from 1589–91.
7. Massimo 1836.
8. Ibid., p. 54.
9. Pignatti 2013.
10. Orsi 1588, f. 24v.
11. Letts 1925, p. 113.
12. Rausa 2005, p. 125, and Granata 2012, pp. 93–6.
13. Hutchinson 1881, pp. 106–8.
14. Letts 1925, p. 113; Granata, 2012, p. 251.
15. See Rausa 2005, pp. 107–15, for examples.
16. See the *c*.1680 inventory (Appendix 1) for their positions.
17. Granata 2012, p. 216. Martinelli was not entirely reliable, attributing the Hercules fresco on the ceiling, described by Orsi 1588, p. 25r, to Domenichino (1581–1641). He also mentions in the loggia 'Li Quattro Evangelisti del Viola ... à guazzo', which Granata, p. 206, identifies as 'Quattro Quadri a guazzo senza cornice' listed in 1696 in the Palazzo alle Terme, clearly moveables and thus no evidence for Viola's involvement in the original decorations of the loggia (see also note 20 below).
18. See note 3 above.
19. Massimo 1836, p. 46; Ostrow 1996, pp. 9–19.
20. Massimo 1836, p. 54, attributed the lunettes to Paul Bril (*c*.1554–1626) and Giovanni Battista Viola (1576–1622), citing Pinaroli 1725, pp. 380–1, who mentions landscapes by 'Paolo Brillo Olandese' as being 'nella galleria', which might be the lunettes; Pinaroli does not however mention Viola (see also note 17 above). Massimo also quotes the Naples, 1733 edition (p. 163) of Baglione 1642, which stated that Viola painted a fine large landscape in Cardinal Montalto's villa, in rivalry with Brill. Extracts recently published (Granata 2012, pp. 294–5) from Cardinal Alessandro Peretti Montalto's accounts for 1607 (shortly after he had come into possession of the villa) record payments totalling 100 *scudi* to both artists, in each case for two landscapes in the 'Palazzotto del nostro Giardino'. These could be the lunettes, but it is worth noting that there are landscapes in nine other rooms in the Palazzo Felice and the Palazzo alle Terme, as described by Massimo, including four, two long and two short, in the substantial inner room of the eastern apartment on the ground

floor of the Palazzo Felice, an apartment which Massimo (p. 50) notes as not described by Aurelio Orsi in his *Perettina*, suggesting that its painted decorations are later (Cardinal Alessandro moved the chapel downstairs at this period). These landscapes could well be those in the 1607 accounts. It may be added that Massimo (p. 133) praises a large overdoor painting by the stairs behind the gallery of the Palazzo alle Terme as 'da ottimo stile' [in the best style] and attributes it to 'Paolo Brillo'. Might this have been the large landscape by Viola, mentioned by Baglione? It is relevant that Paul Bril probably arrived in Rome in about 1575 to join his brother Mathias (1550–1583), who worked extensively in the Vatican for Gregory XIII. Paul was to be part of the team which decorated the Lateran Palace for Sixtus V in the late 1580s and, with his Vatican contacts, would have been known to him long before that (Cappelletti 1996, pp. 218–19).
21. Massimo 1836, p. 50.
22. The list of his virtues in Ciacconio 1630 (cols. 1790–1) comprises 'Modestia, lenitas, moderatio, humanitas, clementia, mansuetudo, facilitas in concedendo, animi magnitude in donando' [modesty, mildness, moderation, humanity, clemency, gentleness, courtesy in concession, magnaminity in donation] and 'aeturnum arcanorum silentium' [endless silence in keeping secrets].
23. Annibale 1999, p. 365.
24. Granata 2012, p. 301: from other payments it is clear that this was Persio Lucidi; further payments were made at this period to a cabinet-maker ('ebanista') named Adriano Fiamengo.
25. Cresti 1988, p. 69.
26. Granata 2012, pp. 96–106, 219–31 (two inventories).
27. Massimo 1836, p. 80.
28. Ibid., p. 77.
29. Vordret 1993, pp. 42–5.
30. Bevilacqua 2009, p. 97.
31. This right to the Peretti inheritance had been hard won in a court case terminated in 1633 between Paolo Giordano Orsini, Duke of Bracciano (1591–1656), son of Flavia Peretti Damasceni (1574–1606), and his cousin by marriage, Bernardino Savelli, in which the latter triumphed (Ademollo 1883, pp. 51–3).
32. Granata 2012, pp. 146–7.
33. Gatta 2010, p. 122.
34. Squarzina 2003, 3, pp. 275–83.
35. Caterina Giustiniani Savelli Inventory 1724, ff. 178v–272v, furnishings (ff. 131–78 are pictures).
36. Ademollo 1883 gives an account of this imbroglio.
37. Bevilacqua 2009, pp. 35–6.

FIVE
THE YOUNG HENRY HOARE

The mortal remains of Henry Hoare (1705–1785) lie in the churchyard at Stourton; his monument, once on the chancel wall, stands in the south aisle of the church; his fame resides in Stourhead garden which unfolds some 100 yards beyond the church porch (frontispiece). Henry owned the Sixtus Cabinet before he began this garden; the great lake and the Pantheon, the finest of its temples, were creations of the 1750s. The garden, beautiful and complex, lies outside the scope of this book.[1] How did this wealthy banker become an aesthete, connoisseur and art collector? This chapter considers his upbringing and the artists and craftsmen with whom he associated, while the next will examine his continental tour of 1739–41.

HOARE'S BANK, FLEET STREET

Any assessment of Henry Hoare (fig. 146) begins at the family bank, founded by his grandfather in the late seventeenth century and continuing as an independent business to this day. Henry became a partner soon after his father's death in 1725 and the senior partner in 1750, when his uncle Benjamin died. The business had developed from goldsmiths' trading to banking proper and lending money to the wealthy whose assets – acres – were cast-iron security. Henry made a speciality of mortgages. The bank's customers respected partners who owned country estates which, if not equal in size to their own broad acres, were reassuringly ample. So the Hoares purchased land, frequently from those owing them money. In 1700 Sir Richard Hoare, 1st Kt, the bank's founder, had bought 242 acres at Staplehurst in Kent from the wife of his debtor, Sir Samuel Gerrard.[2] Henry Hoare's father acquired the Stourhead estate in 1717 from the impecunious Stourton family. In 1730 Benjamin Hoare purchased the New Hall estate in Essex, adjacent to his Boreham House, from another debtor, the Duke of Montagu. In 1732 Henry Hoare bought the manor of West Knoyle, close to Stourhead, from a mortgagor.[3] Ten years later Henry's brother,

Sir Richard Hoare, 2nd Kt, acquired Barn Elms on the bend of the Thames between Hammersmith and Barnes (or began to assemble the estate from various owners).

Ledger entries demonstrate the bank's prosperity during the eighteenth century. In 1720 deposits stood at £223,000, reaching over £1 million by 1791.[4] Henry Hoare took half the profits and, after his brother's death in 1754, about two-thirds. Thus, in 1765 he claimed £17,841 from profits of £26,761. Later he reverted to a half share (in 1782, he received £14,468 from £28,935). He also benefited from marriages, receiving the portion of £10,000 when his first wife, Anne Masham, died and £14,000 after he married Susan Colt.[5] At the end of the avenue of family and banking stood Stourhead.

THE EARLY YEARS

Henry Hoare, as he will be called, except where the context requires differentiation, was 19 when his father died.[6] 'The early part of his life was chiefly spent at the family house at Quarley in Hampshire, in the society of many gay and fashionable young men, who were fond of hunting, and sacrificed rather freely at the shrine of Bacchus.'[7] This hedonistic spell broke in 1725. On his father's death, Henry felt morally obliged to reinvest his inherited wealth in the bank. It was a condition of his father's will that he maintain Stourhead, where his mother, Jane Hoare (1679–1742), was to live out her days (fig. 147). She was the daughter of Sir William Benson, a London merchant and friend of Henry's grandfather. Jane shared her husband's philanthropic bent; moreover, they were devout. Henry Hoare I (1677–1724/5) supported the Tories; if he had Jacobite leanings, he kept them private. He purchased a bust of *Charles I* by Le Sueur, but otherwise confined his art-collecting to portraits and decorative paintings. Architecture was a different matter. Henry Hoare I served as a commissioner for Building Fifty New Churches in London and would have met Christopher Wren, John Vanbrugh and Nicholas

FIG. 146
Henry Hoare II on Horseback, by Michael Dahl and John Wootton, signed by both artists and dated 1726. Oil on canvas, 130 x 120 in, 330.2 x 304.8 cm.
First recorded in the Hall at Stourhead in 1742. National Trust.

FIG. 147
Jane Benson, wife of Henry Hoare I, attributed to Jonathan Richardson the elder, *c.*1725. Oil on canvas. 30 x 25 in, 76.2 x 63.5 cm. The portrait is first recorded at Stourhead in 1822. National Trust.

Hawksmoor. Yet when, in 1720, he came to build Stourhead he chose a Whig architect, Colen Campbell, surely on the advice of Sir William's son and namesake, William Benson (1682–1754).

In 1718 William Benson succeeded Wren as Surveyor of the King's Works. It was a political appointment won through the support of the Chancellor, John Aislabie, as a stop-gap while Benson waited for the more lucrative job as an Auditor of the Imprests.[8] He was dismissed as Surveyor some 15 months later, but not before he had made Colen Campbell his Deputy. Benson was 23 years senior to his nephew, Henry Hoare II, and possessed a quiverful of accomplishments that would have appealed to the younger man. He was an amateur architect with an interest in hydraulics and gardening. In 1708 he had rented Amesbury House in Wiltshire (then believed to be by Inigo Jones). Nearby, Benson designed and built Wilbury, a small precocious country house illustrated in the first volume of *Vitruvius Britannicus*.[9] He sold it in 1734 to Henry Hoare. Benson admired Milton and, in 1737, commissioned Rysbrack to carve his bust for Westminster Abbey.[10] He had literary pretensions and published a translation of Virgil's *Georgics* in 1725. An inventory taken after Benson's death listed 2,000 books, for the most part classics with relatively little art or architecture. Henry Hoare probably discovered from Benson the pleasure, in his own words, 'of looking into books and the pursuit of that knowledge which distinguishes only the Gentleman from the Vulgar'.[11]

It is tantalizing that Henry left no record of his library either at Stourhead or at his house on Clapham Common. J.B. Nichols published the *Catalogue of the Hoare Library* shortly after the death of Sir Richard Colt Hoare, whose collection incorporated books inherited from Henry; but it is no longer possible to differentiate the two components because the Stourhead library was dispersed at auctions in 1883 and 1887.[12] In the following chapters there are references to Nichols's catalogue and the inference is made that Henry Hoare *could* have possessed the books listed therein published before his death in 1785. The only surviving record of Henry Hoare's taste in reading is a list of books jotted down on a spare page in an account book kept for him during his continental tour.[13]

To revert to Henry's relatives, his uncle, Benjamin Hoare (1693–1749/50), was 12 years his senior. It was their task to form a new banking partnership. Benjamin must have been a good teacher and Henry an apt pupil because the business prospered. Benjamin and Henry worked and played together. At Boreham, Benjamin consulted the architect Henry Flitcroft when he demolished the old house and built a new one. Benjamin and Henry patronized the same artists and craftsmen; for example, the painters John Wootton, Jeremiah Davison and Arthur Pond and the upholsterer Robert North.

ARTISTS AND CRAFTSMEN

At the family bank and at Westminster, in city coffee houses and private residences, Henry Hoare encountered fashionable taste in the arts. He read Alexander Pope and Jonathan Richardson and visited Chiswick and Painshill. He formed friendships with artists and they would have helped refine his sensibilities. The architect Henry Flitcroft (1697–1769) opened an account with Hoare's bank in 1724 and continued with the partners until his death.[14] His patron, the third Earl of Burlington, also banked there.[15] Flitcroft was prominent in the Office of Works; in 1748 he succeeded Kent as Master Mason and Deputy Surveyor and ten years later he became Comptroller of the King's Works. He enlarged Wentworth Woodhouse for the first Earl of Malton (later first Marquess of Rockingham), *c.*1735–70, and rebuilt Woburn Abbey for the fourth Duke of Bedford, 1748–61. Henry went to Flitcroft for all building designs at Stourhead. When the architect died his son sent Henry a drawing, 'as the best (tho' inadequate) acknowledgement in my power to make of the great obligation I am under to you on my Father's account & my own'.[16]

Arthur Pond (1701–1758) was a painter whom Henry Hoare patronized over a long period. Pond was the son of a surgeon and considered himself a gentleman-artist. He went to Italy in 1725, where he diversified from painting into dealing and shipping casts. In 1727, Pond sold Henry Hoare 'Two Views of Venice at 16 Guineas each', 'Two Views of Rome at 8 Guineas each', 'Cascade of Tivoli by Horizonti £12-12' and 'Ruins of Rome by Gio: Paolo Pannini £31-10'.[17] Pond was elected a fellow of the Royal Society and of the Society of Antiquities, the only artist of his generation to secure both honours. His importance rested upon his promotion of Italian art through prints published with Charles Knapton. Pond's *Italian Landscapes* (1741–8) comprised engravings after Claude and Poussin and his *Roman Antiquities* (1745–51), engravings after Panini. Henry purchased prints from Pond in 1742.[18] It is conceivable that he sought his advice before setting out for the Continent.

The portrait painter Jeremiah Davison (*c*.1695–1745) also copied old masters. He trained in Scotland but made his career in London, where he charged 32 guineas in 1740 for a full-length portrait.[19] Between 1728 and 1732 Henry Hoare paid him £176.[20] This considerable sum probably included the two large copies after Guido Reni, now in the Staircase Hall at Stourhead (fig. 148).[21] Henry may have placed them first at his London house or at Wilbury. Their purchase suggests that, before he went to Italy, Henry had already joined the fashionable scramble for replicas of large *seicento* art.

Henry admired classical landscapes by Claude Lorrain, which were in short supply. Alongside equestrian portraits and battle scenes, John Wootton (*c*.1682–1764) produced copies, or variations, of landscapes by Claude and Gaspard Poussin. Wootton banked with Hoares and between 1727 and 1730 Henry Hoare became a regular customer, purchasing paintings to the tune of £477.[22] A single bill survives from Wootton.[23] By 1784 there were ten Woottons at Stourhead.[24] The artist was also a dealer; an entry in Henry Hoare's ledger for 20 July 1758 noted a payment to Wootton for 'a History by Sebas[n] Ricci'.[25] Wootton was a clubbable man and on friendly terms with his patron. He witnessed the agreement between Henry Hoare and Rysbrack for the Pantheon *Hercules*.[26]

In 1727 Michael Rysbrack (1694–1770) (fig. 150) sold Henry a bust of *Inigo Jones* along with a statuette of the latter and of *Palladio* (these are no longer at Stourhead).[27] The contract for the great marble *Hercules* for the Pantheon was signed in 1747. Four years later, Henry purchased the sculptor's *Bacchus*, a near life-size marble, again after the antique (sold from Stourhead in 1883).[28] He went on to commission a *Flora* as companion to *Hercules* and a bust of *King Alfred*.[29]

During their long professional relationship, their friendship grew. Henry was steadfast in supporting Rysbrack when he fell out of fashion in the 1750s, and probably paid over the odds for the *Hercules* and *Flora*.[30] He referred to the sculptor with affection: 'I thought old Rysbrach would have wept for Joy to see His offspring placed [in the Pantheon] to such advantage. He thinks it impossible for such a space to have more magnificence in it & striking awe than He found there.'[31] At the sculptor's auction in 1766 Henry purchased three reliefs and five drawings.[32] Rysbrack bequeathed Henry the terracotta model of *Hercules*.[33] Patron and sculptor were attuned in other respects. Rysbrack amassed a stock of statuary and exotic marbles and may well have imparted some of his knowledge and enthusiasm to Henry Hoare. Rysbrack's auction in 1766 included an array of 'Black and Yellow Marble Tables', 'Purple Marble Tables', 'Ægyptian Marble Tables', 'Veined and Black Tables', 'Spanish Marble Tables' and 'Dove Marble Tables'.[34] This litany calls to mind Henry

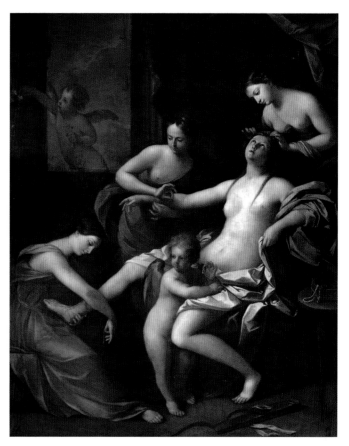

FIG. 148
The Toilet of Venus, by Jeremiah Davison, after Guido Reni, 1728–45. Oil on canvas, 103 x 81 in, 261.6 x 205.7 cm. First recorded in the Saloon at Stourhead in 1754. National Trust.

Hoare's appetite for pietre dure. It was a taste shared by other wealthy collectors.

Rysbrack, a prime exponent of classical sculpture, never visited Italy and depended on models, drawings and prints of antiquities. Over the years he assembled a formidable collection. Henry could have learned the use of engravings from him. Did Rysbrack guide lesser Stourhead sculptors, Benjamin Carter (1719–1766) and John Cheere (1709–1787)? Carter's bas-reliefs for the Pantheon are copies of antique panels, engraved by Bartoli (fig. 149). The *River God* in the Stourhead Grotto is an original and unique lead sculpture supplied by John Cheere and derived from an etching by Salvator Rosa (which Rysbrack may have owned).[35] Such adaptation would have come naturally to Rysbrack. Did he suggest the image to Cheere and did he give Cheere the confidence to undertake the commission with such panache? Henry Hoare commissioned John Boson to carve the decorations for the Sixtus Pedestal. His four giltwood statuettes are classical and close relatives of the female virtues and mourners on Rysbrack's funerary monuments (fig. 151). From 1735 Boson lived in Savile Row, close to Rysbrack in Vere Street. Early in their careers both were employed by Lord Burlington and it is easy to imagine the two as associates.

Henry Hoare's taste and appetite to collect works of art and visit the Continent must have been shaped and sharpened both by his relatives and these coteries of artists and craftsmen.

FIG. 149
Interior of the Pantheon, Stourhead, by Samuel Woodforde, R.A., *c.*1784. Oil on canvas, 48 x 36 in, 121.9 x 91.4 cm. Beneath the dome,
Benjamin Carter's rectangular plaster bas-reliefs are visible. In the centre niche, Rysbrack's *Hercules*; flanked on his right by *Flora* and on his left,
Livia Augusta as Ceres. National Trust, Stourhead.

1. For a full account of the garden see Woodbridge 1982a.

2. Hutchings 2005, pp. 43–6. The appellations '1st' and '2nd' Knight distinguish Richard Hoare (1648–1718/9), founder of the bank and Lord Mayor of London 1712–13 and Richard (1709/10–1754), his grandson, partner in the bank and Lord Mayor 1745–6.

3. Clay 1994, p. 124.

4. H.P.R. Hoare 1955, p. 85.

5. Clay 1994, pp. 123 and 135–7.

6. Because boys were habitually christened 'Henry' among the Hoare family, as adults they were distinguished formally and in genealogies by adding the name of their residence, for example, Henry Hoare of Stourhead, Henry of Mitcham Grove and so on (see Hoare 1844, Addenda to, 'The Hundred of Mere', pp. 13–14, 'Pedigree of Hoare'). However, Henry Hoare of Beckenham (1744–1785) was affectionately known in his lifetime as 'Fat Harry' and is referred to thus by Henry Hoare (WSA Ailesbury Estate Collection 9/35/165 and 1300/4296). Richard Colt Hoare was likewise referred to as 'Colt' by his grandfather (ibid., 1300/4294). The first published use of the sobriquets 'Good Henry' for Henry Hoare I and 'Henry the Magnificent' for Henry Hoare II occur in H.P.R. Hoare 1932, p. 35.

7. Stourhead Library, shelfmark C.7.14, Sir Richard Colt Hoare Bt, 'MS. History of Some of the Hoares 1724–1812'.

8. Eavis 2002, p. 13.

9. Campbell 1715, vol. I, pls 51–2.

10. Eavis 2002, p. 25. In 1738 Benson commissioned Rysbrack to carve two busts of Milton, as a youth and in old age, and these his grandson, William Benson Earle, bequeathed to Sir Richard Colt Hoare in 1796. The latter placed them in the Library at Stourhead. NT 732892 , Young Milton and NT 732893 Old Milton.

11. C. Hoare & Co. HFM/9/10, Henry Hoare to his nephew, Sir Richard Hoare, 1st Bt, December 1755.

12. Nichols 1840; Sotheby, Wilkinson & Hodge 1883 and 1887.

13. WSA 383.28, Henry Hoare's pocket account book, 28 June 1738–6 Sept 1739.

14. C. Hoare & Co. Customer Ledgers, Flitcroft, 1724/5–69.

15. Ibid., Customer Ledgers, third Earl of Burlington, 1717–71.

16. WSA 383.907, Henry Flitcroft junior to Henry Hoare, 4 September 1769, sending 'a drawing of my Father's from a celebrated design by Inigo Jones'. This cannot be traced at Stourhead.

17. WSA 383.4.1, bill 15 January 1727 for £94-10-0, receipted by Pond and annotated by Sir Richard Colt Hoare, 'I remember these pictures in H Hoares Villa at Clapham RCH'.

18. Henry Hoare Accounts 1734–49, 27 November 1742 'Mr Pond for prints pd by Mr Adams' £1-7-6.

19. Rosalind K. Marshall, 'Jeremiah Davison', ODNB 2004, vol. 15, pp. 484–5.

20. C. Hoare & Co. Customer Ledgers, Henry Hoare, Lr/fol. 29/318, 30/1, 33/113.

21. NT 732314, Perseus and Andromeda and NT 732315, The Toilet of Venus, both by Jeremiah Davison, after Guido Reni, 1728–45. Paintings were first mentioned, and attributed to Davison, in the Stourhead Catalogue 1754.*

22. C. Hoare & Co. Customer Ledgers, Wootton, 1727–56; Customer Ledgers, Henry Hoare, Lr/fol. 29/318, 30/1, 30/303.

23. WSA 383.4.1, 'Pictures Painted for Heny Hoare Esqr', receipted 9 January 1728 by Wootton, 'A Large Landskip' £73-10-0, 'A Sketch of the Bloody Shoulderd Arabian Horse' 15 guineas and 'A Small Landskip a Sunsett' 10 guineas.

24. Stourhead Catalogue 1784, listed nine paintings by Wootton but not, curiously, Henry Hoare II on Horseback by Wootton and Dahl (NT 732232). There are three paintings by Wootton at Stourhead today (and a fourth, lent to C. Hoare & Co.), none of which is a landscape. The landscapes hung in the Staircase Hall at Stourhead and perished in the 1902 fire.

25. Henry Hoare Accounts 1749–70, 20 July 1758, 'Mr Wootton for a Picture of Phocion, a History by Sebasn Ricci; & for refreshg & improving the Sun Set with Hercules Farnse in it sent by R: Hoare' £105.

26. WSA 383.4.1, agreement between Rysbrack and Henry Hoare for Hercules, 1 July 1747. NT 562911 .

27. Ibid., agreement between Rysbrack and Henry Hoare, 10 October 1727, 'a Bustow of Inigo Jones in Statuary Marble' £35-0-0, 'a Pedestall' £2-10-0 and 'two Figures of Inigo Jones an[d] Palladio in Plaster' £1-10-0. Langford 1766, first day of Rysbrack's sale , p. 4, lot 69, 'Two figures of Palladio and Inigo Jones, the original models for the figures of Lord Burlington, at Chiswick'. Julius Bryant, 'Exempla Vertutis, Designs for Sculpture', Weber 2013, p. 17, figs 2 and 3, and p. 551, marble busts of Jones and Palladio at Chatsworth attributed to G.B. Guelfi after lost terracotta busts by Rysbrack.

28. C. Hoare & Co., HB/5/A/6, Partnership Ledger 1742–51, Henry Hoare, 3 October 1751, 'Mr Rysbrack in full for a Bacchus' £71-18-10.

29. WSA 383.4.1, agreement between Rysbrack and Henry Hoare, 14 March 1759, 'To make a Figure of Flora in Statuary Marble from the Antique', receipted 9 December 1760; NT 562912 . Henry Hoare Accounts 1749–70, 12 May 1764, 'Mr Rysbrach in full for a Bust & pedesl of Alfred' £100; NT 732917.

30. Ibid., 16 July 1757, 'Mr Rysbrach a Gratuity for ye Hercules beyond ye contract' £50 (the contract was for £300); 11 December 1760, 'Mr Rysbrach for The Flora in part' £200; 14 Dec 1761, 'Mr Rysbrach for The Statue of Flora in full' £200.

31. WSA, Ailesbury Estate Collection 1300/4280, Henry Hoare to his daughter Susannah, Lady Bruce, 23 October 1762.

32. Henry Hoare Accounts 1749–70, 19 Feb 1767, 'Mr Rysbrachs sale 5 Drawgs & 3 Bass Relievo's' £41-9-6.

33. NT 732894.

34. Langford1765 included 31 marble table tops; Langford 1766 included 18 marble tops.

35. The Dream of Aeneas, etching and drypoint by Salvator Rosa, signed, c.1663–4, 34.9 x 23.7 cm. Langford 1764, 18 February, Rysbrack's sale, Books of Prints, lot 55, 'Works of Salvator Rosa'.

FIG. 150
The sculptor John Michael Rysbrack with his terracotta statue of Hercules, by Andrea Soldi, 1753. Oil on canvas, 45¼ x 35⅞ in, 114.8 x 90.8 cm. Rysbrack (1694–1770) points to the terracotta Hercules which became the model for his over-life-size marble version (1747–52) in the Pantheon at Stourhead. The Yale Center for British Art, Paul Mellon Collection.

FIG. 151
Preliminary drawing for a female figure standing on a pedestal by Michael Rysbrack, inscribed twice 'CL 1740' and with scale in feet. Pen and wash, 9½ x 7½ in, 24 x 19 cm. The Victoria & Albert Museum.

SIX
HENRY HOARE'S GRAND TOUR

Four eighteenth-century descriptions of Stourhead state that Henry Hoare acquired the Sixtus Cabinet at a convent in Rome.[1] He could have seen it in the summer of 1739 or on his return to the city that winter and bought it in person, or through an agent then or later. The Cabinet is first documented in England in 1742.[2] No bill or ledger entry records the price; indeed the paper trail for Henry's continental tour is so sparse that Kenneth Woodbridge, master historian of Stourhead, passed it by in a short paragraph. What follows is an attempt to wed documents and deductions. Ledger entries are transcribed in Appendix III in the hope that they will stimulate further research which will no doubt refine and correct the present narrative.

Henry Hoare left for the Continent in March 1739 and returned in September 1741; he was away for two and a half years. His tour coincided with the outbreak of the war of the Austrian Succession (1740–8) and, by 1743, Britain and France were in conflict. Given his love for Italian landscape paintings and the classical world, it is surprising that Henry delayed visiting Europe. There are several possible explanations. The bank's profits had built from zero in 1725 to £16,532 in 1732, dipped to £6,012 two years later, and did not exceed £10,000 again until 1738.[3] Henry was elected a member of parliament for Salisbury in 1734. He also had family on his mind; above all he longed for an heir. He had married his second wife, Susan Colt, in 1728 (fig. 153). Their first child was born and died the following year. Then came Henry (1730–1752), Susannah (1732–1783), Colt (1733–1740) and Anne (1737–1759). When Henry judged that he might be temporarily released from these responsibilities, he was 34 and, to quote his grandson, Sir Richard Colt Hoare, 'With an enlightened mind, the natural scenery of Italy attracted his notice, and the study of the fine arts, occupied that attention abroad, which the pursuit of a fox had hitherto done at home.'[4]

While travelling, Henry Hoare would surely have written to his brother, kinsmen and Joshua Cox who kept an eye on his business affairs. But no such correspondence survives to illuminate his journey. Sir Richard browsed his grandfather's papers and would have preserved any letters or journals that he found. The year 1740 was popular for eminent Grand Tourists: the Countess of Pomfret, Lady Mary Wortley Montagu, Thomas Gray, Joseph Spence and Horace Walpole were all in Paris and Rome, but none of these celebrities mentions Henry. The *London Evening Post*, for 3–6 March 1739, reported, 'Henry Hoare Esq, Member for Parliament for Salisbury, being in a Consumption, is set out for the South of France by the Advice of his Physicians.' Did Henry, nervous lest bank-customers or friends in Parliament consider him frivolous, put it about that he travelled for his health and was his grandson correct in diagnosing his true purpose? It transpires that both reasons were accurately reported.

BUSINESS ARRANGEMENTS

Bankers keep records and Henry Hoare's account books help both riddle and unriddle the story. The ledger of his expenditure in England ceases after 4 March 1739 when he 'Carry^d this ball^{ce} to France'.[5] Entries resume on 28 September 1741. In the interim, payments made on his behalf by the bank, at home and abroad, were logged in the Partnership Ledger.[6] These entries are (almost) duplicated in two pocket-size account books kept by his brother, Sir Richard Hoare, 2nd Kt.[7] They overlap from June to September, 1739, which could indicate that the latter mailed them to Henry, a notion reinforced by Henry's *aide memoire* and reading list jotted on a spare page of the first notebook. Taking the period from his departure until March 1742/3 (which allows customs and freight charges for purchases shipped a few months after his return), his expenses abroad totalled about £6,300, a figure that puts him among the heavy-spending tourists of the era.[8] Payments made on Henry Hoare's behalf to recognizable continental bankers and agents are transcribed in Appendix III. Entries fall in two categories: shippers and agents who dealt with packing and customs; and, more importantly, bankers who offered a variety of services.

FIG. 152
Architectural Capriccio with the Sacrifice of Iphigenia, by Francis Harding, 1745–54. Oil on canvas, 66 x 56 in, 167.6 x 142.2 cm.
In imitation of Panini. On the right, the Mausoleum of the Julii from Glanum (St Rémy-de-Provence). On the left, the Arch of Constantine;
in the background, the pyramid of Cestius, Trajan's column and Colosseum, Rome. Recorded in the Hall at Stourhead in 1754; subsequently
moved to the Italian Room. National Trust.

FIG. 153
Susan Colt, second wife of Henry Hoare II, by Hans Hysing. Signed and dated 1733. Oil on canvas, 50 x 40 in, 127 x 101.6 cm. First recorded in the Hall at Stourhead in 1822. National Trust.

ITINERARY

There are difficulties in trying to extrapolate an itinerary from bank accounts, not least because of the delays between transactions. Henry Hoare set out from England with a man-servant in early March 1739.[9] They headed for Paris, where the engagingly named Parisian banker Alexandre Alexander provided credit and cash from March to May. Henry then travelled south, probably calling at Aix-en-Provence to reconnoitre, on to Marseilles and then by boat to Genoa or Leghorn. This was a recognized route for tourists unwilling to tackle Alpine passes. Before June Henry had reached Venice, where he encountered the celebrated Joseph Smith ('Consul Smith'), who combined the role of diplomat, banker, shipper and dealer as well as being an avid art collector and a bibliophile. Hoare's bank paid Smith £102-9-6 on 9 June 1739.

Henry did not linger in Venice but travelled south, reaching Rome, where he met Girolamo Belloni who was, according to Lady Mary Wortley Montagu, 'the greatest Banker not only of Rome but all Italy'.[10] Hoare's bank first recorded payments, on Henry's behalf, in June 1739. Altogether Belloni received £1,031-18-1 from Henry. His two surviving letters are of particular interest because they record Henry's encounter with the antiquary and dealer Mark Parker (*c*.1698–1775) (Appendix III). The letters show that Henry visited Florence around August 1739.

However, the second indicates that Henry was at Aix by October. Henry had returned to France to meet his wife and their reunion was reported in the press.[11] Susan Hoare (d.1743) had travelled to Paris with an escort, where she shopped and drew money from Alexander.[12] Payments to Belloni recommenced in October so Henry, having settled his wife, probably returned to Italy. Mrs Hoare remained in France, financed by Alexander and other merchants, notably Messrs Vernet, Whatley and Gambert in Marseilles, who received payments on behalf of the Hoares from October 1739 to March 1740/1 amounting to £988.

Hoare's bank had made a final payment to Belloni on 2 April 1740. May we then deduce that Henry quit Italy before April 1740 and that husband and wife remained in France for a year? Aix was a spa city, with a benign climate and an English colony, so the Hoares could have lingered as a rest-cure. Susan Hoare returned to England in June 1741.[13] Henry evidently delayed his journey home until the autumn.[14] While in France, Henry swopped bankers. The first payment to Sir John Lambert, a modest £50, was made on 7 October 1740; the next, in May 1741, when Henry and Susan had arrived in Paris. In June of that year Sir John received just under £2,400 from Hoare's bank. This sum, far above their daily needs, accommodation, coaches and so forth, suggests they shopped heavily.[15]

Is there an alternative explanation? Did Henry shuttle from Marseilles to Italy during the 'lost year'? There is a second difficulty in interpreting the ledgers. Continental bankers could arrange credit with agents in other cities and countries, thus extending the travelling possibilities (and generating commissions along the chain). Alexander and Sir John Lambert would have had agents in Italy to fund Henry Hoare and such 'delegation' would not show up in his London accounts. But Henry Hoare was a wily banker who would be unlikely to countenance double commissions when he had a working relationship with Belloni.

If the notion of sub-agents is rejected and the ledgers are taken literally, Henry made two expeditions in Italy: first, from May or June 1739 to September 1739, when he visited Venice before going south to Florence and Rome; the second from autumn 1739 until April 1740, when he returned to Rome and may, or may not, have continued to Naples and other cities.[16]

ITALY

Some tourists travelled through Italy at leisure, others made brisk progress. In 1730 the scholar Johann Georg Keyssler accompanied the sons, or grandsons, of Count Bernstorff, the prominent Hanoverian statesman, to Italy. Keyssler's four published volumes describing the tour, in letters, are packed with accounts of antiquities, churches and palaces.[17] If the dates on the letters are trustworthy, he was able to see and absorb an astonishing amount in a short time. A week in Florence yielded 71 pages and three weeks in Rome over 300. The ninth Earl of Lincoln (1720–1794), nephew of the first Duke of Newcastle, the politician and a customer of Hoare's bank, travelled through Italy in 1739 with Joseph Spence.[18] They took five weeks in Florence

FIG. 154
The Death of Dido, engraved by Sir Robert Strange, after Guercino, 1776. 18¾ x 23 in, 47.6 x 58.5 cm. The original painting, and a version of Guido Reni's *Abduction of Helen*, hang in the Palazzo Spada, Rome where Henry Hoare could have seen them. He acquired full-size copies of both for the Saloon at Stourhead. The British Museum.

and five months at Rome, interrupted by an excursion to Naples.[19] Half a century later, Sir Richard Colt Hoare advised a minimum of five weeks to see Rome.[20] So Henry Hoare, earnest, enthusiastic and wealthy, could have 'done' Venice, Florence, Rome and other cities en route in the two tours identified.

The monuments which Henry commemorated on the Pedestal for the Sixtus Cabinet are an idiosyncratic selection and suggest that he knew Rome well (see pp. 163–5). There were several famous bear-leaders. Belloni may well have introduced him to Mark Parker. This intriguing *cicerone*, from Cardinal Albani's circle, was both antiquary and dealer. He acted as an agent to Horace Walpole and was employed by Lady Pomfret, who described him as:

> a gentleman who goes about with the English to shew them what is most remarkable; assisting them also in buying what pictures, prints, and other curiosities, they fancy most: he also hires lodgings, servants, &c.: for

which he has a present of some zechins (the gold coin here) when they go away.[21]

Sir Horace Mann evidently found him a useful agent, if a slippery one.[22] Parker was involved with other Grand Tourists (see p. 24). What Parker bought on behalf of Henry Hoare in 1739 is a mystery, although the first sum involved, £142, was significant, and almost twice the amount Horace Walpole paid Parker in 1740 for a medley of purchases, comprising medals, busts and the first instalment on the 'Livia' (the statue he commissioned for his mother's monument).[23] Parker wanted to work for as many English travellers as possible and found it hard to accept that his reputation would suffer when he assisted self-professed Jacobites.[24] His daughter married Joseph Vernet, the celebrated 'moonlight painter', and when Parker was eventually expelled from Rome in 1765 he followed them to Paris, making sure that his association with Henry Hoare continued by writing promptly and

FIG. 155
The Interior of St Peter's at Rome, possibly by Francis Harding, after Giovanni Paolo Panini, *c.*1730–42. Oil on canvas, 45 x 63 in, 114.3 x 160 cm.
First recorded in the Parlour (Music Room) at Stourhead in 1754. National Trust.

offering to procure a picture by his son-in-law.[25] From 1759 Henry had used Thomas Jenkins as his agent in Rome.[26]

According to Keyssler, a tourist could easily gain admittance to private residences in Rome. He wrote, 'An *Italian* prince [...] places his grandeur in adorning his palaces with curious decorations, that foreigners may be induced to visit them, and talk of their magnificence wherever they go.'[27] Henry was fond of quotation, visual and literary, and, when he needed old master copies, he may well have selected originals which he had admired in Rome (and in Paris). For example, at the Palazzo Spada he would have seen *The Abduction of Helen* after Guido Reni and Guercino's *Death of Dido*, versions of which he purchased for Stourhead (fig. 154).[28] Henry also acquired copies of two landscapes by Claude Lorrain in the Galeria Doria-Pamphilj.[29] In the Casino dell'Aurora at the Palazzo Rospigliosi he admired the celebrated *Aurora* by Guido Reni and subsequently acquired a hand-coloured print of this masterpiece and commissioned a version by William Hoare (fig. 161).[30] Henry must have seen Guercino's *Cleopatra before Octavius Augustus* in the Palazzo Sacchetti before it reached the Capitoline Collection in 1748 because he later commissioned Mengs to paint the same subject (fig. 158).[31] In the courtyard of the Palazzo Farnese,

Henry would have admired the famous *Hercules* and *Flora*, inspirations for Rysbrack's sculptures for the Stourhead Pantheon (fig. 149). The convent of Santa Maria dei Sette Dolori, a possible vendor of the Sixtus Cabinet, received tourist-visitors (see pp. 121–2). In 1741 Lady Pomfret visited the convent with the son of the French Ambassador.[32] It is tempting to imagine Henry Hoare going there and catching sight of the Cabinet.

Henry would surely have read the Richardsons' influential critique on Italian painting and sculpture and shared their enthusiasm for hard stone:

> The Magnificence, and Beauty of the Churches, and Palaces of *Rome* must be Seen to be Conceiv'd; particularly the Churches; such Profusion of Gold, Silver, Marble &c. and so Artfully dispos'd! Many Chapels as it were Wainscotted with Marble; Pavements of the same, and These in the most Beautiful Figures, and Colours; for the Marble is commonly Antique, and Finer than any is Now found in the World; nor is it known what part of the Globe produce'd This.[33]

In Florence Henry Hoare was guided by Mark Parker and almost certainly met Sir Horace Mann, the British representative, who, in 1758, acted for him in the purchase

FIG. 156
A *Classical Landscape with Sportsmen*, by Gaspard Poussin, *c*.1658–59. Oil on canvas, 60 x 87½ in, 152.4 x 222.3 cm. The painting, and its companion *Mountainous Landscape with Eurydice*, were purchased for Henry Hoare by Sir Horace Mann in 1758. National Trust, Stourhead.

of three significant paintings (fig. 156).[34] Florence had the finest pietre dure in the world, which would surely have caught Henry's eye. The *Cappella dei Principi*, although unfinished, thrilled visitors with its interior clad in polychrome marbles and pietre dure panels. The *Tribuna* of the Uffizi combined old master paintings, sculpture, a celebrated pietre dure cabinet, table and 'several curious pieces of modern *Florentine* work of *Pietre Commesse*' (fig. 219).[35] If Henry gained admittance to the Pitti Palace, then the residence of Maria-Anna Louisa, widow of the Elector Palatine and daughter of Cosimo III de' Medici, he could have seen baroque pietre dure cabinets by Foggini. The Countess of Pomfret, visiting Florence with her husband in 1739–40, described the splendours of the pietre dure both in the Uffizi and the Pitti Palace.[36] And Henry may well have followed the same itinerary, although it is doubtful that he could have aspired to a private audience with the Dowager Electress, as granted Lady Pomfret.[37] But 1739 was not a propitious moment to commission new pietre dure. At the death of Grand Duke Gian Gastone in 1737, the workshops in the Uffizi closed and the craftsmen moved to Naples. The 'Badminton Cabinet', 1726–33, was the last great baroque masterpiece that the workshop would export (fig. 19). By the time the *Galleria dei Lavori* recommenced, under the new dynasty of Habsburg-Lorraine, Henry

had returned to England. Nevertheless, at some point he acquired a superior Florentine casket (see p. 18).

FRANCE

As already established, Henry Hoare called at Aix-en-Provence in September 1739 to settle his wife before returning to Italy and the couple were reunited in the following spring and remained at Aix for a year. There is a 1741 plan of the city in the library at Stourhead.[38] The fact that Henry learned French, and not Italian, indicates that he had prepared for a stay in France.[39] The list of books he kept included 16 French titles (out of a total 34).[40] Henry surely recommended Aix to his brother Sir Richard and sister-in-law, when they wished to recuperate after his stint as Lord Mayor of London.[41]

In Paris Sir John Lambert could have introduced him to art dealers and private sellers and found a guide to conduct him around the city. Paris had much to offer the tourist. Germaine Brice's popular four-volume guidebook to the city was first published in 1684 and ran to nine editions before 1752.[42] Henry would have taken an interest in the city's architecture. At Stourhead are seven hand-coloured prints of the city by Rigaud.[43] Henry's over-arching interest

FIG. 157
Salome with the Head of the Baptist, by Pompeo Girolamo Batoni, after Guido Reni, *c.*1740. Oil on canvas, 103 x 69 in,
261.6 x 175.2 cm. Reni's version hung in the Palazzo Colonna which Henry Hoare could have visited in Rome. The painting
is now in the Art Institute of Chicago. Batoni's version was first recorded in the Saloon at Stourhead in 1754. National Trust.

FIG. 158
Cleopatra before Octavius Augustus, by Giovanni Francesco Barbieri, 'Guercino', 1640. Oil on canvas, 98⅜ x 109 in, 250 x 277 cm. Henry Hoare must have seen this painting at the Palazzo Sacchetti, Rome, in 1740. Twenty years later, he commissioned Anton Raphael Mengs to depict the same subject and corresponded with their go-between, Thomas Jenkins, about Guercino's painting. Mengs's neoclassical version now hangs in the Picture Gallery at Stourhead as companion to Maratti's *Marchese Pallavicini guided to the Temple of Virtù by Apollo*. Pinacoteca Capitolina, Rome.

lay in Italian paintings of the sixteenth and seventeenth centuries and in antique sculpture. He saw Paris through Roman eyes. This would have taken him to the king's *Cabinet des Tableaux*, the Luxembourg Palace, the *Galerie d'Orléans* and the Crozat collection. The last, formed by Joseph-Antoine Crozat, created Marquis de Tugny, was displayed at no. 17 Place Vendôme. Henry would have known the collection – strong in his favourite schools – from the magisterial publication *Cabinet Crozat*.[44] These *grand luxe* volumes also included old master paintings assembled by the Duc d'Orléans Regent of France, 1715–23. His collection was housed in the Palais-Royal and comprised 500 paintings, predominantly Italian High Renaissance and Baroque and particularly rich in the Venetian school. This chimed with Henry's taste and evidently he spent time studying both the paintings and their arrangement. There is no visual record of the Palais-Royal galleries, but much can be gathered from descriptions included in the contemporary guidebook.[45] The Duc d'Orléans mixed sacred and profane subjects and crowded them on the walls, practices Henry Hoare would adopt at Stourhead. The galleries were hung with red damask and furnished with marble-top tables and ebony cabinets with pietre dure, following the character of the *Tribuna* at Florence. This was a style of presentation which Henry later emulated at Stourhead (see pp. 148–52). The *Galerie à la lanterne* at the

FIG. 159
Mars and Venus with Cupids and a Horse, after Paolo Veronese,
eighteenth century. Oil on canvas, 79½ x 63 in, 201.9 x 160 cm.
This copy was first recorded in the Hall at Stourhead in 1769.
National Trust.

Palais-Royal held the best Italian paintings and was top-lit, a feature which Henry Hoare copied when he added the Skylight Room to Stourhead in 1758–9. Henry would also have visited Versailles, famous for the sculpture and casts which Louis XIV had commissioned, and where Louis XV and his court were tourist attractions.[46] By then the grounds at Versailles would have looked *vieux jeu* to English visitors.[47]

PURCHASES

No bills survive from Henry Hoare's continental travels so there is nothing to colour the outline of his payments to bankers and shippers. The 1742 Stourhead Inventory mentioned a Picture Room with 35 unnamed paintings, which could represent the 'haul' from his Grand Tour.[48] The 1754 Catalogue listed a comparable number and is the earliest, if incomplete, record of Henry's old master collection; it included the Sixtus Cabinet (Appendix II transcribes the list in full and cross-references it to the surviving picture collection at Stourhead).

On 4 August 1742 Henry paid his shipper, Edward or Edmund Fowler, £37-1-6 for, 'D° [Customs& Charg⁵] 10 Cases of Cabinetts from Leghorn'. This was his most expensive shipment from Leghorn. 'Cabinetts' *plural*

is noteworthy and could refer to the Sixtus Cabinet and the pietre dure caskets and other cabinets recorded at Stourhead (see Appendix VI). Whatever their identity, these had reached London before December.[49] The 1754 Catalogue confided that the Sixtus Cabinet 'was admired at Rome where Mʳ Hoare bought it in a Convent, to whom a Nun the last of the Pope's Nephew's (or Peretti) Family left it'.[50] Did Henry himself inspect the Cabinet and did Belloni or Mark Parker arrange the purchase? Mark Parker applied for permissions to export pictures, marble table slabs and sculpture to England in 1739–58. The records omitted the names of his clients and made no plausible mention of the Sixtus Cabinet. An application from Parker, dated 13 October 1740, listed '8 quadri moderni e uno cassetto con diverse medaglie moderne de' Papi di metallo'[51] [8 modern pictures and a box with several modern medals of Popes in metal]. It was normal to understate the merit of exports but, even so, it would stretch credulity to conceal the Sixtus Cabinet within this description. Belloni apparently did not apply for licences for England before 1752.

Up to 1744 Henry paid his primary bankers, Alexander, Belloni and Sir John Lambert £1,214, £1,031 and £2,378 respectively (and they received no further payments before the 1754 Stourhead Catalogue was compiled). Some idea of what Henry paid for the Sixtus Cabinet would help to pinpoint the purchase. In 1769 Sir John Parnell gave a fanciful value of £10,000.[52] There is no payment approaching this magnitude in Henry Hoare's accounts. In 1741 Pietro Rossini, perhaps optimistically, valued the large pietre dure cabinet in the Palazzo Colonna, Rome, at 8,000 *scudi* (about £2,000) (fig. 69).[53] However, it is worth recalling that the great Cabinet for the third Duke of Beaufort was valued in 1732/3 at £500 (and shipped in five cases).[54] The Badminton Cabinet, now in the Liechtenstein Museum in Vienna, is considerably larger than the Sixtus Cabinet and likely, on balance, to have been a more expensive item. If we assume the Sixtus Cabinet cost no more than £500, the purchase is comfortably covered by the sums paid to any one of his three bankers.

Henry reimbursed Fowler for shipping two consignments specifically of 'figures' in 1740–3. Probably these included the antique marble statuettes of *Jupiter* and *Hera* in the Stourhead Saloon (figs 170 and 171).[55] According to an anonymous visitor, writing in 1766, Henry Hoare acquired the large *Livia Augusta as Ceres* in the Pantheon at Cardinal Ottoboni's sale.[56] The Cardinal, famous for his patronage of musicians, artists and women, died in 1740 leaving substantial debts, which were funded by the sale of his collections.

Henry Hoare's later documented acquisitions indicate what he was prepared to pay for pictures; in 1744 Sir John Lambert purchased the large *Judgment of Midas* by Sébastien Bourdon for £45, including shipping.[57] And in 1758 he paid Sir Horace Mann a total of £571-7-0, which included the Maratti painting of the *Marchese Pallavicini guided to the Temple of Virtù by Apollo* and the pair of *Landscapes* by Gaspard Poussin (fig. 156).[58] But when, in 1772, Lambert offered two paintings by Claude Lorrain for 15,000 *livres* (about £700) or 'something less', Henry did not bite.[59]

FIG. 160

Wisdom and Strength, after Paolo Veronese, seventeenth century. Oil on canvas, 103 x 69 in, 261.6 x 175.3 cm. The original is now in the Frick Collection, New York. This copy was first recorded in the Saloon at Stourhead in 1754. National Trust.

FIG. 161
Settee from the Temple of Apollo, Stourhead, *c.*1765. Painted pine, 52 x 87⅝ x 26½ in, 132 x 222.5 x 67.5 cm.
The back decorated with *Aurora*, by William Hoare of Bath, after Guido Reni. National Trust.

How Henry spent the considerable sum of money advanced by the French bankers is most intriguing (see Appendix III). Fowler sent two consignments from French ports, including the most expensive single shipment. Henry and his wife, who was wealthy in her own right, may have splashed out on clothes, jewellery and high living in Paris. Italian paintings were as available there, as in Rome. In Paris Henry probably acquired copies of the two Veroneses in the Palais-Royal (figs 159 and 160) and the copy of Raphael's *Holy Family* (then at Versailles) in a magnificent French frame (fig. 162).[60] Henry acquired other paintings in French frames, notably, Calvaert's *Mystic Marriage of St Catherine* and Poussin's *The Abduction of the Sabines* (now in the Metropolitan Museum of Art, New York). Both are included in the 1754 Stourhead Catalogue, remain in French frames and could have been purchased in Paris (figs 172 and 173). At the Duke of Chandos's sale in 1747,

Henry purchased Poussin's *Choice of Hercules*, also in a fine French frame (fig. 174).

High on the shopping list were pictures for the Stourhead Saloon (figs 148, 157 and 160). The paintings, all but one of which were copies, fitted the wall-space so precisely that the architect, Henry Flitcroft, must have had their dimensions when he designed the room in 1743–4.[61] Henry Hoare would have known the originals in Paris and Rome, and could have acquired the copies during, or immediately following, his tour of the Continent (see Appendix II, 1754 Catalogue p. 198). He continued purchasing and crowding the *piano nobile* of Stourhead. The 1784 Stourhead Catalogue listed 116 paintings, excluding family portraits. Henry was interested in art for display: sculpture, paintings, pastels, hand-coloured prints and pietre dure. He did not collect coins or natural history specimens and evidently he was no connoisseur of manuscripts.

FIG. 162
The Holy Family of François I, after Raphael, seventeenth century. Oil on panel, 24½ x 17 in, 62.2 x 43.2 cm. Frame, 35½ x 25⅞ in, 90.2 x 65.8cm. The original from the French Royal Collection, is now in the Louvre. This copy was first recorded at Stourhead in 1754 and in the Cabinet Room in 1762 where it remained until 1800. Notice the magnificent French frame. National Trust.

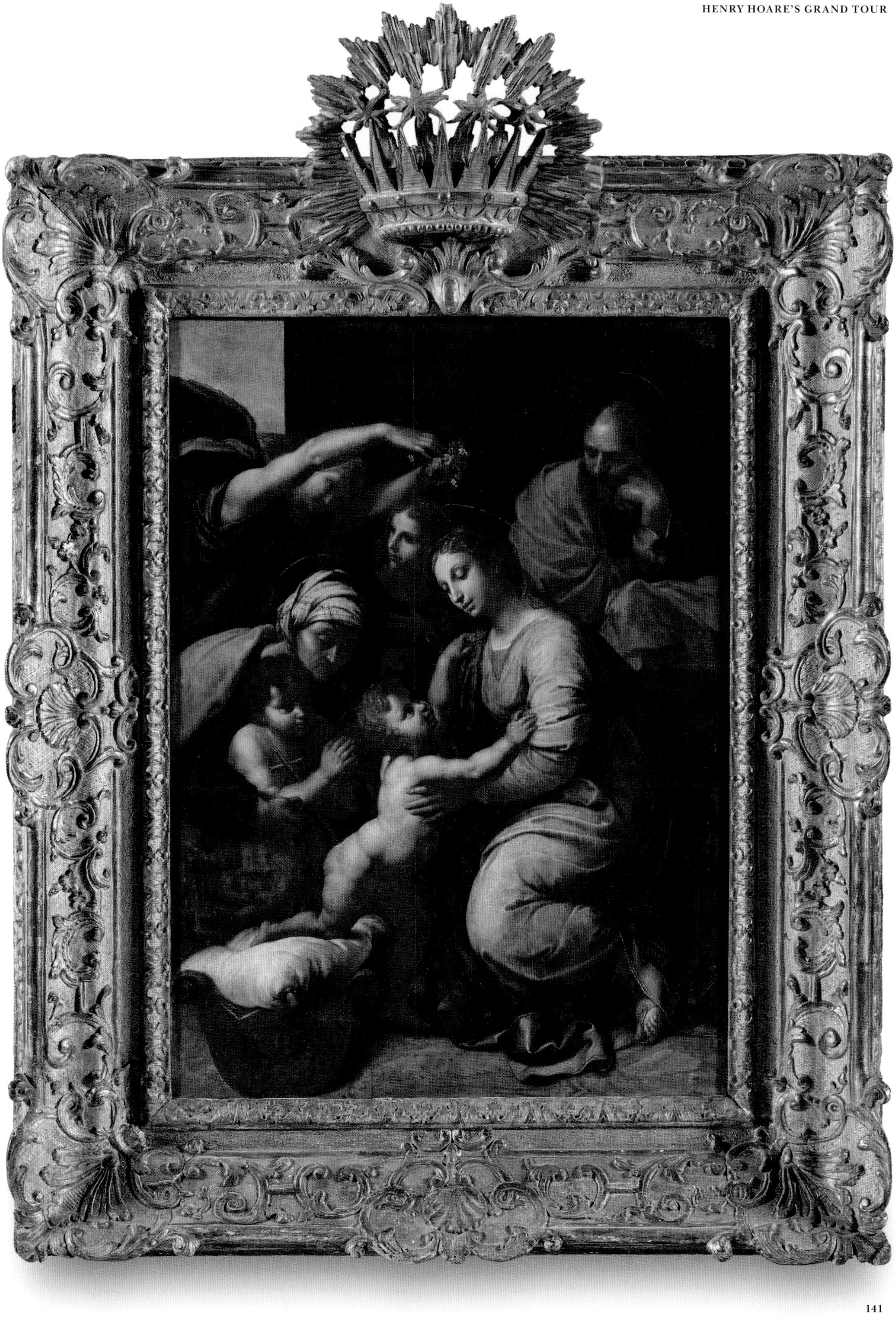

FIG. 163

Architectural Capriccio with the Pantheon and the Maison Carrée, attributed to Francis Harding, manner of Panini, *c.*1745–54. Oil on canvas, 28½ x 18½ in, 72.4 x 47 cm. In the background the Capriccio depicts the Pantheon at Stourhead (1753–61). Henry Hoare may have visited the Maison Carrée at Nîmes, on the left, during his stay at Aix-en-Provence. The painting is not identifiable in the Stourhead inventories. Possibly painted for Sir Richard Hoare, 2nd Kt, who also visited Aix. National Trust.

1. Appendix II. The four descriptions were: Stourhead Catalogue 1754;* Hanway 1756,* p. 88; Burlington 1779,* p. 394; Rezzonico 1787,* pp. 14–15.

2. Henry Hoare Accounts 1734–49, and see p. 160, 3 December 1742, 'Mr Mure for mending ye Fine Cabinet & for a Florence Box', £15-15-0.

3. Clay 1994, pp. 135–7.

4. Hoare 1819, p. 26.

5. Henry Hoare Accounts 1734–49.

6. C. Hoare & Co. HB/5/A/5, Partnership Ledger 1734–42.

7. WSA 383.28, Henry Hoare's pocket account books, 28 June 1738–6 September 1739, including Henry Hoare's reading list, and

25 June 1739–29 August 1740.

8. Black 1992, p. 103, in 1726 Charles Spencer found £500 insufficient annual allowance 'to travel, in any court of Europe'; in 1730–2, Sixth Earl of Salisbury received £3,313 while abroad; in 1740–1, Robert Cartaret spent over £1,850. C. Hoare & Co. HB/5/A/5, Partnership Ledger 1742–51, Henry Hoare's brother, Sir Richard Hoare, 2nd Kt, and party, spent just under £1,350 during his year-long visit to France, 1748–9.

9. Henry Hoare Accounts 1734–49, 29 September 1741, 'Jn Smith being in Full of all disbursm^ts due to Him in France & from Dover to London' £18-8-6; 26 March 1742 'John Smith in Full for 2 years & ½ & 25 Days

Wages at £20 p ann. & Board Wages at 10^s 6^p fr Week to ye 25th Septr 1741 when I returned to England' £96-6-3.

10. Halsband 1966, vol. 2, p. 212, Lady Mary Wortley Montagu to her husband, 23 November 1740.

11. *Country Journal* or *The Craftsman*, 13 October 1739, 'We hear that Henry Hoare Esq, Member of Parliament for new Sarum, who has been abroad some time for the Recovery of his Health, intends to stay at Naples till next Summer. His Lady is gone over to him, and was thirteen Hours in the late great Storm of Lightening, Wind and Rain, passing over from Dover to Calais.'

12. C. Hoare & Co. HB/5/A/5, Partnership

Ledger 1734–42, Henry Hoare, 24, 26 and 27 September 1739 payments made to Alexander on behalf of Mrs Hoare and 5 November 1739, payment to 'Jaˢ Harley attendᵍ Mʳˢ Hoare to France & Expˢ' £6-16-6.

13. C. Hoare & Co. ʜʙ/5/ᴀ/5, the Partnership Ledger 1734–42, Henry Hoare, recorded frequent payments to Mrs Hoare up to 10 September 1739 and these recommence on 15 June 1741. The ledger does not identify payment to a chaperon for her return.

14. *Daily Gazetteer*, 3 October 1741, 'Henry Hoare Esq; the Banker and late a Member of Parliament for Salisbury, who has been for a Year or more in the South Parts of France for his Health, is return'd to England with a very good Share of it, and is since gone to his Seat at Quarley in Hampshire.'

15. C. Hoare & Co. ʜꜰᴍ/ᴍ/9/7-9, 'Henry Hoare Esqʳ his Account Curᵗ wᵗʰ Sʳ Jⁿ Lambert Barᵗ' dated 19 July 1771–2 July 1772. When Henry Hoare visited Paris in 1771, he travelled with his nephew and the latter's second wife. The account itemized the cost of hiring a house at Neuilly: the monthly rent was 135 *livres*, and 200 *livres* per month for the furniture, which totalled just over £15 per month (Sir John Lambert quoted an exchange rate, in 1771, at *livres* 22.25 to one pound sterling). Henry is unlikely to have hired more opulent accommodation in 1741.

16. The sole evidence of Henry Hoare in Naples is the report in *Country Journal* or *The Craftsman*, 13 October 1739. See note 11.

17. Keyssler 1756–7. Nichols 1840, p. 568.

18. C. Hoare & Co. Customer Ledgers, ninth Earl of Lincoln, 1741–59.

19. Ingamells 1997, pp. 601–2.

20. Hoare 1815, p. 70.

21. Seymour 1806, vol. ɪɪ, p. 271, Lady Pomfret to Lady Hartford, 31 March 1741.

22. Lewis, Smith and Lam 1955b 18/2, pp. 238–41, Sir Horace Mann to Horace Walpole, 4 June 1743.

23. Lewis, Smith, Lam and Martz 1971 26/10, Appendix ɪ, pp. 3–8, 'Mark Parker to Walpole 24 September 1740 with other documents about Walpole's purchases in Italy', Parker's bill, sent *c.*24 September, totalled 351 crowns, about £87. (Between 1740 and 1748 a *scudo*, or Roman crown, was worth about 5 shillings sterling.)

24. Lewis 1961, p.120.

25. ᴡꜱᴀ 383.907, Parker to Henry Hoare, 12 October 1765.

26. Ibid., Thomas Jenkins to Henry Hoare, 6 June 1759.

27. Keyssler 1756–7, vol. ɪɪ, p. 213.

28. See Appendix ɪɪ, Stourhead Catalogue 1754, Saloon, p. 198.

29. ɴᴛ 732178 *Procession to the Temple of Apollo on Delos*, attributed to John Plimmer, after Claude Lorrain, 1759–61; ɴᴛ 732157 *The Mill*, attributed to Andrea Locatelli, after Claude Lorrain, early eighteenth century.

30. ɴᴛ 730916 *Aurora leading the carriage of Apollo surrounded by the Hours*, after Guido Reni, hand-coloured engraving by Jacob Frey, Rome, 1722.

31. *Cleopatra before Octavius Augustus*, by Giovanni Francesco Barbieri, 'Guercino', 1640, Pinacoteca Capitolina, Rome, ᴘᴄ 133. ᴡꜱᴀ 383.907, Jenkins to Henry Hoare, 23 April 1760, 'The picture you mention by Guercino

formerly in the [Sacchetti] Pallace now in the Capitol has Merit in it.' Henry commissioned an interpretation by Mengs: ɴᴛ 732099 *Octavian and Cleopatra* by Anton Raphael Mengs, 1759–60.

32. Seymour 1806 , vol. ɪɪɪ, pp. 32–3, Lady Pomfret to Lady Hartford, 11 May 1741, 'the marquis Beauvilliers, son of the French ambassador, came to conduct us to a convent called the Sette Dolori. I cannot imagine why, but this appears to have the fewest nuns I ever saw in such a place. The house is large and pleasant; and each female has two rooms to herself, prettily furnished; and several of the rooms have chimneys. They receive all their friends' visits, both men and women, in parlours without grates. They go abroad with their near relations; and they make no vow, but that of obedience to their superior. They are all people of quality, and live in good esteem. The one that shewed us the house was about six-and-twenty, a very pretty brown woman, with a great deal of wit and good-humour […] she took the habit, which seems rather a convenience than a burden to her. The nuns live well in all respects, without any trouble; and should they wish to marry, they are under no obligation not to do so, though the incident has never yet happened.'

33. Richardson 1722, pp. 325–6. Nichols 1840, p. 629.

34. ɴᴛ 732098 *Marchese Niccolò Maria Pallavicini guided to the Temple of Virtù by Apollo, with a self-portrait of the artist*, by Carlo Maratti, signed and dated 1705; ɴᴛ 732125, *A Classical Landscape with Sportsmen*, and ɴᴛ 732126 *Mountainous Landscape with Eurydice (?)*, both by Gaspard Poussin, *c.*1658–9. Although these Landscapes were purchased in 1758, they were first documented at Stourhead in 1898. The pair may have hung in Henry Hoare's house on Clapham Common, which was inherited by his nephew. They were noted at the latter's house, Barn Elms, in 1792 and subsequently recorded at Wavendon. See p. 219.

35. Keyssler 1756–7, vol. ɪ, p. 437.

36. Seymour 1806, vol. ɪɪ, pp. 77–9, Lady Pomfret to Lady Hartford, 23 October 1740.

37. Ibid., vol. ɪ, pp. 200–3, Lady Pomfret to Lady Hartford, 3 January 1740; pp. 297–9 ditto, 30 July 1740.

38. ɴᴛ 732864, 'Plan de la Ville d'Aix, Capitale de Provence', map by Esprit Devaux, engraved by Honoré Coussin, 1741.

39. Henry Hoare Accounts 1734–49, 4 March 1738/9, 'Monsʳ Le Beau Pin for teachᵍ me French in Full' £3-3-0.

40. See note 7.

41. C. Hoare & Co. ʜꜰᴍ/7/18, notebook and cash accounts kept by Sir Richard Hoare, 2nd Knt in France, 1748–9.

42. Brice 1725. See Berger 1999, p. 125.

43. ɴᴛ 730726, 730735, 730740-4.

44. Crozat 1729–42. ᴡꜱᴀ, 383.28, Henry Hoare's pocket account book 28 June 1738–6 September 1739, included, 'Book contᵗ accᵗ of all yᵉ best engravᵉʳˢ & a List of all their works Number'd'; possibly the 'Cabinet Crozat', if 'Number'd' signified 'with dimensions'.

45. Dubois de Saint-Gelais 1727.

46. Thomassin 1723.

47. Lewis, Lam and Bennett 1961 13-14/1, p. 168, Walpole to Richard West, 15 May 1739,

'The garden [at Versailles] is littered with statues and fountains […] There are avenues of water-pots, who disport themselves much in the squirting up cascadelins. In short 'tis a garden for a great child. Such was Louis Quatorze.'

48. Stourhead Inventory 1742.

49. See note 2.

50. Stourhead Catalogue 1754.*

51. Bertolotti 1880, pp. 79–80, Mark Parker export licences January 1738–November 1758.

52. Parnell 1769,* vol. ɪɪ, f. 102.

53. Rossini da Pesaro 1741, p. 60, at the Palazzo Colonna, 'due Studioli, uno d'Ebano di Basso-relievo dentro, e fuori, del valore di otto mila scudi' [two cabinets, one of ebony with bas-reliefs, inside and external, valued at 8,000 crowns] Rossini went on to value the cabinet with ivory panels at 18,000 crowns. (In 1740–8 a *scudo*, or Roman crown, was worth about five shillings sterling.)

54. González-Palacios 1993, vol. ɪ, pp. 430–1.

55. ɴᴛ 732925 *Jupiter* and ɴᴛ 732926 *Hera* or *Kore*, both Greco-Roman, first or second century. See Vermeule and von Bothmer 1956, pp. 343–4.

56. British Library, Add. ᴍꜱ 6767, ff. 33–4, Anonymous 1766, 'the [Stourhead] Pantheon […] a charming Antique Statue of Livia Augusta, from the Collection of Cardinal Ottoboni, and cost 1000ᵉ [pounds sterling]'. ɴᴛ 562913, *Livia Augusta as Ceres*, first century. Hanway 1756, p. 92. 'Perhaps I should first have mentioned the temple of Ceres [Temple of Flora], which is on the side of the water nearest the village. Here is the figure of the goddess, with her proper emblems, standing in front as you open the door.' The 'Livia' had moved to the Pantheon before 1762 where Walpole described it. Possibly this was the sculpture which Mark Parker applied to export, for an unnamed client, on 13 October 1740, 'una statua antica di marmo al naturale di mediocre scultura figurante una donna in parte ristorata' [a mediocre antique statue in plain marble of a woman with restorations] (Bertolotti 1880, p. 79). See Vermeule and von Bothmer 1956 for an alternative provenance.

57. ᴡꜱᴀ 383.907, Sir John Lambert to Henry Hoare, 1 February 1743/4, reporting the purchase and dispatch of *The Judgment of Midas*, from Paris for 976 French *livres* about £46. (In 1743/4 Lambert quoted an exchange rate of 21.12 *livres* to one pound sterling.)

58. C. Hoare & Co. ʜᴇ/5/ᴀ/7, Partnership Ledger 1751–64, Henry Hoare and see note 34.

59. ᴡꜱᴀ 383.907, Lambert to Henry Hoare, 20 August 1772.

60. ɴᴛ 732146 *Mars and Venus with Cupids and a Horse*, after Paolo Veronese, eighteenth century. Parnell 1769* noted *Mars and Venus* hanging above the Hall chimney piece and therefore opposite *Henry Hoare ɪɪ on Horseback*; surely an intentional juxtaposition? ɴᴛ 732313 *Wisdom and Strength*, after Veronese, seventeenth century. ɴᴛ 732105 *The Holy Family of François ɪ*, after Raphael, seventeenth century.

61. ᴡꜱᴀ 383.907.3, Henry Flitcroft to Henry Hoare, 18 August, 1744, concerning the decoration of the Saloon.

SEVEN
STOURHEAD, THE SIXTUS CABINET AND THE FIRST CABINET ROOM

The arrival of the Sixtus Cabinet lifted Stourhead from the respectable to the remarkable. It possessed many attention-seeking qualities; it was glamorous, it was expensive, it was exotic (for Wiltshire), it was slightly shocking (for its Catholic associations) and, with this single purchase, Henry Hoare created excitement at the house. Sir John Parnell and Mrs Lybbe Powys speculated about its price, but Henry Hoare was not criticized, in print, for extravagance either for the Cabinet or for the house in contrast to his neighbour, bank-customer and friend, Alderman Beckford (1709–1770) of Fonthill. When his house burned in 1755, Beckford rebuilt with greater magnificence and the 10th Earl of Pembroke quipped that Beckford 'wallowed in money and therefore built 2 Houses to get rid of it'.[1] Sir John Parnell considered the ornate marble chimney pieces at Fonthill Splendens 'chosen just by the Sum of Money they would cost and for no other merit [...] mere Expence is always thrown out in Vain to captivate me'.[2] In 1776, Mrs Powys described Fonthill 'where is display'd ye utmost profusion of magnificence, with the appearance of immense riches, almost too Tawdrily exhibited'.[3] Henry Hoare knew that he walked a tightrope at Stourhead: a banker should appear wealthy and prudent, not openly extravagant.[4] Yet he had panache; Henry's life-size equestrian portrait (fig. 146) is as self-advertising as any: but nobody has ever described it as vainglorious, which is a vindication of his later reputation as 'Magnificent'. Anne Masham (d.1727), Henry's first wife, could qualify as a trophy bride, being the daughter of Abigail, Lady Masham, Queen Anne's favourite. And the Sixtus Cabinet was both the cynosure of his collection and a pre-eminent symbol of his wealth.

The impact of the Cabinet on Stourhead may be judged from a description of the house before and after its arrival. When considering the interior of Stourhead it should be borne in mind that, between 1800 and 1820, Sir Richard Colt Hoare refurnished the house, with Thomas Chippendale junior, and the central block was burned out in 1902; so, today, the interiors are an Edwardian evocation of an essentially Regency house.

THE HOUSE

Stourhead (fig. 165) was sufficiently complete by 1724 for Henry Hoare I and his wife, Jane, to move in and, after he died the following year, she stayed on for the remainder of her life (fig. 147).[5] The inventory compiled at her death in 1742 gave no values but listed all the rooms and contents, excepting silver, books and personal effects.[6] The axis of the *piano nobile* lay east–west from the Entrance Hall, through the Staircase or Inner Hall to the Chapel, which rose from the rustic to the *piano nobile*. On either side were rooms which became more private and more sumptuously furnished moving westwards, from the entrance to the park front. Figure 166 suggests how the rooms described in 1742 relate to Campbell's plan of the *piano nobile*. Stourhead was a very early specimen of a Palladian villa, which challenged the Hoares to find appropriate pictures and furniture. This took time and to begin with there were few pictures: portraits, flower pieces and *Elijah Raising the Widow's Son*, attributed to Rembrandt (fig. 168), but also the 35 unnamed paintings in the Picture Room (see p. 138).[7] The 1742 inventory descriptions are of text-message brevity without distinguishing different types of wood or gilding used in the furniture. But each principal bedroom had matching upholstery textiles. Under Jane Hoare Stourhead was decorous and austere, interiors which might have come from the brush of Arthur Devis.

A sketch plan of the *piano nobile* (fig. 167), by Sir John Parnell in 1769 shows alterations made by Henry Hoare.[8] The latter replaced the Chapel with a Saloon, designed by Henry Flitcroft. At the same time Henry enlarged the Breakfast Room as a setting for the Sixtus Cabinet by extending the room into the space occupied by a staircase down to the rustic, shown on Campbell's plan. These stairs he relocated in the south-west corner of the house (also shown by Sir John). To the north of the Hall, Henry made a Study or Library, in the space formerly occupied by the Little Parlour. At the north-west corner of the house he added, in 1758–9, a small picture gallery, opening out

FIG. 164
The Dining Room at Stourhead, by John Buckler, 1824. Pencil, ink and watercolour, 10½ x 14 in, 26.5 x 35.5 cm. In Henry Hoare's time the Sixtus Cabinet stood behind the columns at the far end of the room; its outline is superimposed on the watercolour. The British Library.

FIG. 165
'The Garden or South front of Stourhead in Wiltshire', engraved by Hendrick Hulsbergh, for Colen Campbell, *Vitruvius Britannicus*, London, 1725, vol. III, pl. 43. 9⅝ x 14¾ in, 24.5 x 37.5 cm. RIBA Library Drawings & Archives Collections.

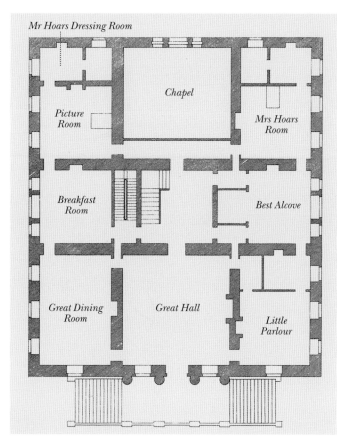

FIG. 166
'Plan of the principal Story of Stourhead as Executed by Mʳ Hoare', engraved by Hendrick Hulsbergh, for Colen Campbell, *Vitruvius Britannicus*, London, 1725, vol. III, pl. 41. 9⅞ x 15¼ in, 25 x 38.5 cm. Overlaid with rooms named in the 1742 Stourhead Inventory. RIBA Library Drawings & Archives Collections.

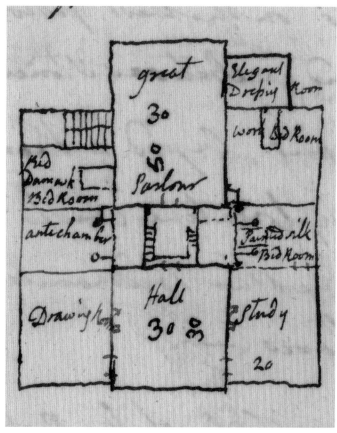

FIG. 167
Stourhead *piano nobile*, sketch plan by Sir John Parnell, 2nd Bt, 1769, vol. II, f. 106. Ink on paper, 2⅜ x 2¼ in, 6.5 x 5.6 cm. The Library of the London School of Economics and Political Science.

of 'the work Bed Room' (the present Column Room). The gallery is visible in John Buckler's drawing of 1811 and watercolour of 1817 (figs 209 and 210). It was lit by a skylight which was a sufficient novelty to lend the room its name. Henry Hoare had probably seen top-lit picture galleries on his continental tour (see pp. 137–8).

From 1740 onwards Henry purchased furnishings from notable London craftsmen such as Giles Grendey, James Moore and James Richards. He seldom recorded in his ledgers destinations for items supplied so it is foolhardy to speculate what was for Stourhead and what for the house at Quarley or his London residence. Grendey probably made the 12 walnut and parcel gilt dining chairs (in the Little Dining Room today) and the 16 mahogany armchairs and settee for the Saloon.[9] A few other pieces at Stourhead are documented as belonging to Henry Hoare: the two 'fox' side tables; a magnificent giltwood table celebrating his marriage to Susan Colt; the Sixtus Pedestal (see Chapter 8); the carved frame for the *Cyrus and Tomyris* silver-gilt salver (fig. 169) and a neoclassical inlaid wine-cooler.[10] A parcel gilt suite of 'Kentian' seat furniture, not securely recorded at Stourhead until the twentieth century, may well have been there since Henry's time.[11]

How many pieces with pietre dure did Henry collect for Stourhead? Shipping costs suggest he bought 'cabinets' and this is confirmed by descriptions of the house. Sir John Parnell counted 3 'florentine chests' and the 1838 Stourhead Inventory listed a coffer and 5 lesser 'cabinets'. Although it is unclear which were caskets, which cabinets, all seem to have incorporated pietre dure panels, being described as 'Mosaic' or 'of different stones'. One Florentine casket was particularly splendid and stood, in Henry Hoare's time, in the Skylight Room, on a sumptuous marble pedestal by the sculptor Benjamin Carter (see p. 18). The *ensemble* was depicted in the Saloon in 1824 but was sold in 1883 (fig. 212). Today there are two small pietre dure cabinets in the Cabinet Room; one, arguably acquired by Henry Hoare, has a complex provenance, while the history of the second is incomplete (see Appendix VI) (figs 68 and 73).

In 1762 Horace Walpole's verdict on the rooms at Stourhead was 'in general too low, but richly furnished'.[12] He would have encountered many grand Roman ingredients. His tour began in the Hall, dominated by three large paintings; the equestrian portrait of Henry Hoare, Maratti's *Marchese Pallavicini guided to the Temple of Virtù by Apollo*, acquired in 1758, and *Octavian and Cleopatra* commissioned from Mengs the following year.[13] In the Parlour stood Rysbrack's *Bacchus*.[14] Walpole also noted there the *Cyrus* salver (framed and hanging like a picture), a copy of Correggio's *Venus with Mercury and Cupid*; and the overmantel, *The Interior of St Peter's at Rome*, after Panini (fig. 155).[15] Next, most Roman of all, the Cabinet Room. Continuing down the south side, Walpole came to the Red Damask Bedroom, its walls dominated by two Old Testament pictures by Imperiali in conspicuous rococo giltwood frames.[16] The dressing room beyond held a mixture of landscapes, the politely titillating *Nymph of the Grotto* by William Hoare of Bath and the miniatures from the Sixtus Cabinet (see pp. 213–5).[17] On the north side of the house Walpole found a similar progress westwards from

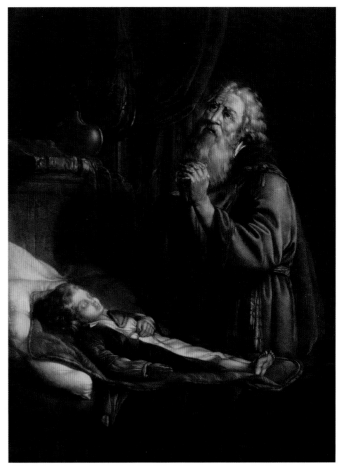

FIG. 168
Elijah Raising the Widow's Son, mezzotint by Richard Earlom, after Rembrandt, 1768. Published by John Boydell, 19¾ x 14 in, 50.3 x 35.4 cm. Inscribed, 'From the Original Picture painted by Rembrandt; In the Collection of Henry Hoare Esq.[r] at Stourhead, Wilts'. The British Museum.

FIG. 169
Silver-gilt salver, with *Cyrus and Queen Tomyris*, by Heinrich Mannlich. Augsburg, late seventeenth century. Salver first recorded at Stourhead in 1762. The painted and part-gilded pine stand was carved by Sefferin Alken in 1777. Stand: 43½ x 55 in, 110.5 x 139.7 cm. National Trust.

FIG. 170
Hera or *Kore*, Greco-Roman, first or second century. Marble, 28½ x 10 x 9 in, 72.5 x 25.5 x 23 cm. Listed in the Cabinet Room at Stourhead in 1784. National Trust.

FIG. 171
Jupiter, Greco-Roman, first or second century. Marble, 32⅝ x 13¼ x 10½ in, 83 x 33.5 x 26.5 cm. Listed in the Cabinet Room at Stourhead in 1784. National Trust.

restraint to opulence; the Library with family portraits and, beyond, two bedrooms, the second with Rembrandt's *Elijah* (fig. 168). Finally came the Skylight Room where 12 old masters were displayed along with paintings by Wootton (now lost) and pastels by William Hoare.[18] The Saloon was a gallery of copies after old master paintings, and one original by Sébastien Bourdon (fig. 212).[19] During the 1902 fire these were rescued, cut from their frames, and 4 now hang in the Stair Hall (figs 148, 157 and 160).

Any picture count must be treated with caution. Nevertheless, the totals for the public rooms are indicative of Henry's voracity; in 1754 there were 42 on the *piano nobile*; the 1784 Catalogue listed 116; and the 1800 guidebook recorded, at minimum, 154. Henry Hoare admitted to his daughter in 1779 that he was running out of space for paintings, 'where to peg Them I know not as We are chuck full'.[20] He hung the best pictures on red damask.[21] To add to the opulence Henry spent generously on gilded frames. A visitor in 1765 described the *piano nobile* with red silk for the south side, the Staircase stone-colour and green and the Saloon, blue. On the north side, the Library was pea-green, the bedroom (Italian Room), blue and the Skylight Room, predictably, hung with red silk.[22]

THE CABINET ROOM

Standing in the Little Dining Room it is easy to imagine the Sixtus Cabinet, centred on the north wall, flanked by two columns of the screen introduced by Henry Hoare, and occupying a dominant position, comparable to that of a state bed in its alcove (fig. 164). From the windows opposite the Cabinet, visitors look onto the south lawn stretching to the valley, with Stourton village and the garden beyond.[23]

The walls were hung with old master paintings in splendid English and French gilded frames. Little is known about the furnishings. In 1762 the Duchess of Beaufort noted, the 'Cabinet very fine of precious Stones, & a Coffre of the same'.[24] Was this the Florentine pietre dure casket that Walpole later described in the Skylight Room?[25] The 1784 Catalogue listed, 'A Statue of Jupiter' and 'A Statue of Juno', classed as 'Antiques'.[26] These must be the two sculptures now in the Saloon, which Henry Hoare probably acquired in Italy (see p. 138) (figs 170 and 171). Henry Hoare's ledger reveals that the Sixtus Cabinet stood on a carpet.[27]

The pictures are well documented and Appendix II indicates how Henry Hoare jig-sawed them around as time

FIG. 172
The Abduction of the Sabine Women, by Nicolas Poussin, *c*.1633–4. Oil on canvas, 60⅞ x 82⅝ in, 154.6 x 209.9 cm. Listed in the Cabinet Room at Stourhead in 1754. Sold in 1883. The Metropolitan Museum of Art, New York.

FIG. 173
The Mystic Marriage of St Catherine, by Denys Calvaert, 1590–5. Oil on copper, 18¾ x 15 in, 47.6 x 38.1 cm.
Frame, 30⅝ x 27¼ in, 78 x 69.2 cm. Listed in the Cabinet Room at Stourhead in 1754. Notice the French rococo frame.
National Trust.

FIG. 174
Choice of Hercules, by Nicolas Poussin, *c.*1636–7. Oil on canvas, 36 x 28⅛ in, 91.5 x 71.5 cm. Frame, 48⅛ x 40⅛ in, 122.3 x 102.1 cm.
Listed in the Cabinet Room at Stourhead in 1754. Notice the French frame. National Trust.

FIG. 175
The Flight into Egypt, by Carlo Maratti, mid-seventeenth century.
Oil on copper, 20¼ x 14¾ in, 51.4 x 37.5 cm. Listed in the Cabinet
Room at Stourhead in 1754. National Trust.

went by. The 1754 Catalogue listed six old master paintings, four religious: 'Herodias and Sᵗ John Baptist Head by Carlo Dulci' (Dolci), 'Our Saviour Sᵗ John and the Virgin from the Duke of Orleans Raphael', 'The 'Marriage of Sᵗ Catherine by Barrochio of Urbin' (Calvaert), 'The Flight into Egypt by Carlo Marat' (Maratti) and 'and two mythological, both by 'Nicolo Poussin', 'Herculas between Virtue and Pleasure' and 'Rape of the Sabins'. It is probably no more than a coincidence that Hercules was a theme of the ceiling of the loggia of the Palazzo Felice where the Sixtus Cabinet once stood, with a cast of Giambologna's *Rape of the Sabines* on a pietre dure table nearby (see pp. 114–5). Henry Hoare intended the Cabinet Room ensemble to evoke a palatial Roman interior fit for a Pope. In 1762 Walpole mentioned a hang of ten or 11 pictures which seems to dilute the earlier ensemble. The 1784 Catalogue described 17 and the 1800 guidebook 21. When Henry Hoare built the Skylight Room, he raided the Cabinet Room, moving Poussin's *Choice of Hercules* (fig. 174), followed, after 1762, by his *Abduction of the Sabine* (fig. 172).[28] The two rooms were then counterpoints: the Cabinet Room resplendent with the Sixtus Cabinet, antique sculpture and Italian old masters; the Skylight Room with even better paintings and the Florentine pietre dure casket.

By 1784 the Cabinet Room was congested; besides the

Italian paintings there were Dutch and Flemish pictures, including Rembrandt's *Elijah*. Henry added a contemporary picture by the young Samuel Woodforde.[29] The largest pictures listed in 1784 were the two copies of Doria-Pamphilj Claudes.[30] Sir Richard Colt Hoare published the first Stourhead guidebook in 1800, before his Library and new Gallery were in use. The Sixtus Cabinet remained in its original setting surrounded by a fresh arrangement of pictures, including contemporary work: Gainsborough's *Peasants going to Market: Early Morning* (moved from the Skylight Room) and family portraits by Reynolds and Angelica Kauffman.[31] This hugger-mugger hang was short-lived; by 1802 Sir Richard had installed the Sixtus Cabinet in his new Cabinet Room and rationalized the pictures in the house.

When Henry Hoare purchased the Sixtus Cabinet it must have been as the culmination of a type coveted by contemporary English Grand Tourists. But its association with Sixtus v, dead a mere 150 years, with an enduring reputation for ruthless energy in rebuilding Rome, was also crucial and reflected in its new Pedestal. However, in 1744 and again in 1779, England was in peril of attack by the French fleet, arousing memories of the 1588 Armada which Sixtus had helped to finance. By hanging his gold Armada medal and Garter George on the Cabinet, perhaps in 1779, Henry Hoare lent it another layer of meaning, as a celebration of England's triumph over Catholic foes (see pp. 216–7).

LIFE AT STOURHEAD

It is curious that Henry Hoare, who so enjoyed and loved country pursuits, did not move permanently to Stourhead in later life. Banking kept him in London for most of the year, when he lived first at no. 41 Lincoln's Inn Fields and, after 1754, at the house which Flitcroft designed for him on Clapham Common where he eventually retired and died. Stourhead was unused by the Hoares for many months in the year but was visited by an ever-growing stream of tourists to both house and garden, as reflected by the many published and manuscript descriptions.

Social life lit up during the summer, when Henry was always resident. Everything which gave salt to English life, Henry brought to Stourhead to delight his guests. Family members were welcomed and, along with his friends, they made prolonged stays. Henry's wife had died in 1743 and nine years later his only surviving son died, aged 21 (see Hoare family genealogy, p. 221). There remained his two daughters. In 1756 Anne, the younger girl, married her cousin, Richard Hoare (1734/5–1787). The alliance was not blue-blooded, but hard-headed and doubtless arranged by Henry himself. He provided the bride with a portion of £20,000. When Anne gave birth to a healthy son, Richard Colt Hoare, in 1758, Henry once more had a male heir *of the blood* who could continue the family name at Stourhead. For his elder daughter Susannah, Henry pursued aristocratic alliances (fig. 177). In 1753 she married Charles Boyle, Viscount Dungarvan. He was the son of John Boyle, fifth Earl of Cork and Orrery, an impecunious peer who that

FIG. 176

'The Dining Room Stourhead Wilts (June. 1900.) H.C. Messer, 29 Castle Street, Salisbury'. Photograph, 7½ x 9½ in, 19 x 24 cm. On the right is *The Abduction of Helen* and around the centre table are the dining chairs attributed to Giles Grendey. Sefferin Alken carved the over-mantel and his frame for the *Cyrus and Queen Tomyris* salver (fig. 169) is seen beside the door on the far wall. The salver stands on a massive side table attributed to Henry Flitcroft. National Trust, Stourhead.

year inherited Lord Burlington's Irish title and who resided close to Stourhead, at Marston. The marriage, which cost Henry £35,000 (including the portion of £25,000), was reminiscent of the opening scene in Hogarth's *Marriage à la Mode* (1743–5). The newly-weds gave Henry his first grandchild; the in-laws gave him a financial headache when they reneged on the agreement with him to manage their debts. In 1759 Lord Dungarvan obligingly died and Sukie, as Susannah was known, was again eligible. A tentative match arranged with the Duke of Somerset (who lived nearby at Maiden Bradley and who was presumably seeking a bride for one of his sons) fell through in 1760.[32] Having tripped twice, Henry persevered and the following year Sukie was betrothed to Thomas, Lord Bruce of Tottenham Park, near Marlborough, youngest son of the third Earl of Cardigan and heir to the fourth Earl of Elgin. The union cost Henry Hoare a further £11,000 and proved a success for all parties. Lord Bruce received more, much more, from Henry. In addition to Sukie's dowry, Henry laid out £13,000 in 1766 to purchase the parliamentary borough adjoining Tottenham.[33] Lord Bruce was created first Earl of Ailesbury in 1776. Henry's letters to his son-in-law and

Sukie survive from 1760–81 and provide an insight to life at Stourhead.[34]

Henry Hoare had three garrulous companions, Messrs Benson, Earle and Rust, who were summer habitués of Stourhead.[35] Besides these were William Hoare of Bath (1707–1792), who became a friend in the 1750s. The artist was not a kinsman but the two men were the same generation and both admired Italian art. One letter, dated 5 June 1760, survives in which William Hoare's voice erupts from the pages with gossip and opinions on the old masters.[36] He had lived in Rome, where he studied with Imperiali and was acquainted with wealthy young British tourists. Between 1759 and 1772 Henry Hoare paid him £1,500.[37] In 1765 Henry's nephew, known affectionately as 'Fat Harry' Hoare, married William Hoare's daughter, Mary. Coplestone Warre Bampfylde (1720–1791) lived at Hestercombe, close to Taunton. Bampfylde was a gentleman-painter, architect and keen gardener. Around 1775 he made two beguiling watercolours at Stourhead.[38] He was a regular visitor and, like William Hoare, he flits through Henry's letters. 'Alderman' William Beckford (1709–1770) was a close friend from the city and neighbour at Fonthill;

he often came to Stourhead and Henry Hoare rode over to Fonthill. Other grandees in the vicinity dined at Stourhead: Lord Ilchester from Redlynch, Lord Pembroke from Wilton and Lord Arundell from Wardour.[39] In August 1776 David Garrick visited.[40] To one and all, Henry liberally dispensed turtle soup, venison and claret.

At times Stourhead was overcrowded.[41] It was not large by country house standards and probably had six, or at maximum, eight guest bedrooms on the first floor, with servants' garrets above. The company dined in the Saloon but breakfasted and congregated in the Hall; in the Parlour (the present Music Room) Henry installed an organ to amuse the children.[42] In the Cabinet Room (Little Dining Room) or Skylight Room William Hoare and Bampfylde busied themselves admiring and copying the paintings. Henry used the Library (the present Cabinet Room) as a retreat, though even this sanctum sometimes served as a studio.[43] When the weather was fine, house guests could amuse themselves beside the lake. It would be wrong to imagine the house as a museum for elderly art-lovers. Young Richard Hoare brought his offspring to Stourhead and Sukie's children often came over from Tottenham Park. Henry Hoare relished young company, along with the pleasures of the table, boating and bathing.

HENRY HOARE'S LEGACY

Place Henry Hoare under a prism and he refracts in many colours: businessman, landowner, farmer, gardener, aesthete, collector and patriarch. To succeed as a banker and landowner was admirable, yet this supremely capable and honourable man longed for recognition as the Olympian of Stourhead. He wanted the place to endure and eventually his dedication to Stourhead out-weighed his commitment to the bank. There was good reason to separate the two aspects of his life: should the bank fail, Stourhead, deemed a business asset, would be sold. In 1783 Henry Hoare, aged 78, decided to make over the property to his grandson, Richard Colt Hoare. The latter was already working at the bank and the gift was to be conditional on his quitting work. Henry had built up the Wiltshire estate to the point that the rents would *almost* pay for the upkeep of the house and garden. By his death it comprised 11,262 acres and yielded an annual income of £10,170.[44] However, that was not quite enough and Henry wished to bolster the estate income by including, in the gift, his London properties, including the bank premises. This sparked a family row. Richard's father and his uncle, 'Fat Harry', were junior partners and considered Henry Hoare to be 'tone-deaf' to their needs.[45] On this pinnacle of discomfort, Henry Hoare capitulated and left the elder Richard the London properties, with the result that Stourhead was under-endowed: and that would have painful consequences.

FIG. 177
Susannah Hoare, Countess of Ailesbury, by Arthur Pond, signed and dated 1757. Oil on canvas, 30 x 25 in, 76.2 x 63.5 cm. In 1761 Henry Hoare's elder daughter, Susannah, married Thomas, Lord Bruce (later created first Earl of Ailesbury). Henry explained to his son-in-law, in a letter dated 7 April 1765, that William Hoare had recently added the feather hat and other Rubenesque touches to the portrait. Listed in the Skylight Room at Stourhead in 1784. National Trust, Stourhead.

1. WSA Ailesbury Estate Collection 9/35/165, quoted in the letter from Henry Hoare to Lord Bruce, 29 August 1763.

2. Parnell 1769, vol. II, ff. 119–20.

3. Mrs Powys 1776, f. 12.

4. Hoare 1819, p. 30, Henry Hoare paid, '£190,000 […] in the purchase of land, and in furnishing his mansion-house at Stourhead'. Alderman Beckford's papers do not survive so it is difficult to gage the cost of Fonthill Splendens; Climenson 1899, p. 166, n. 2, claimed the new house at Fonthill cost £240,000 to build.

5. C. Hoare & Co. HFM/4/7, Henry (Good) Hoare Private Account, 'An Account of House Hold Expenses at Stourton', 16 May 1723–18 February 1724/5, 6 March 1723/4, 'insuring Stourton House' £16-17-6.

6. Stourhead Inventory 1742.

7. The 'Rembrandt' was reputedly the gift of Bishop Atterbury. In 1742 it hung in Jane Hoare's bedroom at Stourhead and left the house in 1883. See Appendix II. Stourhead Catalogue 1754, Green Bed Chamber, p. 197.

8. The Library of the London School of Economics and Political Science, LSE/Coll/Misc/0038, vol. 2, f. 106, Sir John Parnell's sketch plan.

9. Henry Hoare Accounts 1734–49 and 1749–70, payments to Giles Grendey, 29 April 1746, £64; 27 March 1751, £133-2-9; 24 June 1752, £10-17-0. These payments may be associated with the following seat furniture at Stourhead. NT 731638 12 walnut chairs (Little Dining Room).
NT 731607 16 mahogany armchairs.
NT 731608 a long settee (Saloon).
Possibly NT 731628 14 mahogany chairs matching those in the Little Dining Room.

10. NT 731596.1 & 2 a pair of console tables with carved foxes and marble tops, c.1730, Stourhead Inventory 1742, 'In yᵉ Picture Room', 'Marble Slabs wᵗʰ ffox Stands'.
NT 731653 armorial table.
NT 732887.2 salver-frame, WSA 383.4.1, 24, May 1777, 'Henry Hoare Esqr To Seffⁿ Alken To Carving an Oval frame 2ᶠᵗ 8ⁱⁿ by 2ᶠᵗ 4ⁱⁿ a Cavetto neatly enrichd, a torus carv'd with guilloch and flowers two Monsters' £29-10-0.
NT 731646 wine cooler, Henry Hoare Accounts 1770–85, 17 October 1779, 'Mʳ Ward for an Inlaid Sideboard Cistern' £15-11-6.

11. NT 731651 set comprising two armchairs, four single chairs, two stools and a settee, 1730s.

12. Toynbee 1928, p. 41.

13. NT 732098 and NT 732099.

14. Christie's 1883a, lot 49, and now at the Calouste Gulbenkian Foundation Museum, Lisbon, no. 2216.

15. NT 732153 and NT 732268. See Appendix II. Stourhead Catalogue 1754, Parlour, p. 197

16. NT 732123 and NT 732124. See Appendix II. Stourhead Catalogue 1754, Best Bed Chamber, p. 197.

17. NT 730719.

18. NT 730786 *The Infants Christ and John the Baptist with Two Child Angels, a Lamb, and a Still-Life of Fruit* (after Rubens), 1763.
And perhaps NT 730784 *A Nymph: 'Spring'* and NT 730787 *A Nymph: 'Summer'*, c.1765, all by William Hoare of Bath, RA.

19. Appendix II, Stourhead Catalogue 1754, Saloon, p. 198.

20. WSA Ailesbury Estate Collection 1300/4286, Henry Hoare to Susannah, Lady Ailesbury, 28 August 1779.

21. C. Hoare & Co. HB/5/A/7 Partnership Ledger 1751–64, Henry Hoare, 12 August 1758, 'Phil Palmer &ᶜ for damask &ᶜ for Stourᵈ' £263-18-0.

22. Anonymous 1765.*

23. Parnell 1769, vol. 2, f. 107, sketch plan of Stourhead, house and surrounds depicted a statue of 'Apollo' on a pedestal at the far end of the south lawn.

24. Duchess of Beaufort 1762,* p. 41.

25. Walpole 1762,* p. 42.

26. NT 732925 *Jupiter* and NT 732926 *Hera* or *Kore*. See p. 153, note 55. The 1655 inventory of the Palazzo Felice recorded the Sixtus Cabinet displayed with 12 antique marble statues about three feet tall. See Appendix I.

27. Henry Hoare Accounts 1734–49, 10 June 1743, 'Jones for a Wilton Carpet undʳ yᵉ Cabinᵗ' £6-17-8.

28. See Appendix II, Stourhead Catalogue 1754, Cabinet Room, p. 197.

29. Stourhead Catalogue 1784,* *Neptune Calming the Sea and Saint George*, by Samuel Woodforde RA. This picture is no longer at Stourhead.

30. NT 732178 *Procession to the Temple of Apollo on Delos*, attributed to John Plimmer, after Claude Lorrain, 1759–61. Oil on canvas, 59 x 79 in, 149.8 x 200.6 cm. NT 732157, *The Mill*, attributed to Andrea Locatelli, after Claude Lorrain, early-eighteenth century. Oil on canvas, 59 x 78 in, 149.9 x 198.1 cm.

31. *Peasants going to Market: Early Morning*, by Thomas Gainsborough RA. Purchased by Henry Hoare in 1773. Sold in 1883; formerly Royal Holloway and Bedford Colleges.
NT 732329 *Master Henry Hoare, as a boy gardening*, after Sir Joshua Reynolds PRA; copy commissioned by Asher Wertheimer after he bought the Stourhead original in 1883. The latter is now at Toledo Museum of Art, Ohio, object number 1955.31.
NT 732283 *Frances Anne Acland, Lady Hoare* (1735/6–1800), second wife of Sir Richard Hoare, 1st Bt, by Angelica Kauffman RA, c.1773.

32. Stourhead Library (shelfmark C.7.14), Sir Richard Colt Hoare, 'MS. History of Some of the Hoares 1724–1812'.

33. Clay 1994, pp. 127–8, the portions for both daughters and funding given to Lord Bruce. Hoare 1819, pp. 29–30, Sir Richard Colt Hoare recorded that Henry Hoare gave Susannah and 'her connections' £62,000.

34. WSA Ailesbury Estate Collection. Comprising over 100 letters from Henry Hoare to Lord Bruce, to Henry's daughter Susannah, Lady Bruce, and to Harriet Boyle, his grand-daughter.

35. Hoare 1819, p. 29.

36. WSA 383.907.2, William Hoare to Henry Hoare, 5 June 1760.

37. C. Hoare & Co. Partnership Ledgers HB/5/A/7, 1751–64 and HB/5/A/8, 1764–83, recording Henry Hoare's payments to William Hoare. What Henry Hoare purchased is often obscure. The 1784 Catalogue listed four 'pictures' and two drawings. The 1838 Inventory made four attributions. The Stourhead Inventory 1908 (pp. 152–3) included a collection of 22 pastel and crayon portraits and fancy pictures in the Little Dining Room, but most without attribution and some annotated 'from Wavendon'. Among these are 11 pastel portraits, in oval frames, which may have been bequeathed by William Hoare's son, Prince Hoare (1755–1834). See TNA, PROB 11/1842, will of Prince Hoare, 9 December 1831, 'I give and bequeath unto the said Sir Richard Colt Hoare of Stourhead in the County of Wilts Baronet […] all my family portraits painted in Crayon by my father and now hanging in my parlor in New Norfolk Street.'

38. NT 730729 *Stourhead Pleasure Grounds, Wiltshire, View to the Pantheon*, 1775, and NT 730732 *View to the Bristol Cross and Village*, 1775, both by Coplestone Warre Bampfylde.

39. WSA Ailesbury Estate Collection, Henry Hoare's letters record visits by these friends.

40. Ibid., 1300/2947, Henry Hoare to first Earl of Ailesbury, 7 August 1776, 'Mʳ Garrick has not his fellow for Private as well as Publick entertainment. He is active and strong & feelingly alive to each fine impulse. I have held both my sides with laughing till I can hold no longer. like Falstaff He is not only full of wit Himself but the cause of it in others, Mʳ Rust is animated by Him, & forgets he ever had the Gout.'

41. Ibid., 9/35/165/2353, Henry Hoare to Susannah, Lady Bruce, [no date] c.1765, 'We abound in Dingleys, Haslefoots & Hoare's & Brides & Bridegrooms every Room smells of Them.'

42. Ibid., 1300/2941, Henry Hoare to Lord Bruce, 6 May 1776, 'the Organ is kept going by the charming Musicians [grandchildren] alternatively & I believe They would be very happy in having just such an other at Tottenham Park for They like it wonderfully.'

43. WSRO Parham papers, bundle 2/2/2/6, letter 4/78, the Hon. Hester Hoare to Harriet Anne, Lady Bisshopp, Stourhead, Saturday [1783], 'on the right hand side is a Library in which I am now writing t'is a good room and has always an air of comfort owing to its books and to a Young Man being constantly painting in it, he is a protegé of Mr Hoares a self taught painter [presumably Samuel Woodforde]'. (By permission of Lady Emma Barnard and WSRO.)

44. Clay 1994, p. 116.

45. WSA 383. 912, account of the meeting between Henry Hoare, Richard Hoare and 'Fat Harry' Hoare (the author) describing discussions of the inheritance of Stourhead and the bank premises, 1783.

EIGHT
HENRY HOARE'S
'RICH FRAME OR PEDESTAL'
FOR THE SIXTUS CABINET

The National Trust's first guidebook for Stourhead attributed the Pedestal to Thomas Chippendale junior (1749–1822).[1] In fact it was commissioned by Henry Hoare in 1743, some 50 years earlier, and the carving is by John Boson. The error is understandable because the Pedestal is superbly designed and made and Chippendale's name is indissolubly linked with Regency Stourhead. The Pedestal was first described at the house in 1756 and, while it cannot command the reputation of the Sixtus Cabinet, its authority and refinement merit separate attention.

DESCRIPTION

The Pedestal complements, but does not compete with, the Cabinet. It is in the form of a quadriportal triumphal arch. The proportions are noble, the construction robust and the mahogany carving and veneering are of high quality. The carcase is oak.[2] Boson's carvings and relief panels were applied to the veneered carcase, then oil gilded. The façade centres on a large single arch extending from front to rear and intersected by an arch of similar proportions running between the sides. The front breaks forward in the centre to comply with the footprint of the Cabinet. The Cabinet was first displayed at Stourhead in what is today the Little Dining Room, on the wall opposite the windows behind a screen of columns (fig. 164).[3] Accordingly the Pedestal is ornamented at front and sides and, unlike a true quadriportal arch, its back is plain. The structure rests on a shallow unornamented podium, mahogany veneered, matching the superstructure. The side elevations of the Pedestal are decorated with carved double scallop shells at the apex of each arch and swags of leaves, flower-heads and partly open seed pods suspended at the outer corners from rosettes and terminating in vertical drops (fig. 179). Similar embellishments and architectural mouldings are found on designs by William Kent. His Prince of Wales's barge and Kensington Gardens seat make interesting comparisons, as does his temporary arch for the coronation of King George II (fig. 180).[4] However, there is no record in Henry Hoare's accounts of payments to Kent.

The façade of the Pedestal is in a different idiom. Three types of carving may be distinguished: the architectural mouldings, the relief carvings – both the profile portrait and monuments – and, finally, the statuettes. The *ensemble* constitutes an impressive manifesto for the Pope and his works. At the apex of the arch, in place of a keystone, is a carved and gilded medallion profile of Sixtus v triumphant supported by a pair of winged victories in high relief (that on the left with a wing-tip missing). The medallion disc is hollowed out at the back to allow for the egg and dart moulding around the archway. Below the victories, to the left and right of the arch, are miniature representations in high relief of the Antonine Column and the Vatican Obelisk (figs 185 and 183), each identified by inscriptions engraved on tiny gilt bronze plaques set into their bases. The Antonine Column is surmounted by a flame-like pine-cone which looks crude and may be a replacement.[5]

On the upper storey of the arch are four inset panels, with gilded highlights, enclosing relief carvings of monuments in Rome associated with the Pope. The sculptural detail on the reliefs is executed in gilded red wax. The reliefs are so fine as to be better described as models and can be identified from left to right:

- Fig. 187: *Mostra dell'acqua Felice* (also with an inscribed plaque)
- Fig. 188: Façade of *San Girolamo degli Schiavoni*
- Fig. 190: Façade of the *Scala Santa* at the Lateran Palace
- Fig. 189: The *tempietto* in the *Cappella Sistina* at Santa Maria Maggiore

Beneath the relief models are four round-headed niches, devoid of ornamentation but containing giltwood allegorical figures presumably representing the 'virtues' of the Pope, although these seem to lack Christian associations. Their hands and attributes have broken away, rendering iconographic analysis speculative, at best. From left to right:

FIG. 178
Pedestal for the Sixtus Cabinet, carvings by John Boson, structure by 'Mr James', 1742–3, mahogany veneered on oak carcase, partly gilded.
42½ x 52¾ x 35½ in, 108 x 134 x 90 cm. National Trust, Stourhead.

FIG. 179
Left side of Pedestal with applied gilded mahogany carvings. Side arch: 30¼ x 16½ in, 77 x 42 cm. Plinth: 6¼ in, 16 cm.

- Fig. 198: Female holding a viol and a chisel, with an artist's palette and sculpted head at her feet (the 'Arts'?)
- Fig. 199: Female wearing a helmet and breastplate, her left hand resting on a Medusa-head shield, her spear hand snapped away ('Minerva' as 'Wisdom'?)
- Fig. 200: Female with hands snapped at the wrists (henceforth 'Flora')
- Fig. 201: Female with a cornucopia ('Abundance'?)

Each figure is carved in the round and oil gilded. The backs of 'Flora' and 'Abundance' were pared down, before gilding, to fit the niches. Their bases are drilled to slot onto wooden pegs. 'Wisdom' is the odd one out. She is not robed, but dressed in armour and of smaller proportions than her companions, although equal in height, thanks to her plumed helmet. She stands on a rectangular base whereas the other bases have the rear corners chamfered to fit the niches. Her base is drilled with six locating holes whereas the others have a single slot. It is possible that she may have stood elsewhere, although she is evidently not a later addition given the uniform character of the gilding of the statuettes and their discernible 'family' resemblance: all have similar faces with prominent almond-shaped eyes and full cheeks tapering to pimple-like chins. Perhaps they were detachable for easy dusting. Would Henry Hoare have been content with miscellaneous allegoric figures? In 1766 he ordered a selection of lead sculpture with no single theme to fill the exterior niches on the Temple of Apollo at Stourhead.[6] But the Pantheon relief sculptures and furnishings follow a coherent programme of feasting, amorous and rural pursuits. The Pedestal self-evidently celebrates Sixtus v and the statuettes must have been intended to follow this theme.

COMPARISONS

The appearance of the sixteenth-century pedestal is unknown (see p. 103). During the seventeenth century Italian stands for tables and cabinets became heavily sculptural, often with human figures carved in the round; for example, the tables and two cabinet stands in the celebrated *Sala dei Paesaggi* at the Palazzo Colonna (fig. 69).[7] The parcel gilt wooden stand for Bernini's marble *San Lorenzo*, *c.*1617, in the Uffizi (Collezione Contini Bonacossi) is carved with faggots sprouting flames. Henry Hoare possessed figurative furniture, notably the pair of 'fox tables', *c.*1730, now in the Entrance Hall of Stourhead and Sefferin Alken's quaint setting for the silver-gilt *Cyrus and Tomyris* dish: an unusual confection of classical and fantastic motifs (fig. 169).[8] But when Henry came to pietre dure, he was architecturally minded. For his finest Florentine casket, he commissioned a marble stand from Benjamin Carter, 1759–60. Although casket and stand are no longer at Stourhead, Carter's estimate and Sir John Parnell's description, along with his sketch, demonstrate that it too was in the form of a quadriportal arch.[9] This was a ponderous object compared with the sprightly giltwood rococo stand, made *c.*1752 probably by William Vile, for a pietre dure casket at The Vyne (fig. 20).[10] In its architectural

FIG. 180
'The Triumphal Arch Erected and Painted on the West end of Westminster Hall for the Coronation of his Maj[ty] King George the Second and Queen Caroline October the 11th 1727' [detail], engraved by Paul Fourdrinier, after the design by William Kent. 14½ x 10½ in, 37 x 26.5 cm. The British Library.

FIG. 181
Rear of the Pedestal, the oak carcase visible.
Central arch: 30¼ x 18 in, 77 x 45.5 cm.

FIG. 182
'Del Arco di Giano Quadrifronte', engraved by Filippo Rossi, for his
Descrizione di Roma antica formata nuovamente ... , Rome, 1739, vol. I,
p. 288, 4 x 2⅞ in, 10.2 x 7.2 cm. This copy of *Descrizione di Roma* has
Henry Hoare's bookplate. The Arch of Janus on Via del Velabro, Rome,
was erected in the 4th century; the top storey was removed in 1827.
The British Library.

2 March 1742/3	Mr Boson for carving ye Frame & Figures &c on Dᵒ	£33-13
2 March 1742/3	Mr James for ye Mahogany Frame &c of Dᵒ	£29-16-6
24 June 1743	Mr Boson ye Carver's Exʳˢ in Full	£19

It is significant that John Boson charged for carving, not
cabinet work, and that the latter was entrusted to Mr James.
The Dictionary of English Furniture Makers has a three-column
entry on John Boson (*c.*1696–1743).[15] Vertue described
him as a 'carver in Wood a man of great ingenuity, and
undertook great works in his way for the prime people
of Quality & made his fortune, very well in the world'.[16]
Boson began his career carving chimney pieces and
woodwork for the new churches in London and later for
Westminster Abbey. His reputation growing, he worked for
Lord Burlington and Kent. In 1727–8 Boson carved crisp
stone capitals for the portico at Chiswick House and he
subsequently made furniture for the villa.[17] He also carved
(and signed) the marble tabernacle frame for the monument for Anne, Duchess of Richmond (d.1722), in St Peter's
Church, Deene, Northamptonshire (fig. 205).[18] From 1732
he was employed by the Prince of Wales at the royal palaces
of St James and Kew; in 1738 he received £10-15s for
carving a stern-board for the Prince's state barge.[19] Boson
is credited with 43 documented works of which perhaps
10 are traceable today. At St Giles House, Wimborne,
1740–3, he was under the supervision of Henry Flitcroft.
When Boson died in 1743 he was, judging from the Sixtus
Pedestal and Vertue's comment, at the height of his powers.

In 1735 Boson supplied the pair of 'owl' tables and
giltwood looking glasses designed by Kent for Lady
Burlington's rooms at Chiswick. The two tables cost £20
and are heavily embellished with carvings and gilt bronze
escutcheons and loop-handles. Now at Chatsworth, they are
dissimilar in style from the Sixtus Pedestal to an extent that
cannot be satisfactorily explained by the gap of seven years
between them. Different patrons and different functions
played as much a part in such stylistic variations as Boson's
own development, which is difficult to reconstruct.

Boson had worked for Henry Hoare on previous
occasions. He crops up in his building accounts between
1728 and 1733, when he was paid a total of £415 for
unspecified work.[20] Was this for Stourhead or London?
Henry's father built Stourhead and was in the course of
furnishing it when he died in 1724/5. He stipulated that
Henry should continue the work, so it is tempting to
associate Boson with Stourhead. But Boson received the first
payment in 1728, the year Henry remarried and renovated
no. 41 Lincoln's Inn Fields. The latter was destroyed in
1803 and at Stourhead the eighteenth-century woodwork
perished in the 1902 fire, so the puzzle remains.[21] Sir
Richard Hoare, 2nd Kt, Henry's brother, also employed
Boson. More is known about Sir Richard's patronage
because his bills survive. In 1738 he paid Boson £10-5-0 for
'Several Ornements as foliage festoons &c to a head board
foot board & sides of a bedsted done In Mahogany'.[22] It is
frustrating that this is the only Boson bill among the Hoare

CRAFTSMEN

The commissions for the repair of the Sixtus Cabinet and
construction of the Pedestal are recorded in Henry Hoare's
personal ledger:[13]

3 December 1742	Mr Mure for mending ye Fine Cabinet &c & for a Florence Box[14]	£15-15
2 March 1742/3	Mr Giles for cleaning ye Figures &c on yeCabinet	£3-12-6

austerity, the Sixtus Pedestal may be compared with wall
cabinets designed by Horace Walpole and William Kent
in 1743.[11] Walpole's cabinet, and its near twin the Brand
cabinet, are likewise architecture in miniature.[12] They are
resoundingly in the Palladian idiom and, like the Sixtus
Pedestal, clad in handsome wood veneers. Walpole's
cabinet has inset ivory plaques and is surmounted by small
ivory statuettes of Palladio or Rubens, Inigo Jones and
François Duquesnoy, all after Rysbrack. But the intentions
were different: Walpole fêted artists; Henry Hoare used his
Pedestal to vaunt the provenance of the Sixtus Cabinet.

papers and that the bed has vanished.

The architectural models on the Pedestal are so refined and faithful to the monuments that it might be suggested Henry Hoare commissioned these from a craftsman in Italy. He is unlikely to have had the foresight to bring them back from his visits in 1739–40, but he could have ordered them later through an agent when the Pedestal was being designed. However, neither models nor plaques are identifiable in Henry's accounts and the models are carved in the same mahogany (*mahogani swietenia*) as the portrait medallion, the statuettes and the two saints on the Cabinet.[23] Mahogany is a very English choice of wood at this date. Had the carvings been Italian, they would surely be in walnut; hence, they are attributed to Boson. The tiny engraved gilt bronze plaques with Latin inscriptions, which the eighteenth-century antiquarians found so exhilarating, could be English or Italian. They are pretty accurate to the monuments but do not tally precisely with a single published set of transcriptions. It would be curious for a London craftsman to go to more than one printed source, but the engraver, whether in London or Rome, may have used hand-written transcriptions taken from the monuments themselves.[24]

Inscriptions from the Pedestal:

VATICAN OBELISK

SIXTUS. V. PONT.MAX:
OBELISCUM VATICANUM
DIIS GENTIUM
IMPIO CULTU DICATUM
ADAPOSTOLORUM LIMINA
OPEROSO LABORE
TRANS TULIT
A·M·D·LXXXVI · PONT·I

Sixtus the Fifth, Supreme Pontiff,
by a toilsome labour transferred
to the threshold of the Apostles
the Vatican obelisk,
dedicated in unholy veneration
to the gods of the heathen,
in the year 1586, first [second] of his pontificate.

ANTONINE COLUMN

SIXTUS.V. PONT:MAX:
COLUMNAM HANC AB OMNI
IMPIETATE EXPURGATAM
S: PAULO APOSTOLO
AENEAEIVS STATUA
INAURATA IN SUMMO
VERTICE POSITA
DD A·MDLXXXIX·PONT·IV.

Sixtus the Fifth, Supreme Pontiff,
gave as a gift this column, purged
of all wickedness,
to Saint Paul, Apostle,
setting on its topmost summit
his statue in gilt bronze
in the year 1589, fourth of his pontificate

MOSTRA DELL'ACQUA FELICE

SIXTUS.V.PONT.MAX: PICENUS
AQUAM EX AGRO COLUMNÆ VIA
PRAENEST^A: SINISTRORSUM MULTARUM
COLLECTIONE VENARUM DUCTU SINVOSO
ARECEPTACULO MIL XX A CAPITE XXII
ADDUXIT FELICEMQ DE NOMINE ANTEPONT
DIXIT COEPIT PONTI ABSOLVT III.MDLXXXVII

Sixtus the Fifth, Supreme Pontiff, native of Ascoli Piceno,
by the gathering of many rivulets
brought water by a winding channel from the Colonna estate
to the left of the Via Praenestina,
twenty miles from the reservoir, twenty-two from its source,
and called it Felice from his name before his pontificate.
He began it in the first year of his pontificate and completed
it in the third, 1587.

If Boson is an ill-defined figure, James is obscure. A single mention of his Christian name occurs in Hoare's Bank Partnership Ledger, that Henry Hoare paid a 'Thos James the Joyner' in 1744/5.[25] Flitcroft named James in a letter to Henry Hoare and a 'Mr James' received a total of £402 for a variety of tasks at Stourhead and Lincoln's Inn Fields, 1742/3–50.[26] Of the 50 Jameses listed in the *Dictionary of English Furniture Makers* none is a convincing candidate. He cannot have been the architect John James (1672–1746).

DESIGN

Boson and Flitcroft moved in the same circles and the latter is an obvious candidate as designer of the Sixtus Pedestal. Flitcroft trained as a carpenter and was a protégé of Lord Burlington. He was closely associated with William Kent, whose drawings for *The Designs of Inigo Jones* he prepared for publication in 1727 and whom he succeeded as Master Mason and Deputy Surveyor in 1748. Flitcroft was an accomplished draughtsman and it would have been within his capability to provide a drawing for the Pedestal as a variant of a quadriportal arch, just as his Stourhead Pantheon is a sophisticated reworking of the Roman prototype. Three letters survive from Flitcroft to Henry Hoare. On 18 August 1744 he wrote, '[I] must desire Mr James to bring me ye measure of ye Spaces on Each Side ye window in your Lib^y that additional Book-cases may be Accomodated to them Suitable to ye other.'[27] This was written after the Pedestal was made and the earliest recorded payment Henry Hoare made to Flitcroft was in 1745. But the architect and Henry Hoare must have been acquainted before then, either through the bank or his Uncle Benjamin (see p. 126). Flitcroft could turn his hand to designing furniture. In 1741 he supplied drawings for tables at Ditchley Park.[28] His reredos for Saint Andrew's Church at Wimpole, 1748, is in an idiom comparable to the Sixtus Pedestal.[29] His letter to Henry Hoare, just quoted, indicates Flitcroft designed fitted furniture for Stourhead and surely the two lost 'Kentian' side tables for the Saloon must be his (fig. 176 table is visible on the far wall, to right of the doorway).

The sculptor Michael Rysbrack is another candidate for designing the Pedestal. His major commission for Henry Hoare came in 1747, but the two were acquainted in 1727 and became friends (p. 127). If Henry needed precedents for the Pedestal statuettes, Rysbrack would have been well placed to assist, both from his extensive collection of prints and engraved books and from his own drawings. Rysbrack understood architecture; he had worked with James Gibbs in the 1720s and later with Kent; he knew Flitcroft and supplied chimney pieces for Woburn Abbey. He was a proficient draughtsman for monuments in the manner of Kent; furthermore, the giltwood statuettes on the Pedestal are akin to Rysbrack's sculptures (see below).

ENGRAVED SOURCES

The idiosyncratic iconography of the Pedestal was almost certainly beyond either Rysbrack or Flitcroft, but this is more likely to have been devised by Henry Hoare himself, who must surely have chosen the monuments represented. There is a tantalizing reference in the *Catalogue of the Hoare Library*, compiled by J.B. Nichols, to 'Eighteen Prints of Views in Rome in a thin Portfolio'.[30] So Henry may have returned from the Continent with engravings relating to Sixtus v's monuments. Was the choice constrained by prints or drawings that he found? Why, for example, omit the dome of St Peter's, the Lateran Palace or the Palazzo Felice, all of which were Sixtus v's commissions and known from engravings? Was this in order to make room for the *tempietto*, the upper component of the tabernacle in the Cappella Sistina at Santa Maria Maggiore (fig. 118)? It was scarcely an obvious choice. But the *tempietto*, like the Sixtus Cabinet, is miniature architecture and again, like the Cabinet, it is embellished with pietre dure, gilt bronze mounts and statuettes.

Henry Hoare and Boson could have had access to relevant publications, whether from the London book trade, Lord Burlington or Rysbrack.[31] Boson himself subscribed to the English translation of *I quattro libri dell'architettura* by Alberti in 1726 and Isaac Ware's edition of the *Four Books of Andrea Palladio* in 1738. No record survives of Henry's library and the entire Stourhead book collection was sold in the 1880s. Nichols' *Catalogue* does not specify what had belonged to Henry Hoare, but he may reasonably be assumed to have owned the pre-1743 books occuring in the *Catalogue*, which are referred to below.[32]

Nichols listed Montfaucon's *L'Antiquité expliquée*, a work which Henry used, as a source for the plaster relief panels and temple furniture at Stourhead.[33] Henry probably derived the overall design of the Sixtus Pedestal from the Arch of Janus in Rome, which Montfaucon illustrated – in turn acknowledging his source as Lafréry. Filippo Rossi illustrated this arch in *Descrizione di Roma antica formata nuovamente*, a copy of which Sir Richard Colt Hoare presented to the British Museum and which has Henry Hoare's bookplate (fig. 182).[34]

All but one of the monuments represented by the model reliefs are associated with the architect and engineer Domenico Fontana (1543–1607), who was Sixtus v's 'chief executive' in his rapid transformation of Rome (see Chapter 4). In 1590 Fontana published *Della trasportatione dell'obelisco vaticano*, a long and copiously illustrated account of repositioning the Vatican obelisk, which also described buildings and monuments he designed or restored for Pope Sixtus v. It is the obvious source for the Pedestal models.[35] Figures 184, 191, 193 and 197 illustrate the plates in *Della trasportatione* that Boson may have used.

San Girolamo degli Schiavoni is absent because it was designed by Martino Longhi the Elder (d.1591); Pope Sixtus v was patron of the *Schiavoni*, the émigré Croatian community, and he rebuilt their church. There are two further pointers that *Della trasportatione* was not the exclusive source. Fontana included the *Scala Santa*, as plate 5, in his second volume (1604), showing it in elevation, with no roof, whereas the Pedestal model has a roof. And Fontana's transcribed inscriptions on the *Mostra dell'acqua Felice*, Vatican Obelisk and Antonine Column made errors not encountered in the Pedestal tablets.

Numerous guides and descriptions of Rome were published before 1743. Some have illustrations, ranging from crude woodcuts to accurate representations with sufficient detail for a model-maker. In the late sixteenth century Nicolas van Aelst had published large engravings of the Vatican Obelisk and Antonine Column (fig. 186).[36] *Della trasportatione* has full-page engravings of the *Mostra dell'acqua Felice* and the Santa Maria Maggiore tabernacle. Paolo degli Angeli also included a fine illustration of the latter in his monograph on the basilica.[37] In the second half of the seventeenth century G.B. Falda etched general views of the *Scala Santa* and of *San Girolamo degli Schiavoni* (fig. 194).[38] Joachim Sandrart engraved the façade of *San Girolamo* in 1690 (fig. 192).[39] This list demonstrates the wealth of sources available to Boson and the danger of assigning the design to a single publication.

ORIGINS OF THE FIGURATIVE CARVINGS

The portrait medallion of Pope Sixtus v on the Pedestal derives from the medal by Lorenzo Fragni (1538–1619) (fig. 196). If Henry Hoare had owned the medal he would surely have incorporated it, either on the Cabinet or Pedestal. Fragni's portrait was not illustrated in the standard source, Buonanni's *Numismata Pontificum Romanorum*.[40] But it was engraved in the eighteenth century for John Pine's *Tapestry Hangings of the House of Lords* (fig. 237) (see Appendix v, pp. 216–7).[41] Pine showed Sixtus v's portrait-profile reversed and acknowledged the owner, Thomas Sadler, who had premises close to Hoare's Bank.[42] Dr Richard Mead (1673–1754) also possessed a medal identifiable as Fragni's Sixtus v.[43] Henry Hoare and his brother Richard became governors of the Foundling Hospital in 1746, so Boson could have borrowed a medal from Mead or Sadler as a model for the carved version?[44] The medal is not rare; the British Museum has several versions, the finest struck in silver with the portrait on the *obverse*.[45]

The winged figures which hold the relief of Sixtus v probably derive from the genii or victories in the spandrels of triumphal arches, although similar figures are also

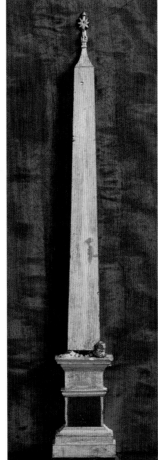

FIG. 183
Model of the Vatican Obelisk.
15 x 2⅛ x 1 in, 38 x 5.5 x 2.5 cm.
Caligula is reputed to have brought the
obelisk from Egypt to Rome in the first
century. Domenico Fontana moved it to
the Piazza San Pietro in 1586.

FAR RIGHT

FIG. 184
'La Guglia finita su la piazza con la fabrica
di San Pietro nel modo, che starà, quando
sara finità', engraved by Natale Bonifacio
da Sebenico, for Domenico Fontana, *Della
trasportatione dell' obelisco vaticano e delle
fabriche di Nostro Signore Papa Sisto .v.*,
Rome, 1590, pl. 35. 15⅜ x 9⅝ in,
39.3 x 24.5 cm. The British Library.

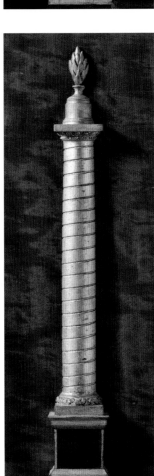

FIG. 185

Model of the Antonine Column.
15 x 2⅛ x 1 in, 38 x 5.5 x 2.5 cm. The
column was erected in the late second
century and restored by Pope Sixtus v.

FAR RIGHT

FIG. 186
'Columna Antonina', engraved by
Ambrogio Brambilla, published by Nicolas
van Aelst, 1589, in George III's 'extended'
copy of Antoine Lafréry, *Speculum Romanae
Magnicentiae*, Rome, 1528–1606, p. 71.
20¾ x 12½ in, 52.5 x 32 cm. Sixtus v placed
the bronze statue of St Paul on the top of
the column. The British Library.

FIG. 187
Inset panels on the Pedestal, 7½ x 5 x ¾ in, 19 x 12.7 x 2 cm.
Model of the *Mostra dell'acqua Felice*, by Domenico Fontana, 1585–7.

FIG. 188
Model of *San Girolamo degli Schiavoni*, by Martino Longhi the Elder, 1588.

FIG. 191

FIG. 192

FIG. 189
Model of the *tempietto* in the Cappella Sistina, Santa Maria Maggiore, by Domenico Fontana, *c.*1587.

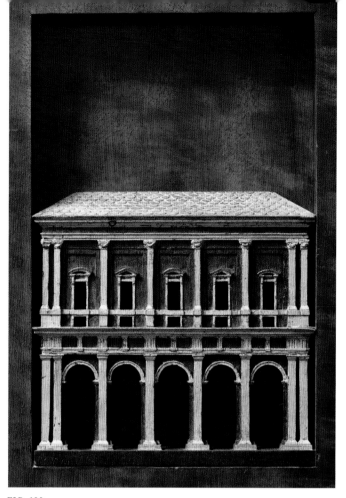

FIG. 190
Model of the *Scala Santa*, Lateran Palace, by Domenico Fontana, 1587.

FIG. 193

FIG. 194

LEFT TO RIGHT

FIG. 191
Mostra dell'acqua Felice [detail], from *Della trasportatione*, pl. 56. 15⅜ x 9⅝ in, 38.5 x 25 cm. The British Library.

FIG. 192
San Girolamo degli Schiavoni, engraved by Joachim von Sandrart, for his *Insignium Romae templorum prospectus exteriores et interiores*, Nuremberg, 1690, pl. 64, 12¾ x 9⅞ in, 33.8 x 25.3 cm. The Victoria & Albert Museum.

FIG. 193
Tempietto [detail], from 'Tabernacolo di metallo dorato', from *Della trasportatione*, pl. 107, 15¼ x 9⅞ in, 38.5 x 25 cm. The British Library.

FIG. 194
Scala Santa [detail], etched by Giovanni Battista Falda for his *terzo libro del' novo teatro delle chiese di Roma*, Rome, *c.*1669–70, pl. 8. 6½ x 11¼ in, 16.5 x 28.6 cm. The British Library.

FIG. 195
Gilded mahogany oval medallion of Pope Sixtus V.
5¾ x 5 x 1¼ in, 14.5 x 12.8 x 3.2 cm.

FIG. 196
Silver medal of Pope Sixtus V (*obverse*) by Lorenzo Fragni, 1585–6.
Diameter: 3 in, 3.75 cm. The British Museum.

found on the original base of the Antonine Column and on Roman sarcophagi (supporting portraits of the deceased). They may also be related to the pairs of angels flanking Papal coats of arms or the athletic pair from the frontispiece of *Della trasportatione.* Boson carved the angels and medallion from a single piece of mahogany. William Kent favoured similar sculptural flourishes: life-size muses recline on the principal door pediments inside the entrance halls at Houghton Hall and Ditchley Park and above the niche in the dining room at Benjamin Hoare's Boreham House.[46]

The standing female statuettes on the Pedestal are also part of an enduring vocabulary minted in classical times and common currency until the nineteenth century. If Henry intended the Pedestal statuettes to mimic the bronzes on top of the Cabinet, he failed. Indeed the Pedestal figures do not derive from Italian renaissance or mannerist sculpture. They belong, in execution if not intention, to the classical baroque tradition of Duquesnoy sustained by Van der Voort and Rysbrack. Louis XIV stocked the park at Versailles with a variety of statues, many after the antique and others in a classical mode by contemporary French sculptors. Thomassin's engravings of these included several illustrations that may have inspired Boson.[47] If they did, he interpreted them through English eyes. 'Abundance' could be based on the marble *Le Travail* at Versailles (fig. 204). The mutilated 'Flora' from the Pedestal ultimately derives from the famous *Farnese Flora* (fig. 203). John Cheere's *Minerva* at Southill, Bedfordshire (fig. 202), is close to the Pedestal 'Wisdom'.[48] Henry Hoare bought lead casts of classical statues from Cheere, including a *Minerva* (in a different pose) for Stourhead. The Stourhead statuette 'Arts' recalls the baroque lead muses ('Music', 'Poetry', 'Painting' and 'Sculpture') by John Nost or Andrew Carpenter, c.1710–30, versions of which are found today at Hardwick Hall and Anglesey Abbey.[49] The Pedestal statuette looks as if the four were compacted into a single figure, made to stand up straight, adopt a classical pose and become 'Arts' united. Indeed, if the Boson statuettes were enlarged, they could serve as models for garden sculpture or supporters in church monuments. Parallels to the Pedestal statuettes occur among Rysbrack's drawings, models and sculpture (fig. 151).[50]

CONCLUSION

Much of this account has been concerned with matters of detail, but the big, original, arguably brilliant, idea was to use a modified triumphal arch as the Pedestal for a heavy Roman cabinet. Again, it seems highly unlikely that this was due to Boson. Flitcroft or Rysbrack are the best candidates, but, as proposed earlier, it is more plausible to suggest that either could have served as the executant draughtsman of an idea supplied by the patron, Henry Hoare, and that he deserves the ultimate credit for a solution at once dignified, congruous and functional.

FIG. 197

The Antonine and Trajan Columns shown with the obelisk in the Piazza del Popolo, engraved by Natale Bonifacio da Sebenico, for Domenico Fontana, *Della trasportatione dell' obelisco vaticano e delle fabriche di Nostro Signore Papa Sisto.v.*, Rome, 1590, pl. 75. Approx. 21¼ x 17⅜ in, 54 x 45 cm. The British Library.

ABOVE: LEFT TO RIGHT
Niches: 11¼ x 5 x 2½ in, 28.5 x 12.7 x 6.4 cm.
Figures: Height 9 in, 23 cm.

FIG. 198
Gilded mahogany figure, 'The Arts'.

FIG. 199
Gilded mahogany figure, 'Wisdom'. In 1766 John Cheere sold Henry Hoare a comparable lead *Minerva*, with helmet but no shield and in a different pose. It now stands on the apex of the portico at Stourhead.

FIG. 200
Gilded mahogany figure, 'Flora'. This allegoric figure, derived from the *Farnese Flora*, could represent 'Peace' without the olive branch and as companion to 'Abundance'. Peace, however, is not an attribute readily associated with Pope Sixtus v.

FIG. 201
Gilded mahogany figure, 'Abundance'. In 1766 John Cheere sold Henry Hoare a comparable lead *Ceres*, with a cornucopia but in a different pose. It now stands on the portico at Stourhead.

FACING PAGE: LEFT TO RIGHT ▶

FIG. 202
Minerva, by John Cheere, lead, *c.*1750. Height *c.*60 in, *c.*160 cm. Southill Park, Bedfordshire.

FIG. 203
'Flora in Ædibus Farnesianis', etched by François Perrier for his *Segmenta nobilium signorum et statuaru*, Rome, 1638, pl. 62. 8¾ x 5¼ in, 22.2 x 13.5 cm. The British Library.

FIG. 204
'Le Travail, figure antique de marbre', engraved by Simon Thomassin, for his *Recueil des statues, groupes, fontaines termes, vases Et autres magnifiques Ornemens du Château & Parc de Versailles*, Paris, 1723, pl. 25. 5¾ x 3¾ in, 14.5 x 9.5 cm. The National Art Library, Victoria & Albert Museum.

FIG. 205
Monument to Anne, Duchess of Richmond, carved by John Boson, the bust by Giovanni Battista Guelfi, 1730. 187 x 92 x 11½ in, 475 x 234 x 29 cm. Bust height 40 in, 102 cm. St Peter's Church, Deene, Northamptonshire.

1. Lees-Milne 1948, p. 26.

2. Piper Pedestal Report 2008, p. 3, 'The pedestal [...] employs the very best materials, slow grown and fine-grained Baltic oak for the substrate and well figured mahogany veneers, the best broken "roe" figure of alternate contrasting light and dark streaks for the plinth and a more subtle "stop-mottle" for the superstructure. The plinth base-board, and the back and top of the superstructure are of panelled construction, the rest of the superstructure comprises of oak boards clad over framing in "cavity wall" fashion to accommodate the niches and inset architectural reliefs. All the oak boards in the superstructure are orientated vertically.'

3. Parnell 1769,* vol. II, f. 102.

4. Vardy 1744, pl. 38, 'A Seat in Kensington Gardens', 23.9 x 16.8 cm, and pl. 53, 'A Window in the Prince of Wales's Barge', 22.7 x 16.3 cm.

5. The name, *Colonna di Antonino Pio*, derives from a mistaken reading of the dedication, correctly addressed to Marcus Aurelius.

6. WSA 383.4.1, 'Henry Hoare Esqr Dr to Mr Cheere 1766', included, 'five Drapery Statues of yc Vestal Ceres Pomona Minerva & <u>Venus Belface</u> allmost naked [...] at 25 Guineas each'. Bill receipted 19 January 1767.

7. Safarik 2009, figs 259, 270 and 458.

8. See p. 147.

9. Jervis 2007, pp. 247–9. WSA 383.4.1, c.1759/60, Benjamin Carter, 'An Estimate of the Pedestal for to carry the Florence Box for Henry Hoare Esqr – To be Executed in Statuary, Genoa Green and Sienna Marble, with a Black Marble Plinth the Cornice, Imposts and Bases to be of Genoa Green the other parts Sienna and Statuary According to the design, the Front Ornaments to be a carv'd Rams head & festoons of fruit & flowers – Exclusive of the Vase [glass case] – About £50.' Henry Hoare Accounts 1749-70, 15 November 1760, 'Mr Carter for the Great Glass frame & Pedestal for Florence Box at Stourd in full of all Demds' £50-6-10.

10. Coleridge 1963, p. 215.

11. V&A w.52: 1, 2-1925. Cabinet for miniatures and enamels veneered in padouk wood on a pine carcase.

12. Christie's 2012, lot 5.

13. Henry Hoare Accounts 1734–49. Any balance on the total due to James for the Pedestal is not identifiable in subsequent payments to him.

14. Harris and Sons, 1935, p. 20, cites 'Hutcheson More', cabinet-maker from an unidentified newspaper advertisement in 1745. Might this be Stourhead's 'Mr Mure'?

15. Beard and Gilbert 1986, pp. 88–9; Roscoe 2009, pp. 123–6;. Weber 2013, pp. 170, 244–5, 290–1, 468–70, 506–7, 511–12, 561, 574.

16. Vertue 1934, p. 116.

17. Spence 1993, p. 526. Rosoman 1985, p. 676. Weber 2013, p. 507, figs 9.4 and 18.53.

18. Inscribed, 'Joannes Baptista Guelfi, Romanus fecit', '[Joan]nes Boson Anglus Sculpsit', 'Andreas Pallad[io] Vicentinus Invent'. Roscoe 2009, p. 124, bust by G.B. Guelfi. Total cost of monument £211 in 1734. Julius Bryant, 'Exempla Vertutis, Designs for Sculpture', Weber 2013, p. 574, the tabernacle is based on the frontispiece, dated 1730 (30 x 19.8 cm), drawn by Kent, for the third Earl of

Burlington's edition of Palladio c.1735–40.

19. Roscoe, p. 125 John Boson's bill, 1738, for ornaments for the state barge made for Frederick, Prince of Wales, including a carved taffrail or stern board (designed by William Kent) for £10-15-0, citing Duchy of Cornwall, vouchers book, vol. VIII, f. 253. Boson was paid six years after the main contract with the carver, James Richards.

20. C. Hoare & Co. Customer Ledgers, Henry Hoare Building Accounts, Lr/fol. 30/1, 30/303, 33/293.

21. Gomme and Norman 1912, p. 50.

22. NAL, 86.NN.3, Sir Richard Hoare, 2nd Kt, Tradesmen's Bills, no. 12.

23. Piper Pedestal Report 2008, p. 10.

24. The Pedestal engraver substituted 'U's for 'V's on the monuments. The inscription on the miniature Vatican obelisk occupies eight lines (seven on the monument), the third line reads DIIS (for 'DIS', on the monument) and the final line 'A·M·D·LXXXVI · PONT·I' (for 'ANNO M·D·LXXXVI PONT·II'); on the model Antonine Column the inscription occupies eight lines (nine lines on the monument) and unites 'AENEA EIVS' in a single word; on the model *Mostra dell'acqua Felice* the inscription occupies seven lines (on the monument, seven lines in the upper storey and one in the frieze) and the engraver rendered 'COLUMNÆ' (for 'COLUMNAE') and altered two abbreviations on the monument so that the third line reads 'PRAENESTᴬ' (for 'PRAENEST[INA]') and 'MVLTARVM' (for 'MVLTAR') and united 'A RECEPTACVLO' in a single word.

Fontana 1590, p. 36, on the Vatican Obelisk, Fontana transcribed DIIS (for 'DIS' on the monument), and abbreviated 'AN.' (for 'ANNO'); p. 99, on the Antonine Column, Fontana transcribed the papal year incorrectly as 'PONT. II.' (for 'PONT·IV'); pl. 56, from the frieze of the *Mostra dell'acqua Felice*, he omitted the date 'MDLXXXVII'.

Buonanni 1699, vol. 1, p. 398, transcribed the Antonine Column inscription on eight lines and omitted the word, 'OMNI' from the second line; p. 404, the *Mostra dell'acqua Felice* text was copied on nine lines making good the letter cutter's abbreviations with 'PRÆNESTINA', 'MVLTARVM' and 'FELICEMQVE' and misreading as 'MILL.XX. CAPITE XXIII' (for 'CAPITE XXII' on the monument) and 'M.DLXXXVIII.' (for 'MDLXXXVII').

Rossi 1739, vol. 1, p. 370, the Antonine Column inscription copied in nine lines with different punctuation and 'IMP ETATE' (for 'IMPIETATE' on the monument); p. 380, Vatican obelisk inscription copied on eight lines with different punctuation and 'DIIS' (for 'DIS') and the year 'PONT I' (for 'PONT II') – the two errors found in the engraved plaque on model.

Fontana 1590 and Bonanni 1699 are listed in Nichols 1840, respectively, pp. 607 and 601. Rossi 1739, the copy in the British Library (658.a.13), with Henry Hoare's book plate; and possibly referred to in Henry Hoare Accounts 1734–49, 20 January 1743/4, 'Chars Wray for Rossi's Statues' £2-18-0.

25. C. Hoare & Co. HB/5/A/5, Partnership Ledger 1742–51, Henry Hoare, 26 February 1744/5, 'Thos James the Joyner' £120.

26. Henry Hoare Accounts 1734–49 and 1749–70 record ten payments from 1742/3 to

1750 and totalling £402-0-6. Those to Mr James specifically for Stourhead and subsequent to the Pedestal: 20 June 1743, 'for yᵉ Stourhᵈ SkyLight 2 Vases &c in full' £31; 10 April 1744, 'on Accᵗ of work at Stourhᵈ' £50; 3 July 1745, 'for Work at Stourhᵈ & Lincoln Inn Fields &c in full of all Demands' 20-5-0.

27. WSA, 383.907.

28. Gomme 1989, citing Oxford Record Office, Dillon Papers, Dil 1/p/3a, 3b.

29. Adshead 2007, p. 45 citing the drawing, NT 206203. The reredos survives, adapted to accommodate windows.

30. Nichols 1840, p. 583.

31. Langford 1764, Rysbrack's book sale included, p. 6, 16 February, lot 52, 'Erecting of the Obelisk of the Vatican by *Fontana*' [Fontana 1590?]; lot 55, 'Templi Vaticani Historia [Buonanni 1696?]; 22 February, p.16, lot 60, 'Antonine ditto, [Column] *in ditto* [*red morocco*]'; 24 February, p. 20, lot 50, 'Triumphal Arches in Rome, by *Bartoli*'; 25 February, p. 22, lot 55, 'Montfaucon's *Antiquities* with the *Supplement*, 15 vol.'.

32. Page numbers in Nichols 1840 are given in the endnotes when these refer to books cited as sources for the Pedestal.

33. Dodd 2007, pp. 18–20.

34. Montfaucon 1719, vol. III, pt I, bk v, p. 178 and pl. XCIX; Rossi 1739,vol. I, p. 288 (British Library 658.a.13).

35. Fontana 1590. The second printing by Constantino Vitale at Naples in 1604, repeated plates from the first as *Libro Primo*, and added 18 new plates as *Libro Secondo*. Nichols 1840, p. 607 (1590 edn) and also in Rysbrack's library. See note 31.

36. Lafréry 1528–1606, George III's 'extended' *Speculum* (British Library MAPS 7 TAB.1).

37. degli Angeli 1621, pl. 170 (British Library 664.i.1 inscribed, 'Presented by Sir Richard Colt Hoare Barᵗ 1825').

38. Falda 1669–70, pls 8 and 38.

39. Sandrart 1690, pl. 64.

40. Buonanni 1699. Nichols 1840, p. 601.

41. Pine 1739, Charts IX and X. Nichols 1840, p. 290.

42. C. Hoare & Co. HB/10/A/2/22 , copy will dated 17 November 1716 of John Cox of Eltham, Kent, fishmonger, included the bequest of house on east corner of Salisbury Court fronting Fleet Street, formerly known as the White Lyon now in the possession of Mr Thomas Sadler, goldsmith. TNA Probate 11/933, will of Thomas Sadler, 'gentleman of Salisbury Court Fleet Street', 1767.

43. Langford 1755, Dr Mead's sale, 8th Day, 19 February 1755, p. 208, lot 49, included this medal, '*a* SIXTVS V. PONT.MAX. *b* NE DETERIVS VOBIS CONTINGAT'. Toderi 1998–2000, vol. II, pp. 742–3, and illustrated, vol. III, table 435, medal no. 2333, by Fragni, 34.5 mm, with both inscriptions and, on the *obverse*, the profile bust of Sixtus V.

44. Nichols and Wray 1935, p. 358.

45. British Museum M.1428. Attwood 2003, vol. I, p. 407 and fig. 107.

46. Fell-Smith 1914 , pp. 54–60. Boreham House was built in 1720s by Benjamin Hoare and sold by his descendant in 1789. C. Hoare & Co. HB/5/A/4, Partnership Ledger 1725–34, Benjamin Hoare paid 'James Dryhurst Carver' 31 December 1729 – 22 July 1731 £167,

presumably for Boreham. Boson is not mentioned in this account.

47. Thomassin 1723. Langford 1764, Rysbrack's book sale included, 22 February, p.16, lot 54, 'Figures and Groups &c. at Versailles', which is presumably an edition of Thomassin.

48. Roscoe 2009, pp. 263 and 267.

49. Hardwick Hall, Derbyshire NT 1129355.1 (Poetry), NT 1129356.1 (Music), NT 1129357.1 (Painting), NT 1129360.1 (Sculpture). Anglesey Abbey, Cambridgeshire NT 515148 (Sculpture) and NT 515149 (Painting); both from the Temple of Concord and Victory at Stowe, Buckinghamshire.

50. Clifford 2010, pp. 116–18. Figs 6–7 illustrate a pair of pearlware figures of *Prudence* and *Fortitude* by Enoch Wood, Burslem, c.1790, H 53.5cm. Fitzwilliam Museum, Cambridge (no. C.902A & B–1928). Clifford points out their resemblance to a pair of terracotta figures, signed by Rysbrack and dated 1743, the models for his failed commission for the monument to the second Duke of Argyll.

NINE

SIR RICHARD COLT HOARE AND THE SECOND CABINET ROOM

Sir Richard Colt Hoare, 2nd Bt (1758–1838) (fig. 206) celebrated the Sixtus Cabinet, moving it to a room adjacent to his new Picture Gallery and embellishing it with a sumptuous carved and gilded frame from which hung a gold-fringed, blue velvet curtain. He used superlatives sparingly but described the Sixtus Cabinet as 'very splendid' and 'this exquisite piece of workmanship'.[1] He surrounded it with his finest landscape paintings. Yet in the guidebook he omitted the convent provenance, perhaps because he himself was ignorant or sceptical of the story. Sir Richard placed the pietre dure casket, another prized possession of Henry Hoare, in the Saloon. John Buckler depicted it in a prime position under the central window on the axis of the house (fig. 212). He moved the lesser pietre dure pieces (Appendix VI) out of the state rooms, probably because he wished to distil the best from his grandfather's collection. He may have had an ulterior motive; pietre dure was a symbol of wealth, collected by the likes of William Beckford and the Prince Regent. Sir Richard did not consider himself a rich man and he shunned extravagance. Pietre dure, porphyry and precious marbles were not on his continental shopping list (the polychrome marble monument to his wife in Stourton Church is the elegant exception). It is time to consider the singular career of Sir Richard Colt Hoare.

He was born on 9 December 1758; his father was Richard Hoare, the nephew of Henry Hoare. His mother, Anne, was the latter's younger daughter. Anne died the following year and Richard remarried. Throughout his life, Richard Colt Hoare got on well with his step-mother and four step-brothers but between father and son there was rivalry that neither could entirely put aside, because they were both potential heirs to Henry Hoare. Young Richard joined the bank and rented a house in Lincoln's Inn Fields. In 1783 he married The Hon. Hester Lyttelton. When Henry Hoare learned of their betrothal, he handed over Stourhead to him on the condition that he quit the bank. Richard Colt Hoare had reached the hinge in his life. Looking back on the event, in his seventieth year, he recalled with some bitterness:

By the persuasion of my Uncle ['Fat Harry' Hoare], my gran^dfather [Henry Hoare] made a new will, by which he excluded <u>me</u> (his rightful heir) from any concern in the banking house; for in his <u>former</u> will he had made me a principal in it [...] Had the 'auri sacra fames' been my ruling passion, this event would have been a severe mortification: and if I had been imprudent in engaging in a <u>second</u> marriage, & had a large family like two of my brothers, I should have been the poorest man of my family.[2]

The year 1785 was equally fateful for the Hoares. In August Hester died at Stourhead shortly after the birth of her second son. On 8 September Henry Hoare expired at Clapham and on the last day of the month Hester's newborn son was buried. Richard Colt Hoare deserted his surviving son, Henry, and departed, with a friend, for the Continent. Apart from a brief interlude in England in 1787–8, which coincided with his father's death, he lived abroad until 1791. For the most part he travelled in Italy.

Sir Richard, who inherited the baronetcy at the death of his father, financed his travels from the Stourhead income and a bank loan.[3] He shopped for books assiduously, purchasing guides, histories and art historical works. In Venice he had the good fortune to acquire ten drawings from the *Dodici Solennità Dogali*, by Canaletto (sold in 1883).[4] The majority of his old master paintings he purchased between 1788 and 1791, among them a masterpiece, *The Adoration of the Magi* by Cigoli (fig. 207).[5] He also commissioned small marble and alabaster vases and statuettes from the Florentine sculptor Pietro Pisani, but he bought no antique sculpture.[6] The artist Samuel Woodforde accompanied Sir Richard for some of the time abroad.[7] Sir Richard himself was a competent draughtsman; he hired topographical artists to record his travels, notably Philip Hackert and Carlo Labruzzi, and he bought watercolours from Abraham Louis Ducros.

These years were a chrysalis time for Sir Richard: he left England as a widower and a banker deprived of his trade,

FIG. 206
Sir Richard Colt Hoare, 2nd Bt with his son Henry, by Samuel Woodforde, R.A, 1795–6. Oil on canvas, 100 x 66 in, 254 x 167.6 cm.
The artist, a protégé of the Hoare family, was resolved to excel in this portrait. Sir Richard, then in his late thirties, cuts a tall and graceful figure with pale aesthetic features. He grasps a drawing in one hand, a portfolio in the other and he pays no attention to his eleven-year-old son, Henry, tugging at his arm. The psychology is accurate; Woodforde's intimate knowledge of his patron paid off. National Trust, Stourhead.

FIG. 207
The Adoration of the Magi, by Lodovico Cardi, 'Cigoli', signed and dated 1605. Oil on canvas, 136 x 92 in, 345.4 x 233.7 cm.
Sir Richard Colt Hoare purchased the painting in 1790 from the Albizzi Chapel in recently demolished San Pier Maggiore,
Florence. National Trust, Stourhead.

he returned fully plumed as an artist, a scholar and an *arbiter elegantiae*.[8] The transformation was not total: he retained a banker's ability to write in a legible hand, to log his expenditure and to file bills. Throughout his life Sir Richard was a champion compiler. He published four volumes of his travel journals.[9] Even in manuscript these are dry, sparing both in his enthusiasms and his prejudices. His prose, except to his immediate family, was not a window on the inner man; it was a shutter to his soul.

Sir Richard returned to England on 30 July 1791. He had taken ample time to ponder his lot: he possessed Stourhead to enjoy, to maintain and to pass on. The annual rent-roll was above £10,000,[10] an income which he considered inadequate, or at least precluding extravagance. He was fortunate to have an heir, no romantic attachments and to have a range of interests – the word 'pastime' does not fit the man – that he would develop. He was perhaps too purposeful. At Stourhead he began a planting regime that transformed his grandfather's pleasure grounds with a wide variety of new species, notably the *Rhododendron ponticum*. He collected geraniums and, by 1821, he was an authority, owning 600 varieties.[11] His taste was austere. In the garden, Henry Hoare had happily mingled the classical, baroque, Chinese, Turkish, Gothic and Gothick styles. Sir Richard preferred the Roman and Gothic and he expunged these other delectable touches. And, as will be shown, he transformed the house.

When the Continent became too dangerous for gentlemen-travellers, Sir Richard set about exploring Britain. Wales in particular caught his imagination. He relished sketching the scenery, he was attracted by the ancient history and by the obscurity it had hitherto enjoyed. In 1796 he stayed at Lake Bala for the summer and liked the spot so much that he later built a villa, 'Fach Ddeilliog' ['Leafy Nook'], on the lake shore and visited each summer.[12]

The first decade of the new century found Sir Richard fully occupied. He was a Justice of the Peace and served as High Sheriff of Wiltshire in 1805. He met neighbours interested in local archaeology, which he took up with such enthusiasm that by 1806 he could assume responsibility for writing up their findings and theories. The result was *The Ancient History of Wiltshire*, published in three magnificent volumes between 1812 and 1821.

At the beginning of each year Sir Richard went to London, either staying with his stepmother or at Miller's Hotel in Jermyn Street.[13] In 1792 he was elected to the Society of Dilettanti and the Society of Antiquaries. When the British Institution was founded in 1805 to exhibit British painters, Sir Richard became a member and purchased their pictures.

During the years 1810–20 Sir Richard followed a similar pattern: regular winter visits to London, summers in Wales and the intervening months in Wiltshire to fulfil his responsibilities as landowner. He became a prolific author, publishing *A Tour through the Isle of Elba in 1789* (1814), *A Journal of the Shrievalty of Richard Hoare Esquire, in the years 1740–1* (1815), *Hints to Travellers in Italy* (1815), *Recollections Abroad* (four volumes, 1815–18) and *Pedigree and Memoirs of the Families of Hore* (1819).[14] He enjoyed seeing his own

FIG. 208
Sir Richard Colt Hoare, 2nd Bt, by Stephen Catterson Smith, *c.*1830. Chalk on paper, 7¼ x 5 ½ in, 18.5 x 14 cm. National Trust, Stourhead.

words in print; indeed publishing himself was perhaps his sole indulgence. He took on an ambitious project to record the history and topography of his county since Roman times. It was to become the *The Modern History of South Wiltshire*, compiled in lapidary rather than Augustan prose. This was the decade of the celebrated Stourhead gatherings: a week every winter when Sir Richard played host to topographers and historians along with men from the new class of professional archivists. The purpose was ostensibly to enjoy Stourhead and use the Library. At these sessions Sir Richard would coax his guests into writing for *Modern Wiltshire*.[15]

At the age of 70 Sir Richard was failing physically. A life-long martyr to gout, he found travel exacting (fig. 208). In 1829 he made a final visit to London.[16] Thereafter, he journeyed to Bath for the mineral water or to Weymouth for a salt-water cure.[17] He was as assiduous about his ill-health as his literary pursuits. His waking hours were occupied writing and editing contributions to *Modern Wiltshire*. The lamp-lit ritual of proofreading became a religion.

In 1836 Sir Richard's son, Henry, died, aged 52, leaving behind a broken marriage, a daughter and creditors who badgered Sir Richard.[18] Henry had proved a disappointment in every respect. His character and temperament were the opposite of his rock-steady father; he was unreliable, work-shy, pleasure-seeking and timidly extravagant. Although Sir Richard cannot have been an easy father, the distance between the two is chilling. Sir Richard made no mention of Henry's demise in the *Stourhead Annals*, where, the previous year, he had recorded the death of his man-servant.[19]

FIG. 209
'South West View of Stourhead, Wilts, July 1811', by John Buckler, pencil, 10¼ x 14⅜ in, 26 x 36.5 cm. Note the west façade with triangular pediment designed by Henry Flitcroft, 1743–4; the Skylight Room is on the extreme left. The British Library.

Henry has a memorial in Stourton Church; it is a brass plaque placed, *by his daughter*, beside the family pew. Under Sir Richard's will, his half-brother, Henry Hugh, would now inherit Stourhead.[20] Henry Hugh was a partner in the family bank and so Sir Richard's wish was fulfilled:

> that the time may come when the streams of the Stour, may be added once more to those that flow from the Golden Barrell – for the experience of forty years has proved to me that all the landed property attached to the owner of Stourhead, will not, of itself maintain a large family, & keep the place in that order which it merits.[21]

THE REGENCY HOUSE

When Sir Richard returned from the Continent in 1791 he settled at Stourhead as his principal residence. The villa, adequate for his grandfather's summer seasons, was crowded with pictures, his private and state rooms intermingled and the upstairs was decrepit.[22] To resolve this he built large pavilions on each side of the house, one for his library, the other for the picture collection (fig. 210).

Sir Richard was a competent draughtsman and probably acted as his own architect with the builders, Moulton & Atkinson, from Salisbury. The shells were completed in 1794 at the cost of £3,466-1-0. He also renovated his own apartment, the service quarters in the basement and built a peach house and vinery, which added £2,000.[23] Then came a pause of five or six years – Sir Richard was busy planting on a ducal scale in the garden and woods.[24] Indeed he ran short of money.[25] In 1800 he set to again and spent a further £3,800 on building work and £5,000 on furnishings.[26] These amounts tally with comparable improvements elsewhere. Sir John Soane's alterations to Port Eliot, 1804–9, cost just over £6,000. His more extensive interventions at Wimpole Hall, 1791–5, totalled almost £18,000.[27] Nash's top-lit picture gallery at Attingham Park amounted to £13,000.[28] Building a new house was a more expensive undertaking, although few competed with William Beckford, who paid £270,000 for Fonthill Abbey.[29]

'Tactful' is the apt description of Sir Richard's east façade. Would the first architects of Regency Britain – Holland, Soane or Nash – have handled the new work with *quite* such reticence?[30] Moving to the south front, Sir Richard's projecting Library wing inevitably destroyed the symmetry of Campbell's garden façade (fig. 209). Flitcroft's west front endured until it was clumsily rebuilt in 1903.

Sir Richard transformed the *piano nobile* of Stourhead. The new Library and Gallery form an *enfilade* along the entire east front. He placed the Sixtus Cabinet in the former Library or Study. Writing in 1807 Richard Fenton described how the house was arranged,

FIG. 210
'North East View of Stourhead House', by John Buckler, signed and dated 1817, watercolour, 6 x 9¼ in, 15.3 x 23.4 cm. The Regency Picture Gallery is in the foreground, the Library on the far left and Henry Hoare's Skylight Room on the extreme right. National Trust, Stourhead.

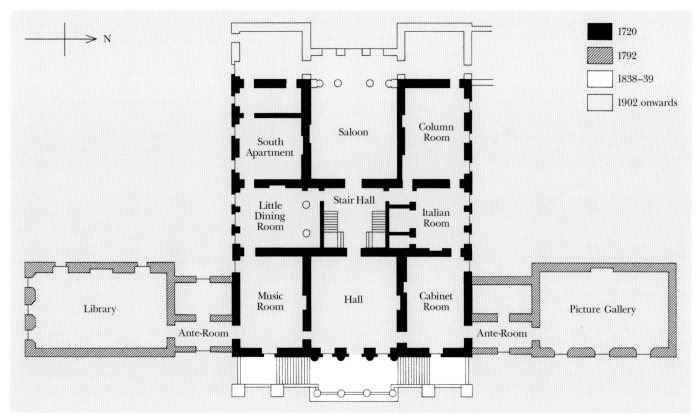

FIG. 211
Plan of the *piano nobile* of Stourhead.

FIG. 212
The Saloon at Stourhead, by John Buckler, 1824. Pencil, ink and watercolour, 10⅜ x 14 in, 26.5 x 35.5 cm. In the centre window stands the pietre dure casket which Henry Hoare prized (see p. 147). The British Library.

FIG. 213
The Library at Stourhead, by John Buckler, 1811. Pencil, ink and watercolour, 10¼ x 14⅜ in, 26 x 36.5 cm. The British Library.

To avoid the inconvenience of a show-house, so that the family might not be liable to intrusion, or the visitors to disappointment, it has been divided into two compartments, separated, as it were, by the entrance hall and staircase. The division to the right [of the Hall], dedicated to show and the public, contains all the most valuable original pictures &c. &c. [Cabinet Room, Picture Gallery and ante room]; that on the left, dedicated to study, convenience, and domestic comfort, contains only the inferior pictures [Music Room, Library and Little Dining Room].[31]

Sir Richard modified this arrangement in the following years. By 1815 he had acquired sufficient pictures by living British artists to oust the lesser old masters from the Music Room.[32] He then dedicated the room to the display of contemporary paintings.[33]

The best old masters were destined for the new Picture Gallery (fig. 214). Here Sir Richard could have followed the precedent of the Skylight Room and top-lit the paintings. Such galleries were becoming fashionable, but he built the Gallery with an upper register of three east-facing 'clerestory' windows with tall windows below. Sidelighting was considered preferable for small cabinet paintings hung low, so, arguably, he achieved the optimum conditions for the collection.[34]

The new Library represents the essence of Sir Richard (fig. 213). Despite the loss of his books, it looks like a place of learning worthy of the *School of Athens* depicted in the stained-glass lunette. This window and the painted lunette of *Parnassus*, both designed by Samuel Woodforde, were reminders of Sir Richard's studies in Italy. Above the chimney piece were arranged the ten Canaletto drawings and a portrait of *Pietro Landi, Doge of Venice* (all sold in 1883). The sphinx-head chairs and tables may have been inspired by French furniture of the late 1790s and also by Sir Richard's recollection of the Egyptian Room at the Villa Borghese. Nevertheless, the Library is overwhelmingly

British, opulent with gold-embossed book spines, sober in the plain mahogany furniture by Thomas Chippendale junior.

The east–west axis, the central spine of Stourhead, had a different character. In the Entrance Hall Sir Richard marshalled family portraits. He wrote,

They remind us of the genealogy of our families, and recall to our minds the hospitality, &c. of its former inhabitants, and on the first entrance of the friend, or stranger, seem to greet them with a SALVE, or welcome.[35]

Passing through the Stair Hall 'allotted to pictures of the second class', the guest entered the Saloon, the showpiece of Henry Hoare.[36] In homage to his grandfather, Sir Richard laid a light hand on this great room.

He was able to reclaim the *piano nobile* bedrooms for his own use. He took the north side for himself, sleeping in what is now the Italian Room, using the adjoining Column Room as a sitting room and spreading beyond into the former Skylight Room. Joseph Hunter described this den in the 1820s:

Sir Richard usually breakfasted in his own apartments, where he occasionally admitted one or two of his guests, when he was seen with his tables and the floor strewed with books, manuscripts, and loose papers, engravings, seals, charters and all the other paraphernalia of the antiquarian student, with abundance of copy, and proof-sheets, and fragments of his own work, on which he wrought daily with great assiduity.[37]

On the south side, Sir Richard, having removed the Sixtus Cabinet, created a private dining room (fig. 164). It opened into the South Apartment and small adjoining room. Sir Richard gave these over to his son until he married and moved away in 1808, when Sir Richard converted the rooms into a much-needed overflow for the Library. Henceforth,

FIG. 214
The Picture Gallery as redecorated in 1994. Satinwood furniture by Thomas Chippendale junior.

FIG. 215
'The Entrance Hall Stourhead. This photo was taken on the Day of the fire; On Wednesday April 16th 1902.' National Trust, Stourhead.

he moulded Stourhead ever more closely to his needs.

The walls of the private apartments were close-hung with the pictures which Sir Richard most appreciated. It is hard today to admire the mass of gold-framed bistre drawings (48 are listed in *Modern Wiltshire*) by Jacob Seydelmann of Dresden (1750–1829) and James Rouby (1750–1812) depicting details from Sir Richard's favourite Italian paintings. His 13 large watercolours by the Swiss watercolourist, Abraham Louis Ducros (1748–1810), offer something more dramatic. Of greater importance were eight watercolours of Salisbury Cathedral by Turner. This combination of old master details and topography lent a didactic flavour to the private rooms.

To furnish Stourhead Sir Richard returned to Thomas Chippendale junior whom he had engaged in 1779 to equip his house in Lincoln's Inn Fields.[38] The furniture that Chippendale supplied is renowned for its originality of design and the excellence of its craftsmanship. Sir Richard's letters to Chippendale do not survive, so there is no way of telling who was the innovator. Sir Richard chose plain mahogany for the south side and satinwood for the 'public' rooms. He continued his grandfather's practice of commissioning top-quality gilded picture frames so that the close-hung walls would have sparkled. Chippendale supplied gilded curtain cornices and looking-glass frames. In terms of swagger the Gallery marked the climax to the house but, even there, only the frames, window cornices and three candelabra pedestals were gilded. The preference for plain wood at Stourhead is comparable to Chippendale's furniture for Paxton House, Berwick-upon-Tweed.[39] At the opposite end of this spectrum stood the magnificence of Harewood, Yorkshire, where Chippendale senior and junior supplied giltwood furniture *in excelsis*. As always cost was a crucial factor.

There is little evidence of the Regency colour schemes beyond the watercolours of the interiors already referred to. The Little Dining Room had red walls, the Library, green and the Saloon, pale blue. In the bills, Chippendale described the curtains and upholstery in some detail but none survive. The Gallery had yellow and black textiles, the Cabinet Room, blue and black, the Music Room and Saloon, blue curtains with crimson linings. The rooms along the main enfilade are quintessential Regency and collegiate in feeling, reminiscent of a gentleman's club. There was neither a drawing-room nor a boudoir at Stourhead. However, the *piano nobile* was enlivened by pot plants and flowers arranged in nine large jardinières that Chippendale made for the window embrasures.

THE NEW CABINET ROOM

Sir Richard would recognize the Cabinet Room today despite certain fundamental changes in the aftermath of the 1902 fire (fig. 215). He might have christened it the 'Landscape Room' because here he gathered together his finest landscape paintings.

In the eighteenth century English collectors set aside rooms for landscapes, a notable survival being the Landscape Room at Holkham Hall, Norfolk. Badminton in 1800 provides a particularly close parallel; in the North Breakfast Room the fifth Duke of Beaufort surrounded his uncle's great Grand Tour trophy, the Badminton Cabinet, with landscape paintings.[40] The concept derived from Italy when, in Renaissance times, rooms in grand houses were decorated with frescoed landscapes. In Rome Sir Richard – and probably Henry Hoare – visited the Palazzo Doria Pamphilj and saw the Landscape Room filled with huge paintings by Gaspard Poussin. The *Sala dei Paesaggi* at the Palazzo Colonna was given over to seventeenth-century landscapes, as the name implies.[41] And it was here that the two celebrated Colonna cabinets, one ebony and pietre dure, the other with ivory, stood.[42] Thus Sir Richard had both Italian and English precedents for combining landscape paintings with the Sixtus Cabinet.

FIG. 216
'The "Cabinet" Room Stourhead Wilts (June 1900)'. Note the giltwood 'cornice' by Thomas Chippendale junior surrounding the cabinet-niche. National Trust, Stourhead.

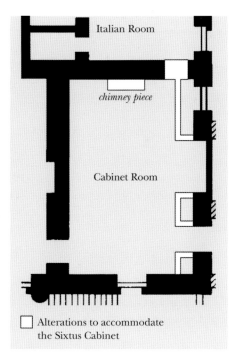

FIG. 217
Ground plan showing the configuration of Cabinet Room in 1802–1902.

While his selection of pictures had a unified theme, he could have further restricted the choice to landscapes in the manner of Poussin and Claude by introducing the versions that Wootton had sold to his grandfather. But these he relegated to the Stair Hall. Instead he combined different styles and schools in the Cabinet Room, hanging copies of Claude alongside eighteenth-century pictures by Zuccarelli and Vernet and the British artists Marlow and Wilson. By 1822 Gainsborough's *Peasants going to Market: Early Morning* held place of honour above the chimney piece where it usurped an overmantel glass.[43] In 1815 Sir Richard added *The Lake of Avernus*, which he commissioned Turner to paint after a drawing he himself had made in Italy.[44] The finest landscapes in the room (17 out of the 30) were sold in 1883.[45]

Before the fire, the Cabinet Room was configured differently and this is apparent in the 1900 photograph (fig. 216). Sir Richard's building accounts for 1801 indicate there was an inner wall along the north side, blocking the door to the Italian Room and masking the three north-facing windows (fig. 217).[46] The first window was covered in; the middle became the niche for the Cabinet; the third, the doorway to the Gallery ante room. After the 1902 fire Sir Richard's false wall was removed and the door to the Italian

FIG. 218
The Cabinet Room in 2013, looking towards the Picture Gallery.

Room reinstated, as was the blind north-facing window. The niche became shallower, so that the Sixtus Cabinet projects about half a metre into the room. Sir Richard's fireplace was on the west wall; after 1902 a new chimney piece was placed on the south side. The original doors were painted deal; Sir Richard had reserved mahogany for the double doors to the Gallery and Library.[47] All doors on the *piano nobile* were replaced in solid mahogany after the fire.

It may seem curious that Sir Richard did not place the Sixtus Cabinet on the south wall where it would face visitors entering from the ante room and they would have been able to inspect its front and sides. There are several possible explanations. His house-guests would have entered from the Hall and met the Cabinet head-on. He may have borrowed the idea of sheltering it in a deep niche from the *Tribuna* of the Uffizi. The Ferdinando I de' Medici cabinet was dismantled in 1780 but its appearance and setting were well known from descriptions and drawings; it is conspicuous in the background of the famous conversation piece with Sir Andrew Fountaine (fig. 219).[48] The 1838 inventory of the Cabinet Room lists a hand-mirror, plausibly to allow visitors to inspect the sides of the Cabinet or to direct light onto it.[49] Sir Richard had a penchant for

recesses. In the Library, Rysbrack's busts of Milton are set in oval niches. He placed bookcases in the embrasures in the North and South Apartments.[50] It is possible that the curious remodelling of the handsome English eighteenth-century marquetry commode (now in the Saloon) resulted from its position in the centre window embrasure of the Column Room.[51] Chippendale supplied a dressing table specifically made 'to fit into the recess of a Window'.[52]

Sir Richard gave no description of the Cabinet Room furnishings in either his guidebook or *Modern Wiltshire*. Knowledge of its contents comes from Chippendale's bills and from the inventory compiled at his death in 1838 (see Appendix II, p. 204). The giltwood frame, or 'cornice', which Chippendale made to encompass the niche perished in the 1902 fire but is visible in the early photographs (figs 216 and 235). Chippendale described

> A large Circular Lath with Cornice Richly carved and finished in Bumishd Gold with the Popes tiara and other insignias. 2 quilld Columns and pedestals to ditto. Gilt in Burnishd Gold and Iron fastenings &c £27-10-0.
>
> Silk oes thread and time Making a blue Velvet drapery Curtain for the Nich with gold fringe and tassells lined with blue sarsnet £2.[53]

FIG. 219
Sir Andrew Flountaine and Friends in the Tribune, by Giulio Pignatta, 1715. Oil on canvas, 57⅛ x 46⅞ in, 145.5 x 119 cm. In the background stands the mighty pietre dure cabinet of Ferdinando I de' Medici draped in a blue-green cloth. It was dismantled *c*.1780. Private collection. Norwich Castle Museum & Art Gallery.

He also supplied '28⅜ Yards of Rich blue Velvet' at 16 shillings per yard lined with '25¼ Yards of blue Sarsnet' at 6s. 6d. per yard. Sir Richard must have purchased the fringe and tassels himself because Chippendale did not invoice for them. In round terms the latter charged £61 for the Cabinet curtain and cornice and £78 for the window curtain and cornice for the Cabinet Room.

Chippendale made satinwood furniture with ebony inlay, including eight dazzlingly elegant and original armchairs which remain in the room. He also supplied two companion bergères, a pair of pole screens and, in 1804, two satinwood gout stools covered in red morocco leather. These pieces survive but his 'sarcophagus' jardinière is missing.[54] The 1838 inventory lists more furniture, some found in other Chippendale bills but not designated for the Cabinet Room, notably a large mahogany oval table which he made in 1801. The satinwood card table and Pembroke table may have come from the drawing-room of the house in Lincoln's Inn Fields which Chippendale had furnished in 1779–80.[55]

Chippendale was willing to adapt pieces and renovate them. The tall pier glass in the Cabinet Room is an example. It was described in 1838 as,

A magnificent Pier Glass with Tablet over plate 7 feet 2 inches high 4 feet 8½ inches wide in two compartments and in good condition.[56]

Chippendale specified how, in 1802, its frame was fluted to match his papal 'Cornice'.[57] A looking glass of this size would be a dominant feature in the room. It must have hung on the south wall and faced the Sixtus Cabinet so that its reflection would greet visitors entering from the ante room. It probably perished in the 1902 fire. Immediately preceding the pier glass in the 1838 inventory is 'A half circular Commode under Pier Glass'. This general description precludes certain identification, but this is probably the fine elliptical commode of satinwood now in the Picture Gallery (fig. 220).[58] It was made in the early 1780s and, although no bill survives, the commode is stylistically attributable to Chippendale junior. It is unequivocally, if comically, described in the 1908 inventory in the Cabinet Room.[59] This grand ensemble of pier glass and commode would have mirrored the Sixtus Cabinet to spectacular effect.

None of the descriptions indicates how the walls were decorated; the close hang of pictures would have largely obscured them. Photographs show wallpaper in 1895. Red was perhaps always the wall colour for the Cabinet at Stourhead. Chippendale described the furnishing fabrics in some detail. Blue was the dominant colour of the textiles, but what weight and what patterns? The window curtain was 'blue satin with black spots' lined in 'blue tammy' (wool). The cushion covers and upholstery were in 'blue Rosette Callico' (cotton) trimmed with black ribbon and the case covers for the pole screens in 'blue Star Callico'.[60] Also unrecorded is the pattern and colour of the original Brussels carpet that flowed uniformly through the Picture Gallery and ante room to the Cabinet Room and sadly no textile fragments have survived.

LIFE WITH SIR RICHARD COLT HOARE

What of society at Stourhead? Visitors not acquainted with Sir Richard were shown around the house by a servant instructed to keep them in order.[61] As to house-guests, descriptions suggest an exclusively male society of scholars and enthusiasts, in contrast to Stourhead when Henry Hoare was in residence, surrounded by grandchildren and guests, male and female.

It is said Stourhead enjoyed a golden age under Sir Richard and in the sense the collection reached a zenith, that is true. Art on paper was his forte. Sadly Turner's watercolours of Salisbury Cathedral were sold in 1883, along with the ten Canaletto drawings.[62] His old masters and contemporary British pictures were not highly regarded in his own day, neither has their reputation grown with the years; *Girl Deploring the Death of a Pheasant, A Shepherdess with a Lamb in a Storm* or *Distress by Land* are better appreciated as characteristic effusions of Regency sentiment than as art.[63] William Beckford is said to have sneered 'Sir Richard had no taste'.[64] The ever-waspish Hazlitt admired the Canaletto drawings and Guido Reni copies and added, 'The rest of this Collection is, for the most part, *trash*.'[65] Among patrons of contemporary art, Sir Richard was less discerning than his friend Sir John Leicester (first Baron de Tabley) and less ambitious than the wealthy third Earl of Egremont. Sir Richard did not participate in the bonanza of buying in France led by Lord Yarmouth (who succeeded as third Marquess of Hertford in 1822) and the Prince Regent. Their taste for Dutch seventeenth-century pictures, eighteenth-century French furniture and Sèvres porcelain contrasts with Sir Richard's preferences. He would have replied that he lacked the means. But in truth, his interests lay elsewhere. He was a thorough-going bibliophile. His library of British history and topography ranked of national importance and its dispersal is arguably the saddest loss from Stourhead. Looking back, Sir Richard could be proud that he had exceeded his grandfather's expectations; preserved and enriched Stourhead; passed it to safe hands and, through his writings, he won an enduring reputation for himself, independent of his inheritance.

FIG. 220
Satinwood Commode, attributed to Thomas Chippendale junior, *c.*1780–5. Veneers and marquetry of harewood, satinwood and purplewood; mahogany and oak carcase, 34½ x 66⅛ x 26⅛ in, 87.5 x 168 x 66.3 cm. National Trust, Stourhead.

1. Hoare 1822,* p. 76.
2. C. Hoare & Co. HFM/11/13, f. 5, MS memoir by Sir Richard Colt Hoare, quoting Virgil, *Aeneid*, bk III, lines 56–7:
   Quid non mortalia pectora cogis,
   auri sacra fames?
as Dryden translated (bk III, lines 80–1):
   O sacred Hunger of pernicious Gold,
   What bands of Faith can impious Lucre hold?
3. C. Hoare & Co. HB/5/H/6, Money Lent Ledger 1783–94.
4. Hoare 1822, p. 75.
5. NT 732100 *The Adoration of the Magi*, by Lodovico Cardi, 'Cigoli'. Signed and dated 1605. Visitors today admire the large dog in the lower left corner of the altarpiece which was remarked upon in the early eighteenth century by Filippo Baldinucci. (*Notizie de' Professori del Disegno* ... , 21 vols, Florence 1717–23, vol. 9, edn. Milan 1812, p.111, 'un ritratto d'un Cane, della bellissima e grande razza d'Ingleterra, a cui per parer vivo, altro non manca, che il moto.' [a life-like portrait of a dog belonging to a fine and important English breed]).
6. WSA 383/4/1, three bills for Sir Richard Colt Hoare from Pietro Pisani, receipted 2 March 1787; 6 April 1789; 5 October 1789.
7. Samuel Woodforde RA (1763–1817). Henry Hoare had financed his study at the Royal Academy Schools in 1782; Sir Richard Colt Hoare continued his allowance. Today there are 21 oil paintings by (or attributed to) Woodforde at Stourhead, his largest being NT 732279 *Parnassus*.
8. C. Hoare & Co. HB/2/D/1, Sir Richard Colt Hoare to Henry Merrik Hoare, *c.*December 1828, advising on rebuilding the bank premises.

9. Sir Richard Colt Hoare, *Recollections Abroad: Journals of Tours on the Continent between the years 1785 and 1791*, 4 vols, privately printed, Bath, 1815–18.
10. Clay 1994, p. 116.
11. Woodbridge 1982a, p. 35.
12. Thompson 1983, pp. 18–19.
13. WSA 383.911, bills (1802–16) from Robert Miller of Miller's Hotel, 87 Jermyn St, London (which became the Cavendish Hotel in 1836).
14. Nichols 1840, pp. xix–xxvi, the complete bibliography of Sir Richard Colt Hoare.
15. Hunter 1851, pp. 16–27. Joseph Hunter (1783–1861), a Presbyterian minister and antiquary, lived in Bath before moving to London in the 1830s. He was appointed Assistant Keeper of the new Public Record Office in 1840.
16. WSA 383.936, Sir Richard Colt Hoare Journals, vol. III, 1815–33.
17. Ibid., visits to Weymouth and Bath 1830–3.
18. WSA 383.14, 'List of Claims sent to Mess.rs Karslake and Crealock by the Tradesmen Servants and other persons claiming to be Creditors of the late Henry Hoare Esq.re' [1836] totalling £2,667-11-10.
19. Stourhead Library G.10.26, Stourhead Annals, vol. I, entry for 1834–5, 'R. Davis My old (86) & faithful servant died (Sept 1st) after a service of 56 years.'
20. TNA Prob 11/1898, will of Sir Richard Colt Hoare, 31 October 1836.
21. C. Hoare & Co. HFM/11/13, f. 5, MS memoir by Sir Richard Colt Hoare.
22. WSRO Parham papers, bundle 2/2/2/6, letter 4/78, the Hon. Hester Hoare to Harriet Anne, Lady Bisshopp, Saturday 1783, 'the

upper part of the House [Stourhead] is very bad, the rooms being few and sadly furnish'd'. (By permission of Lady Emma Barnard and WSRO.)
23. WSA 383.66, 'Sundry Building Accounts for Sir Rich.d C Hoare Bart. at Stourhead' 1792–1805, Abstract 1792–4.
24. Stourhead Library G.10.26, Stourhead Annals, vol. I, 1801, Summary of trees planted 1798–1833, total 620,800.
25. C. Hoare & Co. HB/5/H/7, Money Lent Ledger 1794–1805, by 1797 Sir Richard had borrowed £6,200 from Hoare's bank. He paid off part of this in 1800 and borrowed a further £5,000.
26. WSA 383.66, Sundry Building Accounts 1792–1805, 'Abstract of the whole business' 1800–05'. Goodison 2005, p. 58.
27. Dean 1999, pp. 65 and 103.
28. Cornforth 1981, p. 12.
29. Wilson and Mackley 2000, p. 241.
30. The Hoare family had dealings with leading architects of the day. WSA 383/4/1, William Wilkins to Sir Richard Colt Hoare, 1815, for 'Designs for a Grecian lodge in N.o 4 finished drawings' £60-18-0. It was not built. In 1800 John Nash designed Luscombe Castle, Devon, for Sir Richard's half-brother, the banker Charles Hoare.
31. Fenton 1811, letter 8 November 1807, pp. 180–1.
32. Stourhead Catalogue 1808.
33. Hoare 1822, pp. 72–3.
34. Compton 1991, p. 37.
35. Hoare 1822, p. 70.
36. Ibid., p. 81.
37. Hunter 1851, p. 25.

38. WSA 383.5.70a, 'Richd Colt Hoare Esqr
To Thomas Haig & Co D^r' 21 Sept 1779–30
November 1780. Dodd and Wood 2011,
pp.113–22.

39. Gilbert 1972, pp. 254–66.

40. Warner 1801, pp. 246–8, Excursion II,
Letter III, 14 September 1800, Badminton, in
'the *north breakfast- room*, where the first object
which commands attention is
a most splendid cabinet [fig. 19] [...] This
room contains also the following pictures, to
the right of the cabinet:– Christ accompanying
his two disciples to Emmaus, a large landscape,
by C. Lorraine; remarkable for its trees in the
foreground, and its beautiful distances. Large
Landscape, by Vander Stecten [Hendrik van
der Straaten]. Over the chimney, Landscape,
by Wootton, in imitation of C. Lorraine.
The softness of the tints and glory of the sky,
approach to the best manner of the great
master whose style he has here attempted.
Landscape, by Vander Stecten; a companion
to the one above. – Landscape, by Romanelli;
Pan in pursuit of Syrinx and her nymphs.–
Landscape, by Suanevelt [Herman van
Swanevelt].– Landscape, by Wootton; but
here he worked without his great model, and
has fallen short of the effort described above.
–Landscape, by Claude Lorraine; representing
the temptation of Christ by the Devil.– All these
pictures are of a large size.'

41. Hoare 1815, pp. 72–4, described both
palaces; however, he ignored the Colonna
cabinets. Safarik 2009, pp. 155–7.

42. Rossini da Pesaro 1741, p. 60. See p. 143
note 53.

43. Hoare 1822,* pp. 76–7.

44. Woodbridge 1970, p. 243.

45. Christie's 1883b. Stourhead Library C.7.34,
Alda, Lady Hoare's copy of Hoare 1818, with
her annotations, pp.13–5.

46. WSA 383.66, 'Sundry Building Accounts
1801, Cabinet Room, '19.9 Cube of fir w.
partitioning in sundry parts of room' £4-3-10.

47. Ibid., 1801, 'Mahogany Doors' for new
Library and Picture Gallery, at the total cost
of £80-7-10.

48. Heikamp 1988, pp. 58–9.

49. Stourhead Inventory 1838,* Cabinet Room,
p. 28, no. 307, 'A Circular hand Mirror
(damaged)'.

50. Ibid., South Apartments, p. 74, no. 1016,
'Two mahogany Book Shelves in recess of
windows'; North Apartments, p. 80, no. 1093,
'Two inlaid Mahogany Book Cases in two other
ditto [window recess]'.

51. Ibid., North Apartments, p. 80, no. 1092,
'Inlaid Cabinet in centre window recess'.
NT 731613.

52. WSA 383.4a, 'Sir Richd Colt Hoare Bar^t
D^r To Thos Chippendale', 31 August 1811–15
August 1812, entry 11 April 1812.

53. Ibid., 'Sr Richd Colt Hoare Bar^t To Thomas
Chippendale' 27August 1802–September 1803,
entries 20 September 1802 ('oes' were curtain
rings).

54. Goodison 2005, pp. 82–3.

55. Dodd and Wood 2011, p. 49.

56. Stourhead Inventory 1838,* Cabinet Room,
p. 28, no. 306.

57. WSA 383.4a, 'Sr Richd Colt Hoare Bar^t
To Thomas Chippendale' 27 August 1802
to September 1803, entry 20 September 1802,
'Taking out the plates of Your large Glass frame
New polishing silvering and Making perfect'
£21. 'Fluting the frame and regilding in
Burnishd Gold' £9-4-0.

58. NT 731559. Dodd and Wood 2011, pp. 53–71.

59. Stourhead Inventory 1908, Cabinet Room,
p. 104, 'The 5' 3" handsome Sheraton semi-
circular Cabinet with two folding doors
under, enclosing two circular compartments,
surmounted by two drawers, locks and key,
each door is inlaid with figures of Grizalli and
Angeli Coughton; each of the four supporting
legs are surmounted by Ivory Cameos.' The
'inlaid' figures and the 'Ivory Cameos' are in
fact grisaille paintings on copper; 'Grizalli and
Angeli Coughton' is presumably a corruption
of '*en grisaille* by Angelica Kauffman'.

60. WSA 383.4a, 'Sr Richd Colt Hoare Bar^t
To Thomas Chippendale' 27 August 1802–
September 1803, entries 20 September 1802.

61. Simond 1817, vol. I, pp. 260–1. Simond
(1767–1831) was French by birth but lived
in the United States. In 1810–11 he toured
Britain and wrote of the experience in terms
critical of English society, politics and culture.
Stourhead did not escape his venom. He
criticized the garden and paid scant attention
in the house; he ignored the Sixtus Cabinet.
'These apartments are full of pictures, none
of which are very remarkable. One of the ladies
and myself having sat down a moment to look
at a picture more conveniently, a young girl
who showed the house, told us as civilly as she
could, that it was *the rule of the house not to allow
visitors to sit down*. This is a rule of which that
gentleman (a rich banker) has the merit of the
invention. We have not met with any thing of
this sort anywhere else.'

62. Christie's 1883b, lots 18–35.

63. NT 732260 ; NT 732266 ; NT 732137

64. As recorded by Joseph Farington,
16 October 1806, Cave 1982, vol. VIII, 1982,
p. 2888.

65. Hazlitt 1824, pp. 137–9.

TEN
THE LATER HISTORY
OF THE SIXTUS CABINET

After the death of Sir Richard Colt Hoare in 1838, the Sixtus Cabinet enjoyed a period of quiet obscurity. Stourhead was inherited by his half-brother, Sir Henry Hugh Hoare, who died in 1841, having published the last two volumes of *Modern Wiltshire* and the *Catalogue of the Hoare Library* and built the portico at the house. His son and successor, Sir Hugh Richard Hoare, cherished and improved the estate until his death in 1857. Stourhead was then inherited by his nephew, Sir Henry Ainslie Hoare, 5th Bt (1824–1894), the darkest and most intriguing of the five baronets resident at Stourhead. All seemed set fair; he possessed charm, ambition and ideas, but he lacked the business temperament and lasted a very short time at the family bank. This Sir Henry had a passion for horse-racing and gambling. He was adept at wheedling hand-outs from Hoare's bank, to top up his annual allowance. In the 1860s he tried politics and was elected the Liberal MP, first for New Windsor, then for Chelsea, which he represented 1868–74, thus adding a further unimaginative way of spending money. Stourhead was expensive to maintain. Sir Henry, reluctant to sell land in a falling market, resolved to raise money by disposing of heirlooms. As the life-tenant, he needed a private Act of Parliament to do this, as well as the consent of the next-in-line, who was a cousin.[1] These he won: Christie's auctioned the best pictures and some *objets d'art*, and Sotheby's sold the library.[2]

The family could not agree whether to sell the Sixtus Cabinet. Trustees for Henry Hugh Arthur (1865–1947), the heir-apparent, held out against this and it seems they reached a compromise; Sir Henry sold the wax miniatures and the trustees removed the Cabinet to a 'safe house', Wavendon in Buckinghamshire.[3] This sporting estate had belonged to the Hoares since 1796; it passed to Henry Hugh Arthur on the death of his father in 1873. Wavendon was a comfortable house furnished primarily from Barn Elms at Barnes. The comfortable hugger-mugger is recorded in two watercolours.[4] That was what young Henry Hugh Arthur grew up with and what his wife would recreate for him when he inherited Stourhead. Sir Henry, as he would

become, married in 1887. He was Victorian to the core, a countryman at heart and he did not work at Hoare's bank.

When this Sir Henry moved to Stourhead in 1895 he brought with him all the contents of Wavendon, including the Sixtus Cabinet. Sir Henry and Lady Hoare then set to and renovated the house, installed electric lighting, decorated the rooms with Morris-like wallpapers, rearranged the contents and, fortunately as it transpired, photographed the *piano nobile*. Wavendon paintings filled the gaps on the walls left by the sales and Wavendon books restocked the library. The Regency furniture remained at Stourhead, so the arrival of more belongings created something of a log-jam. In the Cabinet Room Lady Hoare recreated Sir Richard's arrangement of landscape pictures and returned the Sixtus Cabinet to its niche where it rose amid a minestrone of possessions (fig. 216).

In 1902 a chimney fire in a bedroom went undetected and spread to the roof timbers, where efforts to extinguish it failed. Before the roof collapsed, the contents of the *piano nobile*, including the Cabinet, were snatched to safety (fig. 215). Sir Henry and Lady Hoare did not flinch in rebuilding the house with insurance money and their erstwhile friend, the church-architect Edward Doran Webb – a task completed in 1906.[5]

After the death of their son in 1917, the Hoares entertained only close friends and selected family members. They ate formally in the Saloon and *en famille* in the Little Dining Room. The remainder of the *piano nobile* became a series of sitting rooms. The house was shown to visitors one afternoon a week. To keep the place alive – and the servants on their toes – Lady Hoare moved her 'headquarters' from room to room with the change of seasons. In each setting she required furniture suitable for conversation, reading, writing, interviewing and dismissing servants (these last two became principal pastimes). Hence the profusion of chairs, upholstered and upright; tables, desks and shelf space of every kind were there to answer her needs. The encyclopaedic Stourhead Inventory of 1908 reflected the plethora of furniture and ornaments, listing windows, doors, walls and ceilings as well as moveables, presumably for the insurance company. Compiled by Walton, the furniture store in Mere, it is certainly not for connoisseurs, but the 500-word entry on the Sixtus Cabinet is particularly full and conscientious. At the time there was lively commercial and academic interest in English furniture. Ralph Edwards stayed with the Hoares in 1923 and was delighted to be shown Chippendale junior's bills.[6] The first edition of his *Dictionary of English Furniture* illustrated 15 pieces from Stourhead.[7] Henceforward, the house would be celebrated for Chippendale's beautiful, idiosyncratic furniture. Successive editions of the Stourhead guidebook show the change of emphasis and the eclipse of the Sixtus Cabinet.[8]

Sir Henry died in 1947 having given Stourhead and a portion of the estate to the National Trust. After the Trust took over, it united the Sixtus Cabinet with the two smaller pietre dure Cabinets.[9] There was scepticism about the traditional provenance of the Sixtus Cabinet; it was admired but mis-diagnosed as mid-seventeenth century and Florentine. Following the sale of the Badminton Cabinet in 1990 and the rearrangement of pictures at Stourhead during 1993–4, the Trust took a fresh look at the Sixtus Cabinet.[10] At the time it was being slow-cooked by the central heating boiler installed in the basement immediately below. So high was the insurance value for the Cabinet that the Trust decided to repair it on site, building a workshop in the Column Room and imaginatively opening windows into this studio so that visitors could see the work progress. They watched, fascinated, as the distinguished conservator, Colin Piper, dismantled the Cabinet and worked intently for more than a year stabilizing the structure, cleaning the alabaster, marbles, pietre dure and bronzes, replacing missing mouldings and so on. He completed the task in 2008. The Trust dismantled the studio and for two years displayed the Cabinet isolated and spot-lit, before returning it to its niche in the Cabinet Room. The total cost of the exercise amounted to £51,000. The newly resplendent Sixtus Cabinet was thus re-established as the star at Stourhead.

1. Acts of Parliament, 45 and 46 Victoria, Chapter 5, pp. 1–12, Stourhead Settled Estates Act 1882.

2. Christie's 1883b; Christie's 1883a; Christie's 1884; Sotheby, Wilkinson & Hodge 1883 and 1887.

3. WSA 383.20, correspondence concerning the sales, principally between the solicitors for the parties; Messrs Longbourne, Longbourne & Stevens of 7 Lincoln's Inn Fields (for Sir Henry Ainslie Hoare) and Henry Tylee of Messrs Tylee, Wickham, Moberly & Tylee of 14 Essex Street, Strand (for the trustees of his cousin, Henry Arthur Hoare).

4. NT 730748 *Interior at Wavendon: the Drawing Room*, and NT 730749 *Interior at Wavendon: the Library*; both *c*.1840 and attributed to Frances Annette Hoare (elder sister of the 5th Bt).

5. Dodd 1978, pp. 112–27.

6. Stourhead Library shellmark F 9.27, Visitors' Book October 1923.

7. Macquoid and Edwards 1924–7, vol. I, p. xiii, Sir Henry Hoare was a subscriber.

8. Sweetman 1913, p. 42, Cabinet Room, in addition to the Sixtus Cabinet, listed 'a fine specimen of an Inlaid oval Cabinet, with medallions by *Angelica Kauffman*. [...] a very fine specimen of an English mahogany and satinwood Cabinet, exhibited at the Earl's Court Exhibition, 1908 [...] a fine specimen of old English Lacq. (a Cabinet with two mirrors in front).' Sweetman 1925, p. 64, omitted the lacquer cabinet and added 'a set of twenty-two chairs, table with legs harp-shape, two fire screens, and three gout stools, all in satinwood, by CHIPPENDALE. The centre table is an inlaid Rent Table, with centre well. The two walnut writing chests are by CHIPPENDALE.'

9. See Appendix VI.

10. Cornforth 1994, pp. 64–7.

ELEVEN
CONCLUSION

Wilkie Collins's *The Moonstone* is recounted by a sequence of different narrators, each with particular insights, biases and blind spots. Those who have soldiered through to these final remarks may feel that what they have read has been equally various in its perspectives, while those who habitually turn first to last chapters should be warned that this one does not follow a steady and seamless assemblage of information, lacking gaps and uncertainties. Indeed the attempt to present a three-dimensional picture of the context, nature and vicissitudes of an extraordinary masterpiece, which has hitherto attracted scant scholarly attention, has involved accepting many absences of evidence. Nonetheless, solid foundations have been excavated, the chronicle (some uncertainties are ironed out in what follows) has few gaps and the combination of direct insights and raking sidelights may, it is hoped, have illuminated the Sixtus Cabinet as never before.

The prime context for the presence of the Sixtus Cabinet at Stourhead is the English appetite for pietre dure, commencing in the late sixteenth century. The suggestions that a Roman table top at Aston Hall could have been acquired by John Astley, Keeper of the Queen's Jewels and Plate, before the founding of the *Galleria dei Lavori* in Florence in 1588, and that a table top with the Paston arms may have been ordered in Florence in 1638, and the identification of inlaid marble coats of arms on Lady Berkeley's tomb at Cranford as made by 'Sig: Domenica' in Rome in 1639, all tend to suggest that Mildmay Fane's poetic praise of pietre dure tables at Campden House in 1651 reflected an emerging pattern. That Roman pietre dure cabinets of the same type as the Sixtus Cabinet seem to have been acquired by Grand Tourists for Northumberland House in about 1734, for Castle Howard in about 1739, for Arbury Hall in about 1740, for Duncombe Park in 1747 and for the Duke of Chandos's Cavendish Square house by the latter date strongly suggests a specific phase of imitation and

emulation, Henry Hoare emerging with the most desirable trophy of all. Later collectors such as the Prince Regent and William Beckford were even more voracious and when most of the collection of Beckford's son-in-law, the tenth Duke of Hamilton, was dispersed in 1882 the sale included 16 significant pietre dure lots, not including the fine table in the church at Hamilton, sold in 1993, and the Farnese table, perhaps the most important Roman document of all, sold in 1919 and now in the Metropolitan Museum of Art, New York. To these sad losses can be added the Florentine Badminton Cabinet, sold abroad in 1990 and since 2004 in the collection of Prince Liechtenstein in Vienna, and a spectacular early-eighteenth-century octagonal Florentine table from Wrotham Park, sold in 2005. There have been many other departures, but that so much remains speaks for the power of English taste. In the present context it was an exciting discovery that the carved and gilt stand of the great Roman table at Powis Castle has little pears in its Ionic capitals, possibly for Peretti, and that this too may have belonged to Sixtus V.

That there are no papal insignia on the Sixtus Cabinet, although little pears are present and the dominant colours are the heraldic Peretti blue, red, gold and silver, is one reason for suggesting that it was produced or initiated by Cardinal Felice Peretti before he was elected Pope in 1585, as Sixtus V. It stood in the Palazzo Felice, the *casino* which he began to build in 1578 on the Villa Montalto, the great estate above Santa Maria Maggiore which he gradually assembled from 1576 to his death in 1590, and which eventually became the site of Rome's main railway station. Since 1572 Sixtus had been out of favour with Gregory XIII with no prospect of succession, and his villa and its buildings were a private family domain which he vested in his sister to pass on to her descendants. The Sixtus Cabinet, it may be inferred from inventories, was placed at one end of the loggia of the Palazzo Felice, its most magnificent

FIG. 221
The Sixtus Cabinet, drawing of front elevation.

0   50   100 cm

room, whose ceiling paintings included a scene of the nurture of Jupiter on Mount Ida, a direct reference to the Cardinal's humble rustic origins. Overlooking the garden, it was furnished with antique marble figures on painted and gilt stands, doubtless comparable to one in the Victoria & Albert Museum, which supports a bust of Sixtus, and with bronzes by Giambologna on ebony side tables and on a pietre dure centre table. These were probably gifts from the Grand Duke of Tuscany, Francesco I de' Medici, a supporter, whose brother, also a friend, Cardinal Ferdinando de' Medici, then resident in Rome, gave the altarpiece in the Palazzo Felice's chapel. It is noteworthy that it was Ferdinando who in 1588, having doffed his cardinalate to inherit the Grand Duchy from his brother the year before, founded the Florentine *Galleria dei Lavori*.

The iconography of the loggia was predominantly secular, but for three lunettes with biblical scenes incorporating lions and one with St Jerome and the lion (lions were central to Peretti heraldry and Sixtus had a long-standing cult of St Jerome). The most likely explanation for the iconography of the Sixtus Cabinet itself is that the topmost figure represents Minerva or Athena, presiding over the arts and sciences, a theme repeated on a ceiling painting on the ground floor of the Palazzo Felice. One art, music, was incorporated into the fabric of the Cabinet itself in the form of an organ, now lost. Otherwise its function was, externally and internally, display.

Externally the Cabinet, 'a forma d'una facciata di chiesa' [in the form of a church façade], a term used in the 1597 inventory of the Palazzo Pitti, is veneered in ebony, the fashionable wood of the age, and clad in innumerable panels of varied and polychrome pietre dure, mainly set in frames of silver, which were painstakingly fretted out of silver sheet to receive the individually shaped stones, a much more demanding technique than the standard narrow silver stringing, simply butted together. Columns turned from richly variegated alabaster, another demanding technique, articulate three storeys, Ionic, Corinthian and Composite, surmounted by an Attic. Their capitals and bases and many other lively mounts are in gilt bronze, an expensive material, and several friezes are set with gems in silver bezels. Internally numerous doors, drawers and panels (few easily detectable and the last perilously held in position by friction alone) give access to inner compartments and drawers and yet more drawers hidden behind drawers. A demonstration of the Cabinet's secrets must have been a carefully orchestrated performance, culminating, perhaps, in a recital on its organ.

The whole was a complex composite in whose design Sixtus's favourite architect, Domenico Fontana, or his nephew, Carlo Maderno, could have played a part, while the cabinet work may have been orchestrated by the Fleming Giovanni Vasanzio or the Frenchman Flaminio Boulanger. At least some of the gilt bronze mounts can be associated with the Flemish sculptor Jacob Cornelisz Cobaert. In the very late sixteenth century there seems to have been an exclusive fashion for jewelled ('di gioie' or 'gioiellato') cabinets; the rich Florentine banker, Niccolò Gaddi, left one incomplete on his death in 1591 and stated in his will that it could only be alienated if Santa Maria Novella

wanted it for a tabernacle. Indeed the Sixtus Cabinet may be seen as a secular tabernacle, created to serve as the focus of the loggia of the Palazzo Felice and, arguably, of the whole Palazzo.

After Sixtus's death in 1590 the Villa Montalto continued in the possession of his family, whom he had connected to the grandest families in Rome and endowed with great wealth. His great-nephew, Cardinal Alessandro Damasceni Peretti Montalto, was a notable patron of the arts who much embellished the gardens of the villa, notably with Bernini's *Neptune,* and its second palace, the Palazzo alle Terme. The loggia of the Palazzo Felice seems to have been preserved unchanged as the Peretti descent followed the female line, and was still intact in about 1680. But debts accumulated and in 1690, unwillingly, Prince Giulio Savelli, the head of the family, was forced by the Congregazione dei Baroni to sell the contents of the Palazzo. Somehow the Sixtus Cabinet was spared and in 1713 it was listed among the objects transferred to his widow, the Princess Caterina Giustiniani Savelli. It was no longer in her possession at her death and it is a matter for speculation whether she or the Sforza-Cesarini family, the senior Peretti descendants from the notorious marriage of her step-niece, Livia Cesarini, to Federico Sforza in 1673, donated the Sixtus Cabinet to the Roman convent (the best candidates are Santa Maria dei Sette Dolori and Santa Caterina a Magnanapoli) from which Henry Hoare bought it in about 1740, now lacking the organ but its base mounted with wax portraits of the Peretti family.

The translation of the Sixtus Cabinet from Rome to Stourhead, an early Anglo-Palladian villa designed by Colen Campbell, and set in the Wiltshire countryside, was, as noted, a symptom of the pronounced English taste for pietre dure. But, when he left for Rome in 1739, Henry Hoare was not the typical Grand Tourist – young, care-free and aristocratic. He was 34, a seasoned banker with four children, and a member of parliament, whose days of hunting and drinking were long gone. He had a serious interest in architecture, influenced by his uncle, William Benson, an amateur architect whose precociously Palladian house, Wilbury, Henry bought in 1734; in painting, buying views of Rome by Panini from Arthur Pond in 1727; and in sculpture, his patronage of and friendship with Rysbrack going back to 1727, when he purchased statuettes of Inigo Jones and Palladio. Henry's Grand Tour took in Paris, Venice, Rome and Florence in 1739, after which he joined his wife in Aix-en-Provence, and then a further visit to Rome and possibly Naples in 1740, followed by a year in Aix with his wife and a return to England in September 1741. During his absence he employed the best bankers, Alexandre Alexander and Sir John Lambert in Paris, Joseph 'Consul' Smith in Venice and Girolamo Belloni in Rome (bills totalling £1,031 from June 1739 to April 1740) but, tantalizingly, no documents pin down his Roman or other purchases, although a 1742 charge from his shipping agent, Edward Fowler, of £37.1.6 for '10 Cases of Cabinetts from Leghorn' may be relevant.

In 1743 Henry Hoare commissioned an extraordinary Pedestal for the Sixtus Cabinet, formed as an exquisitely detailed quadriportal triumphal arch, veneered in mahogany and ornamented with a medallion of the Pope, flanked by winged victories, allegoric female figures and six reliefs of monuments restored or built by Sixtus V – all gilt. The cabinet work of the pedestal was supplied by an obscure 'Mr James ye Joyner' but its principal ornaments were by John Boson, a famous carver, who had worked for Lord Burlington, William Kent and the Prince of Wales (although the gilt bronze plaques with inscriptions may have been sent from Rome). The likeliest designer is the architect Henry Flitcroft, long a client of Hoare's bank and soon to design the Pantheon at Stourhead. But the concept and the iconography are most probably Henry Hoare's, and it must have been he who placed St Peter and St Paul, also carved by Boson, on the Cabinet: these first unequivocally religious elements were thus, ironically, a Protestant addition.

At Stourhead Henry Hoare recast Colen Campbell's Breakfast Room as the Cabinet Room, enlarging it and inserting a screen of two columns, behind which the Sixtus Cabinet was placed centrally, opposite the window, on a Wilton carpet: in 1769 Sir John Parnell described 'a little Platform about a foot higher than the floor which makes it more conspicuous'. In 1754 the walls, red damask, were hung with a copy after Raphael and paintings by 'Barocci' (in fact Calvaert), Poussin and Maratti in rich gilt frames, an evocation of a Roman palace. In subsequent decades Henry Hoare constantly enriched his collection and the hang became denser and more diffuse. The Sixtus Cabinet was a cynosure much admired by visitors, both for its intrinsic splendour and for its historic association with Sixtus V, which gained extra piquancy when, before 1784, in a period of naval threats from France, it was hung with a Garter George and a gold medal struck to commemorate the defeat of the Armada, backed by Sixtus, in 1588.

Henry Hoare transferred Stourhead to Sir Richard Colt Hoare, his favourite grandson, in 1784. In August 1785 Sir Richard's wife died, followed rapidly by his grandfather in September; almost immediately he sought consolation in a prolonged Grand Tour, which took him to France, Spain, Germany and, above all, Italy and lasted, but for a break 1787–8, until July 1791. Although Sir Richard acquired old masters in Italy, his great love was landscape, both as a serious topographer with antiquarian interests and as a painter of landscapes and collector of landscapes by others. Back at Stourhead, he preserved Henry Hoare's landscape garden, enriching its planting and softening its lines, and removing the Chinese Alcove, the Turkish Tent and the Druid's Cell, 'to render the gardens as chaste and correct as possible and give them the character of an Italian villa'. His grandfather had called the view of the Pantheon 'a charming Gaspd. Picture', alluding to Poussin's brother-in-law, Gaspard Poussin: under Sir Richard Stourhead was, even more, an evocation of the Roman Campagna.

He also considerably enlarged the house in 1792 by the addition of the Library and the Picture Gallery, and converted his grandfather's study into a new Cabinet Room, with an arched niche for the Sixtus Cabinet. Shortage of money postponed furnishing until 1802, when Thomas Chippendale junior fitted the niche with a richly gilt cornice carved 'with the Pope's tiara and other

insignias', hung with blue velvet curtain with gold fringe and tassels. Opposite was a broad satinwood commode by Chippendale with a great mirror above (another large mirror was over the chimney piece), while the room was completely hung with landscapes by Turner and others. The play of reflections, the rich drapery, amid landscapes picturesque and sublime, and the even greater emphasis on its papal provenance amounted to a transfiguration of the Sixtus Cabinet, in a setting to rival the loggia of the Palazzo Felice.

After Sir Richard died, old and infirm, in 1838 there was a long limbo. In the 1880s the Sixtus Cabinet escaped sale and was removed to Wavendon in Buckinghamshire. But in 1895 it returned and, although Stourhead had to be rebuilt after a 1902 fire, the Cabinet Room was recreated, not quite to its original conformation and splendour, but splendid nonetheless. Sir Henry Hoare gave Stourhead to the National Trust in 1946, at a time when faded walnut was more appreciated than gilt bronze and pietre dure, and since then the Sixtus Cabinet has remained *in situ*, its papal provenance regularly but sceptically recited, and its manufacture attributed to Florence, not Rome.

The earliest extant description of the Sixtus Cabinet as 'Studiolo uno fatto a Tabernacolo' identifies its essential purpose as a focal showpiece. Its scale, about the height of a man even without its stand; the complexity and ingenuity of its construction, incorporating some 130 drawers and compartments; the opulence of its materials, including gilt bronze, silver, lapis lazuli, coral, agates, jaspers and richly variegated alabasters; the brilliance of their colours, all set against the black sheen of ebony; the brilliant modulation of congruous but never identical ornamental patterns on its component panels: all these contribute to the Cabinet's sensual appeal. Its architectural design, full of movement in plan and vertical thrust in elevation, is a supercharged version of a Roman church of the late sixteenth century, triumphal arch piled on triumphal arch, all articulated by the Roman orders and reusing ancient Roman materials. Technical virtuosity, the opulence of nature, and artistic ambition informed by classical learning all play their part: the Cabinet was calculated to astonish.

At Stourhead the provision of the Pedestal, at once distinguished and effective as architecture and learned and apposite in its celebration of Sixtus V, naturalized the Sixtus Cabinet, and it was emphatically integrated into the fabric of the house in two successive Cabinet Rooms (and a third post-fire), each expressing the aesthetic and historic values of their generation. But the extent to which the Sixtus provenance continued to be celebrated – even as a foil for the Armada – is exceptional, if not unique. The Cabinet and its pedestal possess great sensual and artistic appeal, no doubt (think of their glitter and shimmer by candlelight), but their layers of association also deserve to be appreciated: Sixtus V, the loggia of the Palazzo Felice and the generations of Peretti descendants who preserved this heirloom – and the Hoares – are integral to the complex history of this extraordinary composite.

APPENDICES

APPENDIX I INVENTORIES AND DESCRIPTIONS OF THE SIXTUS CABINET IN ROME

Text for the item identified as the cabinet now at Stourhead is in **bold**.

PALAZZO FELICE AT VILLA MONTALTO, 1655

Archivio Storico Capitolino, Rome: Sez.v, prot. 4, fo. 69ff., Posthumous inventory, 3 May–30 July 1655 of Cardinal Francesco Damasceni Peretti (1595–1655), compiled for his nephew and heir, Abate, later Cardinal, Paolo Savelli (1622–1685).

Extract listing the contents of the loggia of the *piano nobile* of the Palazzo Felice at Villa Montalto.

[f.897v] *20. Piano al Palazzo felice*
Scabelli due di noce alla Napolitana
Scabelli due dipinti
Tavola una di marmo con sua armatura di legname

Nella Saletta
Portiera una di damasco rosso con sue Colonne di raso vellutato
No. otto Sedie di Cordovano rosso con sui Braccialetti
Un scabellone grande di Legname indorato sopra una Statua di marmo di una vecchia
Buffetti Quattro di canna d'India Indorati all'Indiana con sui corami sopra
No. 11 Ritratti di diversi signori in piede pal 8 circa con sue cornice rabescati d'oro
Un quadro tondo con un Ritratto d'una Signora con cornice indorata
Un quadro a due faccie di pietra di Lavagnio con un Christo morto da una parte e dall'altra con un Christo che porta La Croce con suo scabellone intagliato indorato

1a Stanza
Un Paramento di damasco Rosso e brocatello giallo con due sopraporte e una

[f.898] Portiere della medema robba
No. 9 Sedie di Corame rosso trapuntate coll'appoggio a sbranche
Due Sedie de medesmo con il solo appoggiatore
Una tavola di marmo paragone con sua Cornice di marmo rosso con suo Corame e armature di legno sotto con sopra un Ercole di metallo con piedestallo di ebano
Termini tre di alabastro con sue fette nere
Un scabellone di noce intagliato con una testa il busto di Sisto v
Un quadro di Pio v. con sua Cornice indorata
Un quadro di' un Ritratto d'una Signora a sedere con cornice nera e oro mischiata

Un quadro di tre palmi incirca con Christo all'orto con Cornice indorata
Quadri due di sopraporte tondi con figure dentro con Cornice quadra nera e oro

Nella 2a Camera
Un paramento di Damasco verde e Broccatello rosso e bianco e giallo con due sopraporte e sua Portiera simile
Quattro sedie di Corame rosso trapuntate
Un Cortinaggio con Coperta e altri sui finimenti dell'istessa robba del Paramento
Una lettiera di noce con sue Colonne e pomi indorati

[f.898v.] Un inginocchiatore coperta dell'istesso Damasco e due Cuscini simili
Tre matarazzi con suo Capezzale
Seggietta con suo Vaso coperta dell'istessa robba del paramento e L'orinale
Un scabellone dipinto e indorato con un quadro musaico sopra
Un altro scabellone simile con quadro ovalo con figure di marmo di mezzo rilievo
Un Buffetto di Ebano intarsiato di avorio con suo studiolo di Ebano intarsiato di avorio sopra con tre Statuine di metallo e suoi piedestalli e due Cagnolini del medemo metallo
Una tavola di marmo pedocchioso con suo corame sopra telaio di noce
Una Statuetta di metallo rappresentante un Centauro & una donna ignuda abbracciata con suo piedestallo
Doi Colonnette di due palmi di marmo con figurine di metallo sopra
Un quadro con una Madonna Christo e S. Gioseppe con sua Cornice d'ebano intagliata
Un quadro con una Susanna con sua Cornice d'ebano intagliata
Un quadro di una Arianna con suo Cornice di noce intagliata e oro
Un quadro alto palmi cinque incirca con la Madonna, Christo e S. Giovanni

[f.899] con Cornice nera rabescata di Bianco
Un quadro con S. Gerolimo con sua Cornice d'ebano

3a Camera
Paramento di Damasco giallo con sue Colonnette di rasetto con sue Sopraporte dell'istesso
Un tavolino in ottangolo di marmo mischio con sua Armatura di noce intagliata con sua Coperta sopra di Corame con una Statuetta di metallo che rappresenta un Cacciatore
Quatro Sedie di Corame rosso trapuntate
Un Buffetto di Ebano intarsiato di avolio con sua Scrivania Simile sopra Cinque Stauette di Bronzo con piedestalli
Due Animali di Bronzo con suoi piedestalli
Tre Scabelli di Legno con tre Statue di marmo sopra di pal tre incirca
Due quadri in Paesi sopraporti con sue Cornici intagliate noce e oro
Sedici quadretti con diversi figure con sue Cornici di Ebano 12 e Quattro di Cornici di legno

Segue La Loggia nel Piano nobile
Studiolo uno fatto a Tabernacolo con organo dentro con diece colonne di alabastro nel primo solaro otto nel secondo e sei al terzo con sette figurine, e due a sedere con

sportelli di diversi pietre preziose con suo

[f. 899v] **piede con figure indorate e suo Padiglione di Dobletto rosso con trine d'oro e frangie**
Tavolino uno tondo Commesso di diverse pietre con il suo piede dinanzi intagliato
Gruppo uno di tre figure di metallo con suo piede con fette indorate
Scabelloni 12 rabescati dipinti con l'Arme dorate del Sig. Cardl. Montalto
Statuette dodici alte pal 2½ L'una incirca
Buffetti due sommessi [*sic*] di avolio e Ebano & Legno di Lionato
Cavallucci due di Bronzo con Base uno di Ebano e Lo altro di legno nero
Leoncino uno sopra un toro di Bronzo con sua Base di Ebano
Tori due di Bronzo piccolo con sue Basi Una di ebano e l'altra di legno nero
Leoncino uno di Bronzo sopra un Cavallo con sua Base di Ebano
Sedie quattro do Cordovano rosso imbottite di seta gialla con frangie di Seta gialla e rossa a Scabello sopra Tavolino uno di corame rosso con frangie dorate
Tende tre di velato torchina & li fenestroni della loggia con suoi ferri e cordoni tutti rotti
Un ritratto in Tavola isolate di D. Alvaro

Camerino che segue
Paramento di Damasco verde con colonne di ragetti [?] con due sopraporte

[f.900] Lettiera una di Legno di riposo con un matarazzo di drappetto rigato con quattro cuscini simili
Sedie quattro di Corame imbottite
Scabelli tre rabescati indorati con sopra figurine sei di marmo di altezza di pal. 2. incirca
Quadri Sei marittimi in tavola con Cornice tutta indorata
Mercurio uno di Metallo con la sua base di marmo a Zampa di Leone
Tavolino uno di alabastro occaso con Collarino di marmo giallo e bianco con il suo Corame sopra
Venere una che dorme con un Satiro con la sua base di Legno nero

Stanza attaccata al Camerino
Paramento uno di Damasco rosso con le Colonne di velluto rosso a fogliame con due sopraporte e Portiera del medemo drappo
Cortinaggio uno di Catalusto [?] rosso e giallo con sua Coperta e tutti i suoi finimenti
Seggetta una coperta del medesimo e orinale uno del medesimo
Inginocchiatore uno con sui cuscini del medesimo drappo del Paramento
Lettiera una di noce con Colonne dorate con suoi pomi intagliati dorati sopra à Leone, matarazzi tre di berliccio [?] bianco con suo capezzale
Quattro Sedie d'appoggio trapuntate di Seta

[f.900v.] Tavolino uno di Alabastro con suo piede di noce con quattro figure con sua coperta di Corame sopra il Tavolino
Studiolo uno di Ebano con profili d'argento con diversi Lavori
Un Christo alla Colonna di argento dorato con due manigoldi con sua base di ebano

ad ottangoli
Due Guglie d'argento trasforate con base di
argento
Quadro uno di Christo con la Corona in
testa e Veste rossa con sui cornici indorate
intagliate
Quadro uno di S Gio: Batta alto pal. 3 con
Cornice tutta dorata
Una Madonna con S. Gioseppe e S. Giovanni
con sua Cornice d'Ebano nero

Segue L'altra Stanza
Paramento uno di Damasco giallo con sue
Colonne di velluto pavonazzo con due
Sopraporte & sua portiera
Scabelli quattro rabescati di legname dorati
e sopra quattro Statue di marmo di pal. 4
incirca
Una sfinge di marmo giallo con una testa di
marmo e suo piedestallo quadrato di marmo
Sedie cinque di Corame rosso imbottite
Tavolino uno di marmo rosso con suo telaio
di noce con quattro Colonne, e suo corame
sopra

[f.901] Una Cassetta di noce con suoi
spartimenti piena di lumache marine con
suo […] e ramata sopra
Una Casetta con suoi spartimenti
Quadro uno della Resurrettione di Christo con
sua Cornice dorata di pal. 3
Quadri due compagni coll Istoria delle Sabine
con Le Cornici nere e oro
Quadro uno in tavola con Nettuno con figure
marittimi con sua Cornice Torchina e oro
Quadri due con Christo che porta La Croce, e
L'altro di Christo in Croce di ebano ad onde
Quadro una testa di S Franco. Con sua Cornice
di Ebano
Quadro uno di S. Michele Arcangelo con sua
Cornice di noce intagliata e oro
Quadretto uno di Christo morto con la sua
Cornice nera & oro

PALAZZO FELICE AT
VILLA MONTALTO, 1659

British Library: Sloane MS. 2142, Journal of
Francis Mortoft's travel through France and
Italy in the years 1658–9.

Extract from the section, dated 20 January
1659 describing 'A Pallace that was formerly
belonging to Cardinal Montalto of the Family
of Xistus Quintus' as transcribed in Letts 1925,
pp. 110–15.

In another [chamber] **A very high and Rich
Cabinett of inlaid worke, with many Aggat
pillars to the number of 15.** A great old Urne.
Two Representations in Brasse of that rare statue
in the Capitol of A lyon devouring a horse. The
late Cardinal's Dwarf's picture upon a Board.

PALAZZO FELICE AT
VILLA MONTALTO, 1665

Archivio di Stato di Roma: 30 Not.
A.C. Simoncellus, vol. 6645, ff. 1181–377.

Posthumous inventory of Cardinal Francesco
Damasceni Peretti, 1665, a copy, with few

variations, of the 1655 inventory partly
transcribed above.

[f. 1145v] **Studiolo uno fatto a tabernacolo con
organo dentro con diece colonne d'alabastro
nel primo solaro otto nel secondo e sei al terzo,
con sette figurine e due a sedere & sportelli di
diverse pietre pretiose & suo piede con figure
Indorate e suo padiglione di dobletto rosso
con trine d'oro, e francie**

PALAZZO FELICE AT
VILLA MONTALTO, c.1680

Archivio Storico Capitolino, Rome: Fondo
Cardelli, n. 91, ff. 1–76, *Inventario delle Statue,
suppellettili ed altro esistenti nel Palazzo Peretti alle
Terme*, probably compiled in about 1680–5.

Extract from the section (ff. 43–69), listing
the contents of the Palazzo Felice (taken from
Barberini 1991, pp. 47–8).

[f. 69] Galleria
Incomincia a man dritta e gira intorno
Una Statua di Appollo nudo a sedere coll'arpa
p.mi 3
Una Statua di Cupido di marmo bianco con
appresso arco e carcasso di marmo rosso
p.mi 3
Sopra il p.o tauolino d'ebano. In mezzo
Un leone che sbrana un cauallo nel modello
di Campidoglio è di metallo sopra base di
ebano legno tinto p.mi 2
Mettono in mezzo il sud.o Leone
Doi Tori amendue di metallo e sopra base di
ebano p.mi 1½ l'uno
Seguita
Una Statua di Venere che si asciuga ha un uaso
appresso p.mi 3
Nello studiolo grande che è in mezzo
**Venti sette pezzi di statuette e terminetti di
metallo dorato.**
**Lo studiolo è di ebano commesso di varie
pietre preziose delle quali anche ui sono
compartite uintiquattro colonnette di
diversa altezza**
Seguita
Una Statua di Venere con una conchiglia in
mano et coll'altra si tiene una gamba.
Ha un sciugatoro et un uaso p.mi 2½
Seguita la Galleria
Sopra l'altro tauolino d'ebano in mezzo
Un Leone che sbrana un toro di metallo.
La base è di legno intagliato
Mettono in mezzo il suddetto Leone
Doi cavalli conformi di metallo et sopra base
di ebano p.mi 1½ l'uno
Seguita
Una Statua di Satiro a sedere con sampogna in
mano p.mi 2
Una Statua di Mercurio sopra un dragone,
tiene in mano un testa tronca p.mi 3
Una Statua di un Satiro a sedere con sampogna
in mano p.mi 2
Una Statua di Marsia p.mi 3
Una Statua di Diana coll'arco et con un cane
appresso p.mi 3
Una Statua di Venere che abbraccia un Idolo
con ghirlande. La base sotto è di marmo.
p.mi 3
Una Statua di Cupido con un Lepre in mano

p.mi 2½
Una Statua di Appollo a sedere coll'arpa in
mano p.mi 3
In Mezzo
Un tavolino tondo commesso di uarie pietre
con cornice di Affricano diam. p.mi 5
Sopra ditto tauolino
Un gruppo di tre figure di metallo. Il
piedestallo è di legno tinto p.mi 5

PALAZZO FELICE AT THE
VILLA MONTALTO, JANUARY 1696

Archivio di Stato di Roma: Notai A.C. Marco
Giuseppe Pelosi, vol. 5616, fol. 138r–134v and
137r–139v. *Inventario de mobile esistenti ne Palazzi
del Giardino di Termini*, compiled on 26 January
1696.

Extract from the section (138r–139v) listing
the contents of the first-floor 'Corridore', here
identified as the loggia, taken from Gatta 2010,
pp. 118–22.

[f. 139v] Nel Corridore che siegue
Otto sgabelli indorati e dipinti con sette busti
sopra et una figurina in piedi di marmo
Quattro sgabelli di Cordovano trapuntati
Due tavolini ebano e avorio
Una tavola grande di Pietramischia con cornice
gialla
Un ritratto d'un nanno in tavola

FURNITURE FOR THE PRINCESS
CATERINA GIUSTINIANI SAVELLI,
JULY 1713

Archivio di Stato di Roma: *Giustiniani*, b. 68,
fasc. 277.

Extracts with cabinets (*studioli*) and a 'Ciborio',
the first item, here identified as
the Sixtus Cabinet, in a list of goods, made on
1 July 1713, sent from the Palazzo Savelli, after
the death of Prince Giulio Savelli in 1712, to
the Palazzo Giustininiani, by Princess Caterina
Giustiniani Savelli, taken from Squarzina 2003,
3, pp. 277–82.

**Un Ciborio alto circa dieci palmi ripieno
di Colonnette d'Agata, Capitelli, e Base
di Bronzo dorato, e tutto il Materiale
composto di diverse pietre fine di Stima,
e moltissime incassate ad uso di Anello
in Bronzo ò sia rame, ò Ottone dorato
guarnito di diverse Statuette di metallo,
come sopra dorate, e situato detto Ciborio
ad un gran Piedestallo de legno negro, e
dorato**
E più uno Studiolo di Lunghezza circa 6. Palmi,
alto 4. con sua cima sopra, tutto ripieno di
diversi ritrattini in Rame antichi incirca
n. 50. Detto Studiolo di Ebbano negro
interziato d'avorio, e statue di bronzo dorate
con due tiratorini le fila per parte di essi,
li Prospetti di quale vi è intagliato sopra
diverse Istorie antiche con suo Piedestallo di
legno verde e dorato.
[…] Due Studioli longhi circa 4. palmi con
suoi Tiratori in tutto intersiato d'avorio con
figurine sopra

[…] E piú uno Studiolo longo circa 3 palmi con
Tiratori profilati di argento [note in right
margin: 'Manca il di contro studiolo']

E piú un altro Studiolo piccolo con Tiratori
intersiati avanti di mistura verde [note in
right margin: 'Manca']

A di detto uno Studiolo mezzano con Tiratore
tutto coperto di punto francese di Seta
[note in right margin: 'Manca']

E piú un altro Studiolo mezzano di pero
negro interziati li tiratori, e tutto d'argento
profilato [note in right margin: 'Manca']

E piú un altro Studiolo grande con intagli
attorno di legno dorato, coperto di punto
francese [note in right margin: 'Manca']

E piú un altro studiolo intarziato di filetto
d'argento con suoi tiratori [note in right
margin: 'Manca']

[…] Uno Studiolo largo tre palmi, alto due, e
mezzo incirca d'ebbano interziato d'avorio,
ben custodito con dentro li suoi spartimenti
ad uso di scanzia, e si apre di sopra, con
denro circa cento Libretti tutti messi à oro,
e legati alla francese

PALAZZO FELICE AT VILLA MONTALTO 1836

Vittorio Massimo, *Notizie Istoriche della Villa
Massimo alle Terme Diocleziane con un'Appendice di
Documenti*, Rome, 1836

Extract with a description of the loggia or
gallery, pp. 53–54

… porta, che mette nella galleria esposta verso
la Villa, le cui pitture sono forse le più belle di
tutto il palazzo.

Questa galleria, lunga palmi 56, larga 24½,
segnata in pianta lettera L, è aperta a guisa di
loggia con tre arcate che danno sopra la Villa,
e formano il primo piano del palazzo Peretti da
quella parte incontro al monte della giustizia.
La sua volta a canna contiene tre quadri , due
de' quali sono stati miseramente danneggiati
ed in gran parte scrostati da un fulmine,
che cadde sù questo palazzo il 22. Maggio
della scorso anno 1835. Nel primo viene
rappresentata la nascita di Giove, raccolto ed
officiosamente servito dalle ancelli; il quadro
di mezzo, che è il più grande, e maggiormente
danneggiato rappresenta Ercole al bivio fra
il vizio e la virtù, che sceglie quest'ultima via
guidato da Pallade; e nel terzo si vede lo stesso
Ercole, il quale non ostante gli ostacoli, che
gli si attraversano giunge al tempio meta del
suo viaggio, dove viene incoronato dalla virtù.
Non sarebbe stato tanto facile interpretare il
soggetto di questi quadri in gran parte rovinati,
senza la scorta del nostro Aurelio Orso, il quale
descrivendo al naturale questa bella galleria
con 49. versi della sua Perettina, da noi indicate
alla nota 22, applica poeticamente quelle
pitture a Sisto v., che dalla sua infanzia sempre
seguitò il sentiero della virtù finchè guinse al
Pontificato, meta della sua carriera. Il restante
della volta è carico di ornate rappresentanti
ogni genere di grottesche, emblemi, ed animali,
trammezzati da quattro piccoli soggetti della
favola in altrettanti ovatini, ed agli spigoli
vedonsi otto genj, che sostengono quattro
pitture allegoriche con cornici fatte a front-

espizio, il tutto eseguito con vivacissimi colori.

Anche le pareti di questa galleria hanno il
loro sommo pregio, e forse ancora più della
volta, quantunque non vi siano dipinti, che
quattro grandi Paesi, ma toccati con tale
maestrìa, che recano meraviglia a vederli;
cesserà per altro la sorpresa quando si saprà,
che furono lavorati a gara da due celebri
paesisti di quel secolo, quali furono Paolo
Brilli, e Gio: Battista Viola, come si rileva da
varj autori, che hanno descritto Roma, e fra
gli altri dal Pinaroli nel suo Trattato delle cose
memorabilia di Roma, e dal Baglioni nelle vite
de' Pittore etc. Le parole di quest'ultimo sono
le seguenti, parlando di Gio: Battista Viola,
a pag 163: *Nella vigna di Alessandro Cardinal
Montalto tra il colle Viminale, ed Esquilino dipinse
un paese grande molto bello fatto con quella sua
maniera a concorrenza di Paolo Brillo Fiammingo.*

In uno di questi paesi a man sinistra
entrando vedesi rappresentata la morte del
Profeta disubbidiente, il quale tornando da
Betel sul suo asino fu strangolato da un leone,
che rimase accanto al suo cadavere, lasciandolo
intatto, come anche l'asino; secondo leggesi
nel lib. 3 de' Re al Cap XIII. L'altro paese a man
destra è un soggetto ignoto, non vedendovisi
altro, che un deserto con altissimi scogli, ed un
uomo che li stà considerando. Negli altri due
paesi grandi, che occupano le pareti minori
sulle porte laterali, è dipinto a man destra
Sansone, che squarcia il leone, ed a mano
sinistra Daniele nel lago de' leoni; il quali
soggetti, come anche il primo, forse furon scelti
dai pittori perchè vi figura il leone, che era la
parte principale dell'arme del Card. Montalto.
Questi paesi sono coloriti in altrettante arcate,
le quali con le tre delle finestre, e con quella
della porta d'ingresso, formano intorno alla
galleria otto archi sostenuti da pilastri dipinti
con monti e stelle a chiaroscuro sul fondo
rosso, e trammezzati da pilastri jonici, che
arrivano sotto la volta, ornati d'arabeschi
ed emblemi del Card. Montalto parimente
a chiaroscuro sul fondo giallo. Nei triangoli
laterali a ciascun arco si veggono delle figure
muliebri sedute a guisa di accademie dorate sul
fondo azzurro, ed ai quattro angoli della sala
s'incalzano otto contropilastri arabescati di
bianco sullo stesso azzurro. Finalmente anche
il zoccolo tutto intorno è dipinto a varie pietre,
e niente manca per rendere questa galleria
la più magnifica stanza del palazzo, tanto per
le pitture dalle quali è tutto intiera coperta,
quanto per sua bella esposizione verso Levante
dalla quale si gode di tutta la sotto posta Villa.*

*Per avere una piccolo idea del pregio in
cui era anticamente tenuta questa Galleria,
chiamata la loggia del piano nobile, basterà
dare un'occhiata al seguente elenco di una
porzione de' mobili co' quali era ornate l'anno
1655. come si rilieva da un inventario di quell'
anno; vi si vedera [there follow extracts of the
list of contents of this room from the 1655
inventory transcribed above, commencing
with the 'studiolo' identified as the cabinet
now at Stourhead]

APPENDIX II DESCRIPTIONS OF THE SIXTUS CABINET AT STOURHEAD

This appendix gathers together references, in publications and manuscripts, including inventories and heirloom lists, to the Sixtus Cabinet at Stourhead. In some cases the transcripts include a description of the room and of the paintings displayed with the Cabinet, and of other pietre dure objects in the house. It was rare for eighteenth-century authors to comment on individual pieces of furniture[1] and exceptional to give a provenance, so the references to the Sixtus Cabinet are remarkable and indicate the care that Henry Hoare took to bring it to the attention of visitors and to supply its history. The 13 eighteenth-century travel-writers and catalogue compilers quoted here described the Sixtus Cabinet. (Two authors who failed to remark on the Cabinet when they visited the house are omitted.[2]) Of the 13, all but three associated the Cabinet with Sixtus v and four gave the convent provenance. Mrs Powys alleged it was bought for 'an immense price, so great that he [Henry Hoare] says he never will declare ye sum'. Seven years previously, Sir John Parnell reported its value at £10,000.

The texts, prefaced by brief introductions, are in chronological order, beginning in 1754 and including Sir Richard Colt Hoare's description in his *Modern Wiltshire* (1822). Two years later William Hazlitt was unimpressed by the majority of paintings at Stourhead and omitted to mention the Cabinet.[3] Thereafter travel-writers ceased to visit and the appendix concludes with the inventory taken at the death of Sir Richard.

STOURHEAD CATALOGUE 1754

Longleat House Archives, North Muniment Room 8963.9, a MS catalogue headed 'In the Hall at Stourton' and endorsed with the date 1754 (included by permission of the Marquess of Bath)

This catalogue forms part of an artificial sequence of material relating to Stourton and the Stourtons, apparently arranged in the nineteenth century by Canon J.E. Jackson for the fourth Marquess of Bath. When it is compared to the 1742 Inventory of Stourhead,[4] it emerges that the 'Longleat' compiler omitted private rooms on the *piano nobile* (the Little Parlour and Mrs Hoare's Room), as well as sculpture, flower paintings and family portraits, apart from 'Mr Hoare on Horseback', all of which were listed in 1742; the overlaps are shown below in square brackets. Possibly the catalogue was based on notes provided by Henry Hoare and is here given in full, as the first account of Stourhead to mention the Sixtus Cabinet. It is also the earliest record of his continental purchases.

In the Hall at Stourton

Two Landskips by Wootton [1742]

Four Sea Pieces by Monamy [1742]

Mr Hoare on Horseback by Dahl and Wootton [1742]
NT 732232 *Henry Hoare II on Horseback*, by Michael Dahl (1656–1743) and John Wootton (1681/2–1764), signed by both artists and dated 1726, oil on canvas, 330.2 x 304.8 cm (Entrance Hall) (fig. 146).

Over the Chimney the Sacrifice of Iphigenia by Hardinia
NT 732300 *Architectural Capriccio with the Sacrifice of Iphigenia*, by Francis Harding (fl. *c*.1730–1760), 1745–54, oil on canvas, 167.6 x 142.2 cm (Italian Room) (fig. 152).

In the green Bed Chamber

The Triumph of Bacchus and Ariadne In Hannibal Carrachu's Gallery by Dominichino
Christie's 2 June 1883, sold, lot 62, a version of the fresco in the Palazzo Farnese. Copies of Annibale Carracci were often ascribed to Domenichino, for the prestige of his name.

Elijha praying over the Dead Child by Rembrant [1742]
Elijah raising the widow's son is recorded in the 1742 Stourhead Inventory. From 1754 onwards the painting was attributed to Rembrandt. The first printed guidebook to Stourhead (Hoare 1800, p. 11, no. 12) stated that Bishop Atterbury (1663–1732), a declared Jacobite and a friend of Henry Hoare I, gave the family the painting. Richard Earlom made a mezzotint of it in 1768 (fig. 168). The painting was sold in 1883 (Christie's 2 June 1883, lot 69, bought in). Sumowski 1983–94, vol. IV, p. 2596, no. 1723, the Earlom mezzotint; the painting, neither illustrated nor located, is attributed to Jan Victors (1619–1676).

The Nativity by Trevisani

Bachinals by Titian

Our Saviour St John and the Virgin by Andrea del Sarto
NT 724306 *Madonna and Child with St John the Baptist*, after Andrea del Sarto (1486–1530), seventeenth century, oil on canvas, 69.9 x 55.2 cm. Can this be the painting referred to in the will of Robert Nelson (1656–1714/5), the London philanthropist? He bequeathed Henry Hoare I, 'my picture, being the Madonna of Andrea del Sarto, which hangs in my Parlour, with the frame that belongs to it' (TNA probate 11/544, will dated 18 December 1714). If this is the painting, it is arguably the cornerstone of the Stourhead picture collection (Picture Gallery).

A Madonna and Child by Carlo Cignani
Perhaps NT 732132 *The Madonna and Child*, by Francesco Trevisani (1656–1746), *c*.1700, oil on canvas, 84.5 x 65.4 cm (Picture Gallery).

In the Parlour

The Inside of St Peters Church at Rome by Paulo Pannoni
NT 732268 *The Interior of St Peter's at Rome*, possibly by Francis Harding (fl. 1730–1760), after Giovanni Paolo Panini, 1730–42, oil on canvas, 114.3 x 160 cm (Music Room) (fig. 155).

In the Cabinet Room

Herodias and St John Baptist Head by Carlo Dulci
Christie's 2 June 1883, sold, lot 65.

Herculas between Virtue and Pleasure by Nicolo Poussin
NT 732103 *Choice of Hercules*, by Nicolas Poussin (1594–1665), 1636–7, oil on canvas, 88.3 x 71.8 cm (Picture Gallery) (fig. 174).

Our Saviour St John and the Virgin from the Duke of Orleans Raphael – Italian

Rape of the Sabins by Nic.^o Poussin
The Abduction of the Sabine Women, by Nicolas Poussin (1594–1665), *c*.1633–4, oil on canvas, 154.6 x 209.9 cm. Christie's 2 June 1883, sold, lot 63, now at the Metropolitan Museum of Art, New York (accession number 46.160) (fig. 172). This picture remains in a distinctive late-seventeenth-century French frame – probably from its time in the collection of Bénigne de Ragois de Bretonvilliers.

The Marriage of St Catherine by Barrochio of Urbin
NT 732108 *The Mystic Marriage of St Catherine*, by Denys Calvaert (*c*.1540–1619), 1590–5, oil on copper, 47.6 x 38.1 cm (Picture Gallery) (fig. 173).

The Flight into Egypt by Carlo Marat
NT 732107 *The Flight into Egypt*, by Carlo Maratti (1625–1713), mid-seventeenth century, oil on copper, 51.4 x 37.5 cm (Picture Gallery) (fig. 175).

In the best bed Chamber

Noah Sacrificing by Imperiali
NT 732123 *The Sacrifice of Noah*, by Francesco Fernandi , called Imperiali (1679–1740), *c*.1720, oil on canvas, 137.2 x 255.3 cm (Picture Gallery).

Rachel Concealing the Household Gods by Imperiali
NT 732124 *Rachel sitting on the Household Gods of Laban*, by Imperiali, *c*.1720, oil on canvas, 137.2 x 255.3 cm (Picture Gallery).

The Holy Family after the King of France's Raphael at Versailles – Italian
NT 732105 *The Holy Family of François I*, after Raphael, seventeenth century, oil on panel, 62.2 x 43.2 cm (Picture Gallery) (fig. 162). The original was in the French Royal Collection and is now at the Louvre (inv. 604, oil on canvas, 207 x 140 cm).

David and Goliah's Head by Julius Romano
NT 732115 *David with the Head of Goliath*, Italian (Emilian) School, 1600–29, oil on panel, 57.1 x 41.9 cm (Picture Gallery).

A Lanskip by Claude Lorrain

As Companion
Henry Hoare Accounts 1734–49, 5 December 1746, 'Mr Wootton for a Picture, a Comp^n to my Claude L^n' £36-15-0.' He subsequently acquired two copies of Claudes in the Palazzo Doria-Pamphilj; NT 732157 and NT 732178 one by Locatelli (1695–1741), the other, a generation later, by Plimmer (fl. 1755–1761).

In the best dressing Room

A Battle Piece by Bourgognon
NT 732091 *A Battle Scene*, by Jacques Courtois, Il Borgognone (1621–1676), 1647–76, oil on canvas, 81.3 x 114.4 cm (Picture Gallery anteroom). WSA 383.907.2 possibly purchased on behalf of Henry Hoare, who received a letter from his son dated 25 December 1750, reporting pictures he saw in galleries in Paris, 'The claude you desire me to describe is remarkable [...] it is a pleasant picture, but not a Warm one. & neither that nor any of the others are in good preservation enough for you to buy. I mentioned to you before the only one I thought worth anything, the Bourgognone.'

The Woman washing our Saviours feet after Paul Veronese by Sebastian Bourbell
Christie's 2 June 1883, sold, lot 55. 'Bourbell' is Sebastiano Bombelli (1635–1719), another instance of varnishing a copy with a reputed artist's name.

A Night Piece Landskip by Rembrant
Christie's 2 June 1883, sold, lot 68. The 'Night Piece' is the *Landscape with the Rest on the Flight into Egypt*, by Rembrandt, 1647, purchased for the National Gallery of Ireland, Dublin (inv. NGI 215, oil on panel, 34 x 48 cm).

A Storm by Wootton

A Sun Set by Wootton

A Galatea on Glass – Italian

Ruins &c in Water Colour's by Marco Ritzi

In the Salloon

Venus and the Graces by guido, Copy by Davison
NT 732315 *The Toilet of Venus*, by Jeremiah Davison (c.1695–1745), after Guido Reni, 1728–45, oil on canvas, 261.6 x 205.7 cm (Staircase Hall) (fig. 148). A version from the studio of Guido Reni hung at Kensington Palace, and later at Windsor Castle, until William IV gave it to the National Gallery, London in 1836 (inv. NG 90, c.1620–5, oil on canvas, 281.9 x 205.7 cm).

Judgment of Mydas by Sebastian Bordon
The Judgment of Midas, by Sébastien Bourdon (1616–1671). WSA 383.907, Sir John Lambert to Henry Hoare, 1 February 1743/4, reporting the purchase and dispatch of this painting from Paris for 976 French *livres*, about £46. (In 1743/4 Lambert quoted an exchange rate of 21.12 *livres* to one pound sterling.) It was rescued from the fire at Stourhead in 1902 but not reinstated. In the Stourhead Catalogue 1898 Stourhead Archive, 'Catalogue of the principal Paintings & Drawings at Stourhead July 6th 1898', p. 14, MS annotation by Alda, Lady Hoare noted that Sir Henry Hoare, 6th Bt gave *The Judgment of Midas* to the Victoria Art Gallery, Bath, in 1907. Current whereabouts unknown.

Andromeda by guido Copy by Davison
NT 732314 *Perseus and Andromeda*, by Jeremiah Davison, after Guido Reni, 1728–45, oil on canvas, 261.6 x 205.7 cm (Staircase Hall). The copy was made from a painting, after Guido Reni, which hung at Kensington Palace, and later at Windsor Castle, until William IV gave it to the National Gallery, London in 1836

(inv. NG 87, oil on canvas, 280 x 205.7 cm). The original is in Palazzo Rospigliosi-Pallavicini, Rome (1635–6, oil on canvas, 271 x 217 cm).

Minerva accompanied by Hercules by Paul Veronese, Copy
NT 732313 *Wisdom and Strength*, after Paolo Veronese (1528–1588), seventeenth century, oil on canvas, 261.6 x 175.3 cm (Staircase Hall) (fig. 160). The original hung at the Palais Royal, Paris, where Henry Hoare probably saw it. The painting is now in the Frick Collection, New York (Accession no.1912.1.128, c.1576, oil on canvas, 214.6 x 167 cm).

Herodias's daughter by guido, Copy
NT 732316 *Salome with the Head of the Baptist*, by Pompeo Girolamo Batoni (1708–1787), after Guido Reni, c.1740, oil on canvas, 261.6 x 175.2 cm (Staircase Hall) (fig. 157). The original hung in the Palazzo Colonna, Rome, where Henry Hoare probably saw it. The painting is now in the Art Institute of Chicago (1639–40, oil on canvas, 248.5 x 172 cm).

Rape of Helen by guido, Copy
The Abduction of Helen, after Guido Reni, c.1740, oil on canvas approx. 250 x 310 cm. In 1907 Sir Henry Hoare, 6th Bt, gave this copy to the Victoria Art Gallery (Accession no. BATVG:P1907.3). The original in the Louvre (inv.539, 1629, oil on canvas, 253 x 265 cm) and a contemporary copy attributed to Giacinto Campagna (c.1600–1650) is in the Palazzo Spada, Rome (inv.106, oil on canvas, 250 x 250 cm), where Henry Hoare could have seen it.

King Charles Children – Vandyke, Copy by Davison
NT 732288 *The Three Eldest Children of Charles I*, after Sir Anthony Van Dyck (1599–1641), c.1740, oil on canvas, 147.3 x 147.3 cm (lent to Montacute House). Original in the Royal Collection (inv. RCIN 404403 1635–6, oil on canvas, 133.8 x 151.7 cm).

Death of Dido by guerciho, Copy
The Death of Dido, after Guercino, c.1740, oil on canvas approx. 250 x 310 cm. In 1907 Sir Henry Hoare, 6th Bt, gave this copy to the Victoria Art Gallery (Accession no. BATVG:P1907.4). The original is in the Palazzo Spada, Rome (inv.132, 1631, oil on canvas, 287 x 335 cm) (fig. 154).

The Cabinett or rather Organ was made by The direction of Pope Sextus Quintus for his holiness's Apartment in the Vatican. This Pope was Cotemporary with Elizabeth Queen of England, and he was originally a Pig driver.

This is the first of four assertions that the Cabinet once housed an organ. Hanway 1756, Walpole 1762 and Burlington 1779 followed.

The Bust of the Pope and his Nephew and the Princess (who was once a Laundress) of each side of him, with others of the Peretti Family are represented on the black Pedestal, to the Life in a Curious Composition.

The several Orders of Columns are all different sorts of Oriental Alabaster, The Green Stones in the Pedestals of the lower range of Columns are very rare and of the root of Emerald.

In the Frizes of the Entablatures and in the Center Door are severall precious Stones Viz[t].

Emeralds, Rubys, Amathists &c
The General work is of Oriental Stones set in Silver
The two large Oval Stones in the Sides are Egyptian Pebbles
The Architecture & diminishing form up to the Top was admired at Rome where M[r]. Hoare bought it in a Convent, to whom a Nun the last of the Pope's Nephew's (or Peretti) Family left it.

The first of four assertions of the convent provenance; Hanway 1756, Burlington 1779 and Rezzonico 1787 followed. The lapse of years between the writers indicates that the story endured.

HANWAY 1756

Jonas Hanway, *A journal of eight days journey from Portsmouth to Kingston upon Thames ... in a series of sixty-four letters: addressed to two ladies of the partie ... by a gentleman of the partie*, London, 1756, pp. 86–101

Jonas Hanway (1712–1786), born in Portsmouth, sought his fortune in London. He was a merchant in Lisbon from 1729–41 and later led delegations to St Petersburg and to Persia. The success of his *Historical Account of the British Trade over the Caspian Sea* (4 vols, 1753), encouraged him as an author. In 1755 he returned to Hampshire and in 1756 published *A journal of eight days journey*. The country houses Hanway visited included Wilton, Longford Castle, Eastbury, Blandford (Bryanston) and Stourhead. He had an introduction to Henry Hoare and stayed several days with him, so Stourhead was the highlight of the tour. Hanway's account is important, because his *cicerone* was the owner himself. He described the garden in transition; the great lake was formed but the Pantheon incomplete. He went boating on the lake with Henry. Hanway rounded off his description of Stourhead with a character-sketch of Henry Hoare as 'liberal without prodigality and charitable without ostentation' (pp. 93–4). Hanway then dilated on the perils of wealth and the possession of worldly goods, somehow absolving his host. Hanway was not admired by Samuel Johnson, who claimed he had 'acquired some reputation by traveling abroad, but lost it all by traveling at home'. Hanway continued to profit from the Russia Company and was a notable philanthropist, his main concern being orphaned city children.

Jonas Hanway's account of Stourhead appeared, with minor alterations, in *The London Chronicle or Universal Evening Post*, no. 73, 16–18 June 1757, p. 578.

Letter XXX: pp. 86–8 [extracts]

The saloon has something peculiar; it pleases extremely, by having, at once, all the charms of a grand apartment, and all the comfort of a small one. [...] The FLORENCE boxes, placed on the marble tables, in this saloon, deserve great notice: they are set with many curious, and with some costly oriental stones.

In the drawing-room is a cabinet supported by a rich frame or pedestal, which I understood was once the case of an organ. This cabinet formerly belonged to pope SEXTUS V. The effigies of this pope, and the PERETTI family, from whom one of his nephews descended, are taken from the life, and set in the cabinet in round recesses, with glasses before them, in order to preserve them. The last of this family was a nun, who left the cabinet to a convent in ROME, where Mr. H**** made a purchase of it. The whole is a great curiosity, and of high value. In this apartment are also many excellent painting of the first masters. Within this is a smaller room, which is also a cabinet of pictures.

DUCHESS OF BEAUFORT 1762

John Harris, 'The Duchess of Beaufort's *Observations on Places*', *Georgian Group Journal*, x, 2000, p. 41; citing the Badminton Muniment Room, FM K1/1/4

Elizabeth Berkeley (d.1799) was daughter of John Berkeley of Stoke Gifford. She married the fourth Duke of Beaufort in 1740 but was widowed 16 years later. She wrote a journal of her Grand Tour 1769–74, which reveals her as an intelligent and observant commentator. Prior to that she compiled her *Observations on Places*, recording her travels in England, commencing in 1750. Her first interest lay in landscape gardening and architecture but she also remarked on interior décor and listed the subject and attributions of pictures at Wilton and Longford. At Stourhead she described the house and, briefly, the garden; she admired paintings by Maratti, Imperiali, Titian and Rembrandt.

16 July 1762 [extract]

In ye Cabinet room Cabinet very fine of precious Stones, & a Coffre of the same.

WALPOLE 1762

(ed.) Paget Toynbee, 'Horace Walpole's Journals of Visits to Country Seats &c.', *The Walpole Society*, vol. XVI, 1927–8, pp. 41–4, 'xxvi Journey to Stourhead, Redlynch, Longleate, Haselgrove, Melbury, and Abbotsbury in July 1762'

In the journal Horace Walpole (1717–1797) was concerned with recording painting collections. As well as listing old masters, he included portraits, often with biographical information. He had a taste for genealogy and empathized with ancient families. Furniture he mentioned when it was out of the ordinary: state beds, chairs of state, an ebony suite at Longleat and the sea-dogs table at Hardwick Hall.[5] He seldom discussed the provenance of furniture, which makes his remarks on the Sixtus Cabinet exceptional. His account of the collection at Stourhead is in note form, whereas for the majority of houses he wrote narrative.

In the Cabinet-room [pp. 41–2]

Three views of Venice, by Canaletti.

The prodigal Son, by Sebastian Ricci.

Holy Family, after Raphael.

Flight into Egypt, by Carlo Maratti.

Rape of the Sabines, by Nicolo Poussin.

Marriage of St Catherine, by Baroccio.

Holy Family, after the Raphael at Versailles.

Ruins of Rome, over doors by Paoli Anesi.

A magnificent Cabinet, inlaid with precious Stones, which formerly was an organ belonging to Sixtus Quintus. Round the bottom are medalions in wax coloured & finely executed, of the Pope & his brother's family, called Peretti.

[extract]

In the dressing room [adjoining the red damask bedchamber, the present South Apartment], A great many small Italian heads in rounds; a family; in oil.

[extract]

In the sky-light room, A fine Inlaid Florentine box, on a marble pedestal.

ANONYMOUS 1765

MS description of Stourhead in August 1765 (private collection, Norwich)

The transcription below was supplied by the owner of the manuscript. It is a closely written account of a series of journeys, the first undertaken in 1765 from London to Bath and Bristol and surrounding places of interest. While the account of the Sixtus Cabinet reveals nothing new, the description of the colour schemes on the *piano nobile* of Stourhead is useful and, uniquely, the author identified the staircase as 'Stone' – describing the colour or material?

[extract]

having viewed the Gardens, we went to the house, which is a Modern building, You assend by a handsome Hight of steps to the Hall, which is a very grand one, theris the picture of Mr Hoare on Horseback and many others, on the left hand you enter a genteel parlour furnished with Crimson silk damask beyond that is the Cabinet room furnished with the same, the Cabinet is the most curious of the kind I ever saw it is beyond discription the chiefest part of it is Agate & Mock Stone, it is a great height & sharp at the Top with pillars up the Front, I next entered the Crimson Silk Damask Bed Chamber, & through that to the Dressing room, furnished with the same, and adorned with many pretty pictures, the Dressing Table is set out with B and Gold India Boxes & a curious little link Silver Basket in fillegree, we then crossed the hall to the Library, which is furnished with Pea Green, beyond that is a Bed Chamber furn: Blue Lutestring, the bed in India work in a small Pattern & Quilted, lined with Blue, there is many fine pictures in the room which show to great advantage on that colour, the Mouldings are mostly Gilt, & every Cornish a different pattern in Stucco, the last Bed Chamber was Crimson furniture, the Bed worked in a large pattern upon Dimity, lined with Sattin, the Dressing room beyond it was very elegant, the Table large & Boxes the same as the former but finer, in the middle

was an Ornament looked like a little trunk of Agate, the furniture Crimson Damask, against the Wanscot was a fine piece of Horodicus Daughter with John Baptists head in a Charger, also Elijah raising the Widows Son, we then entered the Saloon furnished with Blue silk damask & lined with fine Paintings, can only remember the Death of Queen Dido, it is a very large and elegant room, returned through the Hall, passed by the staircase which is Stone, hung upon Geometry, Painted Green & Ornamented with Stucco, I then took my leave of that most agreeable place, which is upon the whole the finest I ever saw.

ANONYMOUS 1766

British Library, Add. MS 6767, ff. 36 and 37

The author set off from Manby in Lincolnshire on 26 May 1766 and travelled south to Wiltshire. He visited Thoresby, Chatsworth and the Leasowes without mentioning the interiors of these houses. He described rooms at Hagley briefly but with approval and then travelled to Oxford, Winchester, Portsmouth and on to Salisbury. He did not go inside Wilton. At Longford Castle he admired paintings by Claude Lorrain, Poussin and Holbein. Fonthill he found incomplete but noted expensive chim-ney pieces 'by Moore of London'. Longleat was 'badly furnish'd' but contained some good family portraits. He wrote extensively about the grounds of Stourhead. He admired scenery, natural and man-made, he was knowledgeable about pictures, but was not otherwise a 'contents' person.

[extracts]

The House is modern – the entrance is adorned with Columns of the Corinthian order. It is in every respect most superbly furnish'd. The Cabinet, which once belonged to Pope Sixtus 5th is esteemed a great curiosity, and is indeed very fine […] There is a small but good Collection of Paintings – some admirable copies of the most capital Pictures in Europe, by the most eminent living Masters – Raphael Mengs, Pompeio Battoni &c. several of the[m] from the most esteemed of Raphael and Guido Reni. The rape of the Sabines by Nicolo Poussin, is a fine Picture. The Judgement of Hercules which Strange has engraved – two very fine Rembrandts, and some by Salvator Rosa.

PARNELL 1769

The Library of the London School of Economics and Political Science, Archives Collection Misc. 0038, 'Journal of a Tour thro' Wales and England, anno. 1769' by Sir John Parnell, MS, 4 vols, vol. II, ff. 79–114

After graduating at Trinity College, Dublin, Sir John Parnell, 2nd Bt (1745–1801) studied Law at Lincoln's Inn. He sat in the Irish Parliament and the parliament at Westminster, rising to become Chancellor of the Irish Exchequer in 1785. From May 1769–April 1770 he toured England to gather ideas for improving Rathleague, his property in Queen's County. Sir John's interests lay in estates: farms and husbandry, parks and gardens, then architecture. He gave long descriptions, with sketches, of the gardens at Shugborough, Painshill, Claremont, Prior Park, Stourhead, Hagley and the Leasowes. In vol. II, Sir John described the journey from Bath, through the Longleat estate, to Stourhead to which he allotted 36 pages. His account of the Stourhead garden was published in 1982.[6] Sir John's description of the house is unusually discursive; he seldom noted pictures or *objets d'art* and it is surprising he was taken by the Sixtus Cabinet and the pietre dure caskets. He visited with seven friends, who may have persuaded him to pay greater attention indoors.[7]

Description of the house on
26 September 1769 [extracts]

[f. 98] I need say Little of the House as the two fronts and Ground Plan are in the Vitruvius Brittannicus

[f. 99] I must only observe that there is a convenience grandeur neatness, and at the same time a degree of comfortableness in its Inside that tempts me to Pronounce it the most desirable House for a man from 2000 to 10000 a year I Ever was shewn and a strong contrast to the waste of Rooms and throw away size and Expense of M[r] Beckfords w[ch] I saw the day following

[ff. 101–160] as I thought M[r] Hoares House so desirably furnishd I took a memorandum of what struck me

the Hall about 30 cube a coved ceiling on the left Hand a great Picture of the Present M[r] Hoare on Horseback–

over the chimney Henry the fourth of france and the Belle Gabrielle his Mistress under the characters of Mars and Venus–

at Each side the Door Leading to the Vestibule two Large Pictures one Cleopatra supplicating Augustus Beautifully painted by Mincks

on the other the marquis Pallavicini Lead on by his genius to the Temple of fame &c Carlo Maratti painting his Picture – by Carlo Maratti Mem[dm] [memorandum] they Breakfast & spend All the morning in this Hall, the Prospect Lovely from the Door, but Nothing of M[r] Hoares Improvemn[ts] to signifie to be seen from any Part of his House–

on the Right Hand the Hall is the Small Dining Parlour 30 by 20 or rather Drawing Room Hung with Red Damask & Pictures – within it an anti-chamber to the Red Damask Bedchamber in it an Exquisite cabinett of florintine Inlaid marble with cameos &c & alabaster Pillars. Originally belonging to Pope Sixtus quintus and Valued at £10000 this stands in a little Recess formed by two Pillars taking up about 8 feet the Roof and is Placed upon a Little Platform about a foot higher than the floor which makes it more conspicuous – [Sir John's 'Platform' could be the plain plinth on which the Pedestal arch rests.]

the next Room's the Bedchamber & within it a small closet – all the Rooms of this side the House are hung with crimson Damask & some Excellent pictures but small figures in general

as the Rooms are not great on the other side the Hall stands the Library consisting of a Long sett of shelves without glass but Properly ornamented of the side of the Room opposite the windows and two pair Presses in the same taste one at Each side a window in the End of the Room the other side is where the windows are and the other End the fire Place and Door – within this Room is a Most Beautifull Bed-chamber the Bed stands in an alcove where the great cabinett stands in the fellow Room on the other side the House the Bed Painted silk Exquisitely Beautifull the ceiling done in grotesque very Prettily the walls ornamented with Drawings in water colours a recess in which an Indian Cabinett the Room furnished a lite Blue

the next Room's a Bedchamber with a work Bed India Dimity Embroiderd with worsteds in an Elegant taste and Lined with crimson Sattin over the chimney the fine Picture of Rembrant Elisha Raising the widows son one of the finest Rembrants in the world the Room hung with crimson Paper. I liked this Room Least of any, but within it was a Dressing Room so Elegant that it was like one Entire cabinett The chimney Piece tho small was Beautifully wrought in white & Sienna Marble I think the Prettiest chimney Piece I Ever saw tho I have seen Hundreds more Expensive in this Room there were no windows but lighted at the top as Lord charlemonts ante Room to his Library the walls Hung with the Best

Small Pictures which M[r] Hoare cou[l]d procure at one End stood a florentine chest of fine Inlaid Marbles and Jaspers &c on a little Pedastle of grey & sienna marble formd of four Pillars & four arches on the Chest festoons of flowers & fruit formd in Pretious stones under the Arch lay a sleeping Cupid – there were two others of these florentine chests but not so fine as this in the other Bedchamber fill'd with Dryd Rose Leaves[8] [Parnell sketched the chest and stand]. These chests Particularly Those placed on Marble Stands Look very Elegant & cooling in summer but I can not make out any absolute use in them

Directly opposite to the Hall door stands the Door to a Vestibule Round which goes the stairs and opposite to that the Entrance to the Great Dining Parlour – 50 feet and High as the Hall these two Rooms having nothing over them the two side suits an attic and this forms the House with Excellent offices under the whole [Parnell sketched the ground plan, see fig. 167] in the Elegant Dining Parlour are framed Paintings a copy of the Herodias of Guido by Pompeyo Battone two copies of the Rape of Helen & the Death of Dido the Judgment of Midas not very Pleasing Pictures the furniture Blue Damask ceiling coved, the Room I think look Rathur Bleak and Inadequate to the rest of the House, the window[s] looking to Nothing before Obelisk […]

MRS POWYS 1776

British Library Add. MS 42168, Caroline Powys, Journals and Recipe-Book of Caroline Powys, 14 vols, vol. IX, 'Journal of a Five days Tour in a Letter to a Friend 1776', Stourhead, ff. 14–27

The manuscripts are published, see (ed.)

Emily J. Climenson, *Passages from the Diaries of Mrs Philip Lybbe Powys of Hardwick House, Oxon. AD 1756–1808*, London, 1899, pp. 168–73.

Caroline Powys (1738–1817) married Philip Lybbe Powys of Hardwick House, Whitchurch, Oxfordshire, in 1762. John Girle, her father, had encouraged her to keep a diary and after her marriage she continued to record her social life and visits to country houses. In so doing she left a record of 'polite' society in the later eighteenth century. Mrs Powys was less interested in paintings than furnishings. Her description of the Sixtus Cabinet is among the fullest. She set out to see Stourhead on 5 August 1776 with 'M[r] Annesley, my Brother [-in-law], M[r] Powys […] in two Phaetons' (f. 2). They made a leisurely journey, calling at Long-ford, Wilton and Fonthill before arriving, on the fifth day, at Stourton. When she reached Stourhead she complained that there was no catalogue available (f. 20). The party went on to see Stonehenge and spent the night at Amesbury, where they met Horace Walpole and Robert Adam (the architect?), 'whom we were exceedingly well acquainted with' (f. 30). Her reference to the date '1677' on the 'Antique Cabinet' is puzzling.

ff. 23–4: the Cabinet Room [extract]

in the third room shown us, is the so much talked on Cabinet, that once belong'd to Pope Sixtus V, which M[r] Hoare purchas'd at an immense price, so great that he says he never will declare ye sum. It is indeed most Beautifully Ornamental, as well as valuable for on the outside are many fine Jems a Border goes around ye frame 4 feet from ye ground, a[re] set in Frames Pope Sixtus['s] picture and those of his Family, drawn you may be sure after he was rais'd from his original obscurity; some <u>time</u> after the purchase, in some inner private drawers were found Seventy two other miniatures some in the old English dress others that of Spain Italy &c the date on this curious Antique Cabinet is 1677 in a Closet out of this room is a most inimitable portrait of Titian by himself at 92 years old; small place[?] round this are hung the 72 miniatures above mention'd.

CURWEN 1776

George Atkinson Ward, *Journal and Letters of the late Samuel Curwen … an American refugee in England … 1775–1784*, London, 1842, pp. 78–9

Samuel Curwen (1715–1802), born in New England, was a life-long anglophile. He fought the French, rose to be a Judge of the Admiralty and, at the outbreak of the War of Independence, quit America to come to London. His published letters describe British towns, institutions and politics. He was often in the South-west, where small seaside villages were becoming health resorts. He was less interested in country houses. In the vicinity of Stourhead he visited Redlynch and Longleat but not, apparently, Wardour, Fonthill or Wilton. Curwen mistook Lord Arundell (of neighbouring Wardour Castle) as the owner of Stourhead. Describing the Cabinet, his reference to prints in metal frames is puzzling.

Did he mean the miniatures? If so, this is the first mention of their return to the Cabinet drawers. In August the same year Mrs Powys, a more reliable commentator, had seen the miniatures in the closet adjoining the Cabinet (see above). Sir Richard Sulivan found them on show there in 1778 (see below).

23 September 1776

Rode through Lord Ilchester's park, passing by the late Lord Berkeley's estate, and through a vale to Lord Arundle's. One passes on a flight of noble steps to the centre door letting into the hall; – the walls are adorned with paintings of the most celebrated artists. There is a cabinet of Pope Sixtus Quintus, which stands on a mahogany frame; – the front is of ebony; and amber pillars, set with sapphires, emeralds and other precious stones, and mini-atures of all the Perotti family from which he sprang, and elegantly executed in white alabaster. In the drawers are prints of the principal royal and noble families of Europe in metal frames.

SULIVAN 1778

Sir Richard Joseph Sulivan, *Observations made during a tour through parts of England, Scotland, and Wales, in a series of letters*, London, 1780 pp. 52–60 Letter VI, July 1778

Sir Richard Joseph Sulivan (or Sullivan), 1st Bt (1752–1806), began his career with the East India Company and after his return to Britain in 1784 he took a tour of the country, which he described in the *Observations*. In 1787 he stood as a MP and continued as a politician. In 1804 he was granted a baronetcy by Pitt. Horace Walpole annotated his copy of the *Observations* (NAL, Dyce, T., 4 to 9578) witheringly: 'This is one of the worst of our many modern books on travels. It is silly, pert, vulgar, ignorant; aims at florid diction, which is no merit, unless when absolutely necessary to description of prospects; it is larded with affectation often and crass sentiment. The blunders & false spellings are numerous; and the whole betrays total want of taste. H.W.'

Caves were a highlight for Sulivan, notably Wookey Hole in Somerset and Poole's Hole near Buxton. He called at the great country houses and was duly impressed by Longford Castle, Wardour Castle and Wilton.

A shortened version of Sulivan's text appeared in Mavor 1800, vol. III, pp. 1–152 (Stourhead, pp. 32–6).

pp. 55–6 [extracts]

In the cabinet room, A Grecian lady, by Angelica Kauffman. The departure from Egypt, by Carlo Moratti. The meeting of Jacob and Esau, by Roza de Tivoli. A holy family, copied from Raphael. A holy family, by Carlo Moratti. A morning and evening, by Luccotelli. A cabinet of Pope Sixtus V. heavy, and rich, though not elegant. A holy family, from the school of Raphael. An antique amber cabinet. The marriage of St. Catherine, a most beautiful and highly-coloured painting, by Barocci of Urbin.
"And heavenly choirs
"Their Hymenean sung,

"Glory to God in the highest,
"And on the earth peace,
"Good will towards men."
In the dressing-room to that chamber [state bed chamber] [...] 79 miniature pictures, many of them of English Monarchs, found in the cabinet of Pope Sixtus V [...]
Pleased with the paintings, and satisfied altogether with the stile and furniture of the house, we next entered upon a verdant lawn.

BURLINGTON 1779

Charles Burlington, David Llewellyn Rees and Alexander Murray, *The Modern Universal British Traveller*, London, 1779, p. 394

The *Traveller* described Wiltshire in 24 pages of double columns. It mentioned the towns, Stonehenge and a selection of country houses: Longford, Amesbury Abbey and Stourhead it covered briefly, but omitted Longleat. The authors gave an eight-column account of Wilton House, leaning heavily on the published guidebook, which they neglected to acknowledge. The description shows some interest in semi-precious stones. They noted in the Cube Room 'a Jasper marble table' and 'an alto relievo of Pyrrhus the son of Achilles; it is an oval and has a splendid aspect as of a very large gem, the face is porphyry, which the cardinal Mazarine so much valued as to finish his dress with a helmet of different coloured marble' (p. 387).

This account of Stourhead was published in abbreviated form in *A New Display of the Beauties of England*, 2 vols, London, 1787, vol. II, pp. 365–6.

p. 394 [extract]

In the drawing-room is a great curiosity, having formerly belonged to the famous pope Sixtus Quintus. It is a fine cabinet supported by a rich pedestal, said to have been once the case of an organ. On the cabinet are fine paintings of the pope, and others of the Peretti family, the last of whom was a nun, who gave it to a convent at Rome, where Mr. Hoare purchased it.

STOURHEAD CATALOGUE 1784

WSA 383.715, copy deed, ff. 57–64, 'The Catalogue or Particulars of the Pictures Prints Statues and other Things in ... Stourhead ... mentioned in the Indenture whereunto the same is annexed.'

The catalogue is attached to the Settlement of 27 January 1784 whereby Henry Hoare transferred Stourhead, the surrounding estates and the heirloom contents of the house to trustees for his own use, then for Richard Colt Hoare and his successors during their lives. On 30 September 1784 Henry renounced his interest in favour of his grandson. This is an 'heirloom list' – neither an inventory of the house, nor a complete record of the pictures. Conspicuously, it omitted the equestrian portrait of Henry Hoare in the Hall by Dahl and Wootton.

In the Cabinet Room

Pictures

The Flight into Egypt By Carloe Marratti

Jacob and Esau Meeting By Rosa of Tivoli

The Holy Family By Hannibal Carrachi

Cattle and Figures By Cuyp

The two Claudes in the Pamphili Palace at Rome By Luccatelli

Two Views of Venice By Canaletti

The four Elements By Brugen and Van Balen

A Sea View and Rocks By Salvator Rosa

The Holy Family at Versailles From Raphael

Elijah praying over the Dead child By Rembrandt

The Marriage of Saint Catherine By Barrocio

Ruins of Rome over the Doors By Paoli Aucoi

Neptune Calming the Sea and Saint George By Woodforde

David and Goliath By Mola

Statues

A Statue of Jupiter – Antiques

A Statue of Juno

Cabinet &c.

A Superb Cabinet and Pedestal on it

A Medal of Queen Elizabeth and the George and Dragon hanging under it in Gold

In the Sky Light Room [extract]

Inlaid box &c.

A Florence Inlaid Box with a Pedestal and Boy under it in Marble by By Fiamingo

COUNT CARLO GASTONE DELLA TORRE DI REZZONICO 1787

Viaggio in Inghilterra di Carlo Castone Gaetano della Torre di Rezzonico Comasco, (ed.) P. Gamba, Venice, 1824, pp.14–15

Count Carlo Gastone della Torre di Rezzonico (1742–1796) was a relative of Pope Clement XIII, a scholar and poet. He toured England in 1787–8; among the gardens he visited were Painshill, Blenheim, Castle Howard, Chatsworth, Kedleston and Stourhead. When he came to the latter in 1787, he described the garden and the house, where he admired the picture collection and the Sixtus Cabinet and he identified the Armada 'Dangers Averted' medal (see Appendix V, pp. 216–17). In the light of the Count's comments it is worth noting that Henry Hoare also possessed a miniature of Mary Queen of Scots.[9]

[extract]

Ma non debbo tacere la più bella rarità che qui vidi, cioè il Gabinetto portatile di pietre preziose, di statuette e di picciole colonne, d' iscrizioni e di ritraiti, che fu già di Sisto V, e dove si veggono effigiati i fasti della famiglia Peretti: lavoro ammirabile che pie namente gareggia colla ricchezza della materia. L'ultima della pontificia casa fu mo naca, regalò questo gabinetto ad un convento in Roma, ed il sig. Hoare lo ha poscia comperato. Vidi qui posta la medaglia unica e rarissima della regina Elisabetta dopo la vittoria che riportò sull' armata *invincibile* di Filippo II. La medaglia si gira sovra un perno per essere veduta da' due lati, ed è: custodita sotto cristalli con cerniere dorate. Ella è di smalto a più colori col ritratto della regina, che ben si vede non essere stata mai bella, nè degna d'entrare in contesa per ciò colla rivale Marie di Scozia. Il rovescio è un alloro in mezzo al mare con leggenda intorno.

But I cannot be silent about the most beautiful and rare object on display, the freestanding Cabinet of precious stones, with statuettes, inscriptions and portraits which belonged to the late Sixtus V. One sees the likenesses and splendours of the Peretti family: a wonderful piece of work that does justice to the sumptuous materials. The last of the Pope's family was a nun who donated the cabinet to a convent in Rome where Mr Hoare later purchased it. Placed upon it one can see the unique and rare medal of Queen Elizabeth I after the victory over the *invincible* Armada sent by Philip II. The medal turns on a pin so that one can see both sides and it is kept under a glass cover with a gold clasp. It is decorated with enamel of several colours and displays a portrait of the Queen who can be seen to have never been beautiful and thus not worthy of comparison with her rival Mary of Scotland. The reverse has a laurel tree in the middle of the ocean with an inscription around.

GUIDEBOOK 1800

Anonymous [Sir Richard Colt Hoare, Bt], *A Description of the House and Gardens at Stourhead … with a Catalogue of the Pictures &c.*, Salisbury, 1800, pp. 14–17

The guidebook does not describe the new Library and Picture Gallery and the Sixtus Cabinet remained in Henry Hoare's setting (the present Little Dining Room). Paintings marked with an * were also recorded in the Cabinet Room by the 1784 catalogue.

Cabinet Room

This Cabinet belonged to Pope Sextus V.; around it are Portraits in wax of the Peretti Family, of which he bore the name. His own portrait is in the centre.

Upon it is fixed a curious and scarce medal of gold, struck during the reign of Queen Elizabeth, upon the defeat of the Spanish armada.

28 A View of St. Mark's Place at Venice, by Canaletti.

29, 30 Two smaller Views of Venice, by Canaletti.*

31 A Landscape, with Peasants going to Market at break of Day, by Gainsborough.

32 St. John preaching in the Wilderness, by Breughel.

33 The four Elements, by Breughel and

Van Balen.*

34 Portrait of the Emperor Charles the Fifth, by Rubens, after Titian.

35 The Temptation of St. Anthony, by Teniers.

36 Portrait of Lady Hoare, widow of the late Sir Richard Hoare, Bart. by Angelica Kauffman.

37 A Landscape, by Claude Lorrain, engraved by Vivares.

38 A Portrait in the character of St. Agnes, by Titian.

39 A Holy Family, supposed to be painted by Annibale Caracci, or by Guido, in his dark manner.*

40 St Catharine, by Lovino, scholar of Leonardo da Vinci.

41 Flight into Egypt [quote from Bellori omitted], by Carlo Maratti.*

42 Tobit and the Angel, by Francesco Mola.

43 Penelope and Euriclea, by Angelica Kauffman.

44 Portrait of an Old Woman, by Morillio.

45 Marriage of S. Catherine, by Frederico Baroccio.*

46 Portrait of Henry Hoare, Son to Sir Richard Colt Hoare, Bart. by Sir Joshua Reynolds.

47 Democritus, the crying Philosopher, by Salvator Rosa.

48 A Holy Family, a very fine old copy, from the original, by Raphael, which was formerly in the collection of the King of France.*

WARNER 1800

Revd Richard Warner, *Excursions from Bath*, Bath, 1801. Excursion 1, letter 1, to James Cromrie, Esq. Bath, 1 September 1800, pp. 91–117

Richard Warner (1763–1857), clergyman and prolific writer, moved to Bath in 1794. His interests were antiquarian, but his publications commercial rather than scholarly. Doubtless he knew Sir Richard Colt Hoare. Warner described three itineraries in September 1800. The first, south from Bath, included descriptions of works of art in Longleat, Marston, Stourhead, Fonthill, Wardour and Wilton. The second itinerary, northwards, included Badminton. Warner had an eye for marbles and semi-precious stones which he noted at Stourhead, Wardour and Badminton. His description of pietre dure at the latter may be compared with his Sixtus Cabinet at Stourhead.

Excursion II, letter III, 14 September 1800 [extracts]

[p. 244] Badminton Church, 'Beneath the communion-table, a *quarry* of precious marbles spreads itself into a pavement twenty-six feet long and twelve broad, representing, upon a vast scale, the Duke of Beaufort's arms.'

[pp. 246–7] Badminton House, the north breakfast-room , 'where the first object which commands attention is a most splendid cabinet, made in Italy for Christina Queen of Sweden,

and brought from thence by Henry Duke of Beaufort (grand-father of the present Duke) who also collected, at an immense expence, the vast profusion of precious marbles contained in the church, and in every room of the house. This cabinet is formed of black marble and ebony enriched with every precious stone, and fillagreed brass, double gilt. It is about fourteen feet high, and terminated at the top by a clock; the drawers are of cedar.'

At Stourhead, Warner followed the room-order of the 1800 guidebook and copied picture descriptions word for word, with occasional interpolations, thus justifying the observation by Joseph Hunter, a fellow antiquary and Assistant Keeper of Public Records, that Warner 'was deep in no subject. He had read little, made no particular preparations for publication, and began to read in a subject only when he had previously determined to publish upon it.'[10]

Excursion 1, letter 1, to James Cromrie, Esq. Bath, 1 September 1800, p.96 [extract]

The *cabinet-room* takes its name from a most elaborate and expensive piece of workmanship, a cabinet consisting of several stories, constructed of ebony, agate, lapis lazuli, and ornamented with solid gold, and a profusion of every precious stone, except diamonds. It belonged to Pope Sixtus V. and contains in its front the portraits, in wax, of the Paretti family, of which the Pontiff bore the name. The head of Sixtus is in the centre. On it is a very scarce and curious gold medal, struck during the reign of Queen Elizabeth, upon the defeat of the Spanish armada; from which depends a beautiful George, richly enamelled.

BRITTON 1801

John Britton, *The Beauties of Wiltshire*, 3 vols, London, 1801, vol. II, pp. 1–24

John Britton (1771–1857) was befriended by Sir Richard Colt Hoare who provided illustrations for the second volume of *The Beauties*; hence its glutinous dedication to him, 'neither pride nor arrogance ever had dominion in your breast'. Britton had received help from the antiquary and archaeologist William Cunnington, whom Sir Richard also cultivated when he took up archaeology. Britton, impoverished and chippy by nature, quarrelled with them both in 1804. The story of the ensuing rivalry and jealousies is well told by Kenneth Woodbridge.[11] Britton's reference to Stourhead as 'This celebrated seat never yet accurately described' is disingenuous; his account drew on the 1800 guidebook, which he failed to acknowledge. Britton mentioned the new wings to the house, 'one destined for a library, the other for a picture-gallery'.

p. 7 [extract]

The CABINET ROOM, is so called on account of a magnificent piece of ornamental furniture, which has long been stationed in this apartment. This complicated curiosity is ornamented in the centre with a portrait of Pope Sixtus the Fifth, and surrounded with about twenty heads of the Peretti family, from one of whom his nephew descended, and he

retained the name. The last of this family was
a Nun, who bequeathed the cabinet to a convent
at Rome, where Mr. Hoare purchased it.

FENTON 1807

A Barrister [Richard Fenton], *A tour in
quest of genealogy, through several parts of Wales,
Somersetshire, and Wiltshire, in a Series of Letters to
a Friend in Dublin; interspersed with a description
of Stourhead and Stonehenge*, London, 1811,
pp. 179–232

Richard Fenton (1747–1821), the topographical
and historical authority, trained as a lawyer in
London, where he associated with writers and
painters and gained a reputation as a wit. He
returned to Wales as a practising barrister and
took up local history and archaeology. Money
from his father and his marriage enabled him
to retire from the law in 1792 in order to write
a history of Wales. From an uncle, he inherited
property in Fishguard, where he built a new
house, Plas Glynamel. In 1793 Fenton met Sir
Richard Colt Hoare, who shared his enthusiasm
for Welsh scenery and history. They became
life-long friends. Like Sir Richard, he made
a large collection of books and manuscripts.
Fenton's *Tour in quest of genealogy* is a lightly
written account of a journey dedicated to Hon.
Matthew Fortescue, who married Sir Richard's
half-sister, Henrietta-Anne. Fenton wrote about
Stourhead in 1807 under the polite fiction
he had arrived with his friend and fellow-
antiquarian, Theophilus Jones (1758–1812),
whereupon they were taken up by Sir Richard.
The description continued through several
letters. Fenton is the first to describe the new
Library, Picture Gallery and Cabinet Room.

Letter dated 8 November 1807,
pp. 181–2 [extract]

The entrance hall is appropriately hung with
family pictures. The next room, to the right, in
the show wing, is filled entirely with landscapes,
among which three are particularly deserving
of notice, viz. a landscape by Claude Lorrain;
another by Gaspar Poussin; and a night-scene
by Rembrandt. There are also two fine pictures
by Vernet; two by Wilson, whose delightful
imitation of nature struck even me; how much
more then Jones, whose admiration was heightened by nationality, and not very remote kin-
dred; one by Marlow; two by Canaletti; and a
most charming one representing a morning
scene, by our countryman Gainsborough.
This is called the cabinet-room, from a most
sumptuous cabinet that occupies a recess on
one side of it, that originally belonged to Pope
Sixtus v. and ornamented with his own portrait,
and twenty others of the Peretti family,* to which
he was allied. Its structure, which is remarkably
elegant, involves every order and style of
architecture, and among its superb decorations
its variegated inlay displays specimens of all the
richest marbles, and of all the known precious
stones in the world, the diamond excepted.
The festooned curtain of blue velvet, richly
fringed with gold, issuing out of a gilt mitre
over the centre of the arched recess, and
falling in fine folds of drapery on each side,
is disposed of with great taste and effect.

* Fenton and Britton counted 21 portraits in
total but there are only 11 'sockets' for the
waxes around the base. Were they inaccurate or
were some miniatures displayed alongside?

STOURHEAD CATALOGUE 1808

'A Catalogue of Pictures Prints Drawings Busts
Statues and other things in the Capital Messuage
or Manor House of Stourhead and the Garden
or Pleasure Ground thereto belonging referred
to in the foregoing Indenture of Settlement'
(WSA 383.714, copy deed, ff. 127–32)

The settlement dated 3 February 1808 was made
by Sir Richard Colt Hoare on the marriage of
his son, Henry (1784–1836). Under its terms
ownership of Stourhead was vested in new
trustees and Sir Richard and his heirs were
tenants for life without power to sell the house,
grounds and heirlooms.

In the Cabinet Room [extract]

Superb inlaid Cabinet with a Medal of Queen
Elizabeth and George and Dragon hanging
under it.

SKINNER 1808

British Library, Add. MS 33635, Revd John
Skinner, 'Journals of tours in the South of
England, Sketches in Somerset, Devon and
Cornwall', ff. 154, 158–9

John Skinner (1772–1839) was an unhappy
clergyman and a spirited antiquary with
an appetite for field archaeology and a
stronger one for interpreting the finds. He
was befriended by Sir Richard Colt Hoare
and stayed as a guest at Stourhead in 1812.
Skinner was jealous of his host and resented
him appropriating his theories. His hobby of
etymology tried the patience of his friends.
Today Skinner is remembered for his journals,
transcribed by his brother. The relevant volume
comprises an account of the life of the Revd
R. Graves, the diary of a tour to the South-
west from Wells to Land's End in 1797 and
memoranda of visits to Stourhead. His travels
are noteworthy for the breadth of his interests,
ranging over topography, history, archaeology,
mining and fishing industries in Cornwall.
Skinner paid his first visit to Stourhead as a
tourist in 1808; his second visit, in 1812, was
in the company of Peter Hoare, as guests of
Sir Richard Colt Hoare. Peter Richard Hoare
(1772–1849), half-brother of their host, was
a barrister and lived at Kelsey Park, Kent.

Memoranda of an excursion from home to
Stourhead, and Longleat: October 5th 1808
[extracts]

[f. 158, transcribed by Russell Skinner, his
brother] we ascended by a flight of stone steps,
to the front door, where we found the house-
keeper, expecting our arrival, in the hall.
[Cabinet Room] we were also shown a richly
worked Cabinet, said to have been made for
the Pontiff Pius VI.

[f. 154v, in John Skinner's own hand] on the
beginning of September: 1812 I received an

invitation from Mʳ P Hoare who was staying
with his brother at Stourhead to spend a week
at that delightful place.

[f. 159v] the next room [Cabinet Room] to the
right filled with Landscapes amongst which
there are particularly deserving of notice – one
by Claude Lorrain – another by Gaspar Poussin
& a night piece by Rembrant – there are also
two fine subjects by Vernet two by Wilson one
by Marlow two by Canaletti and a morning
scene by Gainsborough – There is in this room
a most sumptuous Cabinet originally belonging
to Pope Sextus 5.

BECKFORD 1814

Boyd Alexander (ed.), *Life at Fonthill 1807–1822
with Interludes in Paris and London from the
Correspondence of William Beckford*, London,
1957, p. 158

William Beckford (1760–1844), connoisseur
and heir to a great sugar fortune, was a neighbour of Sir Richard Colt Hoare. His father had
been a friend of Henry Hoare. The younger
Beckford built the extraordinary Fonthill Abbey.
He was ostracized by society and would have
been unwelcome at country houses, except in-
cognito as a tourist. Beckford's comments were
well informed and waspish. Two days prior to
Stourhead he visited Longleat, where he noted
'miserable cabinets, and a deal of daubs enough
to make one spit' and scorned Wyatville's improvements. In 1817 he went to Corsham Court
where he dismissed the paintings collection but
admired 'the little coffers are fine, rich and
harmonious in the highest degree – their
shagreen background pleases me immensely'.
As the book title implies, this collection of
letters concerns Fonthill Abbey and Beckford's
shopping in Europe. They were addressed to
his confidant and companion Gregorio Fellipe
Franchi. The description of Stourhead in 1814
betrayed Beckford's preoccupation with his
own collection; he had previously observed
'Sir Richard had no taste'.[12]

Wednesday 14 September 1814 [extract]

Sixtus the Fifth's cabinet is divine, I know
– the bronzes are of extreme delicacy and
elegance, and those lovely agates, alabasters
and cornelians, mingled with the glittering
mother-of-pearl, produce a rich effect, agreeable and grateful to the eye. It will be difficult
to surpass, but we must try, and produce something to make people doff their hats, whether
they will or no […]

GUIDEBOOK 1818

Anonymous [Sir Richard Colt Hoare, Bt]
A Description of the House and Gardens at Stourhead,
Bath, 1818, pp.13–15

p. 13, Cabinet Room [extract]

So called, from containing a rich and costly
Cabinet, composed of the greatest variety of
precious stones, agates, marbles, &c. which
formerly belonged to Pope Sextus the Fifth,
whose likeness, as well as those of his family
(Peretti) are recorded by little portraits most

delicately moulded and coloured in wax, and placed round the bottom edge of this valuable piece of furniture.

MODERN WILTSHIRE 1822

Sir Richard Colt Hoare, Bt, *The Modern History of South Wiltshire*, vol. I, pt I, 'The Hundred of Mere', London, 1822, pp. 70–85

Sir Richard's account of the house runs for 16 pages and at its close he apologizes for being 'too minute in the foregoing description'. He described the interior of Longleat in five pages. His guidebook and the 1838 inventory also recorded the painting collection but *Modern Wiltshire* alone identified, with initials, who acquired each painting; Henry Hoare (H.H.) and Sir Richard (R.C.H.).

pp. 76–7, Cabinet Room

We now proceed across the Entrance-hall, to an apartment called the Cabinet Room, from the circumstances of its containing a very splendid Cabinet, embellished with precious stones, marbles, agates, &c. of every description. It formerly belonged to Pope Pius Sextus the Fifth, whose portrait, as well as those of his family, PERETTI, are beautifully moulded in wax, and placed in medallions round the base of this exquisite piece of workmanship. It was purchased by Henry Hoare, Esq. in Italy, who added the base, on which are designed several of the buildings erected by that Pope at Rome and a bas-relief of his portrait.

This room is devoted exclusively to Landscapes, of which it contains a very pleasing variety.

Over the chimney is a painting, representing a Male and Female Peasant, with some Colliers, going to Market at break of day. H.H. By Gainsborough.

Beneath it are two small Landscapes by Momper. R.C.H. And a View of Florence, by Marlow. H.H.

On the sides are a Sea-port and Moonlight. H.H. By Vernet.

The Lake of Nemi, with the Story of Diana and her Nymphs. H.H. By Wilson.

The Lake of Avernus, with the Story of Æneas and the Sibyl. R.C.H. By –Turner, R.A.

This classical subject was painted from a correct sketch taken by Sir Richard Colt Hoare when in Italy, and represents the lake of Avernus in the fore ground, with the temple on its banks; above is the *Monte nuovo*, which was thrown up by volcanic force in one night. In the next distances are the Lucrine lake; beyond it the castle of Baiæ, and the lofty promontory of Misenum, with the island of Capri at the extremity of the horizon.

South side. A View of the Mole at Naples, with Mount Vesuvius. H.H. By Marlow.

A Storm, with the Story of Jonas and the Whale, copied from a celebrated painting by Nicolo Poussin. H.H. By Taverner.

A Landscape, by Claude Lorraine. H.H. Engraved by Vivares.

A Landscape. H.H. by Gasper Poussin, formerly in the collection of Sir Luke Schaub.

A Landscape. R.C.H. By Nicolo Poussin, in his early brown manner.

Two large Landscapes, copied by Lucatelli from the originals of Claude Lorrain, in the Pamphili Palace at Rome. H.H.

Two Landscapes with cattle and figures. R.C.H. By Bout and Baudoin.

A Landscape. R.C.H. by D. Teniers.

A Landscape. R.C.H. By Wilson. This small and simple composition has excited the general attention of artists and connoisseurs, from its very excellent colouring. It was painted in Italy, and presented by Wilson to his friend Zucharelli. This painting pleased me so much at first sight, that I used my utmost endeavours to procure it, but I failed in my repeated applications, At the decease of Zucharelli I became the purchaser of this little jewel.

Beneath it is another painting which merits our attention – a Moon-light Scene, in which some gypsies are reposing by a fire-side. H.H. By Rembrandt. It is engraved by R. Earlom. Over the door is a Landscape. H.H. By C.W.Bampfylde, Esq.

Amphitheatre at Rome. R.C.H. By Gaspero d'Occhiali.

Inside View of a Church. H.H. By H.V. Stein. Diana and her Nymphs. H.H. By Zuccarelli. A very highly-finished picture, and painted, by order of Henry Hoare, Esq. sq. to fit a frame of rich carved work by the celebrated Gibbon.

East side. – Two spirited sketches, of an upright form; the one of a tree, under which a friar is praying, by Francesco Mola; the other, a scene of rocks and water, by Rosa di Tivoli. R.C.H.

Two small Landscapes, with figures and buildings. R.C.H. By Bartolomeo. Bought at the Orleans sale.

Two small Views at Venice. H.H. By Canaletti. Remarkably good, and highly finished.

STOURHEAD INVENTORY 1838

'1838 Inventory of Heir-Looms at Stourhead directed to be taken by the Will of the late Sir Richd Colt Hoare Bar^t. with the state and condition thereof.' WSA 383.16, pp. 26–9 (later annotations in *italics*)

It lists the contents of the Cabinet Room with paintings first (nos 266–90), Sèvres porcelain (nos 291–3) then

294 A magnificent Cabinet composed of Precious Stones, Agates, Marbles et^c. which formerly belonged to Pope Sixtus 5th whose likeness as well as those of his family (Peretti) are recorded by little Portraits most delicately moulded and coloured in Wax, and placed round the bottom edge of this valuable piece of furniture.

295 A polished Grate 36 inches wide.

296 Steel polished Fender Fire Irons with Guard on stand and a Hearth Brush.

297 Brussels Carpet to cover Room, half worn.

298 Hearth Rug and Green Drugget 28 feet by 19 feet *Drugget worn out.*

299 Two Leather Covered Foot Stools.

300 Pair of Inlaid Satin Wood Small Pillar & Claw Tables.

301 A ditto Pembroke Table with Drawer.

302 A ditto Card Table.

303 A Pier ditto to match.

304 A pair of Fire Screens to match.

305 A half circular Commode under Pier Glass.

306 A magnificent Pier Glass with Tablet over plate 7 feet 2 inches high 4 feet 8 ½ inches wide in two compartments and in good condition.

307 A Circular hand Mirror (damaged).

308 Pair of Glass Lusters complete.

309 Two Easy Arm Chairs with Covers & Cushions.

310 Eight Arm Chairs to match with Cane Seats & Cushions.

311 A figured Satin Window Curtain with Cornice pins et^c complete much worn and faded.

312 A tin lined Flower Stand in recess of Window 6 feet long by 2 feet wide.

313 A centre inlaid oval Pillar and Claw Table 5 feet long by 3 feet 9 inches wide.

314 A figured Cover to same.

The following pietre dure

248 – Saloon – A Mosaic Coffer 22 inches wide 22 ½ inches high on a Marble Stand 28 inches high

514 – Nursery – A Cabinet of different Stones (damaged) *in Music Room*

540 – Little Attic – A Cabinet of different Stones damaged *in Picture Gallery*

629 – Yellow Dressing Room – A small Mosaic Cabinet 2 feet high by 2 feet wide. broken and on Wood Stand *In Picture Gallery*

1025 – South Apartments – A Mosaic Cabinet 14 inches high 20 inches wide 16 inches over. *Picture Gallery*

1076 – North Apartments – A Mosaic Cabinet. *In Picture Gallery*

Notes for Appendix II

1. See Jervis 2006, pp. 76–82.
2. Cartwright 1888, vol. II, pp. 42–4, Dr Pococke to his wife, 2 July 1754, description of Stourhead. Ellis 1907, vol. II, pp. 321–3, Mrs Rishton to Miss Burney, 13 April 1773. (Mrs Rishton described the garden at Stourhead and passed by the house in a single sentence.)
3. Hazlitt 1824, pp. 137–9.
4. Stourhead Inventory 1742.
5. Toynbee 1928, p. 30, August 1760, Hardwick Hall, 'The great apartment as it was furnished for the Queen of Scots. [...] A Cabinet of oak carved, with two tables to the sides [...] There are other Tables & cabinets in the apartment in better taste, supported by Lions, like Kent's tables & tortoises for feet'; p. 45, July 1762, Longleat, 'Very fine Cabinet of Silver Japan [...] The Gallery has a table, settee, and 24 chairs of ebony'.
6. Woodbridge 1982b, pp. 59–70.
7. Parnell 1769, vol. I, f. 2 Sir John travelled

from Ireland with 'Mr Smith gentleman Keeper of the Black rod and Mr Fanning of Waterford two very agreeable companions', vol. II, f. 67, on the excursion from Bath 'Exclusive of servants we were just seven in Company Mrs Forster and Miss Forster Captn Erskine and Dive Downes with us three.'

8. See p. 170 note 9.

9. NT 731894 This is an eighteenth-century miniature, reputedly representing Mary Queen of Scots, with a glass and plain fruitwood frame. Henry Hoare Accounts 1749–70, 3 July 1754, 'M^r [William] Hoare for Picture Glass & frame of Mary Q^n of Scots', £15·15 which would have been a high price for the frame and glass alone.

10. Michael Hicks, 'Richard Warner' ODNB 2004, vol. 57, pp. 451–3, citing British Library Add. MS 26527.f.134.

11. Woodbridge 1970, pp. 195–6, 204–5, 207–8.

12. See p. 185 note 64.

APPENDIX III GRAND TOUR DOCUMENTS

CONTEMPORARY TRANSLATIONS OF GIROLAMO BELLONI'S LETTERS TO HOARE'S BANK, FILED WITH THE ORIGINALS IN ITALIAN

C. Hoare & Co. HB/8/M/8

Mess.rs Hoare & Arnold at London
Rome 5th Sept.r 1739

I have the Honour to acquaint you, That Your M.r Henry Hoare having Ordered me by a Letter wrote from Florence to pay a Sum of Mony to M.r Mark Parker, I have accordingly paid s.d Gentleman 600 Roman Crowns as appears by the said M.r Parkers Receit annext, which you will please to keep for the said M.r Hoare, Who has ordered me to reimburse myself on You for such Sum as I shall pay, I have therefore drawn on You for his Account at 40 Days Date
£142:17:2 to the Order of John Baptist Cambiaso the Son of Jn.o Maria & Son of Bartholomew of Genoa
When this my Bill is presented I intreat you to honour it with Acceptance, & pay it when due, observing that with commission at 42 pence and one [?] pound Sterling, it makes exactly my Reimbursement of the said 600 Crowns, which you may Acquaint said M.r Hoare of, and take you Reimbursement on him, I remain with the utmost Readiness to serve you and the greatest Regard Gent.m.

Your most humble & Obliged Serv.t
Girolamo Belloni

Genoa 105 Legh.o 90
Amsterd.m 407/x D.rs. Paris 107⅛

[Translation of M.r Parker's Receipt]

I have received of M.r Girolamo Belloni Six hundred Crowns in Mony paid me on Account by Order of a larger Sum by Order given in my Favour by M.r Henry Hoare at Florence by his 'n of the 4th past, In testimony whereof I have signed this, and another of the like Tenor, both of which are to be accounted but as One[.] Rome the 2.d Septemb.r 1739'

Mark Parker

Sd. 600

[The second letter from Girolamo Belloni, Transcribed the letter of 5 September 1739 with minor variations with this postscript]

We are at y.e 3.d of October, without any of yours the present serves to confirm the Substance of my former contain in the above Copy, and further to acquaint you that by Order of your M.r Henry Hoare I draw on you at forty days Date £94:15:9 to the Order of Fabio & Ubaldo Maggi of Leghorn Value in Account-
Be pleased to Accept & pay it when due,

valuing yourself upon your M.r Henry Hoare, and Observe that the said Draft is for Mony paid by his Order to M.r Parker, as by Receipt – sent to the said M.r Hoare at Aix in Provence from whence I received his Letter, who am, always ready At Your Command & with Tender of my sincerest Respects am

Your most humble Sev.t Girolamo Belloni

Directed To Mess.rs Hoare & Arnold at London

CONTINENTAL AGENTS, BANKERS AND SHIPPERS PAID BY HENRY HOARE, 1739–43

The entries from Henry Hoare's account recorded in two Partnership Ledgers at C. Hoare & Co.[1]

Alexandre Alexander

Alexander (fl. 1727–1751) is listed in the *Almanach Royal*, 1739 (p. 349), among the 'banquiers pour les traités et remises de place en place'. Alexander was in Rue Sainte Apolline during 1729–41. When he went into partnership with Denis Despueches, they moved to Rue Saint- Roch.[2] He acted for clients of Hoare's bank from 1731, including the ninth Earl of Lincoln who made the Grand Tour in 1739–41.[3] He was accompanied by Joseph Spence, who had previously used Alexander as a forwarding address in Paris.[4] Alexander is mentioned by other tourists. In 1730 Edward Mellish collected money at Blois from Alexander, paying £5 commission for drawing £200 on his uncle's London banker.[5] In preparation for his visit to Paris in 1736, the sixth Earl of Salisbury arranged to draw money on Alexander.[6] Horace Walpole wrote to George Montagu on 20 March 1737, 'À Monsieur Monsieur Mountagu [*sic*] racommandé à Monsieur Alexandre Banquier à Paris'.[7] Richard West wrote to Walpole on Monday 24 September 1739, 'au soin de Monsieur Alexander, Banquier, à Paris, France'.[8]

Year	Date	Text	£-s-d
1739	26 Mar.	M.r Alexander	150 – –
1739	5 April	M.r Alexander's bill to M.r Knox & C.o	43-17-2
1739	9 April	M.r Alexander	100 – –
1739	19 May	M.r Alexander	236-17 –
1739	4 Sept.	M.r Alexander	50 – –
1739	24 Sept.	M.rs Hoare's bill to M.r Alexander	105-16-8
1739	26 Sept.	Ditto's [M.rs Hoare's] bill to Ditto [M.r Alexander]	50 – –
1739	27 Sept.	Ditto's [M.rs Hoare's] bill to M.r Pigualt	58-10 –
1739	11 Oct.	M.r Alexander	23-1-6
1739	2 Nov.	M.r Alexander pd 1 Novemb	36-15-6
1739	17 Dec.	M.r Alexander	9-18-11
1740	14 April	M.r Alexander	100 – –
1740	16 June	M.r Alexander	50 – –
1740	24 June	M.r Alexander	100 – –
1740	2 July	M.r Alexander	100 – –
			1,214-16-9

Joseph Smith

'Consul Smith' (*c*.1674–1770) arrived in Venice *c*.1700 to work for the merchant banker Thomas Williams. They were importers of meat and fish and, more glamorously, acted as bankers and agents for tourists. He served as British Consul 1744–60 and was meshed in diplomacy for the remainder of his life. He was famous as a collector of old master and contemporary pictures, notably work by the Riccis, Rosalba Carriera and Canaletto. George III purchased his library, paintings, gems, coins and medals.[9] Smith also ran a publishing business, the Pasquali Press, which produced elegant, scholarly books. The Earl of Lincoln and his tutor, Joseph Spence, called on Smith for £300 in 1741.[10]

Year	Date	Text	£-s-d
1739	9 June	Jos. Smith	102-9-6
1740/1	20 Jan.	Custom & Charges on two Cases of Pictures from M.r Smith of Venice	11-7 –
			113-16-6

Girolamo Belloni

Belloni (1688–1760) belonged to an ambitious dynasty of merchant-financiers from Bologna. His uncle, Giovanni Angelo (d.1729), grew the business; his customers included the third Duke of Beaufort in 1728.[11] Girolamo Belloni became *the* prominent merchant banker in Rome and is remembered for his treatise on economics, *Dissertazione del Commercio*, first published in 1750. He worked for Popes Clement XII and Benedict XIV and purchased for himself the title of a Papal Marchese. To tourists he was indispensible. In 1740 Belloni had acted as mail box for Walpole and as banker to Lady Mary Wortley Montagu.[12] The same year Belloni was the forwarding address for Joseph Spence in Rome and financed him, along with the Earl of Lincoln in 1740–1.[13] Belloni also applied for export licences in his own name from 1752.[14] His reputation was somewhat chequered; in 1744 Cardinal Albani attempted to seize his assets.[15] Sir Horace Mann complained in 1745 that Belloni had assisted a debtor of Mann's escape to Naples.[16] And in 1751 he helped fund the Old Pretender's household in Rome.[17] Robert Adam, writing from Rome to the merchants Innes & Clerk, in 1756, used Belloni as a forwarding address and mentioned that he charged unfavourable exchange rates.[18]

Year	Date	Text	£-s-d
1739	14 June	Guilamo Beloni 50 & 150	200 – –
1739	17 Sept.	Gulᵒ Belloni	72-5 –
1739	22 Sept.	Gulᵒ Belloni's bill to Peter Meyer & Cᵒ	95-4-9
1739	6 Oct.	Gulᵒ Beloni's to Batta Cambirso & Cᵒ¹⁹	142-17-2
1739	3 Nov.	Gulᵒ Belloni's bill to Faber & Cᵒ	94-15-9
1739	13 Dec.	Gulᵒ Belloni's bill to Antoniti & Cᵒ	94-15-9
1739/40	23 Jan.	Gulᵒ Belloni's bill	47-1-2
1739/40	23 Jan.	Ditto [Belloni]	118-9-8
1739/40	24 Mar.	Gulᵒ Belloni's bill to Peter Meyer & Co	47-7-10
1740	2 April	Gulᵒ Belloni's bill	119-1 –
			1,031-18-1

Vernet, Whatley & Gambert

These merchant-agents seem to have operated in Marseilles and are recorded there in 1738.[20] George Whatley supplied Sir Richard Hoare, 2nd Kt, when he wintered at Aix in 1748–9. On 5 February 1749 Whatley wrote (in English) from Marseilles about velvet for new breeches; on 12 March he promised to deliver a 'hamper of wine' and his bill, dated 29 March, amounted to 11,554 *livres* (about £500). On 25 June he wrote about a bulk order including butter, Malaga, garden seeds and 'Venice treacle' (a traditional medical concoction).[21]

Spence drew money from Vernet & Co when travelling with the Earl of Lincoln in 1741.[22]

Year	Date	Text	£-s-d
1739	6 Oct.	Messʳˢ Vernet Whatley & Cᵒ	100 – –
1739	8 Dec.	Messʳˢ Whatley & Gampert	240 – –
1739/40	8 Mar.	Messʳˢ Vernet & Comp.	150 – –
1740	21 June	Whatley & Cᵒ to Messʳˢ Simmondˢ	18-1 –
1740	17 Nov.	Messʳˢ Vernet & Company	120 – –
1740	3 Dec.	Messʳˢ Vernet & Whatley & Cᵒ	200 – –
1740/1	26 Jan.	Messʳˢ Vernet & Whatley & Cᵒ	100 – –
1740/1	6 Mar.	Messʳˢ Vernet & Whatley & Cᵒ	60 – –
			988-1 –

Alexander Hay

Alexander Hay (residence unknown) also helped Sir Richard Hoare, 2nd Kt, in small ways towards the end of his visit to France. In September 1749 he sent Sir Richard a bill for wine supplied during the previous two months at £84-15-0.[23]

Year	Date	Text	£-s-d
1740	6 Aug.	Alexander Hay	100 – –
1740	25 Sept.	Alexander Hay	100 – –
1740	26 Sept.	Ditto [Alexander Hay]	100 – –
1741/2	26 Jan.	Alex. Hay's bill to Alex: Andrews 883.12.9	4-15 –
			304-15 –

Sir John Lambert

There were three generations of Lamberts, each christened John. The first John (1666–1722/3) was reputedly an eminent Huguenot merchant who fled to England in 1685. He was described as 'an opulent London Merchant' and was created baronet in February 1710/11.[24] He lent large sums to Queen Anne but was disgraced after the South Sea Bubble.[25] The second Sir John (1690–1772) was Henry Hoare's banker in Paris. The association began in 1740 and continued throughout Henry's life. In 1743/4 he negotiated, or at least financed, the purchase of Bourdon's *Judgment of Midas* on behalf of Henry.[26] When Sir Richard Hoare, 2nd Kt, visited France in 1748–9, Sir John Lambert was his banker, both in Paris and during his residence at Aix. In total he received £846 from Hoare's bank on behalf of Sir Richard.[27] The latter noted the exchange rate of 23 *livres* to the pound sterling.[28] Evidently the bankers were on cordial terms and Sir Richard dined with Sir John on three occasions during their home-bound visit to Paris.[29] When Henry's son visited France in 1750–2 with his companion John Rust, Sir John acted as their banker.[30] In 1771 Sir John arranged the trip to Paris made by Henry Hoare, his nephew and his wife.[31] Spence included Sir John and Lady Lambert in a list of those met in Paris in 1739.[32] This Sir John Lambert was *the* magno-operator in Paris for the British visitor. He had wide-ranging businesses, although in 1762–8 he burned his fingers financing a slave-trading venture.[33] During 1738–47 John Chute of The Vyne travelled in France and Italy with Francis Thistlethwaite Whithed. Their London banker gave Chute letters of credit enabling him to draw money on bankers in Paris, usually Sir John Lambert.[34] In 1768 James and Thomas Coutts wrote to the Countess of Bute querying an arrangement for Frederick Stuart made with Sir John Lambert for £185-10-0.[35] Walpole received 350 *louis* from Sir John Lambert in 1769.[36] The third Sir John (1728–1799) continued to work as banker and agent for the English in Paris. Frederick Robinson (1746–1792), the brother of Thomas second Baron Grantham (1738–1786), dined with Sir John in Paris 11 April 1778.[37] *Memoirs of Mary Robinson* 'Perdita' described how, c.1783, 'Sir John Lambert, on being informed of her [Mrs Robinson's] arrival, exerted himself to procure for her commodious apartments, a *remise*, a box at the opera, with all the fashionable and expensive *et-ceteras* with which an inexperienced English traveller is immediately provided.' Sir John introduced her to the Duc d'Orléans and the less reputable Duc de Lauzin.[38]

Year	Date	Text	£-s-d
1740	7 Oct.	Sʳ John Lambert	50 – –
1741	23 May	Sʳ John Lambert	100 – –
1741	2 June	Ditto [Sʳ John Lambert] 500, 400, 350, 450	1700 – –
1741	3 June	Ditto [Sʳ John Lambert] 300 & 200	500 – –
1742/3	23 Feb.	Sʳ Jn Lambert's bill to Alexʳ Menuset 962: 2: 5½	28-8 –
			2,378-8 –

Thomas Smith

'Smith of Bologne' was involved with shipping Bourdon's *Judgment of Midas* to Henry Hoare in 1743/4.[39]

Year	Date	Text	£-s-d
1741	11 Sept.	Thos Smith's bill to Ramsay & Strachm	21-18-5
1741/2	10 Mar.	T Smith's bill to A Ramsey	6-19-10
1742	3 June	Knox & Craghead Rect on accᵗ of Smith of Boulogne for Carriage 3 Bales	3-2-6
			32-0-9

Miscellaneous entries

Year	Date	Text	£-s-d
1739	20 Oct.	To Messʳˢ Campagni & Libis[40]	50 – –
1740	31 Oct.	Messʳˢ Luber & Fils	100 – –
1742	15 May	Aleaʳ[?] Ramsey for Freight & Charges of a Picture from Leghorne	3-9 –

Edmund, or Edward, Fowler
Shipping agent used by Henry Hoare.

Year	Date	Text	£-s-d
1739	3 Nov.	Edwd Fowler for Custom & Charges on Pictures	19-2-6
1740	19 June	Edmond Fowlers for Customs & Charges on Figures &cc for Leghorne	9-15-6
1740	15 Oct.	Edmund Fowler's bill for Customs & Charges of things from abroad	22-14 –
1741	24 July	Ed^{wd} Fowlers bill for Customs & Charges of a large Case from Leghorne	19-14 –
1741	24 July	To Ditto' [Fowler's] bill for Ditto of 2 Cases by the St John Baptist from Leghorne[41]	23-7-6
1741	24 Nov.	Edm^d Fowler's bill for Charges of things from Dunkirk by Capt Smith	2-13-9
1741/2	15 Feb.	Edward Fowler's bill to Custom & Charges on Spa Water	1-16 –
1742	1 July	Edm^d Fowler's Bill for customs & charges of 3 cases from Boulogne	47-3 –
1742	1 July	Ditto Bill of Spa Water from Rotterdam	3-11 –
1742	4 Aug.	Edm^d Fowlers bill of Customs & Charg^s on oyl Raisins	2-13 –
1742	4 Aug.	Do [Fowler's] bill of D^o [Customs & Charg^s] 10 Cases of Cabinetts from Leghorn	37-1-6
1742/3	2 Mar.	Edm^d Fowler Custom & Charges of 2 figures fr Livourno	13-5-6
			202-17-3

Notes for Appendix III

1. C. Hoare & Co. Partnership Ledgers HB/5/A/5, 1734–42, and HB/5/A/6, 1742–51.
2. Lewis, Lam and Bennett 1961 13–14/1, p. 184, Richard West to Horace Walpole, 24 September 1739, note 1.
3. C. Hoare & Co. HB/8/M/14/1-3, 5, 6, Letters of credit with Mr Alexander. And Customer Ledgers, ninth Earl of Lincoln, Lr/fol. O/414 and Q/44.
4. Klima 1975, p. 174, Joseph Spence to his mother, 20 June 1737, asking her to direct letters to 'Monsieur Monsieur Spence Recommandé à Monsr. Alexandre Banquier, à Paris'.
5. Black 2003, p. 92.
6. Ibid.
7. Lewis and Brown 1941 9/1, p. 9.
8. Lewis, Lam and Bennett 1961 13–14/1, p. 184.
9. Ingamells 1997, pp. 869–71.
10. C. Hoare & Co., Customer Ledger, ninth Earl of Lincoln, Lr/fol. Q/44, 11 July 1741, Jos. Smith, £200 and 1 August 1741, D^o, £100.
11. González-Palacios 1993, vol. I, pp. 429–30.
12. Lewis, Smith and Lam 1955a 17/1, p. 23, Walpole to Sir Horace Mann, 14 May 1740, 'Continue the letters to the banker; he will keep them for me, if I should be gone'. Halsband 1966, vol. II, p. 212, Lady Mary Wortley Montagu to her husband, 23 November 1740.
13. Klima 1975, p. 340, Spence to Dr Cocchi, 31 December 1740. C. Hoare & Co., Customer Ledgers, ninth Earl of Lincoln, Lr/fol. O/414, and Q/44, £800 paid in four installments to Belloni.
14. Bertolotti 1880, applications December 1752–April 1759, pp. 80–4.
15. Lewis 1961, p. 124.
16. Lewis, Smith and Lam 1955c 19/3, p. 77, Mann to Walpole, 27 July 1745.
17. Lewis 1961, p. 173.
18. Bolton 1922, vol. I, p. 318, Appendix A.
19. This is surely the agent/banker to whom Belloni refers in his letter dated 5 September 1739 to Hoare's bank. See p. 206.
20. Lemarchand 2006, p. 37.
21. C. Hoare & Co. HFM/7/19, Sir Richard Hoare, 2nd Kt, folder of bills 1748–9.
22. Ibid., Customer Ledger, ninth Earl of Lincoln, Lr/fol. Q/44, 17 August 1741, 'Jos Spence's bill to Vernet & Co' £50.
23. C. Hoare & Co. HFM/7/19, Alexander Hay to Sir Richard Hoare, 2nd Kt bill for 30 July–4 September 1749.
24. Burke's 1949, p. 1157.
25. Hancock 1995, p. 209.
26. See note 39.
27. C. Hoare & Co. HB/5/A/6, Partnership Ledger 1742–51, Sir Richard Hoare, 2nd Kt, payments to Lambert recorded from 23 September 1748–25 August 1749.
28. Ibid., HFM/7/18, notebook and cash accounts kept by Sir Richard Hoare, 2nd Kt while in France, 1748–9.
29. Ibid., 'Dined with S^r Jn Lambert' on 7, 15 and 25 June 1749.
30. Ibid., Partnership Ledgers HB/5/A/6, 1742–51, and HE/5/A/7, 1751–64, Henry Hoare Junior.
31. Ibid., HFM/M/9/7-9, Lambert to Henry Hoare, 1 August 1771.
32. Klima 1975, p. 422.
33. Hancock 1995 pp. 209–11.
34. HRO 5M50/ 2097-2109, papers and vouchers of Thomas Puckridge, agent to Francis Thistlethwayte Whithed during his travels abroad 1738–48.
35. Black 2003, p. 93.
36. Lewis and Smith 1939 7/5, p. 408, 'Paris Journals, Expenses 1769'.
37. BLA, L30/14/333/84, Frederick Robinson to Thomas second Baron Grantham, 12 April 1778.
38. Robinson 1895, pp. 191–3.
39. WSA 383.907, Lambert to Henry Hoare, 1 February 1743/4, 'J'ai achêté et dejà expedié le Bourdon a Mr Trotter chez Mr Smith a [sic] Bologne pour vous être envoié par le premier Navire […] £45-3-8 a l'ordre de M. Blampain' [I have bought and already dispatched the Bourdon to Mr Trotter at Mr Smith's in Bolougne to be sent to you by the first boat].
40. Further references apparently to this firm: C. Hoare & Co. Customer Ledger, ninth Earl of Lincoln, Lr/fol. O/414, 1 January 1740, 'Jos Spence's bill to Campani Libri' £100.

Lewis, Smith and Lam 1955a 17/1, pp. 81–2. Mann to Walpole, 1 July 1741, Mann reported Parker had drawn on Compagni and Libri for 70 crowns, about £17-10-0.
41. *St John the Baptist* was a recognized name for a ship. For example, Treasury Warrant, 6 December 1744: 'Ship's name "St. John Baptist"; Master. John Harvey', 'From Leghorn, &c., with oil'. http://www.british-history.ac.uk/report.aspx?compid=92060.

APPENDIX IV
THE PIETRE DURE MATERIALS OF THE SIXTUS CABINET

The words 'pietre dure' [hard stones] refer to semi-precious stones. 'Commesso di pietre dure' [assemblage of hard stones] refers to the fitting together of shaped hard stones in a panel to form a pattern or picture. However, such panels and the technique employed to produce them are in common usage (as in this book) referred to as pietre dure, used both as an adjective and as a collective noun (this was long Englished as 'pietra dura'; the Italian words used to be italicised as *pietre dure*, but more recently, as in the Metropolitan Museum of Art, New York's 2008 catalogue, *Art of the Royal Court, Treasures in Pietre Dure from the Palaces of Europe*, 'pietre dure' has become normal usage). Despite its name pietre dure often incorporates *pietre tenere* [soft stones], such as alabaster.

There follows a summary vocabulary of the materials used on the panels of pietre dure and elsewhere on the Sixtus Cabinet. It should be noted that the more transparent stones are often backed with gold or silver foil, to increase reflections; that a few of the smaller stones are drilled, having once been used as beads; and that two engraved gems are incorporated (both carnelians).

This list is also followed by a visual analysis of the pietre dure of one of the richest areas of the Cabinet, incorporating no fewer than eighteen different materials.

- **Agate**: banded, black and white, brown, grey, grey and white, moss, orange, pink, pink mottled
- **Alabaster**: Egyptian, fiorito, green, green Algerian, di Palombara, a pecorella, *a tartaruga*, white
- **Amethyst**: tinted with hematite
- **Aventurine**
- **Bianco e nero antico**
- **Bloodstone**
- **Breccia**: various
- **Brocatello**: Spanish
- **Carnelian**
- **Chalcedony**: green chrome, white
- **Chrysoprase**
- **Citrine**
- **Coral**
- **Crystal**: rock
- **Emerald**
- **Garnet**: alamandine
- **Glass**: Roman, blue [some fire damaged]
- **Jasper**: di Barga, brown, dark brown, green, green and red, mottled green and brown, mottled red, mottled yellow, orange, red, red variegated, red and white, Sicilian, yellow, yellow and red
- **Lapis lazuli**
- **Mother-of-pearl**
- **Onyx**
- **Paragone**
- **Paste**: green, orange, purple, red, yellow
- **Plasma**: green
- **Prase**: green
- **Quartz**: smoky
- **Sealing wax**: [once!]
- **Semesanto**: Skyros
- **Serpentine**: green and yellow, verde, yellow
- **Serpentinite**
- **Smaragdite**
- **Turquoise**
- **Verde di Prato**

FIG. 222.2
Roman glass

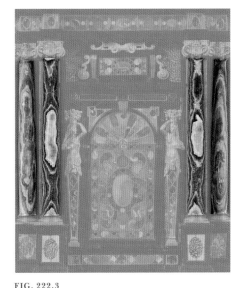

FIG. 222.3
Alabaster *a tartaruga*

FIG. 222
The centre of the Ionic first storey

FIG. 222.1
Lapis lazuli

FIG. 222.4
Paste of various colours

FIG. 222.8
Turquoise

FIG. 222.6
Coral

FIG. 222.9
Garnet

FIG. 222.12
Agate of various colours

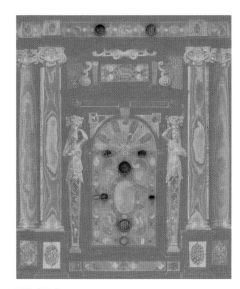

FIG. 222.7
Carnelian

FIG. 222.10
Mother-of-pearl

FIG. 222.13
Jasper of various colours

FIG. 222.11
Banded agate

FIG. 222.5
Emerald

FIG. 222.16
Serpentine

FIG. 222.14
Amethyst

FIG. 222.17
Prase

FIG. 222.15
Moss agate

FIG. 222.18
Bloodstone

APPENDIX V
LOSSES, ASSOCIATIONS AND ADDITIONS TO THE SIXTUS CABINET

THE ORGAN

The 1665 and 1665 inventories of the Palazzo Felice (see Appendix I) describe the Sixtus Cabinet as 'con organo dentro' [with an organ inside], but the organ goes unmentioned in the later Roman references to the Cabinet, which suggests that it may have stopped working and/ or been removed. In 1754 the Cabinet is called 'the Cabinett or rather Organ' and in 1756 Jonas Hanway, slightly garbling this description, states that the Cabinet is 'supported by a rich frame or pedestal, which I understood was once the case of an organ' (this was repeated in the 1779 *Modern Universal British Traveller*), while in 1762 Horace Walpole states that the Cabinet 'was formerly an organ' (see Appendix II). It seems likely that when Henry Hoare acquired the Cabinet in Rome in 1740 he was informed that it had contained an organ, but this part of its story was first muddled and then evaporated well before his death in 1785.

The clear vestiges of a keyboard in the centre of the Cabinet's podium (see p. 67 and fig. 81) and the fact that it incorporates an extensive void behind its serried ranks of drawers con-firms existence of the organ. For a cabinet to have been fitted with a musical instrument was far from unique, although the Sixtus Cabinet, if indeed of the 1580s, is an early instance. In 1582 Duke Wilhelm V of Bavaria gave his uncle, Archduke Ferdninand II of Tyrol, a mechanical organ in an ebony case, with fictive silver trumpeters, whose movement was by the Augsburg goldsmith Hans Schlottheim, a specialist in automata.[1] Its ancestry includes a mechanical organ on a different scale, the water organ in the garden at Tivoli, constructed by Lucha Clerico (Luc de Clerc) and Claude Vénard from 1568–72.[2] This was seen in 1576 by Erasmus Mayr, the Augsburg cathedral organist, who carried the secret of its drum mechanism back to Augsburg, where a number of craftsmen exploited the technique.[3] Also in 1576 the organist Gregor Aichinger, independently, saw a mechanical organ in Regensburg.[4] There is no reason to suggest that the Sixtus Cabinet's organ was mechanical, but it shared that mannerist delight in miniaturization and concealment reflected in such devices. A marquetry cabinet in Munich, probably made in the Tyrol in about 1580, incorporating a virginal which slides out from a compartment in its base, is paralleled by a cabinet from the same workshop with an organ now in Stuttgart.[5] A small ebony cabinet in New York dated 1598 and signed by Laurentius Hauslaib of Nuremberg, who seems to have specialized in such instruments, incorporates a virginal and an organ.[6] Later instances include a pipe organ in the Stipo Tedesco [German cabinet] in Florence, of 1619–25, the removable mechanical virginal by Samuel Bidermann I (1540–1622) in the Gustavus Adolphus cabinet in Uppsala, of 1625–31, and a virginal, again by Bidermann in a work table in Dresden, of 1628 at the latest, all three assembled by the great impresario of the cabinet, Philipp Hainhofer (1578–1647).[7] It may be added that Sixtus V had some interest in organs: in 1585 he ordered that the small portative organ in Santa Maria in Aracoeli, made by Dario de Mezzana in 1583, be replaced by a great organ to be made by Domenico Benvenuti (d.1587) with a chair organ by Francesco Palmieri.

Apart from clear indications of its having contained a keyboard, the Sixtus Cabinet's lost organ has left no external traces, and internal evidence – various blocks glued to the sides of the case, pieces knocked away, shadows of pieces and cut-outs – are enigmatic. No specific vestiges survive of the stays for pipes, key action, bellows or of supports for a wind-chest. Apertures for a means to work the bellows or an oblong hole for an air-trunk to penetrate the baseboard are absent. A possible explanation is that, as in a roughly contemporary design by Agostino Ramelli (1531–1600) for an artificial nest of singing birds, there was a hidden slot in the wall behind the cabinet, allowing it to be operated, invisibly, from the next room (fig. 225).[8] One tantalizing piece of evidence in the Corinthian storey is a double groove evidently worn away by rope being moved repeatedly, which might suggest movement of a bellows or feeder. The spaces at the back of the Ionic and Composite storeys are open, perhaps to let the sound out (fig. 224). Evidently the organ would have been supplied by a specialist, and may have been tailored to the space and constructed so that it could be inserted – and eventually removed – as a more or less self-contained unit with minimal structural connections to the Cabinet itself.

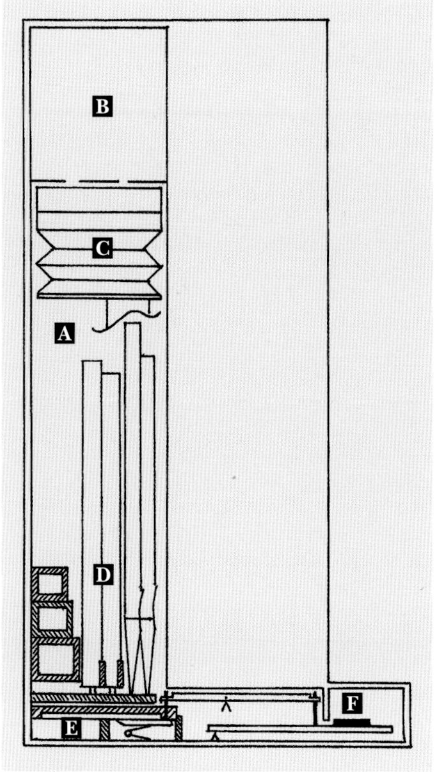

A. The main rear void. Internal dimensions 43¾ x 47⅛ x 11⅝ in, 113 x 119.6 x 29.6 cm.
B. Its narrower Composite third storey section. Internal dimensions 12¾ x 27½ x 11⅝ in, 31.6 x 70 x 29.6 cm.
C. Bellows, reservoir and feeder above the pipes, a usual position in a small organ of this period (although Italian organs often had a pair of bellows, lifted alternately, projecting from their backs); the Cabinet's bellows were operated with ropes.
D. Pipes, the longest and widest wooden and horizontal (and possibly connected to a vertical toeboard). The very longest would be the full width of the void, so an octave higher than the unison. If stopped it could be unison, but that was unlikely in Italy, and there is nothing wrong – and possibly it was not even unusual – in having an 'octave' organ. The second tin rank of pipes would be an octave higher. All the vertical pipes may have been tin.
E. Windchest (soundboard and pallet box) placed on the baseboard, to allow the maximum height for pipework. The soundboard a single piece of wood with grooves fanning out towards the back in chromatic order.
F. The available width, 26⅞ in, 68.2 cm, allows a keyboard with 45 notes. The available height, 4⅞ in, 12.5 cm, allows keys pivoted at the tail, with action to a lever (backfall), taking the action over the pallets.

FIG. 223
Possible configuration of the organ.

FIG. 224
The open void, which once housed the organ, behind the Ionic first storey.

FIG. 225
'Vaso musicale' [musical vase], engraving, possibly by Ambroise Bachot, for Agostino Ramelli, *Le Diverse et Artificiose Machine*, Paris, 1588. The organ formerly in the Sixtus Cabinet might have been operated by a comparable 'hole-in-wall' device.
12⅜ x 8 in, 31.5 x 20.5 cm.

The organ historian and builder, Dominic Gwynn, has observed that there is space for more than one stop of pipes, but no trace of stop controls, either holes for stop shanks, or slots for levers:

> Italian organs of this period do share certain characteristics. They tend not to use stopped pipes except where it is not possible to accommodate the length of open pipes. They tend to have a tonally homogeneous chorus, i.e. with all the pipes of the same type as far as possible, either pine or tin. The largest pipes might be pine, so they can be mitred, a way of accommodating longer pipes in a small organ. They tend to have soundboards made of a single board rather than a frame, with grooved channels from the pallets to the pipe holes (which means that the grooves can be fanned out to accommodate the larger pipes). They have keys pivoted at the tail, and not at an intermediate pivot point (which is only encountered in organs for the first time in England at the end of the 17th century).[9]

Clearly any number of arrangements are possible, but Gwynn has sketched a schematic diagram which demonstrates one possible disposition, and also that the inclusion of an organ was entirely feasible (fig. 223).

THE WAX PORTRAITS

> The Bust of the Pope, and his Nephew and the Princess (who was once a Laundress) of each side of him, with others of the Peretti Family are represented on the black Pedestal to the Life in a Curious Composition.

This description, in the 1754 Longleat manuscript (see Appendix II), is the first reference to this prominent but unusual feature of the Sixtus Cabinet. In the later descriptions Horace Walpole (1762) adds most by describing the portraits as 'in wax coloured & finely executed', an account repeated in the 1818 guidebook. Other references add that the waxes were recessed and glazed, and set in frames.[10] (Misinformation was also provided: the portraits were described as 'elegantly executed in white alabaster' or as 'fine paintings', while their reported numbers expanded from eleven to twenty-one.[11]) The portraits are mentioned in nineteenth-century guidebooks to Stourhead, routinely reprinted, without amendment, until Edwardian times. Finally, Alda, Lady Hoare, wife of the 6th Baronet, annotated her copy of the 1894 edition, writing against the waxes 'all sold'.[12] They are absent from Christie's Catalogue of the Stourhead Heirlooms, auctioned on behalf of Sir Henry Ainslie Hoare, 5th Baronet, in 1883. It seems probable that this Sir Henry, who inherited in 1857, had earlier sold them privately. It is hoped that they may yet re-emerge and be identified.

The physical evidence for the waxes (see p. 69) establishes that they were 11, that their insertion postdates the removal, or at least suppression, of the organ, last noted in 1665, and that, allowing for frames, they were probably about 2¼ inches (5.5 cm) in diameter. Sixtus V was self-evidently central, flanked by his sister Camilla and, probably, his great nephew Cardinal Alessandro Peretti Montalto. There is no evidence for the identities of the eight remaining family members, but the absence of this feature of the Cabinet from all the Roman descriptions, ending in 1713, suggests that the waxes may have been introduced subsequently, and that later generations formed part of this display of family and ancestry. It is difficult to conceive that Henry Hoare could have commissioned such a group in England. He was certainly a patron of Isaac Gosset (1713–1799), the Huguenot frame-carver and wax-modeller, who produced both contemporary and historic portraits, his payments beginning in 1753, a year before the portraits were first described.[13] But Gosset worked in natural, uncoloured wax, and it would surely have been well-nigh impossible to find models for 11 members of the Peretti dynasty in London around 1750.

Perhaps Henry Hoare bought 11 Peretti waxes in Rome and had them installed in his Cabinet there or in England. This is feasible, but it seems more likely that, presumably after 1713, the family had already rendered the Cabinet an even more eloquent Peretti heirloom and memorial by adding these portraits, which might have been to hand or specially commissioned, using medals and other images as models. Unfortunately, the history of wax portraiture in Rome is a vacuum, although a mention in the 1724 inventory *post mortem* of Caterina Giustiniani Savelli of 'Un ovato rappresentante Il Retratto del Principe D. Andrea Giustiniani In cera con cristallo e cornice negra' [an oval representing Prince D. Andrea Giustiniani in wax with glass and a black frame] – that is her father who had died in 1667 – suggests some tradition.[14] A possible candidate for the waxes on the Sixtus Cabinet, if they were indeed supplied after 1713, is Johann Georg Sindler (1669–1732), a sculptor from Styria who settled in Rome in that year and executed two wax reliefs of Pope Benedict XIII (r. 1724–30), one dated 1726, now in the Victoria & Albert Museum.[15] However, although relatively few have survived, the making of wax reliefs was an essential stage in the making of medals and, with the addition of colour, this technique could easily be adapted to produce independent wax relief portraits, a formula pioneered by the medallist Antonio Abondio (1538–1591). Sindler can hardly have been alone.

THE MINIATURES

In 1762 Horace Walpole remarked in the dressing room adjoining the red damask bedchamber, 'A great many small Italian heads in rounds; a family; in oil.'[16] Mrs Powys gave their history: 'some <u>time</u> after the purchase [of the Sixtus Cabinet] in some inner private drawers were found Seventy-two other miniatures some in old English dress others that of Spain Italy &c [...] in a Closet out of this room is a most inimitable portrait of Titian by himself, at 92 years old; small place [?] round this are hung the 72 miniatures above mention'd.'[17] Presumably as a result of the growth of his picture collection, Henry Hoare returned

FIG. 226
Marie Louise of Orleans (see p. 215), derived from a portrait by Juan Carreño de Miranda (1614–1685). Oil on copper, 2¼ x 1⅞ in, 5.6 x 4.8 cm.

FIG. 227
Philip III of Spain (granted Michele Peretti the title of Prince of Venafro), derived from a portrait by Frans Pourbus the younger (1569–1622). Oil on card, 2¼ x 1⅞ in, 5.6 x 4.8 cm.

FIG. 228
Pope Clement VIII Aldobrandini (friend and supporter of Cardinal Alessandro Peretti Montalto), derived from a portrait attributed to Antonio Scalvati (1569–1622). Oil on copper, 2⅜ x 1⅞ in, 5.9 x 4.7 cm.

the miniatures to the Cabinet and, in 1776, Samuel Curwen mentioned that: 'In the drawers [of the Cabinet] are prints of the principal royal and noble families of Europe in metal frames.'[18] Prints, they are not; framed in oval ormolu mounts they are. The miniatures pass silently through the nineteenth century. Sir Richard Colt Hoare had probably stored them.[19] By 1900, however, they were on display, a framed set of miniatures being visible, propped beside the Cabinet, in a photograph taken then (fig. 235), and, set in two rectangular frames, they were recorded in the library in 1908[20] and photographed there some time after 1913.[21] The National Trust removed these two outer frames and displayed

the miniatures in rows in a table-top show-case.

The 73 miniatures (one more than Mrs Powys counted) comprise two groups: a set of 56 in larger oval frames (3 x 2½ in, 7.6 x 6.3 cm) with 26 men and 30 women; and a set, in smaller frames (2¼ x 1⅞ in, 5.7 x 4.6 cm), with Pope Clement VIII and 16 women. The paintings are in oil on copper, rather than being miniatures in the strict technical sense, backed by modern cardboard and lack identification beyond the old National Trust inventory numbers pencilled on their reverses. The oval gilt bronze frames have a pin-hole drilled in the narrow side; the smaller frames are also drilled on a long side but these holes have been stopped and gilded over.

The story that the miniatures were found in certain of the Cabinet's secret drawers may sound fanciful, and their connection to the Cabinet doubtful. However, the discovery that a cabinet which was listed in 1713 immediately after the Sixtus Cabinet, among the goods which the widowed Princess Caterina Giustiniani Savelli took from the Palazzo Savelli to the Palazzo Giustiniani, was full of 'diversi ritratti in Rame incirca n. 50' [various portraits on copper numbering about 50] strongly suggests that the miniatures were associated with the Sixtus Cabinet after this move (Appendix I). There is a disparity in numbers, but the 1713 list is relatively perfunctory in description, and does not claim to be numerically accurate.

FIG. 229
Charles II of Spain (see p. 215), derived from a portrait by Juan Carreño de Miranda (1614–1685). Oil on copper, 2½ x 1⅞ in, 6.2 x 4.8 cm.

FIG. 230
Olimpia Aldobrandini (in 1670 her daughter, Flaminia Pamphilj, married Bernardino Savelli), derived from a portrait by Jacob Ferdinand Voet (1639–1689). Oil on copper, 2½ x 1⅞ in, 6.2 x 4.7 cm.

FIG. 231
Isabella Gioeni Colonna (in 1671 her second son, Filippo Colonna, married Cleria Cesarini), derived from a portrait attributed to Pietro Novelli (1603–1647). Oil on copper, 2½ x 1⅞ in, 6.2 x 4.9 cm.

FIG. 232
Pope Clement VIII Aldobrandini. A smaller
version of fig. 228. Oil on copper, 1¾ x 1⅜ in,
4.5 x 3.4 cm.

FIG. 233
Maffeo Barberini (first cousin of Filippo
Colonna, through his father, Taddeo Barberini's
marriage to Anna Colonna, sister-in-law of
Isabella Gioeni Colonna (see fig. 231), derived
from a portrait by Carlo Maratti (1625–1713).
Oil on copper, 2½ x 1⅞ in, 6.3 x 4.8 cm.

FIG. 234
Camillo Pamphilj (the husband of Olimpia
Aldobrandini (see fig. 230), derived from
a portrait by Giovanni Battista Gaulli
(1639–1709). Oil on copper, 2½ x 1⅞ in,
6.4 x 4.9 cm.

It is difficult to resist the inference that this
unusually large group of miniatures on copper
was a family assemblage and that it seemed
appropriate to insert them into that prime
Peretti heirloom, the Sixtus Cabinet.[22] The
1713 reference does not mention frames, which
are noted in most of its other picture entries,
suggesting that the miniatures were unframed
when they reached England, and that Henry
Hoare had their ormolu frames supplied before
Walpole saw them hanging at Stourhead in
1762, probably by a London maker, although
they are not identifiable in Henry's accounts.

The inventories, valuations and lists
associated with Giulio Savelli and Caterina
Giustiniani Savelli include numerous portraits,
particularly of the Peretti and Savelli families,
which would have supplied ample models
for reduction into oil miniatures.[23] The first
antechamber of the Palazzo Savelli contained
three portraits, those of Charles II of Spain,
of Mariana of Austria, his widowed mother,
who was his regent from 1663, and of his queen
Marie Louise of Orleans.[24] Their prominence
reflected Giulio's role as Spanish ambassador
in Rome, a diplomatic position which echoed
that of his father, Paolo Savelli, who had
served as imperial ambassador in Rome. In
1667 Giulio Savelli was raised to the degree
of Grandee of Spain, first class, anticipating
his eventual succession, in 1683, as ninth
count of Chinchón, thanks to his de la Cerda
y Bobadilla great-grandmother. The presence
among the Stourhead miniatures of a number
of Spanish sitters, above all the unmistakeably
Hapsburg features of Charles II (fig. 229), is
thus entirely explicable, and confirms their
Savelli provenance.

Pinning down the identity of sitters in
miniatures, which may be derived from other
portrait images, is fraught with uncertainty.
The nine miniatures of whose identities the
authors feel reasonably secure are illustrated
here (figs 226–34). The full set may be viewed

FIG. 235
The Cabinet Room, Stourhead, c.1900.
One framed set of Peretti miniatures propped
beside the niche is particularized in the
enlargement.

on the National Trust Collections website
(see p. 222) under the references NT 731901
–731973 and 731985.

FIG. 236
The Sixtus Cabinet: left, St Paul, height:
7⅛ in, 18 cm; right, St Peter, height: 6⅞ in,
17.5 cm. Carved and gilt wood, by
John Boson, London, c.1743.

SAINT PETER AND SAINT PAUL

On 4 December 1587 a monumental gilt
bronze statue of Saint Peter, modelled by
Tomaso della Porta and Leonardo Sormani
and cast by Bastiano Torrigiani, was placed
on Trajan's Column; this was followed on
27 October 1588 by the installation of an
equivalent statue of Saint Paul, by the same
team, on the Column of Marcus Aurelius,
then known as the Antonine Column. Both
columns had been repaired by Domenico
Fontana by order of Sixtus V, and the two
statues were signals of his campaign to
Christianize the pagan monuments of Rome.

The Sixtus Cabinet now has a giltwood
statue of St Peter on the right forward corner
of its Corinthian second storey and another of
St Paul to the left (fig. 236). Both Apostles are
carved in the round, straight-backed, and with
stiff drapery folds similar to those of the figures
on the Pedestal below. They have comparable

FIG. 237
Charts IX and X, engraved by Hubert-François Gravelot, for John Pine, *The Tapestry Hangings of the House of Lords, representing the several engagements between the English and Spanish Fleets in … MDLXXXVIII …*, London, 1739. Inscribed and dated 24 June 1739. 15½ x 24¼ in. 39.5 x 62 cm. The profile head of Pope Sixtus V derives from Fragni's medal which was also the model for his carved medallion on the Pedestal. The British Library.

delicately modelled hands and plain bases and are similarly gilded and carved in the same timber, *mahogani swietenia*.[25] They can thus be securely attributed to John Boson, who supplied the Pedestal carvings in 1743.

Saint Peter holds a book and, in his left hand, a gigantic key, while Saint Paul has a book and, in his left hand, a sword, its blade now missing. The attributes are standard, although, strictly speaking, Saint Peter's key should be in his right hand, as it is on Trajan's Column. Despite this reversal, accounted for by the need for compositional symmetry in confined spaces, the two statues bear a general resemblance to their Roman predecessors, and there seems little doubt that in choosing these subjects Henry Hoare was extending his programme of memorializing Sixtus's Roman monuments from the Pedestal to the Cabinet itself. Prints of the columns available before 1742 depict the poses of the statues, not the detail, and intermediate drawings or engravings used by Boson have yet to be identified.[26] The survival (see p. 96) of a singleton gilt bronze figure suggests that one of the pair originally in these positions had been lost. The Boson statuettes now sit convincingly on the Cabinet's church-like façade, but it probably did not enter Henry Hoare's calculations that they Christianized what is otherwise, arguably, a pagan monument – an unintended echo of Sixtus V.

THE ARMADA MEDAL AND THE GEORGE

The 1784 Catalogue of Stourhead lists 'A Superb Cabinet and pedestal on it a Medal of Queen Elizabeth and the George and Dragon hanging under it in Gold'.[27] In 1787 Count Carlo Gastone della Torre de Rezzonico noted that the medal turned on a swivel to allow both sides to be seen, and was protected by a double-sided glazed and hinged frame.[28] He did not mention the George, described in 1800 by the Revd Richard Warner as hanging from the medal, although in the same year, Sir Richard Colt Hoare mentioned only the medal.[29] The last reference to this ensemble is in the 1808 Catalogue.[30] Of the George there is no further mention, and the medal only surfaces when, on 29 August 1882, Augusta, wife of Sir Henry Ainslie Hoare, 5th Bt, recorded its removal.[31] Drill holes on the Cabinet suggest that it was suspended, with the George below, in front of the splendid foiled amethyst in the centre of the Composite third storey.[32]

Several medals were struck to commemorate the defeat of the Armada in 1588. Rezzonico described 'la medaglia unica e rarissima della regina Elisabetta dopo la vittoria che riportò sull' armata *invincibile* di Filippo II […] Ella è di smalto a più colori col ritratto della regina […] Il rovescio è un alloro in mezzo al mare con leggenda intorno' [the unique

FIG. 238
Great George of the Order of the Garter, English, 1628–9. Enamelled gold, set with 44 diamonds, 2¾ x 2⅜ in, 7.2 x 6 cm. From the regalia of the Garter which belonged to William Compton, first Earl of Northampton created a Knight of the Garter in 1628. Henry Hoare acquired a version of the 'George' to display with the Sixtus Cabinet. The British Museum.

and rare medal of Queen Elizabeth I after the victory over the invincible Armada sent by Philip II [...] It is decorated of enamels in several colours and displays a portrait of the Queen [...] The reverse has a laurel tree in the middle of the ocean with an inscription around]. Mention of the tree suggests that the Stourhead medal was of the 'Dangers Averted' model, which has a bay tree on an island representing Britain on its reverse, with a tablet inscribed 'NON . IPSA . PERICVLA . TANGVNT' [not even dangers can affect it] (figs 239 and 240).[33] Given this identification, Rezzonico was mistaken in describing the inscription as round the reverse. Perhaps he had confused his notes of the *obverse*, depicting Queen Elizabeth, whose inscription indeed forms a border. It might also be supposed that he had confused the medal with the George, in stating that the former was 'di smalto a più colori' [of enamel in several colours], were it not that on 24 February 1723/4 this very medal, with inscriptions correctly described, was shown to the Society of Antiquaries of London: 'The face and neck are likewise enamelled like flesh [...] There were but six of them struck. This belongs to Henry Hoare, esq. There is a loop at the top to hang it by, as a favour; and three loops below, to fasten pearls to or the like.'[34] Evidently the Stourhead medal was an unrecorded and possibly unique enamelled version, fragile enough to require the glazed locket described by Rezzonico, while the presence of lower loops suggests that the George could have been suspended from the central one. Henry Hoare I died on 12 March 1724/5 and the medal is unremarked upon for 60 years.[35] Walpole, Mrs Powys and other commentators would surely have noted if it were displayed at Stourhead. The medal might have belonged to the banking partnership, acquired in payment of a debt, and been kept at their Fleet Street premises. Henry II was 19 when his father died and was at that age more interested in hunting than the arts, so he is an unlikely purchaser. But he was heir to his father's personal belongings as well as Stourhead. A tantalizing single word entry in the 1742 Inventory mentions a 'medal' in Mr Hoare's dressing room; whether this refers to the 'Dangers' medal is impossible to say.[36]

The 'George and Dragon' listed in 1784 was described by the Revd Richard Warner in 1800 as 'richly enamelled'. The insignia of the Order of the Garter includes a 'Great George', with a knight in armour on horseback in the act of killing a dragon on the ground below, which hangs from the Collar of the Order (fig. 238), and a 'Lesser George', a smaller pendant in which the saint is encircled by the Garter. A Great George would have composed better with the 'Dangers Averted' medal, and is more likely to have had enamel as its dominant form of decoration, and it is thus reasonable to assume that this was what was hung on the Cabinet.[37] The regalia of the Order of the Garter traditionally belonged to the monarch and was handed back at the death of a knight. In the eighteenth century this rule was relaxed and the Chancellor of the Order was allowed to receive and keep the collars of deceased knights as a perquisite. The chancellorship went customarily to the Bishop of Salisbury and a warrant was issued in 1782 to Shute

Barrington, on his appointment as Bishop of Salisbury, specifically permitting him to convert the 'Jewels and Ornaments [...] to his own personal use, profit and advantage' while he held office.[38] Henry Hoare was on friendly terms with Shute Barrington's predecessor, John Hume, Bishop of Salisbury, 1766–82, and could well have acquired the 'George and Dragon' through him, although it was not recorded at Stourhead until 1784.[39]

The idea of affixing a medal depicting Queen Elizabeth and commemorating the defeat of the Spanish Armada in 1588 to the Sixtus Cabinet reflected an apposition of Pope and Queen which was current throughout the eighteenth century, finding expression in the very title, *The life of Sixtus Quintus, Pope of Rome in the reign of Queen Elizabeth*, translated from the Italian of Gregorio Leti, published in London in 1724.[40] According to Rapin de Thoyras, a historian admired by Henry Hoare, 'the Pope [Sixtus V] thundered against *Elizabeth* a Bull, absolving her Subjects from their oath of allegiance, and giving her Kingdoms to the first that shall seize them'.[41] In 1739 John Pine published a set of engravings after the Armada tapestries commissioned in 1592 by the commander of the English fleet, Lord Howard.[42] Henry Hoare and his brother Richard subscribed to this publication, which is recorded in the nineteenth century both at Wavendon and Stourhead.[43] Richard's copy survives at Stourhead.[44] The combined charts IX and X (fig. 237) are ornamented with a profile head of Elizabeth I and, below, portraits of Philip II, Sixtus V and the Duke of Parma.[45] The Pope is derived from Fragni's medal (see Chapter 8) with the profile reversed. Henry Hoare had probably read *The History of the Spanish Armada*, published in 1759, whose preface explained the contemporary relevance of 'The Measures that were most prudently concerted for Defence of the Realm against the then threatened Invasion' and praised 'The Spirit and Vigor so seasonably and unanimously exerted by the loyal Nobility, Gentry and Commonalty, for putting those Measures in Execution, and the Success with which it was attended.'[46] In 1779 the French and Spanish fleets lay in sight of Plymouth, only to be driven by winds and the English navy into the Solent, where they abandoned the attack. Henry Hoare received first-hand reports and described his anxiety in a letter to his son-in-law also alluding to the Armada.[47] A poem, *The Spanish invasion, or, defeat of the invincible Armada*, published in London in 1780, had an introduction comparing the contemporary crisis to 'the danger we were in during the reign of Queen Elizabeth'.[48] If, as seems plausible, the medal was affixed to the Cabinet at this juncture, the gesture was not only patriotic, but topical.

The George would seem to have no specific significance in this precise context but its presence underlined those strongly royalist feelings which Henry Hoare expressed in tangible form when in 1762 he began a great brick tower dedicated to the memory of Alfred the Great. He drafted its dedication while the government was negotiating peace with France and Spain: 'In memory of Alfred the Great, the Founder of the English Monarchy. Britons will revere the Ashes of that Monarch by whose

FIG. 239
'Dangers Averted' medal (obverse) bust of Elizabeth I, inscribed, DITIOR . IN . TOTO . NON . ALTER . CIRCVLVS . ORBE. [no other circle in the whole world more rich]. British, 1589. Gold, cast and chased, 2¼ x 2⅛ in, 5.8 x 5.2 cm. The British Museum.

FIG. 240
'Dangers Averted' medal (reverse) a bay-tree uninjured by storms and flourishing on an island; three ships sail in the distance, inscribed, NON . IPSA . PERICVLA .TANGVNT [not even dangers affect it]. The British Museum.

Lessons They have (under the protection of Divine Providence) subdued Their Enemys this year with Invincible Force by Land & Sea, in Europe, Asia, Africa & America, stop'd the Effusion of human blood & given peace & rest to the Earth. Erected, Anno Dom': 1762 in the 3ᵈ Glorious Year of the Reign of our truely British King George the 3ᵈ.'[49] In 1764 he acquired the Bristol Cross, another celebration of royalty with its eight statues of monarchs. This purchase demonstrated Henry's patriotism and his eye for a bargain; the cross had been dismantled and stored in Bristol Cathedral. Henry rebuilt it close to Stourton Church, thus providing a historical foreground for the principal view of the garden – an opportunistic purchase just as he had bought the Sixtus Cabinet to command attention at the house.

Notes for Appendix V

1. Lietzmann 1994, pp. 390–402.
2. Lightbown 1964, pp. 184–6.
3. Lefeber-Morsman 2010, pp. 7–8.
4. Morsman 2006, p. 35.
5. Himmelheber 1977, pp. 18–19 and 69–70.
6. Escalas Llimona 2002, pp. 87–100.
7. Colle 1997, p. 186; Boström 2001, p. 156 and pl. 4; Reinheckel 1981, pp. 45–6.
8. Published in 1588 and illus., Jervis 1974, p. 34 and pl. 178.
9. Abridged from the unpublished report, 'The Pope's Cabinet at Stourhead, Wilts. Quaere: whether there was originally an organ contained within', by Dominic Gwynn, 2006.
10. Hanway1756,* 'with glasses before them' and Mrs Powys 1776,* 'set in Frames'.
11. Curwen 1776,* 'miniatures of all the Perotti family […] in white alabaster'; Burlington 1779,* 'On the cabinet are fine paintings of the pope, and others of the Peretti family'; Fenton 1807,* '[the Cabinet] ornamented with his [Sixtus v] own portrait, and twenty others of the Peretti family'.
12. Stourhead Archive 6787, *Sweetman's Historical Pamphlets* 1894, p. 5.
13. Henry Hoare Accounts 1749–70, 30 March 1753, 'Mr Gosset in full for all my profile Pictures' £23-2-0.
14. Squarzina 2003, 3, p. 290.
15. V&A A.45-1940 (diameter 9.2 cm) and A.6-1996 (diameter 8.5 cm). See Pyke 1973, p. 137.
16. Walpole 1762.*
17. Mrs Powys 1776.*
18. Curwen 1776.*
19. Stourhead Inventory 1838 does not appear to record the miniatures. The entry in North Apartments, p.78, no. 1078, 'Two Frames of Medallions', is more likely to be the two framed sets of impressions by Nathaniel Marchant, today displayed in the Library (NT 731991.1&2 15¼ x 20 in, 39 x 51 cm), and not the Peretti miniatures.
20. Stourhead Inventory 1908, Library, p. 132, 'One 22" x 22" antique black and gold case containing 47 Miniatures, in gilt oval frames. One 23" x 19" do., containing 34 oval and 1. square Miniatures in gilt frames.' This total, 82, exceeds by nine the Peretti collection. Today unrelated miniatures in miscellaneous frames are displayed in the Library (including the rectangular *Young Woman with a Bucket*). These 'strays', which probably account for the disparity in numbers, were included in the two black and gold cases.
21. *Country Life*, Photograph 11577-2, Library, Stourhead. On the folio table are visible the two framed cases of miniatures. The photograph was taken after 1912–13, when the present chimney piece, shown in the companion photograph, was installed.
22. The 1713 entry may be identifiable with one in the 1712 valuation of Giulio Savelli's paintings and sculpture for the 'Gabinetto detto delle ritrattini I quadrucci di detto gabinetto non si stimano per esser proprij della Signora Principessa, come si dice nell'inventario' [cabinet called 'of the little portraits'. The little paintings in the said cabinet are not valued as they are the property of the Lady Princess, as is stated in the inventory], Squarzina 2003, 3, p. 270, under 'Quadri e statue dell'eredità del principe Giulio Savelli. Perizia di Michelangelo

Ricciolini del 24 maggio 1712'.
23. Ibid., 3, pp. 195–339. As well as many individually named portraits there were several large groups – for example, p. 234: 44 little round black frames with various little portraits, 34 little carved and gilt wood frames for little portraits, some with portraits, others empty, nine similar, ten similar, p. 213: 35 portraits of cardinals of the family, 54 portraits of gentlemen and ladies of the family.
24. Ibid., p. 197.
25. Piper Cabinet Report 2008, p. 63.
26. Pietro Bombelli's engravings of the statues are dated 1779.
27. Stourhead Catalogue 1784.*
28. Rezzonico 1787.*
29. Warner 1800;* Hoare 1800.*
30. Stourhead Catalogue 1808.*
31. Stourhead Library, shelfmark E 10.24, MS diary of Augusta, Lady Hoare, 29 August 1882, 'Mr Benjamin came to take away […] the Spanish Armada Medal.'
32. Piper Cabinet Report 2008, figs 149–52 and pp. 71–2. 'The green onyx frieze [above the composite storey] has two small holes bored into it, each to the outer ends of the frieze […] [a second pair of holes on the top of the drawer] may simply be a second fixing […] made necessary when the ribband was found to impede the opening of the drawer […] This proposition is further supported by the deliberate cut-out of the top framing mould beneath the holes, evidently to allow the ribband to hang satisfactorily.'
33. British Museum 1866.1218.1 and Hawkins 1885, vol. I, p. 154, no. 130. Also British Museum, with similar obverse and reverse, M.6903 (in gold); M.6902 (in silver); M.6904, M.6906 and M.6907 (in bronze); Elizabeth I, and no reverse, M.6905, and BNK, ENGM.21 (in bronze). A gold version is in the Fitzwilliam Museum, Cambridge CM.YG.1401-R.
34. John Nichols, *Literary Anecdotes of the Eighteenth Century*, VI, pt 1, London, 1812, p. 158. John Nichols was father of J.B. Nichols, publisher to Sir Richard Colt Hoare and compiler of the 1840 Stourhead Library Catalogue.
35. The medal is not identifiable in Henry Hoare I's record of expenditure.
36. Stourhead Inventory 1742, 'medal print & a [illegible] flower piece in ye Chimney'.
37. Begent 1999, pp. 164–73.
38. Ibid., p. 173.
39. Stourhead Catalogue 1784.*
40. This edition was preceded by another in 1704 and succeeded by yet another in 1754, with later reprints. Leti's work, first issued in Italian in Geneva in 1669, was delicately described by Edward Gibbon as 'a copious and amusing work, but which does not command our absolute confidence' (Edward Gibbon, *The Decline and Fall of the Roman Empire*, London, 1790, 12, p. 392). Gregorio Leti, *Historia o vero Vita di Elisabetta, Regina d'Inghilterra*, Amsterdam, 1693, published in Italian, was the first life of Queen Elizabeth. Leti's position as a Catholic turned Protestant made his chronicles very palatable to an English audience.
41. Rapin de Thoyras 1732–3, vol. II, bk XVII, p. 135. Nichols 1840, p. 79 listed Rapin de Thoyras' *History* in French (1727) and English (1732–47).

42. Pine 1739. From the time of Charles II, the tapestries were displayed where the House of Lords met. The set perished during the fire at Westminster Palace in 1834.
43. Wavendon Book Inventory 1852, 'Library, Bottom Shelf (Folios)', 'Pines tapestry hangings of the house of Lords'. Henry Hoare's copy, Nichols 1840, p. 290.
44. Stourhead Library, shelfmark B10.23.
45. The engraved portrait of the Queen relates to the British Museum, M.6883, a silver medal of Elizabeth I, attributed to Reutlinger, 1574, with the Queen shown in left profile, H 47 x w 41 mm (Hawkins 1885, vol. I, p. 124, no. 70).
46. Anon. 1759, p. i; Nichols 1840, p. 24.
47. WSA Ailesbury Estate Collection, 9/35/165, Coplestone Warre Bampfylde to Henry Hoare, not dated but infer, August 1779, with a description of the preparations at Plymouth to resist the French. Ibid., 1300/4294, Henry Hoare sent this letter on to Lord Ailesbury, 23 August 1779. 'I returned the Bishop of Sarums & Lady Mary Humes Visit at Mr Humes at Gillingham last week here we saw a Letter from The Rams Head wrote by an officer of Plimouth Dock Yard to His son Mr – who says He saw the Ardent beat off 2 Ships of The Enemy & got clear off but other Accounts will have it she struck[.] this East Wind is lamented as the most unfortunate that ever happened to Us by preventing Sr Charles Vardy from coming up I pray God grant us Victory in the day of Battle.' And , as PS, 'I enclose with the Acct We rec'd this morn from the Bishop of Sarum at Mr Humes to keep out of the Hurry of St. sown off afflavit Deus & dissipantur [God sent forth His breath and they were scattered: the motto which Queen Elizabeth had ordered to be struck on medals commemorating the Armada], I hope it will give us time to prepare better for a 2d Attack & bring The opposition to Their senses.'
48. Anonymous, *The Spanish invasion*, London, 1780.
49. WSA Ailesbury Estate Collection, 1300/4281, Henry Hoare to Lord Bruce, 18 November 1762.

APPENDIX VI
FURTHER ROMAN
PIETRE DURE
CABINETS AT
STOURHEAD

TWO SOLD CABINETS

The 1883 Christie's sale of Stourhead heir-looms included two cabinets which were almost certainly, from their descriptions, Roman:

> Lot 46 A HANDSOME ITALIAN CABINET, of architectural design, with four columns and door in the centre, composed of rare agates and jaspers, mounted with chased or-molu, and with four drawers on each side, on blackwood stand.

> Lot 47 ANOTHER, with niche in the centre, two columns, with or-molu capitals, and five drawers, on each side, the front of lapis lazuli, agates, &c.

The first (Lot 46) was purchased by 'Philpots' for £73.10s.: its fate is unknown. The second was bought by the dealer, Charles Davis, acting for the Duke of Norfolk, for £42.[1] No longer at Arundel Castle, it is probably one of a many Italian cabinets sold by Christie's at the Castle in 1945, at a nadir in the taste for such things.[2] Given that Edward Fowler's 1742 charge of £37.1.6 for the transport of 'Cabinetts' from Leghorn is in the plural is it possible that it covers, at least, these two cabinets, as well as the Sixtus Cabinet itself. Descriptions in the 1838 Stourhead Inventory are too generalized to identify them, although they could be numbers 514, 540 or 1076, which all lack measurements (see Appendix II, p. 204).

The Cabinet Room at Stourhead now contains two further Roman cabinets, both of which *could* have been purchased by Henry Hoare, although the provenance of neither is clear.

THE WAVENDON CABINET

The first, called in the 1908 Stourhead Inventory 'The Wavendon Cabinet' (fig. 68), was first documented at Stourhead in a 1900 photograph of the Picture Gallery.[3] The stand bears a label on the underside stating it belonged to Sir Henry Hugh Hoare, 3rd Bt:

> February 1845:
> family picture, brought from York Street,
> St James's Square,
> under the Will of
> Sir H.H. Hoare, Bart.;
> left as an heir loom,
> "To go [to] the several Persons to whom my estates in the Counties of Bucks and Beds are devised; subject nevertheless to the Necessary Wear and Tear of perishable Articles."
> Will dated 27 April, 1839

In his will Sir Henry mentioned that it came from Barn Elms, the house which had descended to him from his grandfather, Sir Richard Hoare, Henry Hoare's younger brother.[4] Neither Sir Richard nor his son, also Sir Richard, the 1st Baronet, had been on the Grand Tour, but the former was close to his brother Henry and, after he acquired Barn Elms in the 1740s, he employed artists and craftsmen who had worked at Stourhead including Henry Flitcroft who advised him on improvements to its garden.[5] The cabinet might have been given by Henry Hoare to his brother before the latter's death in 1754, or might have been in Henry's villa in Clapham, which he left, with its contents, to his nephew, the 1st Baronet, who sold the house after Henry's death in 1785, having taken his pick of the pictures and furnishings either for his London residence or for Barn Elms, which was sold to the Hammersmith Bridge Company in 1825.

At some point after the 3rd Baronet's death in 1841, the cabinet was moved from London to Wavendon, the Hoare property in Buckingham-shire, and was recorded, in its 1852 and 1895 inventories.[6] Wavendon then belonged to Sir Henry Hoare, 6th Bt, who removed its contents to Stourhead, in whose 1908 Inventory it is listed in the Picture Gallery:

> The 36" x 15" Rosewood Wavendon Cabinet, with Mosaic, Ormolu, and silver enrichments., this Cabinet stands upon a quaint black and gold carved Wood stand 26" high, on four brass claw feet., the lower tier consists of centre door with Corinthian Column each side, and drawer under. To the right and left are three small drawers, and at each end is a large centre drawer, smaller one end, with square inlaid marble at each side; over this tier are three large drawers with colonnade on each end, and six gilt busts., at each end of the Cabinet is a large brass handle.[7]

To this description should be added that wave mouldings frame the two tiers of three drawers; the carcase wood is chestnut and the drawer linings of walnut; the veneer is not rosewood but African blackwood; and the side handles, oil-gilt, appear late.[8] The cabinet shares many features with one of the Cini bequest examples (630 Cini), at present on view in the Palazzo dei Conservatori, and probably dates from about 1625. Its stand, not 'carved', but with delicately fretted foliate brackets, probably dates from about 1750, although its present black and gold japanned finish appears Regency, as do the in-filling of the chamfers on the insides of its legs and its massy gilt bronze paw feet. A date of about 1750 would accord with its being pro-vided to Henry Hoare's brother, Sir Richard when he was particularly active at Barn Elms, but it could equally have been for his London house, or for Henry's Clapham villa.

THE STOURHEAD CABINET

The second cabinet, visible in a second 1900 photograph of the Picture Gallery[9] and called in the 1908 Inventory 'The Stourhead Cabinet' (fig. 73), has no further provenance.[10] It might be one of the three cabinets listed in the 1838 Inventory, but, as with the two sold cabinets described above, it cannot be identified there. It is veneered in African blackwood with panes of partridge wood and with overlay of ebon-izing varnish; the carcase is of chestnut, the drawer linings in walnut. Its front, with a central columned swan-neck pediment and empty niche, has four drawer fronts to each side faced with pietre dure panels. Its stand, with glass panels painted to resemble pietre dure in its frieze, has square tapering legs and gilt brass bun feet.[11] The cabinet itself is of formulaic Roman design, but reasonably well executed and may date from about 1650. Its stand has clearly been made or converted to match the cabinet, possibly in about 1825. This would suggest that it could have been in the house under Sir Richard Colt Hoare. If so it *may* also have been there since the reign of his grandfather, Henry.

Notes for Appendix VI

1. Jervis 2005, p. 242.
2. Christie's 1945, possibly Lot 151 'An Italian cabinet, with architectural centre supported by columns and numerous drawers, entirely overlaid with coloured stones and mounted with two bronze-gilt figures of amorini, on stand similarly inlaid – 3 *ft. 7 in. wide'.
3. NT 732424.
4. TNA PROB 11/1952.
5. Miller 2010, pp. 195, 201.
6. Wavendon Inventory 1852, Saloon, 'An antique Cabinet with numerous drawers & the front inlaid with various stones & ornamented with ormolu (1 pillar split & one stone ch^d. [chipped] A stand for d° with gilt claws'. Wavendon Inventory 1895, the Drawing Room, p. 92, 'Inlaid Ebony Cabinet 3ft x 1ft 10 supported on antique Table 3ft 3 x 2 ft 1. 5 pieces missing from front of Cabinet'.
7. Stourhead Inventory 1908, p. 117.
8. Wavendon Cabinet. NT 731577. 21⅜ x 38½ x 15½ in, 55.5 x 97.7 x 39.5 cm. Stand 26 x 41 x 18 in, 66 x 104 x 46 cm.
9. NT 732425.
10. Stourhead Inventory 1908, p. 117, '3 6" x 15" (a) Ebony Stourhead Cabinet, with Mosaic, Marble, and Silver enrichments, the centre forming a drawer (b) with Corinthian Columns, one drawer under and one over, with five each side.[struck out and supplemented with MS pencil notes] (a) Standing on 4 square pillars. Total height 4' 6" (b) drawer with niched front with Classical figure* Corinthian Columns & Gothic surmount – each side of this is 4 drawers locked & underneath these 2 draws without locks all richly moulded with ebony, silver inlaid & ormolu escutcheons.* arms of figure missing.' This latter may be the poor-quality gilt bronze statuette now attached at the right side of the Composite third storey of the Sixtus Cabinet.
11. Stourhead Cabinet. NT 731578. 23⅜ x 42½ x 16¼ in, 60 x 108 x 41 cm. Stand 33⅞ x 42½ x 17 in, 86 x 108 x 43 cm.

APPENDIX VII
GENEALOGIES

PERETTI GENEALOGY

This diagram is selective, but includes
virtually all those mentioned in the text.
In a few instances, for clarity of presentation,
the general rule of 'oldest to the left' has
been overridden.

† Cardinal

Maria
Leonora de
la Cerda y
Bobadilla

Alfonso
Cavazzi della
Somaglia

1. Margherita
Cavazzi della
Somaglia (d.1613)

Camilla Damasceni
Peretti (1596–1668)

Bernardino
Savelli
(1604–58)

1. Anna
Aldobrandini
(d.1653)

Flaminia
Pamphilj
(1651–1709)

Domizio
Baroni
Mattei

Costanzo
Costantini

Giacomo de
Monte Alto

Michele
Damasceni
Peretti (1577–1631)

Giulio
Savelli
(1626–1712)

Bernardino
Savelli
(1653–72)

Maria Felice
Damasceni
Peretti (1603–50)

2. Caterina
Giustiniani
(1648–1712)

Cornelia
Cesarini

Fiore
Costantini
Peretti
(1541–73)

Andrea Baroni
Peretti Montalto
(1572–1629)†

2. Anna
Maria Cesi
(d.1647)

Francesco
Damasceni Peretti
(1595–1653)†

Alessandro
Savelli
(1624–28)

Anna
Cesarini

Maria Felice
Cesarini

Piacentina
Peretto

Fabio
Damasceni
(d.1595)

Alessandro
Damasceni
Peretti Montalto
(1571–1623)†

Paolo Savelli
(1622–85)†

Camilla
Cesarini

Giambattista
Mignucci

Maria Felice
Mignucci Peretti
(1552–84)

2. Muzio Sforza
(1577–1622)

Francesco
Savelli
(1621–27)

Giulia
Cesarini

Camilla Peretti
(1519–1601)

Francesco
Mignucci Peretti
(1549–81)

Felice
Orsina
Damasceni
Peretti
(b.1573)

Margherita
Savelli
(d.1690)

Filippo
Colonna
(1642–86)

Piergentile
de Monte Alto
Peretto (d.1554)

2. Vittoria
Accoramboni
(1557–85)

1. Marcantonio
Colonna
(1575–95)

Cleria
Cesarini
(1655–1735)

Felice Peretti
de Monte Alto,
Sixtus V (1521–90)†

Flavia
Damasceni
Peretti
(1574–1606)

Giuliano
Cesarini
(1618–65)

Mariana
da Frontillo

Paolo
Giordano
Orsini
(1541–85)

Alessandro
Cesarini
(d.1656)

Maria
Francesca
Giustiniani
(1707–83)

Paolo Giordano
Orsini (1591–1656)

Filippo
Cesarini
(d.1685)

Giovanni
Giorgio Cesarini
(d.1653)

Virginio
Orsini
(1572–1615)

Vittoria
Conti
(d.1743)

Sforza
Giuseppe
Sforza Cesarini
(1705–44)

Cosimo I
de' Medici
(1519–74)

Eleonora
de Toledo
(1522–62)

Livia
Cesarini
(1646–1711)

Valerio
Santacroce

1. Isabella
de' Medici
(1542–76)

Gaetano
Sforza Cesarini
(1674–1727)

Federico
Sforza
(1651–1712)

Margherita
Sforza Cesarini
(1704–40)

220

THE HOARES OF STOURHEAD

A selective genealogy

Owners of Stourhead are in **bold**

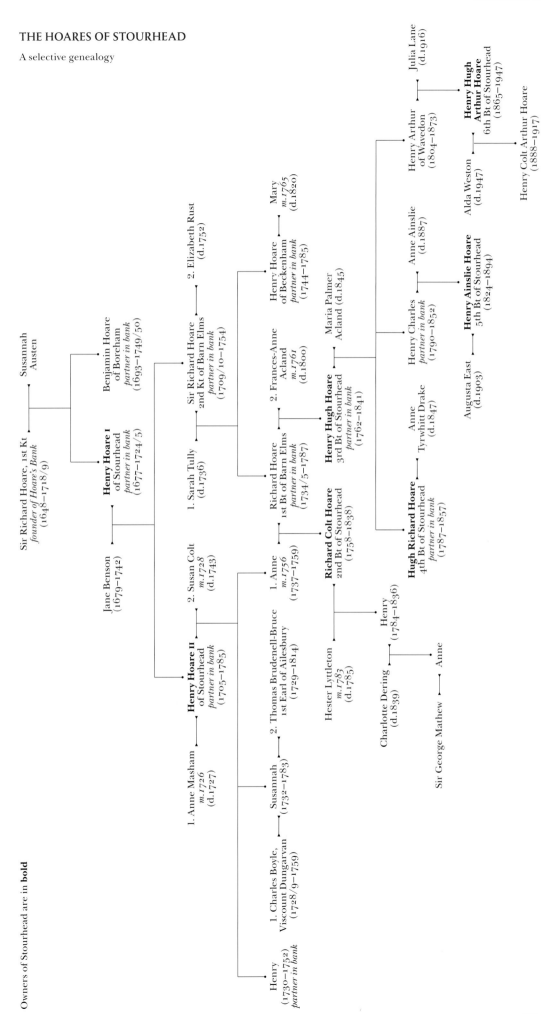

BIBLIOGRAPHY

National Trust Collections website
(www.nationaltrustcollections.org.uk)
has individual photographs of the contents
of Stourhead. These may be accessed by
entering, in the search box, the six digit
numerical code quoted in the endnotes.

ABBREVIATIONS

BLA
Bedfordshire & Luton Archives, Riverside
Building, Borough Hall, Bedford MK42 9AP

C. Hoare & Co.
C. Hoare & Co., 37 Fleet Street,
London EC4P 4DQ

Christie's
Christie's London, King Street,
London SW1Y 6QT

HRO
Hampshire Record Office, Sussex Street,
Winchester SO23 8TH

NAL
National Art Library, Victoria & Albert
Museum

Stourhead Archive
Stourhead, Stourton, Warminster,
Wiltshire BA12 6QH

NT
Prefix to the National Trust's collection
management system coding

ODNB
Oxford Dictionary of National Biography,
Oxford, 2004

Sotheby's
Sotheby's, 34–35 New Bond Street, London
W1A 2AA

TNA
The National Archives, Kew, Richmond,
Surrey TW9 4DU

V&A
Victoria & Albert Museum, Cromwell Road,
London SW7 2RL

WSA
Wiltshire & Swindon Archives, Cocklebury
Road, Chippenham, Wiltshire SN15 3QN

WSRO
West Sussex Record Office, County Hall,
Chichester PO19 1RN

* Denotes quoted in full or part in Appendix II,
Descriptions of the Sixtus Cabinet at Stourhead.

ARCHIVES

Alexandrinae mensae descriptio
British Library, BM Add. MS 8297 fols. 207–13,
'Alexandrinae Mensae Descriptio Philippo
Hispaniarum atque Indiarum Regi Catolico
Potentissimo ac Invictissimo Vincentius Stampa
Mediolanensis Civis Romanus S.' [1587].

Anonymous 1765*
Private collection, Norwich, MS description of
Stourhead in August 1765.

Anonymous 1766*
British Library, Add. MS 6767, ff. 36 and 37,
description of Stourhead in 1766.

Arundel Inventory 1816
Arundel Castle Archives, MS. IN 16
'An Inventory of furniture etc appraised at
Arundel Castle on the 27th of January 1816
and the following days by James Lear.'

Caterina Giustiniani Savelli Inventory 1724
Archivio de Stato di Roma, Rome, ASR 30
Notai capitolini, uff. 17, notai A. Ficedula,
gennaio [January] 1724, Inventarium Bonorum
Haereditorium Clarae Memoriae Principessae
D. Catherinae Justinianae Sabelli.

Codrington 'Gathering Moss' 1947
Liddell Hart Centre for Military Archives,
King's College, London, GB0099K CLMA
Codrington, Lt. Col. John Alfred Codrington,
'Gathering Moss', 1947, typescript memoir.

Gori *Relazione* 1771
Biblioteca degli Uffizi, Florence, MS. 60, I,
ins. 36, 1771–9, Relazione dell'arte di lavorare
in scagliola di Lamberto Gori allievo di
Hugford Enrico monaco vallombrosano.

Gray Long Gallery Report 2010
Powis Castle, National Trust, Margaret Gray,
Research and Conservation of marble statuary,
the Return of the Caesars and other issues,
unpublished report, October 2010.

Henry Hoare Accounts 1734–49
C. Hoare & Co., HFM/9/1, Henry Hoare Ledger
of Personal Accounts 1734–49; the so-called
'Wilberry' ledger.

Henry Hoare Accounts 1749–70
WSA, 383.6, Henry Hoare Ledger of Personal
Accounts 1749–70.

Henry Hoare Accounts 1770–85
C. Hoare & Co., HFM/9/5 Henry Hoare Ledger
of Personal Accounts 1770–85.

Mobili nel Palazzo Montalto 1591
Archivio Storico Capitolino, Rome, Archivio
Cardelli, Appendice Savelli, vol. 29 1591
Inventario e vendita dé Mobili ed oggetti
esistente nel Palazzo Montalto.

Parnell 1769*
The Library of the London School of
Economics and Political Science, Archives Coll.
Misc. 0038, 'Journal of a Tour thro' Wales and
England, anno. 1769' by Sir John Parnell, MS,
4 vols.

Piper Cabinet Report 2008
Colin Piper, 'The National Trust: Stourhead,
Wilts. The Pope Sixtus v Cabinet (STO.F.31)
Condition & Treatment Report', unpublished
report 9 August 2008.

Piper Pedestal Report 2008
Colin Piper, 'The National Trust: Stourhead,
Wilts. The Pedestal to the Pope Sixtus v Cabinet
(STO.F.32) Condition & Treatment Report',
unpublished report 26 August 2008.

Mrs Powys 1776*
British Library Add. MS 42168, Caroline Powys,
Journals and Recipe-Book of Caroline Powys,

vols 14, vol. IX, 'Journal of a Five days Tour in
a Letter to a Friend 1776'.

Skinner 1808*
British Library Add. MS 33635, Revd John
Skinner, 'Journals of tours in the South of
England, Sketches in Somerset, Devon and
Cornwall'.

Stourhead Inventory 1742
C. Hoare & Co., HB/1/B/4, 'An Inventory
of Goods and ffurniture in the House at
Stourhead belonging to Henry Hoare Esq
taken the 24th day of June 1742'.

Stourhead Catalogue 1754*
Longleat House Archives, North Muniment
Room 8963.9, MS catalogue headed 'In the Hall
at Stourton' and endorsed with the date 1754.

Stourhead Catalogue 1784*
WSA, 383.715, copy deed, ff. 57–64, 'The
Catalogue or Particulars of the Pictures Prints
Statues and other Things in … Stourhead …
mentioned in the Indenture whereunto the
same is annexed.' The catalogue is attached
to the Settlement of 27 January 1784 made
by Henry Hoare (1705–1785).

Stourhead Catalogue 1808*
WSA, 383.714, copy deed, ff. 127–32,
'A Catalogue of Pictures Prints Drawings
Busts Statues and other things in the Capital
Messuage or Manor House of Stourhead
and the Garden or Pleasure Ground thereto
belonging referred to in the foregoing
Indenture of Settlement'. The catalogue was
attached to the Settlement of 3 February 1808
for the marriage of Henry Hoare (1784–1836).

Stourhead Inventory 1838*
WSA, 383.16, '1838 Inventory of Heir-Looms
at Stourhead directed to be taken by the Will
of the late Sir Rich[d] Colt Hoare Bar[t]. with the
state and condition thereof'.

Stourhead Catalogue 1898
Stourhead Archive, 'Catalogue of the principal
Paintings & Drawings at Stourhead July 6th
1898'.

Stourhead Inventory 1908
Stourhead Archive, 'Stourhead. Wilts.
Inventory of Furniture, Bedding, Carpets,
China, Plate, Pictures, Curios, and other effects
on the premises of the Mansion the property
of Sir Henry Hugh Arthur Hoare Bt, January
1908. John Walton & Co: Ltd. Mere, Wilts.'

Wavendon Inventory 1852
Stourhead Archive, 'Inventory of Furniture
& Effects at Wavendon House Woburn, Beds
as let to Frederick Woodbridge Esq. June 1852.
Banting & Sons 27 St James Street.'

Wavendon Book Inventory 1852
WSA, 383.17, 'Inventory of Books on the
Premises Wavendon House, Woburn, Beds on
the Property being let to Frederick Woodbridge
Esq[re] June 1852 Bantings & Sons, 27 St James
Street'.

Wavendon Inventory 1895
WSA, 383.18, 'Inventory of The Furniture and
Effects in Wavendon made on behalf of Sir
Henry H. A. Hoare. Bart John Walton valuer
Mere. Wilts' [1895].

PUBLICATIONS

Abel-Smith 1996
Abel-Smith, Lucy, 'The Duke of Beaufort's Marble Room', *Burlington Magazine*, vol. CXXXVIII (1996), pp. 25–30.

Ademollo 1883
Ademollo, A. *Il Matrimonio di Suor Maria Pulcheria* (Rome, 1883).

Adshead 2007
Adshead, David, *Wimpole: Architectural Drawings and Topographical Views* (London, 2007).

Aguiló Alonso 2009
Aguiló Alonso and María Paz, 'Para un Corpus de las Piedras Duras in España', *Archivio Español de Arte*, vol. LXXV (2009), pp. 255–67.

Alcouffe, Dion-Tenenbaum and Lefébure 1993
Alcouffe, Daniel, Anne Dion-Tenenbaum and Amaury Lefébure, *Le Mobilier du Musée du Louvre*, I (Dijon, 1993).

Alexander 1957*
Alexander, Boyd (ed.), *Life at Fonthill 1807–1822 with Interludes in Paris and London from the Correspondence of William Beckford* (London, 1957).

Andrews 1936
Andrews, C. Bruyn (ed.), *The Torrington Diaries*, 3 (London, 1936).

Annibale 1999
Annibale, Claudio, Review of John W. Hill, *Roman Monody, Cantata and Opera from the Circle round Cardinal Montalto*, Oxford 1997, *Early Music History*, vol. XVIII (1999), pp. 365–98.

Anon. 1759
Anonymous, *The History of the Spanish Armada* (London, 1759).

Art Journal 1851
Art Journal Illustrated Catalogue (London, 1851).

Attwood 2003
Attwood, Philip, *Italian Medals, c.1530–1600 in British Public Collections*, 2 vols (London, 2003).

Bachrach and Collmer 1982
Bachrach, A.G.H. and R.G. Collmer (eds), *Lodewijk Huygens, The English Journal, 1651–1652* (Leiden, 1982).

Baglione 1642
Baglione, Giovanni, *Le vite de' pittori, scultori, architetti ed intagliatori* (Rome, 1642).

Baglione 1733
— *Le vite de' pittori, scultori, architetti ed intagliatori* (Naples, 1733).

Baldini 1979
Baldini, Umberto, Annamaria Guisti and Anna P. Pampaloni Martelli, *La Cappella dei Principi e le Pietre Dure a Firenze* (Milan, 1979).

Barberini 1991
Barberini, Maria Giulia, 'Villa Peretti Montalto-Negroni-Massimo: la collezione di sculture', in Elisa Debenedetti (ed.), *Studi sul Settecento Romano, 7, Collezionismo e ideologia, mecenati, artisti e teorici dal classico al neoclassico* (Rome, 1991), pp. 15–90.

Barbieri, Barchiesi and Ferrata 1995
Barbieri, Costanza, Sofia Barchiesi and Daniele Ferrata, *Santa Maria in Vallicella, Chiesa Nuova* (Rome, 1995).

Barker, Devonshire and Scarisbrick 2003
Barker, Nicolas, Andrew R.B.C. Devonshire, Diana Scarisbrick and Art Services International, *The Devonshire Inheritance: Five Centuries of Collecting at Chatsworth* (Alexandra, 2003).

Barletti 2011
Barletti, Emanuele, *Giovan Antonio Dosio da San Gemignano, architetto e sculptor fiorentino tra Roma, Firenze e Napoli* (Florence, 2011).

Baxter 1992
Baxter, Clare, 'A Pair of pietra dura Cabinets at Alnwick: The History of their Acquisition', *Apollo*, vol. CXXXII (1992), pp. 350–2.

Beard and Gilbert 1986
Beard, Geoffrey and Christopher Gilbert, *Dictionary of English Furniture Makers 1660–1840* (Leeds, 1986).

Beard and Goodison 1987
Beard, Geoffrey and Judith Goodison, *English Furniture 1500–1840* (Oxford, 1987).

Beckford 1805
Beckford, Peter, *Familiar Letters from Italy to a Friend in England* (Salisbury, 1805).

Bedon 2008
Bedon, Anna, 'Venture e sventure finanziarie del Cavalier Domenico Fontana', in M. Fagiolo and G. Bonaccorso (ed.), *Studi sui Fontana, Una dinastia di architetti ticinese a Roma tra Manierismo e Barocco* (Rome, 2008), pp. 39–44.

Begent 1999
Begent, Peter J. and Hubert Chesshyre, *The Most Noble Order of the Garter 650 Years* (London, 1999).

Berger 1999
Berger, Robert W., *Public Access to Art in Paris: A Documentary History from the Middle Ages to 1800* (Pennsylvania, 1999).

Bertolotti 1880
Bertolotti, A., 'Esportazione di Oggetti di Belle Arti da Roma per l'Inghilterra', in Fabio Gori (ed.), *Archivio Storico, Artistico, Archeologico e Letterario della Città e Provincia di Roma*, vol. IV, anno VI, f. 2 (Spoleto, 1880), pp. 74–90.

Bevilacqua 2009
Bevilacqua, M., *S. Caterina da Siena a Magnanapoli* (Rome, 2009).

Black 1992
Black, Jeremy, *The British Abroad: The Grand Tour in the Eighteenth Century* (New York, 1992).

Black 2003
— *France and the Grand Tour* (Basingstoke, 2003).

Bohr 1993
Bohr, Michael, *Die Entwicklung der Kabinettschränke in Florenz* (Frankfurt am Main, 1993).

Bolton 1922
Bolton, Arthur T., *The Architecture of Robert & James Adam*, 2 vols (London, 1922).

Bonnaffé 1874
Bonnaffé, Edmond, *Inventaire des Meubles de Catherine de Médicis* (Paris, 1874).

Borghini 2004
Borghini, Gabriele (ed.), *Marmi antichi* (Rome, 2004).

Bosman 2005
Bosman, Lex, 'Spolia and Coloured Marbles in Sepulchral Monuments in Rome, Florence and Bosco Marengo, Designs by Dosio and Vasari', *Mitteilungen des Kunsthistorischen Institutes in Florenz*, vol. XLIX (3) (2005), pp. 353–76.

Boström 2001
Boström, Hans-Olof, *Det underbara skåpet, Philipp Hainhofer och Gustav II Adolfs konstskåp* (Uppsala, 2001).

Bracken 2003
Bracken, Susan, 'The Early Cecils and Italianate Taste', in Edward Chaney (ed.), *The Evolution of English Collecting: Reception of Italian Art in the Tudor and Stuart Periods* (Newhaven and London, 2003).

Brennan 1993
Brennan, Michael G., 'The Travel Diary (1611–1612) of an English Catholic, Sir Charles Somerset', *Leeds Philosophical and Literary Society Proceedings*, vol. XXIII (1993).

Brennan 2004
— (ed.), 'The Origins of the Grand Tour', *Hakluyt Society*, III, vol. XIV (2004).

Brice 1725
Brice, Germain, *Nouvelle description de la ville de Paris ...*, 8th edn rev., 4 vols (Paris, 1725).

Brighton 1995
Brighton, Trevor, 'The Ashford Marble Works and Cavendish Patronage, 1748–1905', *Bulletin of the Peak District Mines Historical Society*, vol. XII (1995), pp. 58–67.

Britton 1801*
Britton, John, *The Beauties of Wiltshire*, 3 vols (London, 1801).

Brown and Lorenzoni 1993
Brown, Clifford Malcolm and Anna Maria Lorenzoni, *Our Accustomed Discourse on the Antique* (New York and London, 1993).

Brown and Lorenzoni 1999
— 'The "studio del clarissimo Cavaliero Mozzanico in Venezia", Documents for the Antiquarian Ambitions of Francesco I de' Medici, Marco Bevilacqua, Alessandro Farnese and Fulvio Orsini', *Jahrbuch der Berliner Museen*, vol. XLI (1999), pp. 55–76.

Buitoni 2010
Buitoni, Antonio, *I reliquarii della Basilica di San Petronio* (Bologna, 2010).

Buonanni 1696
Buonanni, Filippo, *Numismata summorum pontificum Templi Vaticani fabricam indicantia, chronologica ejusdem fabricæ narratione* (Rome, 1696).

Buonanni 1699
— *Numismata pontificum romanorum quæ à tempore Martini v. usque ad annum M.DC.XCIX*, 2 vols (Rome, 1699).

Burke's 1949
Burke's Peerage (London, 1949).

Burlington 1779*
Burlington, Charles, David Llewellyn Rees and Alexander Murray, *The Modern Universal British Traveller* (London, 1779).

Burton 1960
Burton, Gerald, 'Sir Thomas Isham, An English Collector in Rome in 1677–8', *Italian Studies*, vol. XV (1960), pp. 1–21.

Bustamente and Marías 1991
Bustamente, Agustin and Fernando Marías, *Dibujos de Arquitectura y Ornamentacion de la Biblioteca Nacional* (Madrid, 1991).

Butters 1996
Butters, Suzanne B., *The Triumph of Vulcan: Sculptors' Tools, Porphyry, and the Prince in Ducal Florence* (Florence, 1996).

Camiz 1991
Camiz, Franca Trinchieri, 'Music and Painting in Cardinal del Monte's Household', *Metropolitan Museum Journal*, vol. XXVI (1991), pp. 213–26.

Campbell 1715
Campbell, Colen, *Vitruvius Britannicus, or the British Architect*, 2 vols (London, 1715).

Campbell 1725
— *The Third Volume of Vitruvius Britannicus* (London, 1725).

Cannata 2011
Cannata, Pietro, *Museo Nazionale del Palazzo Venezia, Scultore in Bronzo* (Rome, 2011).

Cappelletti 1996
Cappelletti, Francesca, 'Dalla 'Minuzia e Diligenza' all''Aerea Morbidezza': Cenni sull'Attività di Paul Bril e i suoi Contatti con l'Ambiente Romano', in S. Danesi Squarzina, *Natura morte, pittura di paesaggio e il collezionismo a Roma nella prima meta del Seicento; Italia, Flandre, Olanda, il terreno di elaborazione dei genere* (Rome, 1996).

Carlton House 1991
Carlton House, The Past Glories of George IV's Palace (London, 1991).

Cartwright 1888
Cartwright, James Joel (ed.), *The Travels Through England of Dr Richard Pococke*, 2 vols (London, 1888).

Cave 1982
Cave, Kathryn (ed.), *The Diary of Joseph Farington*, 16 vols, vol. VIII (London, 1982).

Chancellor 1908
Chancellor, E. Beresford, *The Private Palaces of London* (London, 1908).

Chaney 1985
Chaney, Edward, *The Grand Tour and the Great Rebellion, Richard Lassels and the 'Voyage of Italy' in the Seventeenth Century* (Geneva, 1985).

Chaney 1998
— *The Evolution of the Grand Tour* (London, 1998).

Christie's 1882
Christie, Manson & Woods, Messrs (Christie's), *Tassie Collection, Catalogue of Original Portraits in Wax and Opaque Paste ... 20 April 1882.*

Christie's 1883a
— *Stourhead Heirlooms Catalogue of Old Sevres, Chelsea, Worcester and Oriental Porcelain, Wedgwood Ware, Italian Cabinets and Caskets and a Fine Statue by Rysbrack which (by Order of Sir Henry Hoare, Bart.,) will be Sold by Auction ... 1 June 1883.*

Christie's 1883b
— *Stourhead Heirlooms Catalogue of the Pictures, Old Masters of the Italian, French, and Dutch Schools; Fine Works of the Early English School, and Drawings by A. Canaletti and J.M.W. Turner, RA which (by Order of Sir Henry Hoare, Bart.,) will be sold by Auction ... 2 June 1883.*

Christie's 1884
— *Catalogue of Handsome Jewels, the Property of Thomas Gee, Esq ... Handsome Silver Plate, being a portion of the Stourhead Heirlooms sold by order of Sir Henry Hoare, Bart ... 2 July 1884.*

Christie's 1945
— *Catalogue of Decorative Furniture Objects of Art and Pictures, The Property of His Grace the Duke of Norfolk, K.G., Arundel Castle, Sussex, 19 September 1945*

Christie's 2004
— *The Badminton Cabinet*, London 9 December 2004.

Christie's 2012
— 'Exceptional Sale', Sale no. 5702 5 July 2012.

Ciacconio 1630
Ciacconio, Alphonso, *Vitae et Res Gestae Pontificum Romanorum* (Rome, 1630).

Clay 1994
Clay, C.G.A., 'Henry Hoare, Banker, his Family, and the Stourhead Estate', in F.L.M. Thompson (ed.), *Landowners, Capitalists and Entrepreneurs, Essays for Sir John Habakkuk* (Oxford, 1994), pp. 113–38.

Clifford 2010
Clifford, Timothy, 'William Kent, John Michael Rysbrack and English Ceramics', *Keramos*, vol. 210 (October 2010), pp. 111–20.

Climenson 1899
Climenson, Emily J. (ed.), *Passages from the Diaries of Mrs Philip Lybbe Powys of Hardwick House, Oxon. AD 1756–1808* (London, 1899).

Cock 1747
Cock, Mr, *A Catalogue of all the Genuine Houshold Furniture ... of His Grace James, Duke of Chandos ... At his late Seat call'd Cannons* (Cannons, 1747).

Cockcroft 1979
Cockcroft, Irene, '"Used in the Mansions of the Nobility": The Rise and Fall of a Slate Company', *Country Life*, vol. CLXV (1979), pp. 493–4.

Coen and Fidanza 2011
Coen, Paolo and Giovan Battista Fidanza (ed.), *Le Pietre Rivelate* (Rome, 2011).

Coffin 1991
Coffin, David R., *Gardens and Gardening in Papal Rome* (Princeton, 1991).

Coffin 2004
— *Pirro Ligorio: the Renaissance artist, architect and antiquarian* (Philadelphia, 2004).

Coleridge 1963
Coleridge, Anthony, '18th-Century Furniture at the Vyne', *Country Life*, vol. CXXXIV (25 July 1963), pp. 214–16.

Coleridge 1967
— 'English Furniture and Cabinet-makers at Hatfield House – I: c.1600–1750', *Burlington Magazine*, vol. CIX (1967), pp. 63–8.

Coleridge 1968
— *Chippendale Furniture, The Work of Thomas Chippendale and his Contemporaries in the Rococo Style* (London, 1968).

Collard 1996
Collard, Frances, 'Town and Emanuel', *Furniture History*, vol. XXXII (1996), pp. 81–9.

Colle 1997
Colle, Enrico, *I Mobili di Palazzo Pitti, Il Periodo dei Medici 1557–1737* (Florence, 1997).

Colle 2000
— *Il Mobile Barocco in Italia* (Milan, 2000).

Colle and Bartolozzi 2005
— and Massimo Bartolozzi, *Guido Bartolozzi Catalogo* (Florence, 2005).

Collins 1955
Collins, A. Jefferies, *Jewels and Plate of Queen Elizabeth, The Inventory of 1574* (London, 1955).

Collins Baker and Collins 1949
Collins Baker, C.H. and Muriel I. Collins, *The Life and Correspondence of James Brydges, First Duke of Chandos, Patron of the Liberal Arts* (Oxford, 1949).

Compton 1991
Compton, Michael, 'The Architecture of Daylight', in Giles Waterfield (ed.), *Palaces of Art, Art Galleries in Britain 1790–1990* (London, 1991), pp. 37–47.

Cordier 2012
Cordier, Sylvain, *Bellangé Ébénistes* (Paris, 2012).

Cornforth 1981
Cornforth, John, *Attingham Park* (London, 1981).

Cornforth 1988
— 'Princely Pietra Dura', *Country Life*, vol. CLXXXII (1 December 1988), pp. 160–5.

Cornforth 1994
— 'Stourhead, Wiltshire', *Country Life*, vol. CLXXXVIII, (8 September 1994), pp. 64–7.

Cresti 1988
Cresti, Carlo, 'La Cappella dei Principi: Un Panteon Foderato di Pietre Dure', in Annamaria Giusti (ed.), *Splendori di Pietre Dure, L'Arte di Corte nella Firenze dei Granduchi* (Florence, 1988), pp. 61–73.

Croft-Murray 1970
Croft-Murray, Edward, *Decorative Painting in England*, 2 vols, vol. II, *The Eighteenth and Early Nineteenth Centuries* (London, 1970).

Crook 1981
Crook, J. Mordaunt, *William Burges and the High Victorian Dream* (London, 1981).

Crozat 1729–42
Crozat, Joseph-Antoine, *Recueil d'estampes d'après les plus beaux tableaux et d'après les plus beaux desseins qui sont en France: dans le Cabinet du Roy, dans celuy de Monseigneur le Duc d'Orléans, & dans d'autres Cabinets; divisé suivant les differentes écoles ...*, 2 vols (Paris, 1729–42).

Dacos, Grote, Giuliano, Heikamp and Panuti 1980
Dacos, U., N. Grote, A. Giuliano, A. Heikamp and D. Panuti, *Il Tesoro di Lorenzo il Magnifico, Repertorio delle gemme e dei vasi* (Rome, 1980).

Dakers 2010
Dakers, Caroline, 'Furniture and Interior Decoration for James and Alfred Morrison', *Furniture History*, vol. XLVI (2010), pp. 189–216.

Dakers 2011
— *A Genius for Money, Business, Art and the Morrisons* (Newhaven and London, 2011).

Dean 1999
Dean, Ptolemy, *Sir John Soane and the Country Estate* (Hampshire, 1999).

de Bellaigue 1995
de Bellaigue, Geoffrey, 'Daguerre and England',
in *Bernard Molitor 1755–1833* (Luxembourg,
1995), pp. 157–79.

degli Angeli 1621
degli Angeli, Paolo, *Basilicae S. Mariae Maioris
de Urbe a Liberio Papa I. usque ad Paulum V. Pont.
Max, lib. XII* (Rome, 1621).

Devonshire 1982
Devonshire, Duchess of, *The House, A Portrait
of Chatsworth* (London, 1982).

di Castro 1994
di Castro, Alberto, 'Rivestimenti e Tarsie
Marmoree a Roma tra il Cinquecento e
il Seicento', in Valentino Martinelli (ed.),
*Marmorari e Argentieri a Roma e nel Lazio tra
Cinquecento e Seicento* (Rome, 1994), pp. 9–155.

Dodd 1978
Dodd, Dudley, 'Rebuilding Stourhead
1902–1906', *National Trust Studies 1979*
(London, 1978), pp. 112–27.

Dodd 2007
— 'Fit for the Gods: Furniture from Stourhead's
Temples', *Apollo National Trust Annual 2007*,
pp. 14–22.

Dodd and Wood 2011
Dodd, Dudley and Lucy Wood, 'The "Weeping
Women" Commode and other Orphaned
Furniture at Stourhead by the Chippendales,
Senior and Junior', *Furniture History*, vol. XLVII
(2011), pp. 47–124.

d'Onofrio 1957
d'Onofrio, Cesare, *Le Fontane di Roma*
(Rome, 1957).

Dresden 1981
Staatliche Kunstsammlungen, Museum für
Kunsthandwerk, Schloss Pillnitz, *Kunsthandwerk
der Gotik und Renaissance* (Dresden, 1981).

Dubois de Saint-Gelais 1727
Dubois de Saint-Gelais, Louis François,
*Description des tableaux du Palais Royal. avec la
Vie des Peintres à la tête de leurs Ouvrages. dediee
à Monseigneur le duc d' Orléans Premier Prince
du Sang* (Paris, 1727).

Dudley 1990
Dudley, Colin J., *Canterbury Cathedral,
Aspects of its Sacramental Geometry*
(Bloomington, 1990).

Dutton 1969
Dutton, Ralph, *A Hampshire Manor*
(London, 1969).

Eavis 2002
Eavis, Anna, 'The Avarice and Ambition of
William Benson', *The Georgian Group Journal*,
vol. XII (2002), pp. 8–37.

Ellis 1907
Ellis, Annie Raine (ed.), *The Early Diary of
Frances Burney 1768–1778*, 2 vols (London,
1907).

Escalas Llimona 2002
Escalas Llimona, Romá, 'Claviorgans attributed
to Laurentius Hauslaib in New York, Moscow
and Barcelona', *Music in Art*, no. 27 (2002),
pp. 87–100.

Fagiolo and Madonna 1992
Fagiolo, Marcello and Maria Luisa Madonna

(eds), *Sisto V, I, Roma e Lazio* (Rome, 1992).

Falda 1669–70
Falda, Giovanni Battista, *Il terzo libro del' novo
teatro delle chiese di Roma* (Rome 1669–70).

Fanti 2003
Fanti, Mario, *Il Museo di San Petronio in Bologna*
(Bologna, 2003).

Fell-Smith 1914
Fell-Smith, Charlotte, 'Boreham House, Essex',
Country Life, vol. XXXVI (11 July 1914),
pp. 54–60.

Fenton 1811*
Fenton, Richard [A barrister], *A Tour in
quest of genealogy, through several parts of Wales,
Somersetshire, and Wiltshire, in a Series of Letters to
a Friend in Dublin; interspersed with a description
of Stourhead and Stonehenge* (London, 1811).

Fittipaldi 1995
Fittipaldi, Teodoro, *Il Museo di San Martino
de Napoli* (Naples, 1995).

Foister, Roy and Wyld 1997
Foister, Susan, Ashok Roy and Martin Wyld,
Making & Meaning, Holbein's Ambassadors
(London, 1997).

Fontana 1590
Fontana, Domenico, *Della trasportatione dell'
Obelisco Vaticano e delle fabriche di Nostro Signore
Papa Sisto V.* (Rome, 1590).

Ford 1988
Ford, Sir Brinsley, 'A Memoir of Ralph Dutton',
in Christopher Rowell, *Hinton Ampner*
(London, 1988), pp. 42–61.

Foster 1991
Foster, Richard, *Patterns of Thought, The Hidden
Meaning of the Great Pavement of Westminster Abbey*
(London, 1991).

Fothergill 1969
Fothergill, Brian, *Sir William Hamilton,
Envoy Extraordinary* (London, 1969).

Fowler 1994
Fowler, Alastair, *The Country House Poem,
A Cabinet of Seventeenth Century Estate Poems
and Related Items* (Edinburgh, 1994).

Friedman 1975
Friedman, Terry, 'The English Appreciation
of Italian Decorations', *Burlington Magazine*,
vol. CXVII (1975), pp. 841–7.

Fuhring and Bimbinet-Privat 2002
Fuhring, Peter and Michèle Bimbinet-Privat,
'Le Style 'Cosses de Pois', L'orfèvrerie et la
gravure à Paris sous Louis XIII', *Gazette des
Beaux-Arts*, vol. CXLIV (2002).

Furlotti 2010
Furlotti, Barbara, 'Connecting People,
Connecting Places: Antiquarians as Mediators
in Sixteenth Century Rome', *Urban History*,
vol. XXXVII (2010), pp. 386–98.

Garstang 2003
Garstang, Donald, *Master Paintings and Sculpture*
(London, 2003).

Gatta 2010
Gatta, Francesco, '"Pure ed il nome, e le
ricchezze e le grandezze svanirono come il
fumo ..." La dispersion della Collezione Peretti
Montalto: nuove proposte e un inventario

inedito del 1696', *Bollettino d'Arte*, vol. XCV (6)
(2010), pp. 87–122.

Gemmett 2000
Gemmett, Robert J., *The Consummate Collector,
William Beckford's Letters to His Bookseller*
(Wilby, 2000).

Gilbert 1972
Gilbert, Christopher, 'Chippendale Senior
and Junior at Paxton 1774–91', *Connoisseur*,
vol. 180, no. 726 (August 1972), pp. 254–66.

Gilbert 1978
— *The Life and Work of Thomas Chippendale*,
2 vols (London, 1978).

Gilbert 1998
— *Furniture at Temple Newsam House and
Lotherton Hall*, vol. III (Leeds, 1998).

Giusti 1988
Giusti, Annamaria (ed.), *Splendori di Pietre
Dure, L'Arte di Corte nella Firenze dei Granduchi*
(Florence, 1988).

Giusti 2003
— 'Da Roma a Firenze: gli esordi del commesso
rinascimentale', in Annamaria Giusti (ed.),
Eternità e Nobilità di Materia (Florence, 2003),
pp. 197–230.

Giusti 2006
— *Pietre Dure, The Art of Semiprecious Stonework*
(Los Angeles, 2006).

Gnoli 1988
Gnoli, Raniero, *Marmora Romana*, 2nd edn
(Rome, 1988).

Gnoli and Sironi 1996
— and Attilia Sironi (eds), *Agostino del Riccio,
Istoria delle Pietre* (Turin, 1996).

González-Palacios 1981
González-Palacios, Alvar, *Mosaici e Pietre Dure,
Firenze-Paesi Germanici-Madrid* (Milan, 1981).

González-Palacios 1986
— *Il Tempio del Gusto, Il Granducato di Toscana
e gli Stati Settentrionali* (Milan, 1986).

González-Palacios 1988
— 'Itinerario da Roma a Firenze', in
Annamaria Giusti (ed.), *Splendori di Pietre
Dure, L'Arte di Corte nella Firenze dei Granduchi*
(Florence, 1988), pp. 43–52

González-Palacios 1991
— *Fasto Romano* (Rome, 1991).

González-Palacios 1993
— 'Lo stipo del duca di Beaufort', *Il Gusto
dei Principi: arte di corte del XVII e del XVIII secolo*,
2 vols (Milan, 1993).

González-Palacios 2001
— *Las Colecciones Reales Españolas de Mosaicos
y Piedras Duras* (Madrid, 2001).

González-Palacios 2010
— 'Concerning Furniture: Roman Documents
and Inventories. Part I, c.1600–1720',
Furniture History, vol. XLVI (2010), pp. 28–135
(indexed).

González-Palacios 2011
— 'Destino di un capolavoro: un tavolo
ottagonale in pietre dure', *Paragone/Arte*,
vol. LXII, no. 96 (March 2011), pp. 51–6.

González-Palacios and Röttgen 1982
— and Steffi Röttgen, *The Art of Mosaic,
Selections from the Gilbert Collection*
(Los Angeles, 1982).

Gomme 1989
Gomme, Andor, 'Architects and craftsmen
at Ditchley', *Architectural History, Journal of the*

Society of Architectural Historians of Great Britain, vol. 32 (1989), pp. 85–97.

Gomme and Norman 1912
Gomme, Sir Laurence and Philip Norman, *London County Council, Survey of London*, vol. III, Parish of St Giles-in-the-Fields, pt I, Lincoln's Inn Fields (London, 1912).

Goodison 2005
Goodison, Judith, 'Thomas Chippendale the Younger at Stourhead', *Furniture History*, vol. XLI (2005), pp. 57–116.

Granata 2012
Granata, Belinda, *Le passioni vitruose, Collezionismo e commitenze artistiche a Roma del cardinal Alessandro Peretti Montalto (1571–1623)* (Rome, 2012).

Gross 1981
Gross, G.W., *The Diary of Baron Waldstein, A Traveller in Elizabethan England* (London, 1981).

Guidobaldi 2003
Guidobaldi, Federico, '*Sectilia pavimenta* e *incrustationes*: i rivestimenti policromi pavimentali e parietali in marmo o materiali litici e litoidi dell'antichità romana', in Annamaria Giusti (ed.), *Eternità e Nobilità di Materia* (Florence, 2003).

Guinness 1971
Guinness, Desmond, *Irish houses & castles* (New York, 1971).

Halsband 1965–7
Halsband, Robert (ed.), *The Complete Letters of Lady Mary Wortley Montagu*, 3 vols (Oxford, 1965–7).

Hancock 1995
Hancock, David, *Citizens of the World, London Merchants and the Integration of the British Atlantic Community, 1735–1785* (Cambridge, 1995).

Hanway 1756*
Hanway, Jonas, *A journal of eight days journey from Portsmouth to Kingston upon Thames … in a series of sixty-four letters: addressed to two ladies of the partie … By a gentleman of the partie* (London, 1756).

Harris 1986
Harris, John, 'To Oblivion and Back, Dr Bargrave's Museum of Rarities', *County Life*, vol. CLXXIX (1986), pp. 278–80.

Harris 2000*
— 'The Duchess of Beaufort's *Observations on Places*', *Georgian Group Journal*, vol. X (2000), pp. 36–42.

Harris and Sons 1935
Harris, Moss and Sons, *Old English Furniture, Its Designers and Craftsmen* (London, 1935).

Havard 1887–90
Havard, Henry, *Dictionnaire de l'Ameublement et de la Décoration* (Paris, 1887–90).

Hawkins 1885
Hawkins, Edward, *Medallic Illustrations of the History of Great Britain and Ireland to the Death of George II*, Augustus W. Franks and Herbert A. Grueber (eds), 2 vols (London, 1885).

Hazlitt 1824
Hazlitt, William, *Sketches of the Principal Picture-Galleries in England* (London, 1824).

Hay 2010
Hay, Kate, 'Mosaic Marble Tables by J. Darmarin & Sons of Malta', *Furniture History*, vol. XLVI (2010), pp. 157–88.

Heikamp 1963
Heikamp, Detlef, 'Zur Geschichte der Uffizien-Tribuna und der Kunstschrank in Florenz und Deutschland', *Zeitschrift für Kunstgeschichte*, vol. XXI (1963), pp. 193–268.

Heikamp 1988
— 'Lo "Studiolo Grande" di Ferdinando I nella Tribuna degli Uffizi', *Splendori di Pietre Dure, L'Arte di Corte nella Firenze dei Granduchi* (Florence, 1988), pp. 57–61.

Hellwag 1924
Hellwag, Fritz, *Die Geschichte des Deutschen Tischlerhandwerks* (Berlin, 1924).

Hervey 1921
Hervey, Mary S.F., *The Life, Correspondence and Collection of Thomas Howard, Earl of Arundel, 'Father of Vertu in England'* (Cambridge, 1921).

Himmelheber 1977
Himmelheber, Georg, *Kabinettschränke*, Bayerisches Nationalmuseum (Munich, 1977).

Hoare 1932
Hoare, H.P.R., *Hoare's Bank, A Record 1673–1932* (London, 1932).

Hoare 1955
— *Hoare's Bank, A Record 1672–1955* (London, 1955).

Hoare 1800*
Hoare, Sir Richard Colt, Bt, *A Description of the House and Gardens at Stourhead … with a Catalogue of the Pictures &c.* (Salisbury, 1800).

Hoare 1815
— *Recollections Abroad during the years 1785, 1786, 1787* (Bath, 1815).

Hoare 1818*
— *A Description of the House and Gardens at Stourhead* (Bath, 1818).

Hoare 1819
— *Pedigrees and Memoirs of the Families of Hore* (Bath, 1819).

Hoare 1822*
— *The Modern History of South Wiltshire*, vol. I, part I, 'The Hundred of Mere' (London, 1822).

Hoare 1844
— *The Modern History of South Wiltshire*, Addenda (London, 1844).

Hunter 1851
Hunter, Joseph, 'The Topographical Gatherings at Stourhead 1825–1833', *Memoirs Illustrative of the History and Antiquities of Wiltshire and the City of Salisbury*, Archaeological Institute of Great Britain and Ireland (London, 1851), pp. 16–27.

Hutchings 2005
Hutchings, Victoria, *Messrs Hoare Bankers, A History of the Hoare Banking Dynasty* (London, 2005).

Hutchinson 1881
Hutchinson, Margarite (ed.), *A Report of the Kingdom of Congo … Drawn Out of the Writings and Discoveries of the Portuguese Duarte Lopez by Filippo Pigafetta in Rome 1591* (London, 1881).

Impey 1998
Impey, Oliver, *The Cecil Family Collection, Four Centuries of Decorative Arts from Burghley House*

(Alexandra, 1998).

Incisa della Rochetta 1972
Incisa della Rochetta, Giovanni, 'La Cappella di San Filippo alla Chiesa Nuova', *Oratorium*, vol. III, 1 (1972), pp. 46–52.

Ingamells 1997
Ingamells, John, *A Dictionary of British and Irish Travellers in Italy 1701–1800, compiled from the Brinsley Ford Archive* (Newhaven and London, 1997).

Jackson-Stops 1985
Jackson-Stops, Gervase (ed.), *The Treasure Houses of Great Britain* (Washington, 1985).

Jenkins 2005
Jenkins, Susan, '"An Inventory of his Grace the Duke of Chandos's Seat at Cannons Taken June the 19th 1725" by John Gilbert', *Walpole Society*, vol. LXVII (2005), pp. 93–192.

Jenkins 2007
— *Portrait of a Patron, The Patronage and Collecting of James Brydges, 1st Duke of Chandos (1674–1744)* (Aldershot, 2007).

Jervis 1972
Jervis, Simon Swynfen, 'Gothic at No. 95 Piccadilly, New Light on the Taste of John Jones', *Apollo*, vol. XCV (1972), pp. 52–7.

Jervis 1974
— *Printed Furniture Designs before 1650* (Leeds, 1974).

Jervis 1978
— 'Furniture at Arundel Castle', *Connoisseur*, vol. CXCIII (1978), pp. 203–16.

Jervis 1983
— *High Victorian Design* (Woodbridge, 1983).

Jervis 1989
— '"Shadows not substantial things". Furniture in the Commonwealth Inventories', in Arthur Macgregor, *The Late King's Goods* (London and Oxford, 1989), pp. 277–306.

Jervis 1997
— 'Furniture for the First Duke of Buckingham', *Furniture History*, vol. XXXIII (1997), pp. 48–74.

Jervis 2004
— 'From Abbotsford to Australia: A Set of Brustolon Chairs', *Burlington Magazine*, vol. CXLVI (2004), pp. 400–4.

Jervis 2005
— 'Charles Davis, the 15th Duke of Norfolk, and the Formation of the Collection of Furniture at Arundel Castle', *Furniture History*, vol. XLI (2005), pp. 231–48.

Jervis 2006
— 'Furniture in Eighteenth-Century Country House Guides', *Furniture History*, vol. XLII (2006), pp. 63–152.

Jervis 2007
— '*Pietre Dure* Caskets in England', *Furniture History*, vol. XLIII (2007), pp. 245–65.

Jervis 2010
— 'The Tables', in Mark Evans (ed.), *Art Collecting and Lineage in the Elizabethan Age, The Lumley Inventory and Pedigree* (London, 2010).

Jourdain 1924
Jourdain, Margaret, *English Decoration and Furniture of the Early Renaissance* (London, 1924).

Kalas 2013
Kalas, Gregor, 'Architecture and Elite Identity in Late Antique Rome: Appropriating the

Past at Sant'Andrea Catabarbara', *Papers of the British School at Rome*, vol. LXXXI (2013), pp. 279–302.

Ketton-Cremer 1944
Ketton-Cremer, R.W., *Norfolk Portraits* (London, 1944).

Keyssler 1756–7
Keyssler, Johann Georg, *Travels through Germany, Bohemia, Hungary, Switzerland, Italy, and Lorrain. … Carefully Translated from the second edition of the German*, 4 vols (London, 1756–7).

Kirkendale 1979
Kirkendale, Warren, 'Emilio dei Cavalieri', *Dizionario Biografico degli Italiani*, vol. XXII (1979), pp. 659–664.

Klima 1975
Klima, Slava (ed.), *Letters from the Grand Tour, Joseph Spence* (Montreal, 1975).

Koeppe 2008
Koeppe, Wolfram (ed.), *Art of the Royal Court, Treasures in Pietre Dure from the Palaces of Europe* (New York, 2008).

Kunsthistorisches Vienna 1989
Kunsthistorisches Museum, *Guide to the Collections* (Vienna, 1989).

Lafréry 1528–1606
Lafréry, Antoine, *Speculum Romanae Magnicentiae* (Rome, 1528–1606).

Langer and von Württemberg 1996
Langer, Brigitte and Alexander Herzog von Württemberg, *Die Möbel der Residenz München*, II, *Die deutschen Möbel des 16. bis 18. Jahrhunderts* (Munich, 1996).

Langford 1755
Langford, A., *Museum Meadianum, siue, catalogus nummorum, ueteris aevi monumentorum, ac gemmarum … quae vir clarissimus. Richardus Mead M.D. nuper defunctus comparaverat, 11th–19th February 1755*.
Langford 1764
— *A Catalogue of the Capital and Entire Collection of Prints, Drawings, and Books of Prints, of Mr Michael Rysbrack … will be sold by Auction, By Mr Langford and Son … 15th February 1764 and the Nine following Evenings*.
Langford 1765
— *A Catalogue of the Genuine and Curious Collection of Mr Michael Rysbrack … sold by Auction, By Mr Langford and Son … on 20th April 1765*.
Langford 1766
— *A Catalogue of the Genuine, Large and Curious Collection of Models, &c. of Mr Michael Rysbrack … sold by Auction, By Mr Langford and Son … 24th and 25th January 1766*.

Lanzarini 1998–9
Lanzarini, Orietta, 'Il codice cinquecentesco di Giovanni Vincenzo Casale e i suoi autori', *Annali di architettura*, nos 10–11 (1998–9), pp. 183–202.

Lees-Milne 1948
Lees-Milne, James, *Stourhead: A Property of the National Trust* (London, 1948).

Lefeber-Morsman 2010
Lefeber-Morsman, Marieke, 'Augsburger Instrumentenbauer und ein Augsburger Spinett in St Petersburg', *Das Mecanische Musikinstrument*, no. 108 (2010), pp. 7–8.

Lemarchand 2006
Lemarchand, Yannick, '"A la conquête de la science des comptes" variations autour de quelques manuels de comptabilité des XVIIe et XVIIIe siècles, *Écrire, compter, mesurer 2*, available online (Paris, 2006), pp. 34–65. http://www.bldd.fr/ProductDocumentation/9782728803729_0.pdf

Leonardo 1997
Leonardo, L., 'Gli statute dell'Università dei marmorari a Roma: scultori e scalpellini (1406–1756)', *Studi Romani*, vol. XLV, 3–4 (1997), pp. 269–300.

Letts 1925
Letts, Malcolm (ed.), 'Francis Mortoft: His Book being his Travels through France and Italy 1658–1659', *Hakluyt Society*, vol. LVII (1925).

Lewis 1961
Lewis, Lesley, *Connoisseurs and Secret Agents in Eighteenth Century Rome* (London, 1961).

Lewis and Brown 1941
Lewis, W.S. and Ralph S. Brown Jnr (eds), *Horace Walpole's Correspondence with George Montagu*, vol. IX, pt I (New Haven and London, 1941).

Lewis and Smith 1939
Lewis, W.S. and Warren Hunting Smith (eds), *Horace Walpole's Correspondence with Madame du Deffand and Wiart*, vol. VII, pt V (New Haven and London, 1939).

Lewis, Lam and Bennett 1961
Lewis, W.S., George L. Lam and Charles H. Bennett (eds), *Horace Walpole's Correspondence with Thomas Gray, Richard West and Thomas Ashton*, vols XIII–XIV, pt I (New Haven and London, 1961).

Lewis, Smith and Lam 1955a
Lewis, W.S., Warren Hunting Smith and George L. Lam (eds), *Horace Walpole's Correspondence with Sir Horace Mann*, vol. XVII, pt I (New Haven and London, 1955).
Lewis, Smith and Lam 1955b
— *Horace Walpole's Correspondence with Sir Horace Mann*, vol. XVIII, pt II (New Haven and London, 1955).
Lewis, Smith and Lam 1955c
— *Horace Walpole's Correspondence with Sir Horace Mann*, vol. XIX, pt III (New Haven and London, 1955).

Lewis, Smith, Lam and Martz 1971
Lewis, W.S., Warren Hunting Smith, George L. Lam and Edwine M. Martz (eds), *Horace Walpole's Correspondence with Sir Horace Mann and Sir Horace Mann the Younger*, vol. XXVI, pt X (New Haven and London, 1971).

Lietzmann 1994
Lietzmann, Hilda, 'Die Geschichte zweier Automaten: Ein weiter Beitrag zum Werk des Valentin Drausch', *Zeitschrift für Kunstgeschichte*, no. 57 (1994), pp. 390–402.

Lightbown 1964
Lightbown, Ronald, 'Nicolas Audebert and the Villa d'Este', *Journal of the Warburg and Courtauld Institutes*, no. 27 (1964), pp. 184–6.

Litchfield 1907
Litchfield, Frederick, *Illustrated History of Furniture* (London, 1907).

Luce and Jessop 1955
Luce, A.A. and T.E. Jessop (eds), *The Works of George Berkeley, Bishop of Cloyne*, VIII (London, 1955).

Macquoid and Edwards 1924–7
Macquoid, Percy and Ralph Edwards, *The Dictionary of English Furniture*, 3 vols (London, 1924–7).

Mandel 1994
Mandel, Corinne, *Sixtus V and the Lateran Palace* (Rome, 1994).

Markham 1984
Markham, Sarah, *John Loveday of Caversham 1711–1789* (Wilton, 1984).

Marot c.1660
Marot, Jean, *Le magnifique chasteau de Richelieu* (Paris, c.1660).

Marsden 2010
Marsden, Jonathan (ed.), *Victoria & Albert, Art & Love* (London, 2010).

Massimo 1836
Massimo, Vittorio, *Notizie istoriche della Villa Massimo alle Terme Diocleziane con un'appendice di documenti* (Rome, 1836).

Massinelli 1997
Massinelli, A.M., *Scagliola: l'arte delle pietre de luna* (Rome, 1997).

Mavor 1800
Mavor, William, *The British tourists: or Traveller's pocket companion through England, Wales, Scotland and Ireland*, 6 vols (London, 1800).

McClendon 1980
McClendon, Charles B., 'The Revival of *Opus Sectile* Pavements in Rome and the Vicinity in the Carolingian Period', *Papers of the British School at Rome*, vol. XLVIII (1980), pp. 157–65.

McLeod and Hewat Jaboor 2002
McLeod, Bet and Philip Hewat Jaboor, '*Pietre Dure* Cabinets for William Beckford: Gregorio Franchi's Role', *Furniture History*, vol. XXXVIII (2002), pp. 135–43.

Methuen-Campbell 2004
Methuen-Campbell, James, *Corsham Court* (Norwich, 2004).

Michel 1999
Michel, Patrick, *Mazarin, Prince des Collectionneurs* (Paris, 1999).

Middeldorf 1935
Middeldorf, Ulrich, 'Two Wax Reliefs by Guglielmo della Porta', *Art Bulletin*, vol. XVII (1935), pp. 90–6.

Millar 1972
Millar, Oliver (ed.), 'The Inventories and Valuations of the King's Goods 1649–1651', *Walpole Society*, vol. XLII (1972).

Miller 2010
Miller, Sally, '"The Fruits of Industry": The Garden of Sir Richard Hoare at Barn Elms, Surrey, 1750–54', *Garden History*, vol. 38, no. 2 (2010), pp. 195, 201.

Montagu 1996
Montagu, Jennifer, *Gold, Silver and Bronze, Metal Sculpture of the Roman Baroque* (Princeton, 1996).

Montfaucon 1719
Montfaucon, Bernard de, *L'Antiquité expliquée et représentée en figures*, 5 vols (Paris, 1719).

Monfaucon 1724
— *Supplément au livre de L'Antiquité expliquée*, 5 vols (Paris, 1724).

Morgan 1821
Morgan, Lady, *Italy* (London, 1821).

Morrogh 1985
Morrogh, Andrew, *Disegni di Architetti Fiorentini 1540–1640* (Florence, 1985).

Morrogh 2011
— 'La Cappella Gaddi nella Chiesa di Santa Maria Novella', in Emanuele Barletti, *Giovan Antonio Dosio da San Gemignano, architetto e sculptor fiorentino tra Roma, Firenze e Napoli* (Florence, 2011), pp. 299–323.

Morsman 2006
Morsman, Marieke, *Quicquid rarum, occultum et subtile, Augsburg Musical Automata around 1600* (Utrecht, 2006).

Murdoch 2006
Murdoch, Tessa (ed.), *Noble Households, Eighteenth Century Inventories of Great English Houses* (Cambridge, 2006).

Neve 1726
Neve, Richard, *The City and Country Purchaser, and Builder's Dictionary: or, the Compleat Builders Guide*, 2nd edn (London, 1726).

Newman 1995
Newman, John, *Glamorgan* (London, 1995).

Nichols 1840
Nichols, John Bowyer, *Catalogue of the Hoare Library at Stourhead* (London, 1840).

Nichols and Wray 1935
Nichols, R.H. and F.A. Wray, *The History of the Foundling Hospital* (London, 1935).

Nogué 2000
Nogué, José María Luzón, *El Westmorland, Obras de arte de una presa inglesa* (Madrid, 2000).

Orbaan 1910
Orbaan, J.A.F., *Sixtine Rome* (London, 1910).

Orsi 1588
Orsi, Aurelio, *Perettina* (Rome, 1588).

Ostrow 1990
Ostrow, Steven F., 'Marble Revetments in Late Sixteenth-Century Roman Chapels', in Marilyn Aronberg Lavin (ed.), *IL 60, Essays Honoring Irving Lavin on his Sixtieth Birthday* (New York, 1990), pp. 253–76.

Ostrow 1996
— *Art and Spirituality in Counter-Reformation Rome* (Cambridge, 1996).

Palladio 1730
Palladio, Andrea, *Fabbriche Antiche designate da Andrea Palladio*, (ed.) Richard Boyle, third Earl of Burlington, (London, *c.*1735–40, title page dated 1730).

Panuti 1980
Panuti, Ulrico and others, *Il Tesoro di Lorenzo il Magnifico, Repertorio delle gemme e dei vasi* (Rome, 1980).

Peacock and Williams 1995
Peacock, D.P.S. and D.F. Williams, 'Ornamental Coloured Marbles in Roman Britain: An Interim Report', *Asmosia*, vol. IV (1995), pp. 353–7.

Peccolo 1994
Peccolo, Paola, 'Gioielli e Reliquie, Argenti ed Altari', in Valentino Martinelli (ed.), *Marmorari e Argentieri a Roma e nel Lazio tra Cinquecento e Seicento* (Rome, 1994), pp. 159–219.

Pedone 2011
Pedone, Silvia, 'The Marble Omphalos of Santa Sophia in Constantinople: An analysis of an Opus Sectile Pavement of Middle Byzantine Age', in Mustafa Sahin (ed.), *11th International Colloquium on Ancient Mosaics 2009* (Istanbul, 2011), pp. 759–68.

Peill 2007
Peill, The Knight of Glin, James, *Irish Furniture* (Newhaven and London, 2007).

Penny 1991
Penny, Nicholas, 'Lord Rockingham's Sculpture Collection and "The Judgement of Paris" by Nollekens', *J. Paul Getty Museum Journal*, vol. XIX (1991), pp. 5–34.

Perrier 1638
Perrier, François, *Segmenta nobilium signorum et statuaru* (Rome, 1638).

Petraccia 2011
Petraccia, Arianna, 'Flaminio Boulanger "Gallo de Urbe" a L'Aquila nel 1584', *Studi medioevale e moderni*, vol. XV (2011), pp. 85–100.

Pignatti 2013
Pignatti, Franco, 'Orsi, Aurelio', *Dizionario Biografico degli Italiani*, vol. LXXIX (2013).

Pike 1973
Pike, E. J., *A Biographical Dictionary of Wax Modellers* (Oxford, 1973).

Pinaroli 1725
Pinaroli, Giovanni Pietro, *Trattato delle cose più memorabili di Roma tanto antiche come moderne* (Rome, 1725).

Pine 1739
Pine, John, *The Tapestry Hangings of the House of Lords, Representing the several Engagements Between the English and Spanish Fleets in the ever memorable Year MDLXXXVIII … To which are added … Ten Charts of the Sea-Coasts of England …* (London, 1739).

Porzio 2001
Porzio, Annamaria, '"Opere Recuperate" and Riccardo Fusco, "Quid sit Marmor"', *Quaderni di Palazzo Reale*, vol. VIII (2001), pp. 6–19, 32–41.

Price 2007
Price, Monica T., *Decorative Stone* (London, 2007).

Pryke 1996
Pryke, Sebastian, 'Curiosities of a Cabinet', *Country Life*, vol. CXC (1996), pp. 44–5.

Quast 1991
Quast, Matthias, *Die Villa Montalto in Rom* (Munich, 1991).

Radcliffe and Thornton 1976
Radcliffe, Anthony and Peter Thornton, 'John Evelyn's Cabinet', *Connoisseur*, vol. CXLVII (1976), pp. 254–63.

Raggio 1960
Raggio, Olga, 'The Farnese Table: a Rediscovered Work by Vignola', *Metropolitan Museum of Art Bulletin*, vol. XVIII, no. 7 (1960), pp. 213–31.

Rapin de Thoyras 1732–3
Rapin de Thoyras, Paul, *The History of England written in French translated into English … by N. Tindal*, 2nd edn, 2 vols (London, 1732–3).

Rausa 2005
Rausa, Federico, 'L'Album Montalto e la Collezione di Sculture Antiche di Villa Peretti Montalto', *Pegasus*, vol. VII (2005), pp. 97–132.

Reinheckel 1981
Reinheckel, Günter (ed.), *Kunsthandwerk der Gotik und Renaissance* (Dresden, 1981).

Repton 1844
Repton, John Adey, 'Oxnead Hall, Norfolk', *Gentleman's Magazine*, vol. XXI (1844), p. 152.

Rezzonico 1824*
Rezzonico, Count Carlo Gastone della Torre di, *Viaggio in Inghilterra di Carlo Castone Gaetano della Torre di Rezzonico Comasco*, ed. P. Gamba (Venice, 1824).

Richardson 1722
Richardson, Jonathan Sr and Jr, *An Account of some of the Statues, Bas-reliefs, Drawings and Pictures in Italy &c.; with Remarks …* (London, 1722).

Rieder 1974
Rieder, William, 'More on Pierre Langlois', *Connoisseur*, vol. CLXXXVII (1974), pp. 11–13.

Roberts 2000
Roberts, Hugh, '"Quite Appropriate for Windsor Castle", George IV and George Watson Taylor', *Furniture History*, vol. XXXVI (2000), pp. 115–37.

Roberts 2001
— *For the King's Pleasure, The Furnishing and Decoration of George IV's Apartments at Windsor Castle* (London, 2001).

Roberts 2002
Roberts, Jane (ed.), *Royal Treasures: A Golden Jubilee Celebration* (London, 2002).

Roberts 2004
— (ed.), *George III & Queen Charlotte, Patronage, Collecting and Courtly Taste* (London, 2004).

Robins 1832
Robins, George, *Erlestoke Mansion, Nr Devizes Wiltshire* (23 July 1832).

Robinson 1895
Robinson, M.E. (ed.), *Memoirs of Mary Robinson 'Perdita'* (London, 1895).

Rokeby 1986
Rokeby Park (Rokeby, 1986)

Ronfort 1991–2
Ronfort, Jean Nérée, 'Jean Ménard (*c.*1525–1582) Marqueteur et Sculpteur en Marbre et Sa Famille', *Antologia di Belli Arti*, nos 39–42 (1991–2), pp. 139–47.

Roscoe 2009
Roscoe, Ingrid, *A Biographical Dictionary of Sculptors in Britain 1660–1851* (New Haven and London, 2009).

Rosoman 1985
Rosoman, T.S., 'The Decoration and Use of the Principal Apartments of Chiswick House, 1727–70', *Burlington Magazine*, vol. CXXVII, (October 1985), pp. 663–77.

Rossi 1739
Rossi, Filippo, *Descrizione di Roma antica formata nvovamente con le Autorità di Bartolomeo Marliani, Onofrio Panvinio, Alessandro Donati Famiano Nardini ...*, 2 vols (Rome, 1739).

Rossini da Pesaro 1741
Rossini da Pesaro, Pietro, *Il Mercurio Errante Delle Grandezze di Roma* (Rome, 1741).

Rowan 1993
Rowan, Alistair, *Paxton House* (Norwich, 1993).

Rowell 2005
Rowell, Christopher, *Ham House* (London, 2005).

Rowell 2011
— 'Marriage, Divorce and Re-Marriage', *National Trust abc Bulletin* (February 2011), pp. 4–5.

Rowell 2013
— '*Scagliola* by "Baldassare Artima *Romanus*" at Ham House and elsewhere', in Christopher Rowell (ed.), *Ham House, 400 Years of Collecting and Patronage* (Newhaven and London, 2013), pp. 204–21.

Rye 1865
Rye, William Brenchley, *England as seen by Foreigners* (London, 1865).

Safarik 2009
Safarik, Eduard A., *Palazzo Colonna* (Rome, 2009).

Sandrart 1690
Sandrart, Joachim von, *Insignium Romae templorum prospectus exteriores et interiors ...* (Nuremberg, 1690).

Sarti 2006
Sarti, G., *Catalogue No. 7. Fastueux Objets en Marbre et Pierres Dures* (Paris, 2006).

Scarisbrick 1987
Scarisbrick, Diana, 'Gem Connoisseurship: The 4th Earl of Carlisle's Correspondence with Francesco de Ficoroni and Antonio Maria Zanetti', *Burlington Magazine*, vol. CXXIX (1987), pp. 90–104.

Seymour 1806
Seymour, Frances, Duchess of Somerset, *Correspondence between Frances, Countess of Hartford, (afterwards Duchess of Somerset,) and Henrietta Louisa, Countess of Pomfret, between the years 1738 and 1741*, 3 vols (London, 1806).

Simond 1817
Simond, Louis, *Journal of a tour and residence in Great Britain during the years 1810 and 1811*, 2 vols (Edinburgh, 1817).

Simond 1828
—, *A Tour in Italy and Sicily* (London, 1828).

Sitwell 1942
Sitwell, Osbert, 'The Red Folder II', *Burlington Magazine*, vol. LXXX (1942), pp. 84–90.

Sotheby, Wilkinson and Hodge 1883
Sotheby, Wilkinson & Hodge, *The Stourhead Heirlooms Catalogue of the Library removed from Stourhead 30th July–8th August 1883*.

Sotheby, Wilkinson and Hodge 1887
— *The Stourhead Heirlooms Catalogue of the Remaining Portion of the Library removed from Stourhead 9th December–13th December 1887*.

Spence 1993
Spence, R.T., 'Chiswick House and its gardens, 1726–32', *Burlington Magazine*, vol. CXXXV (August 1993), pp. 525–31.

Spiers 1919
Spiers, Walter Lewis, 'The Notebook and Account Book of Nicholas Stone', *Walpole Society*, vol. VII (1919).

Spinelli 2011
Spinelli, Riccardo, 'La cappella Niccolini nella basilica francescana di Santa Croce', in Emanuele Barletti, *Giovan Antonio Dosio da San Gemignano, architetto e sculptor fiorentino tra Roma, Firenze e Napoli* (Florence, 2011), pp. 345–73.

Squarzina 2003
Squarzina, Silvia Danesi, *La collezione Giustiniani*, 3 vols (Turin, 2003).

Starkey 1998
Starkey, David (ed.), *The Inventory of Henry VIII, The Transcript* (London, 1998).

Stillman 1977
Stillman, Damie, 'Chimney Pieces for the English Market: A Thriving Business in Late Eighteenth-Century Rome', *Art Bulletin*, vol. LIX (1977), pp. 85–94.

Strunck 2008
Strunck, Cristina, 'Neue Überlegungen zur Künstlerfamilie Schor – eine Einführung', in Cristina Strunck (ed.), *Johann Paul Schor und die internationale Sprache des Barock* (Munich, 2008), pp. 7–30.

Sulivan 1780*
Sulivan, Sir Richard Joseph, *Observations made during a tour through parts of England, Scotland, and Wales. In a series of letters* (London, 1780).

Summerson 1966
Summerson, John (ed.), 'The Book of Architecture of John Thorpe in Sir John Soane's Museum', *Walpole Society*, vol. XL (1966).

Sumowski 1983–94
Sumowski, Werner, *Gemälde der Rembrandt-Schüler*, 6 vols (Landau, 1983–94).

Sweetman 1894
Sweetman's Historical Pamphlets. Stourhead Mansion, Gardens, Church ... Being a reprint of a pamphlet published in 1822, (Wincanton 1894) Stourhead Archive, 6787.

Sweetman 1913
Sweetman, George, *Guide to Stourhead, Wilts. The Seat of Sir Henry Hoare, Bart.* (Wincanton, 1913).

Sweetman 1925
— *Guide to Stourhead Wilts. The Seat of Sir Henry Hoare, Bart.* (Wincanton, 1925).

Syndram 1994
Syndram, Dirk, *Das Grüne Gewölbe zu Dresden* (Munich, 1994).

Syon Park 2003
Syon Park (Derby, 2003).

Tait 1983
Tait, A.A., 'The Duke of Hamilton's Palace', *Burlington Magazine*, vol. CXXV (1983), pp. 394–402.

Thomassin 1723
Thomassin, Simon, *Recueil des statues, groupes, fontaines, termes, vases, Et autres magnifiques Ornemens du Château & Parc de Versailles* (Paris, 1723, first published in 1694).

Thompson 1983
Thompson, M.W. (ed.), *The Journeys of Sir Richard Colt Hoare through Wales and England 1793–1810* (Gloucester, 1983).

Thornton 1997
Thornton, Dora, *The Scholar in his Study* (Newhaven and London, 1997).

Thornton and Rieder 1972
Thornton, Peter and William Rieder, 'Pierre Langlois, Ebéniste. Part 2', *Connoisseur*, vol. CLXXIX (1972), pp. 107–10.

Toderi 1998–2000
Toderi, Giuseppe and Fiorenza Vannel, *Le Medaglie Italiane del XVI secolo*, 3 vols (Florence, 1998–2000).

Tomlin 1972
Tomlin, Maurice, *Catalogue of the Adam Period Furniture* (London, 1972).

Tomlinson 1996
Tomlinson, John Michael, *Derbyshire Black Marble* (Matlock, 1996).

Toynbee 1928*
Toynbee, Paget (ed.), 'Horace Walpole's Journals of Visits to Country Seats & c.', *Walpole Society*, vol. XVI (1928), pp. 9–80.

Treasures from the Royal Collection 1988
Treasures from the Royal Collection (London, 1988).

Tuena 1988
Tuena, Filippo M., 'Appunti per la storia del commesso romano: il 'Franciosino' Maestro di Tavole e il Cardinale Giovanni Ricci', *Antologia di Belle Arti*, nos 33–4 (1988), pp. 54–69.

Valeriani 1999
Valeriani, Roberto, 'Gli Arredi', in Eduard A. Safarik, *Palazzo Colonna* (Rome, 1999), pp. 256–66.

Vardy 1744
Vardy, John, *Some Designs of Mr Inigo Jones and Mr Wm Kent* (London, 1744).

Verde 2008
Verde, Paola Carla, 'Domenico Fontana, regio ingenere nel Regno di Napoli (1592–1607)', in M. Fagiolo and G. Bonaccorso (eds), *Studi sui Fontana, Una dinastia di architetti ticinese a Roma tra Manierismo e Barocco* (Rome, 2008), pp. 91–6.

Vermeule and von Bothmer 1956
Vermeule, C. and D. von Bothmer, 'Notes on a New Edition of Michaelis: Ancient Marbles in Great Britain, Part II', (October 1956) *American Journal of Archaeology*, vol. 60, no. 4, pp. 321–50.

Vertue Note Books 1934
'Vertue Note Books, Volume III', *Walpole Society*, vol. XXII, (Oxford, 1934).

Vertue Note Books 1955
'Vertue Note Books, Volume VI', *Walpole Society*, vol. XXX (Oxford 1955).

Vodret 1993
Vodret, Rossella, 'La Decorazione Interna', in *Santa Susanna e San Bernardo alle Terme* (Rome, 1993).

Waddy 2002
Waddy, Patricia (ed.), *Nicodemus Tessin the*

Younger, Traictè dela decoration interieure 1717
(Stockholm, 2002).

Wainwright 1989
Wainwright, Clive, *The Romantic Interior*
(Newhaven and London, 1989).

Walker 1991
Walker, Stefanie, 'A Pax by Guglielmo della
Porta', *Metropolitan Museum Journal*, vol. XXVI
(1991), pp. 167–76.

Walpole 1798
Walpole, Horace, *The Works of Horace Walpole,
Earl of Orford* (London, 1798).

Ward 1842*
Ward, George Atkinson, *Journal and Letters
of the late Samuel Curwen ... an American refugee
in England ... 1775–1784* (London, 1842).

Waring 1863
Waring, J.B., *Masterpieces of Industrial Art
and Sculpture at the International Exhibition*
(London, 1863).

Warner 1801*
Warner, Revd Richard, *Excursions from Bath*
(Bath, 1801).

Weber 2013
Weber, Susan (ed.), *William Kent: Designing
Georgian Britain* (New Haven and London, 2013).

Wenley 1990–3
Wenley, Robert, 'Robert Paston and the
Yarmouth Collection', *Norfolk Archaeology*,
vol. XLI (1990–3), pp. 113–44.

Westgarth 2009
Westgarth, Mark, 'A Biographical Dictionary
of Nineteenth Century Antique and Curiosity
Dealers', *Regional Furniture*, vol. XXIII (2009).

White 1999
White, Adam, 'A Biographical Dictionary
of English Tomb Sculptors, *c.*1560–*c.*1660',
Walpole Society, vol. LXI (1999), pp. 1–162.

White 1984
White, Roger, 'Whiston Hall Remodelled',
Architectural History, vol. XXVII (1984), pp. 241–54.

Wilson 1985
Wilson, Gillian, 'A Pair of Cabinets for Louis
XVI's Bedroom at Saint-Cloud: Their Present
Appearance', *Furniture History*, vol. XXI (1985),
pp. 38–45.

Wilson and Mackley 2000
Wilson, Richard and Alan Mackley, *Creating
Paradise: The Building of the English Country House
1660–1880* (London, 2000).

Wolsey and Luff 1968
Wolsey, S.W. and R.W.P. Luff, *Furniture in
England, The Age of the Joiner* (London, 1968).

Wood 1962
Wood, Anthony C., 'The Diaries of Sir Roger
Newdigate 1751–1806', *Transactions of the
Birmingham Archaeological Society*, vol. LXXVIII
(1962), pp. 40–55.

Woodbridge 1970
Woodbridge, Kenneth, *Landscape and Antiquity:
Aspects of English Culture at Stourhead 1718 to 1838*
(Oxford, 1970).

Woodbridge 1982a
— *The Stourhead Landscape* (London, 1982a).
There have been subsequent reprints; the
1982 edition is the author's definitive version.

Woodbridge 1982b
— 'Stourhead in 1768: extracts from an unpublished journal by Sir John Parnell', *Journal
of Garden History*, vol. 2, no. 1, January–March
(London, 1982), pp. 59–70.

Zobi 1853
Zobi, Antonio, *Notizie storiche sull'origine e
progressi dei lavori di commesso in pietre dure*
(Florence, 1853).

PHOTOGRAPHIC CREDITS AND COPYRIGHT

INDEX

Page numbers in *italic* refer to illustrations

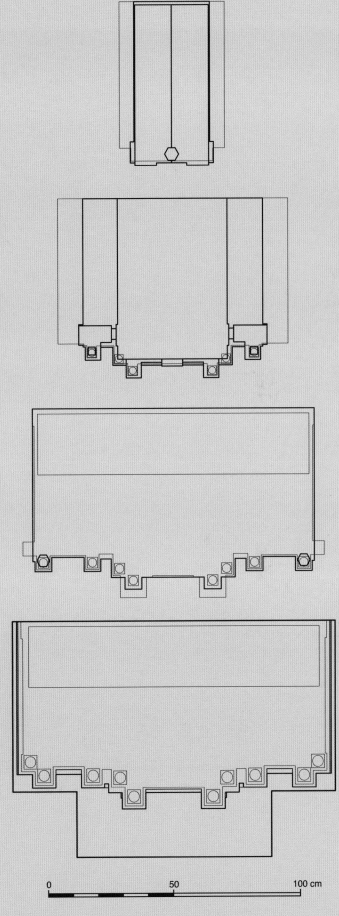

0   50   100 cm

FIG. 241
The Sixtus Cabinet, plans at podium and Ionic first storey,
Corinthian second storey, Composite third storey and Attic levels